THE LAWBOOK EXCHANGE, LTD.

FOUNDATIONS OF THE LAWS OF WAR

GENERAL EDITOR: JOSEPH PERKOVICH

The Foundations of the Laws of War Series presents reprints of works influential in the development of the regulation of armed conflict, humanitarian law, and international criminal law.

AGGRESSION AND WORLD ORDER

Books in the Series

Aggression and World Order
By Julius Stone
With a new introduction by Benjamin Ferencz
Chief Prosecutor for the United States at the Nuremberg War Crimes Trial, author of Defining International Aggression-The Search for World Peace *(1975), Adjunct Professor of International Law, Pace University and founder of the Pace Peace Center*

Axis Rule in Occupied Europe
By Raphael Lemkin
With a new introduction by Samantha Power
Currently affiliated with the Carr Center for Human Rights Policy, Harvard University John F. Kennedy School of Government and author of "A Problem from Hell": America and the Age of Genocide, *winner of the 2003 Pulitzer Prize*
Second Edition (paperback) 2008, with an introduction by William A. Schabas
OC, MRIA, Professor of Human Rights Law, National University of Ireland, Galway, Director, Irish Centre for Human Rights, Global Legal Scholar, University of Warwick, Professor, Queen's University Belfast

Instructions for the Government of Armies of the United States in the Field* [*with*] *Guerrilla Parties Considered With Reference to the Law and Usages of War
By Francis Lieber
With a new introduction by Steve Sheppard
William Enfield Professor of Law, University of Arkansas School of Law

The International Law of Civil War
Edited by Richard A. Falk

Law and Civil War in the Modern World
Edited by John Norton Moore
With a new introduction for this edition by John Norton Moore
Walter L. Brown Professor of Law, Director, Center for National Security Law and Director, Center for Oceans Law and Policy, University of Virginia School of Law

A Manual of the Law of Maritime Warfare
By William Hazlitt and Henry Philip Roche
With a new introduction by William E. Butler
John Edward Fowler Distinguished Professor of Law, Dickinson School of Law, Pennsylvania State University, Founder and Director of the Vinogradoff Institute and former Chair of Comparative Law, University of London

Nuremberg and Vietnam: An American Tragedy
By Telford Taylor
With a new introduction by Benjamin Ferencz
Chief Prosecutor for the United States at the Nuremberg War Crimes Trial, author of Defining International Aggression-The Search for World Peace *(1975), Adjunct Professor of International Law, Pace University and founder of the Pace Peace Center*

A Treatise on the Law of War
By Cornelius van Bynkershoek
With a new introduction by William E. Butler
John Edward Fowler Distinguished Professor of Law, Dickinson School of Law, Pennsylvania State University, Founder and Director of the Vinogradoff Institute and former Chair of Comparative Law, University of London

United Nations Forces: A Legal Study
By D.W. Bowett
With a new introduction by Dame Rosalyn Higgins
President (Ret.), International Court of Justice

AGGRESSION
AND
WORLD ORDER

A CRITIQUE OF UNITED NATIONS THEORIES OF AGGRESSION

by

JULIUS STONE

S.J.D. (Harvard), D.C.L. (Oxford)

Challis Professor of International Law and Jurisprudence, University of Sydney; Solicitor of the Supreme Court, England, of the New Zealand and Victorian Bars. Formerly Professor of International Law and Diplomacy, Fletcher School of Law and Diplomacy, Visiting Bemis Professor of International Law, Harvard University, Visiting Professor of International Law, Columbia University, etc. Associé de l'Institut de Droit International.

New Introduction by Benjamin B. Ferencz

THE LAWBOOK EXCHANGE, LTD.
Clark, New Jersey

ISBN 9781584776017 (hardcover)
ISBN 9781616191467 (paperback)

Lawbook Exchange edition 2011

The quality of this reprint is equivalent to the quality of the original work.

THE LAWBOOK EXCHANGE, LTD.
33 Terminal Avenue
Clark, New Jersey 07066-1321

Please see our website for a selection of our other publications and fine facsimile reprints of classic works of legal history:
www.lawbookexchange.com

Library of Congress Cataloging-in-Publication Data

Stone, Julius, 1907-1985.
Aggression and world order : a critique of United Nations theories of aggression / Julis Stone ; new foreword by Joseph Perkovich ; new introduction by Benjamin Ferencz.
p. cm. -- (The foundations of the laws of war)
Originally published: Berkeley : University of California Press, 1958.
Includes bibliographical references and index.
ISBN-13: 978-1-58477-601-7 (alk. paper)
ISBN-10: 1-58477-601-3 (alk. paper)
1. Aggression (International law) 2. United Nations. I. Title. II. Series.

KZ6374.S76 2005
341.6'2--dc22 2006005521

Printed in the United States of America on acid-free paper

General Editor's Preface

The principle of aggression is at the core of the modern international legal order. The United Nations Charter and the Nuremberg principles have enshrined its peremptory and criminal properties. In this moment when many sober observers view geopolitical upheaval on the horizon, the persistent instability of that core is placed in relief. The inability of international institutions to give effect to the prohibition of armed force and the absence of machinery to ensure the prosecution of parties for aggressive conflict are symptomatic of this state. The uncertain legal position of aggression remains intertwined with the roots of persistent global problems.

The following reprint of Professor Julius Stone's work is prompted by perennial questions of security and order relating to this core principle. Many years after its original publication, there is much to support Stone's underlying skepticism toward the principle as expressed in his two part thesis that i) defining aggression is not vital to human survival and thus not ethically imperative and ii) focus on promoting security actions via the broader concept of breach of the peace would better assist human survival.

However, as Professor Benjamin Ferencz has underscored in his new introduction, important gains have been made in recent years, especially respecting international criminal law. Stone's work focused on the norm of the prohibition of aggression and its place within the nascent United Nations system. He gave less attention to the consequences of the Nuremberg principles for international criminal law. Gains in that latter area have created opportunities to realize a framework that can enforce the prohibition of aggression by codifying the means to adjudge and punish those responsible for its commission. Aiding our historical understanding of Stone's text, Ferencz has imparted in the present introduction his matchless legal perspective beginning prior to his tenure in Nuremberg as a Chief Prosecutor and an Executive Counsel to General Telford Taylor.

If Stone and Ferencz were able to discuss today the basic questions in *Aggression and World Order*, they would likely still disagree on central positions, just as they had – to the profit of their readers – over the course of decades of discourse on the subject in scholarly texts and journals. In any discussion, the like-mindedness of the two humanitarians would doubtless come through. The Foundations of the Laws of War Series is clearly deeply enriched by Ferencz's contribution to the vexing topic set out in Stone's authoritative and provocative treatment.

Joseph Perkovich
November 20, 2005

Paradoxes of a Sharp Legal Mind:
Professor Julius Stone and International Aggression

BENJAMIN B. FERENCZ

Julius Stone was one of the most respected international legal scholars of the past century. Stone, the Challis Professor of Jurisprudence and International Law at the University of Sydney from 1942 to 1972 and then professor at the University of New South Wales from 1972 through 1985, did not hesitate to probe the most contentious jurisprudential problems.[1] His 1958 book, *Aggression and World Order: A Critique of United Nations Theories of Aggression*,[2] explored the United Nations' quest for a definition to identify nations that resorted to the illegal use of armed force. He agreed that aggression was the gravest international crime, yet he was unable to avoid the painful conclusion that the search for a binding definition that would curb aggressive behavior of nations might be a frustrating and futile endeavor. Sovereign states, he observed, are concerned with protecting their own national interests rather than enforcing the rule of law. After almost half of a century since his book was written, it is worth reexamining his thesis to see if it still has merit and what can be done realistically to move toward the humanitarian goals which Stone so fervently shared with peace-loving people everywhere.

Background

Let us recall that after some fifty million men, women and children were killed in World War II, political leaders of the victorious powers held forth the promise that a new structure of international society would be created to preserve the peace. Those who had launched the war and directed the mass murder of millions of innocent civilians were warned that they would be held to account for the purposes of justice and legal precedent alike. The framework of international society's new structure would be the United Nations, built from the rubble of its failed predecessor, the League of Nations, another edifice framed in the aftermath of a catastrophic war.

The Preamble of the United Nations Charter, signed June 26, 1945, begins by expressing the determination "to save succeeding generations from the scourge of war." Paragraph 1 of Article 1 of the Charter declares the UN's purpose to include the exercise of "collective measures for the prevention and removal of threats to the peace, and for the suppression of acts of aggression or other breaches of the peace." Responsibility for preserving the peace is entrusted to the Security Council, composed of fifteen members including five permanent members drawn from the victorious Allied Powers. Chapter VII of the Charter empowers the Council with the *discretion* to determine whether an act of aggression by a state has occurred and to take whatever measures necessary to restore international peace and security.[3] The Charter, however, fails to specify which acts constitute the illegal aggression that triggers a collective defense.[4]

In addition to that framework, the matter of dispensing justice after the vast breach of the peace and establishing precedents for the prevention and punishment of future aggressors still remained for international society's new structure. On August 8, 1945, the four Allied Powers occupying Germany signed the London Agreement in order to create an International

Military Tribunal to try German leaders deemed responsible for the war and its atrocities.[5] The trial was to take place at Nuremberg. The IMT's jurisdiction was limited to Crimes Against Peace, War Crimes, and Crimes Against Humanity. Crimes Against Peace were defined as "planning, preparation, initiation or waging of a war of aggression, or a war in violation of international treaties, agreements or assurances, or participation in a common plan or conspiracy for the accomplishment of any of the foregoing."[6] After a fair trial that was open to the public, and a thorough analysis of the arguments made by the defendants' chosen lawyers,[7] the eminent IMT judges concluded that those who had planned and directed attacks against their peaceful neighbors must have known that they were violating existing international law.

The genesis of modern international criminal law occurred in the interim between the two wars. At the conclusion of the Great War, the Allied Powers convened a special commission of international law experts to address criminal responsibility. Robert Lansing, the U.S. Secretary of State, chaired the Commission on the Responsibility of the Authors of War and Enforcement of Penalties for Violations of the Laws and Customs of War, which issued a Report naming over 850 suspected war criminals and enumerating 32 activities constituting war crimes.[8] Leading up to the Treaty of Versailles, the report asserted that "all persons belonging to enemy countries . . . who have been guilty of offenses against the laws and customs of war or the laws of humanity, are liable to criminal prosecution."[9]

The Treaty of Versailles, 1919, served two basic purposes. It included the Covenant of the League of Nations,[10] the institution designed to establish a pacific world order, and it established the terms of the peace as dictated by the victorious Allies.[11] The long term prospects of the League were not helped by the U.S. Senate's failure to ratify the Treaty and unwillingness to ever join. The Treaty also formed an untenable peace.[12]

In addition to its Report, Lansing's Commission also drafted the "Penalties" section of the Treaty, which included Kaiser Wilhelm II's public arraignment for "a supreme offence against international morality and the sanctity of treaties."[13] In the event, the Kaiser avoided a trial by fleeing to Holland, where the Dutch state refused requests for his extradition. Although the Treaty of Versailles also called for military tribunals administered by the Allied Powers,[14] German war prisoners were ultimately returned, ostensibly to face a special court established in 1921 in Leipzig. The Criminal Senate of the Imperial Court of Justice held just twelve trials, none of which concerned significant figures. The process was highly unpopular in Germany and clearly did not foster any sort of national contrition.[15] In spite of its practical inconsequence for prosecutions, the Treaty of Versaille's precedents for criminal responsibility comprised a step toward the prohibition of force.

In the aftermath of Versailles, France initiated bilateral negotiations with the United States to rehabilitate relations between the former allies eroded in large part because of the United States' unwillingness to forgive France's war debt, which, itself, was linked to German reparations due to the Treaty. These negotiations resulted in a turning point for the proscription of armed force. The multilateral Kellogg-Briand Pact of 1928, signed outside the League of Nations framework by Germany, France, the U.S. and over sixty other countries, outlawed the use of force for the settlement of international disputes.[16] While signatories failed to adhere to its terms, the Kellogg-Briand Pact is nonetheless a critical precedent for international criminal law.

The Pact and the Treaty of Versailles were cited along with many other treaties by the Nuremberg Tribunal and prosecutors to justify the aggression charge as being consistent with existing international law as well as the principles of fair trial.[17] In his June 6, 1945 report to President Truman, Justice Robert Jackson, on leave from the United States Supreme Court in order to act as Chief Counsel for the United States, decried "the sterile legalisms developed in the age of imperialism to make wars respectable."[18] Augmenting the gravity of the available legal precedents, he called for common sense and a firmer enforcement of the laws of international conduct, "so as to make war less attractive to those who have governments and the destinies of people in their power." The IMT judges recognized that the law is not static but must change to meet the needs of a changing world. Aggressive war, that had previously been a national right, was legally condemned as an international crime. International law had taken a significant step forward.

In December 1946, the first General Assembly of the United Nations unanimously affirmed the validity of the IMT trial and judgments,[19] which were followed by subsequent Nuremberg proceedings and war crimes trials in Tokyo. In 1947, the Assembly appointed committees to draft a Code of Offences against the Peace and Security of Mankind – a code expressly to be based on the Nuremberg principles – and prepare for the establishment of a permanent International Criminal Jurisdiction to try those who violated the anticipated new criminal code.[20] Idealistic UN aspirations in support of the rule of law soon confronted political reality. Nations and groups with different national, political, religious and ethical backgrounds had different perceptions of what was right and just. Additionally, as the price for joining the collective UN effort, the permanent members on the Security Council had reserved to themselves an unfair veto power: Any one of the five could block any enforcement action.

The argument was heard that there was no need for an International Criminal Court unless there was an agreed Code of Crimes for the Court to enforce. There could be no Code without including the crime of aggressive war that the Nuremberg Judgment had labeled as "the supreme international crime."[21] It was said that until aggression was more specifically defined, it could not be included in a precise criminal statute. Indeed, the General Assembly determined that a formulation of a criminal statute itself must be suspended until a definition was reached.[22] Defining aggression was the key effort needed to unlock action on the Code and the Criminal Court, the doors of the gateway to the order conceived at Nuremberg. This definition project survived the years immediately following the Nuremberg Tribunal in spite of pronounced difficulties.

In addition to directing the International Law Commission in 1950 to "formulate the principles of international law recognized in the Charter of the Nuremberg Tribunal and in the judgment of the Tribunal,"[23] the General Assembly also appointed successive Special Committees in 1952 (15 members) and 1954 (19 members), to cope with the same problem.[24] Surely, so many lawyers working for so many years would have been able to agree upon an acceptable definition if the powerful states had been ready to restrain their aggressive behaviors. In truth, powerful states were simply not ready or willing to entrust their national security or vital interests to the judgment of any impartial international body.

Preparing Aggression*:* *Skepticism and a Call for Justice*

Through the decade after the Charter of the Nuremberg Tribunal, the crime of aggression remained undefined and illegal wars continued to be waged with impunity in many parts of the world. Professor Stone, in preparation for his Hague Lectures to be given in the summer of 1956, began the study ultimately published as *Aggression and World Order* in 1954. The "politico-legal analysis"[25] proffered in those Hague Lectures did not, in the event, address the particular issue of aggression. However, beginning in the fall of 1956 while a visitor to the Harvard Law School, Stone used North American speaking invitations as an opportunity to apply his analysis to the particular matter of aggression in international law. Contemplating the "meagre results"[26] – indeed, failure – of the UN's apparatus to confront aggression in the dire circumstances of both the Suez Crisis and the Hungarian Uprising, Stone was reinforced in his melancholy conclusion that hope was gradually fading for finding an acceptable definition of aggression precise enough yet flexible enough to cope with the demands that precipitated international violence.[27] He struggled with the tension between immediate security needs and long range aspirations. His Lithuanian Jewish parentage and his sympathies for the beleaguered young state of Israel probably increased his sensitivity to the urgent need for a more humane and peaceful world and the complexities inherent in prohibitions of the use of force. In the final analysis, he still aspired for the UN "to arrest breaches of the peace before these spread into a holocaust for mankind."[28]

Unable to find a legally, philosophically or politically acceptable formulation for aggression, Professor Stone concluded that the most that could be done was to buy time so that moderation, understanding and tolerance might overcome or soften positions and perceptions that had hardened beyond the reach of reason. Although Stone had no illusions about the ability to define aggression as a step toward world order, paradoxically, he made plain that we must not desist from trying to attain an "ambitious theory of justice" that would place effective limits on the use of force by states.[29]

Upon publication in 1958, Stone's book was widely reviewed in English language law journals by prominent scholars and international lawyers.[30] Sir Gerald Fitzmaurice, Chief Legal Adviser to the U.K. Foreign Office and thereby longstanding opponent to any attempt to define aggression, praised Stone's eloquence and erudition and generally agreed with his conclusions. Clyde Eagleton, scholar and U.S. Department of State expert, struck a sympathetic chord with Stone's thesis by inquiring in the pages of the *American Journal of International Law* what use there would be of a definition of aggression until the community of nations was so organized that it could apply and maintain law. Dissonant views were conveyed as well. Covey Oliver of the University of Pennsylvania, critical of Stone's analytical dissection of UN Charter prohibitions, noted that *realpoliik* and force might not be the most effective means to attain justice. Professor Louis Sohn of Harvard Law School argued for a definition and an improved UN as important steps toward a more peaceful world.[31]

Aggression focused on the concept as a peremptory norm proscribing certain conduct by states. Stone devoted less attention to the international crime of aggression applicable to individuals.[32] Throughout his career, Stone espoused this relative weighting of the two roles of the concept. But the events of the intervening decades have demonstrated that the ascent of a criminal law structure able to incorporate the crime of aggression has been clearly the main channel of progress for the matters of international justice and the regulation of force considered so intensively in *Aggression* and revisited periodically in Stone's later work on the topic.

Stalemate, Then Consensus at the United Nations

In the face of the ideological differences among major powers and their allies, the UN delegates were stymied. Little progress was visible in defining aggression or preparing either Code or Court. While revolving committees dithered, outstanding legal scholars filled the breach, seeking to clarify the necessary components of an acceptable system to restrict the use of force in international affairs. Professors McDougal and Feliciano of Yale University Law School, for instance, produced a remarkable book in 1961. *Law and Minimum World Public Order: The Legal Regulation of International Coercion* contained a profound and exhaustive analysis which recognized that a humane world order could not be achieved without bringing national violence and coercion under effective international controls. To achieve those goals it was necessary to invent and put in place new structures of authority which leaders and peoples could be persuaded to accept.[33]

In contrast to the prescriptive scholarship represented by McDougal and Feliciano, Professor Stone, a dozen years after publication of *Aggression and World Order*, used the introduction to the collection of essays *Toward a Feasible International Criminal Court* to reaffirm his earlier observations. Stone asserted that "the capacity of States for denouncing international lawlessness is one thing: their willingness to submit their own conduct or that of their agents to third party judgment on this account, is another."[34] Despite this skepticism, Stone did feel that even a minimalist approach, in which only a few states would agree to be bound by a court with limited jurisdiction, would be well worthwhile. Until there was an agreed definition of aggression, however, there was no hope that delegates would move forward toward creating any International Criminal Court.

On December 14, 1974, in the midst of Soviet-American détente, the General Assembly adopted Resolution 3314, a consensus definition of aggression painstakingly reached by UN Special Committees after almost 30 years of effort. The 138 Member States were by no means agreed on the interpretation of every clause in this definition.[35] Notably, the resolution was not put to a vote. The consensus was the product of compromise achieved by including phrases of such dexterous ambiguity that adversaries could interpret them to suit their own political agendas. The eight articles of the definition began with a general clause based on UN Charter language prohibiting the use of armed force. That was followed by specific illustrations of outlawed behavior, such as invasion or attack. Exculpating clauses were added to placate states that were primarily concerned with protecting the right to self-determination or freedom from alien domination. Adding the vague phrase "in accordance with the principles of the Charter" made the enabling clauses tolerable. The clear articulation that the Security Council had the final word in what would be held to be aggression made the compromise wording acceptable to the permanent members, who wielded veto power.

Nations seemed to have forgotten, or had wished to forget, that the definition was originally intended to form a vital part of a new international criminal code and judicial system. As Professor Stone had foreseen, powerful sovereign states were not willing to yield their prerogatives to use military might when, in their sole judgment, it was necessary to defend or advance their national interests. Robert Rosenstock, the adroit United States delegate who promoted the adoption of the consensus definition, argued nonetheless that it only provided a guide for the Security Council and had no binding legal significance.[36] No doubt, the compromise definition of aggression was actually more sieve than substance. It reflected the fears and hesitations that still prevailed in the world. But its very existence, however feeble, and the prolonged debates in its genesis showed an increasing awareness that human survival might depend upon man's capacity to limit the unbridled use of international force.[37] The 1974 consensus definition finally set the keystone – albeit a porous one – for a construction of the missing Code of Crimes and the International Criminal Court.

The Hopeful Skeptic

Professor Stone's 1977 book, *Conflict through Consensus: United Nations Approaches to Aggression*, revisited the subject matter and findings of *Aggression and World Order.* In defense of his prediction that it was futile to expect a workable definition, Stone meticulously punched holes in practically every substantive paragraph of Resolution 3314. He pointed to discrepancies and inadequacies as well as omissions and ambiguities. He floated the cynical conclusion that the consensus was acceptable only because states wished to use its vague formulations to support their own political objectives. He acknowledged that a definition might be useful for trials of individuals for crimes against peace but not for facilitating instant voluntary international cooperation to halt a military crisis. Such an effective definition, he wrote, would be "rather unattainable, and may not even be worth searching for."[38] While denouncing the consensus, he still – begrudgingly and paradoxically – paid tribute to its existence as a visible reaffirmation of the indomitable hope, shared by most of mankind, that there must be legal limits to the use of armed force.

Stone's basic paradox of being pessimistic and hopeful at the same time appears throughout his writings. He referred to "the noble aspiration of a more peaceful and just world" yet pointed to the "socio-political reality" which led him to believe that its pursuit was a hopeless endeavor.[39] No one expected the definition to include world social reform yet Stone found obstacles that were not even on the table. To demonstrate the futility of a definition he argued that it might require a redistribution of planetary resources, a conclusion he presumably might welcome. He denied any prospective correlation between the definition of aggression and the creation and purpose of an International Criminal Court. He wrote that the existence of the consensus definition of 1974 had "made the creation of such a jurisdiction more improbable than ever" and concluded that it would be "a miracle" if such a court would be accepted.[40]

A year before his death in 1985 at the age of 78, Stone published *Visions of World Order: Between State Power and Human Justice*. He dedicated the little book to his grandchildren "in the hope that their world grows safer and more peaceful than now appears." He remained plagued by his realistic perceptions and his pessimism. The prospect of attaining a peaceful world order was still described as a vague hope "devoutly to be desired."[41] Stone's awareness of the nuclear arms race and the refusal of states to be bound by a common rule of law did not allow his mind to go with his heart's desire. He noted progress made in many fields of international organization but highlighted the extension and proliferation of barriers to world peace rather than emerging signs of advancement in, by his own reckoning, significant areas ranging from the judicial settlement of international disputes to improvements in legal enforcement and fortified human rights protections.[42] In the end he called for the brotherhood of man and counseled: "We should not despair before this task."[43]

Where Do We Go From Here?

A half-century after Stone published his initial comprehensive analysis of problems of aggression and world order, the dilemmas he so carefully dissected then remain with us still. However, there has been significant progress in reaching certain goals he doubted, but hoped, could be achieved. An International Criminal Court was approved, by the overwhelming vote of one-hundred twenty in favor and seven against, in a frenetic five-week conference in Rome in 1998. The Rome Statute entered into force on July 1, 2002 as a result of the deposit of the sixtieth instrument of ratification on April 11, 2002. Currently, one-hundred, thirty-nine states have signed the Rome Statute, with one-hundred having ratified it to become a State Party. The Court has started to prepare for its work in the Hague. Its jurisdiction is strictly limited, subordinated to national criminal jurisdictions.[44] Only crimes of a magnitude to concern the international community as a whole can come within its reach. The new criminal tribunal can deal only with charges of Genocide, Crimes Against Humanity and major War Crimes – all of which were carefully defined. The problem of defining aggression remained unresolved. Stone had recognized that even a minimalist court for a limited number of states would be well worthwhile. His conviction that it would never happen, since aggression could never be defined, has proven to be too pessimistic.

Stone, however, was nearly prophetic. Aggression, the most divisive issue for the Rome Conference Delegates, was sidestepped in a last minute maneuver. The Statute's enumeration of crimes postpones the matter of defining aggression well into the future. Article 5 of the Statute provides that the Court has jurisdiction with respect to four crimes: "(a) The crime of genocide; (b) Crimes against humanity; (c) War crimes; (d) The crime of aggression." While Articles 6, 7, and 8 proceed to define the first three crimes listed in Article 5, the second paragraph of Article 5 renders dormant the Court's jurisdiction over the last crime:

> The Court shall exercise jurisdiction over the crime of aggression once a provision is adopted in accordance with articles 121 and 123 defining the crime and setting out the conditions under which the Court shall exercise jurisdiction with respect to this crime. Such a provision shall be consistent with the relevant provisions of the Charter of the United Nations.

Article 123 provides that seven years after the entry into force of the Statute, the UN Secretary-General shall convene a Review Conference to consider amendments. Article 121 requires a two-thirds majority of States Parties for the adoption of an amendment at a Review Conference or at any meeting of the Assembly of States Parties after that seven year period. However, an amendment will not enter into force until one year after *seven-eighths* of the States Parties have deposited instruments of ratification.

Thus, an aggression amendment cannot be adopted before June, 2009 and even then would still need ratification by a hyper-majority of the States Parties and await a year before actually according the Court jurisdiction over the crime. There is no way of knowing when, or if, the pre-conditions might be met. Until then, no one can be prosecuted by the Court for what the Nuremberg Judgment labeled "the supreme international crime." The Assembly of States Parties has appointed special Working Groups to try to resolve the impasse. Professor Stone's prediction that it would be a frustrating endeavor has, so far, been true. Whether it will also be futile remains to be seen.

Should he prove to be right and the perpetrators of aggression remain immune, it will not bode well for humankind.

Professor Stone, even in his last years, did not hesitate to challenge the views of other legal titans with whom he disagreed in whole or in part. He argued that profound thinkers like Myres McDougal of Yale Law School, Richard Falk of Princeton University, and Wilfred Jenks, Director General of the International Labor Organization, all went too far in their world views.[45] He tried to bring them down to earth by maintaining that they were espousing ethical programs for evolutionary action rather than describing a sociology of existing international law. Stone's understanding of the nature of man and the structure of power did not allow him to take a more optimistic view. While he remained aware of the global dimensions of major problems and the increasing dangers of physical destruction, he warned against exaggerated expectations and utopian visions.[46] Stone's writings should be appreciated for their important insights despite a realism which sometimes verges on disabling pessimism.[47]

Professor Shabtai Rosenne, who represented Israel at the United Nations for many years, is one of the world's leading scholars on both international courts and the law of treaties.[48] As Israel's delegate to the UN's Sixth (Legal) Committee during the preparation of General Assembly Resolution 3314, he roundly criticized the resultant consensus definition of 1974. Like Professor Stone, throughout his highly distinguished career he has expressed a longstanding skepticism about defining aggression and also the efforts to create an International Criminal Court. Yet he has described the establishment of the ICC as one of the two major legal creations that "will shine on the record of the twentieth century..."[49] Like Stone was, he is adept at finding faults, but, unlike Stone, he has perceived that most of the defects were in the process of being repaired. As a statutory matter, the need to expressly define the crime for the Court is clear; as a jurisprudential matter, there is no real need for a new definition of aggression. The definition of the Nuremberg Charter proved adequate for the Nuremberg Tribunal. It was also affirmed by the General Assembly, as well as, after years of study, by the expert International Law Commission. Taken together with existing precedents and coupled with the guidelines contained in the consensus definition, competent judges of the ICC have ample illustrations to enable sound judgments of guilt or innocence to be formed. Although Stone would argue the contrary, the term aggression is no more vague than "due process" or "fair trial," which has never obtained a specific definition.[50] The insistence upon another definition is not motivated by respect for the rule of law but, as Stone feared, by the aim of powerful states to evade it.

Conclusion

Hope is the engine that drives human endeavor. Without the expectation that a more humane and peaceful world is attainable, humankind will lack the enormous energy and creativity needed to save man from himself. The dreams of today can become the reality of tomorrow.

The last century has witnessed political and economic transformations that were previously inconceivable. New international courts to deal with crimes committed in Yugoslavia, Rwanda, and Cambodia, as well as Human Rights courts, now abound. By the universal condemnation of aggression, we can begin to transform human thinking away from a glorified war-ethic to a peace-ethic vital for human survival. It is not sufficient to convict major criminals for crimes against humanity and war crimes. It is far more important that those who plan and perpetrate aggressive wars be shown to be contemptible criminals and not heroes. We must eradicate the power of rhetoric to rationalize the killing of vast numbers of innocent human beings simply because they do not share the race, religion or ideology of their executioners. The murder of innocent men, women and children is a crime and an abomination no matter how sincere the motives or the sacrifices of the executioners. Increased recognition of the crime of aggression, in turn, should improve the recognition by states of their inviolable duty to prevent its commission in the first place.

The communications revolution offers unimaginable new opportunities to influence even the most deeply held convictions. The murderous absurdity in the nuclear age of trying to resolve ideological differences by massive military might must one day yield to human reason if humankind is to survive. McDougal outlined the necessary process, advocating the creation of acceptable new legal structures to control unacceptable coercive actions. Sohn wrote of global peace through a World Law. Stone, despite his despair, pointed to the essential ingredients of how to get from here to there: time, moderation, understanding and tolerance. Such changes cannot come quickly or easily or without blemish and opposition. Courage and perseverance hold the key to further progress.

A retrograde power jeopardizes the hard won progress made through the twentieth century. The United States government has opposed the International Criminal Court for reasons that are misguided and not persuasive. Washington has turned its back on allies such as England, France, Canada, Australia and others who support the Court, as well as the recommendations of the American Bar Association and the American Society of International Law.[51] The National Security Strategy of the United States, as published in 2002, envisages preemptive military strikes without Security Council approval in defiance of the Nuremberg precedents as well as the UN Charter.[52] Aggression cannot be disguised as humanitarian intervention or self-defense.

As this recent exploitation of the leeway in the existing legal apparatus demonstrates, the structure is insufficient for our times. The laws must be improved, not discarded. The International Criminal Court, with or without a revised definition of aggression, is like an infant that must be fostered to maturity. A working framework to adjudge international aggression is what Stone seemed to hope for but never clearly articulated or felt would be accomplished. Through scholarship, Stone and his peers advanced the goal of the establishment of a world order that upholds the rule of law so that all may live in peace and human dignity. It is up to the public and advocates, in the light of such work, to persuade decision makers who do not yet discern that law is better than war.

November 2005

Endnotes

1 *See* Leonie Star, Julius Stone: An Intellectual Life (1992).
2 Julius Stone, *Aggression and World Order: A Critique of United Nations Theories of Aggression* (1958) [hereinafter *Aggression*]. Originally published in London by Stevens & Sons, Ltd., in Berkeley by the University of California Press, and in Sydney by Maitland Publications Pty. Ltd. This reprint edition published in Clark, NJ by The Lawbook Exchange, Ltd., 2006.
3 Hans Kelsen, *Sanctions in International Law under the Charter of the United Nations*, 31 Iowa L. Rev. 499, 519 (1946):

> It may be argued that the enforcement measures determined in Articles 39, 41, 42, and 45, are not "sanctions" since they are not established as reaction against a violation of obligations under the Charter . . . The enforcement actions are purely political measures to be used by the Security Council at its discretion for the purpose to maintain or restore international peace. This interpretation may be confirmed by the fact that according to Art. 39, the first Article of Chapter VII, the Security Council, after having determined the existence of a threat to the peace, breach of the peace, or act of aggression, may not only resort to enforcement action but may "make recommendations."(footnote omitted) It has the choice between two different measures of which only the former could have the character of a sanction.

4 Jochen A. Frowein & Nico Krisch, *Article 39*, *in* The Charter of the United Nations: A Commentary 717, 722 (Bruno Simma et al. eds., 2nd ed. 2002).
5 *London Agreement of 8 August 1945, in* Trial of the Major War Criminals before the International Military Tribunal, Nuremberg, 14 November 1945 - 1 October 1946 8-9 (Nuremberg, 1949) [hereinafter *Trials of the Major War Criminals*]. France, the United Kingdom, the United States and the Soviet Union formed the Agreement.
6 *See id.*, at 11-12, Charter of the International Military Tribunal, Part II. Jurisdiction and General Principles.
7 *But see* B.V.A. Röling, The Tokyo Trial and Beyond 34 (Antonio Cassese ed. 1993). Röling, a judge in the Tokyo Proceedings, perceived a gradual creeping of "Anglo-Saxon features" into the court presided over by predominantly English speaking judges. He attributed it to the Tokyo Charter's "vague provision for 'a fair trial.'" Röling viewed Tokyo's development as consanguine

with the observed occurrence that "the German lawyers [defending the accused at Nuremberg] often did not know how to behave in a procedure which was foreign to them."

8 Paul Bowers, Research Paper 01/39, The *International Criminal Court Bill [HL]*, Bill 70 of 2000-2001 15 (International Affairs & Defence Section, House of Commons Library, U.K. 2001).

9 *Report of the Commission on the Responsibility of the Authors of War and Enforcement of Penalties for Violations of the Laws and Customs of War*, 14 Am. J. of Int'l L. 95, 117 (1920).

10 *Treaty of Versailles articles 1-26 (Part I.), June 28, 1919*, [hereinafter *Treaty of Versailles*] *in* The Treaties of Peace 1919-1923, Vol. 1 121 (Carnegie Endowment for International Peace ed. 1924).

11 *Id.* at articles 27 – 440 (Part II. through Part XV.).

12 *See* John Maynard Keynes, The Economic Consequences of the Peace (1919). *But see* Margaret MacMillan, Paris 1919: Six Months That Changed the World (2002).

13 *Treaty of Versailles, supra* note 10, art. 227.

14 *Id.* at art. 228.

15 *See* Claud Mullins, The Leipzig Trials: An Account of the War Criminals' Trials and a Study of German Mentality (1921).

16 Kellogg-Briand Pact, *opened for signature* Aug. 27, 1928, 46 Stat. 2343. Article 1 provided that the signatories "condemn recourse to war for the solution of international controversies, and renounce it, as an instrument of national policy in their relations with one another." The United States and others still consider this treaty to be in force.

17 *Trials of the Major War Criminals, supra* note 5, at 216. "Violations of International Treaties . . . of principal importance" discussed in the Judgment included, in addition to the Kellogg-Briand Pact and the Versailles Treaty, the Hague Conventions of 1899 and 1907, and various bilateral agreements between Germany and other states in the form of Treaties of Mutual Guarantee, Arbitration, and Non-Aggression. *See also* Susan Lamb, Nullum crimen, nulla poena sine lege *in International Criminal Law*, *in* The Rome Statute of the International Criminal Court: A Commentary 736 (Antonio Cassese, Paola Gaeta, and John R.W.D. Jones eds. 2002). Lamb argued that *nullum crimen*, and its tandem concept, *nulla poena sine lege* emerged as norms of customary international law only after the Nuremberg proceedings and, at

that time, neither concept could have been argued to have been more than a moral maxim and thus not a bar to the application of the crime of aggression.

18 Benjamin B. Ferencz, Defining International Aggression, The Search for World Peace: A Documentary History and Analysis, Vol. 1 171 (1975).

19 G.A. Res. 95 (I), pt. 2, at 1144 (1946).

20 G.A. Res. 177 (II), (Nov. 21, 1947).

21 *Trials of the Major War Criminals, supra* note 5, at 186, Judgment. *See also* Stone in *Aggression* 149-150:

> It is a . . . vast understatement of the real obstacles to suggest, as some have done, that progress in the adoption of the draft Code of Offences against the Peace and Security of Mankind depends on an adequate definition of aggression.(footnote omitted) The difficulties appear to be of a different and far more formidable order; they may lie rather in the inaptness of the concept of "aggression", however defined,(footnote omitted) to perform, in our actual world, the functions designed for it by those who have advocated and promoted the proposed international code.(footnote omitted)

22 G.A. Res. 897, U.N. GAOR, 9th Sess. (Dec.4, 1954).

23 G.A. Res. 177 (II), (Nov. 21, 1947).

24 G.A. Res. 688, U.N. GAOR, 7th Sess. (Dec. 20, 1952); G.A. Res. 895, U.N. GAOR, 9th Sess. (Dec. 4, 1954). The 1952 and 1954 Special Committees were followed by two more in 1959 (21 members) and 1967 (35 members). The final Special Committee culminated in the 1974 definition that became General Assembly Resolution 3314.

25 *Aggression, supra* note 2, at vii.

26 *Aggression, supra* note 2, at 26: "Such a mood may well be both wise and responsible as we observe the Twelfth General Assembly's discussion in 1957 of the meagre results of its latest Special Committee on the Definition of Aggression."

27 *Id.* at 182.

28 *Id.* at 183.

29 *See id.*

30 The following are among the reviews of *Aggression* in English speaking law journals: Sir Gerald Fitzmaurice, *Comment:* Inter Arma Silent Definitiones, 3 Sydney L. Rev. 71 (1958); Clyde Eagleton, Book Review, 52 Am. J. Int'l L. 364 (1958); Covey Oliver, Book Review, 108 U. Pa. L. Rev. 229 (1959); Louis Sohn, *The Definition of Aggression*, 45 Va. L. Rev. 697 (1959); Book Review, 72

Harv. L. Rev. 1403 (1959); Creighton Burns, Book Review, 1 Melb. U. L. Rev. 574 (1958); John Collier, Book Review, 1960 Cambridge L.J. 246 (1960); P.J. Fitzgerald, Book Review, 76 Law Q. Rev. 165 (1960); W.W. Kulski, Book Review 58 Colum. L. Rev. 1108 (1958); J. Roland Pennock, Book Review, 68 Yale L.J. 387 (1958).

31 Ironically, Sohn became the Bemis Professor at Harvard in 1961, assuming permanently the post that Stone had occupied in a Visiting capacity during 1956 while preparing *Aggression.*

32 *Aggression, supra* note 2, at 134 – 150.

33 Myres McDougal & Florentine Feliciano, Law and Minimum World Public Order: The Legal Regulation of International Coercion 122, 260 (1961).

34 Toward a Feasible International Criminal Court xi (Julius Stone & Robert K. Woetzel eds. 1970).

35 *See* Benjamin B. Ferencz, *The United Nations Consensus Definition of Aggression: Sieve or Substance?*, 10 J. Int'l L. & Econ. 701 (1975).

36 1974 U.N.Y.B. 841. In addition to the U.S. delegate, several others, including representatives of Israel, Italy, and the United Kingdom called into question the legal status of the definition, positing "that it would have the same recommendatory status as any other Assembly resolution" thereby providing the "general guidelines" for the Security Council to identify aggression under Article 39.

37 *See* Benjamin B. Ferencz, *A Proposed Definition of Aggression: By Compromise and Consensus*, 22 Int'l & Comp. L. Q. 417 (1973).

38 Julius Stone, Conflict through Consensus: United Nations Approaches to Aggression 14-16 (1977).

39 *Id.* at 113.

40 *Id.* at 162.

41 Julius Stone, Visions of World Order: Between State Power and Human Justice xiv (1985).

42 Benjamin B. Ferencz, Book Review, 79 Am. J. Int'l L. 1084 (1985).

43 Stone, *supra* note 33, at 157.

44 Rome Statute of the International Criminal Court art. 1, Jul. 17, 1998, 2187 U.N.T.S. 90 (entered into force July 1, 2002).

45 *See* Stone, *supra* note 33, at 33. Stone gave extended discussions of the following works: Myres McDougal, *International Law, Power and Policy: A Contemporary Conception*, 82 Hague Recueil 133 (1953); Richard Falk, Statecraft in an Era of Word Order, Delay and Renewal, Arthur F. Yencken Memorial

Lectures, Australia National University (1974); and C. Wilfred Jenks, Common Law of Mankind (1958).

46 *Id.* at 43, 67.

47 *See* Julius Stone, *Hopes and Loopholes in the 1974 Definition of Aggression*, 71 Am. J. Int'l L. 224 (1977).

48 *See* Shabtai Rosenne, *The Law and Practice of the International Court* (3d ed. 1997); Shabtai Rosenne, *The Law of Treaties: A Guide to the Legislative History of the Vienna Convention* (1970); Shabtai Rosenne, *Developments in the Law of Treaties, 1945-1986* (1989).

49 Shabtai Rosenne, *Poor Drafting and Imperfect Organization: Flaws to Overcome in the Rome Statute*, 41 Va. J. Int'l L. 164 (2000).

50 *Aggression, supra* note 2, 119-133. Stone devoted a chapter to the analogy of due process and the criteria of aggression. Stone gave significant attention to contemporary American jurisprudence regarding substantive and procedural due process, contrasting the typical "fact-value complex" at issue in a municipal court with the kind that would be involved in adjudicating aggression in an international forum. Stone, at p. 123, found that:

> the lack of an effective international legislature, and of collective enforcement of legal rights generally, make unavailable to an international applying organ the course charted by [U.S. Supreme Court Justice] Brandeis [in the *Oklahoma Ice Case* (285 U.S. 262 (1931))] of not retreading the path of legislative judgment, but merely testing its results by the limiting notions of what is arbitrary and unreasonable on any reading of the whole situation.

51 Letter from Robert E. Hirshon, President, American Bar Association, to The President of the United States of America (Apr. 11, 2002) (on file with the American Bar Association); Letter from Monroe Leigh, Partner, Steptoe & Johnson, to Henry Hyde, Chairman, House Committee on International Relations (Feb. 21, 2001), attaching memorandum entitled "Misconceptions About the Proposed International Criminal Court" by current and former presidents of the American Society of International Law, Oscar Schacter, Hamilton Fish Professor of International Law and Diplomacy Emeritus & Special Lecturer, Columbia University School of Law; William D. Rogers, Partner, Arnold & Porter; Monroe Leigh, Partner, Steptoe & Johnson; Louis B. Sohn, Distinguished Research Professor and Director, Research and Studies, George Washington University Law School; Peter D. Trooboff, Partner, Covington & Burling; Louis Henkin, University Professor Emeritus and

Special Service Professor, Columbia University School of Law; Edith Brown Weiss, Georgetown University Law Center; Thomas M. Franck, Murray and Ida Becker Professor and Director, Center for International Studies, New York University School of Law; Arthur W. Rovine, Partner, Baker & McKenzie; Stephen M. Schwebel, former Judge, International Court of Justice (Feb. 13, 2001) (on file with Arthur W. Rovine, President, American Society of International Law).

52 The National Security Strategy of the United States of America (2002), http://www.whitehouse.gov/NSC.pdf.

AGGRESSION
AND
WORLD ORDER

A CRITIQUE OF UNITED NATIONS THEORIES OF AGGRESSION

by

JULIUS STONE
S.J.D. (Harvard), D.C.L. (Oxford)

Challis Professor of International Law and Jurisprudence, University of Sydney; Solicitor of the Supreme Court, England, of the New Zealand and Victorian Bars. Formerly Professor of International Law and Diplomacy, Fletcher School of Law and Diplomacy, Visiting Bemis Professor of International Law, Harvard University, Visiting Professor of International Law, Columbia University, etc. Associé de l'Institut de Droit International.

UNIVERSITY OF CALIFORNIA PRESS
BERKELEY and LOS ANGELES
1958

Published in the United States of America by the University of California Press of Berkeley & Los Angeles, California, U.S.A.

Published in Australia by Maitland Publications Pty. Ltd., of 149 Castlereagh Street, Sydney, New South Wales.

Published in the United Kingdom by Stevens & Sons Limited, of 119 & 120 Chancery Lane, London, W.C.2.

Set in Linotype Baskerville

Printed by Halstead Press, Sydney, Australia

In Tribute

to the

Courage and Dedication

of

Harriet Griswold

PREFACE

This study was begun in 1954 as a particular application of a general theme entitled "Problems Confronting Sociological Inquiries Concerning International Law", which I was to present at the Hague Academy of International Law in August, 1956. Limitations of time did not allow me to cover this ground at The Hague, and this was perhaps in the event fortunate. For the circumstances of the later international crisis of 1956-57 were to provide many enriching illustrations of what I had written in outline, and (along with the report of the General Assembly's 1956 Special Committee on the Definition of Aggression) a great deal of verbal grist for the mill of politico-legal analysis.

When therefore I was honoured with invitations to speak at the Annual Dinner of the Canadian Branch of the International Law Association at Montreal in November, 1956, and also to prepare the fifth series of Roscoe Pound Lectures at the University of Nebraska College of Law in April, 1957, it was natural that I should choose to develop my original analysis in the light of the onrushing events. Being at that time Visiting Bemis Professor at the Harvard Law School, I benefited greatly from many stimulating and provocative exchanges with my Harvard colleagues, among whom I hope it will not be invidious for me to mention in particular Professor Milton Katz, and the able group of scholars working with him in the International Legal Studies Programme of the Harvard Law School.

In April, 1957, I delivered three lectures on the subject "Aggression in International Law" at the University of Nebraska in the series of Roscoe Pound Lectures already mentioned, covering an important part of the present ground. In view, however, of the impending publication of this present larger exposition the University of Nebraska authorities kindly agreed that this should serve also as publication of the Roscoe Pound Lectures.

It will become apparent from these pages that there lies behind the grim repulsions of the subject international aggression and its definition, a rich vein of problems and ideas of fundamental juristic and political importance. While the anxieties of the international crisis pressed closely on me during the later phases of writing, my formulation of the theoretical issues long preceded it. And mature reflection after the crisis confirmed my conviction that if we are to escape from the dead ends of thought which we have reached on these issues, we must somehow learn to see and translate them in larger terms than those of any immediate crisis, or indeed of any particular generation. These pages are an effort towards this translation; and the singular coincidence of the Middle East crisis, 1956-57, with the crisis in the United Nations enterprise of defining "aggression", displays the importance of making such an effort far better than any argument of mine.

Besides the application in the international sphere of a number of basic principles of juristic and political theory, the present undertaking has involved a careful examination of the proper limits of the analogical transposition of familiar principles of municipal law to the relations of States. And it has also involved a rethinking, from the foundations upwards, of the role in which so many human hopes have cast the United Nations, and especially the General Assembly, in the maintenance of international peace.

While the present analysis departs in its main lines from the approaches current in scholarly or diplomatic endeavour, I have nevertheless felt a heavy obligation to understand and build upon the many notable attempts of the last two generations to found a system of international peace and security on a definition of aggression. If my conclusions are correct, and we are still only at the beginning of the development of an adequate body of theory in this area, it would follow that existing thought, void though it may yet seem of practical fruit, cannot be lightly discarded. It must rather be preserved, ready for re-interpretation as an adequate body of theory emerges. For this and other reasons shortly to be mentioned, I have tried (while keeping the text readable for the non-specialist) to provide in the footnotes an accurate and reasonably complete guide back into the existing body of literature and diplomatic documentation. The lay reader should feel no compulsion to read the footnotes; but I trust he will also be indulgent of their presence for the sake of the extension of knowledge in this critical field.

This book was originally to have been addressed to three main groups of readers: first, the general reader interested in international and United Nations affairs, second, the specialists of the law schools and departments of government of Universities, and third, the legal and diplomatic officers of foreign offices and United Nations delegations. My experience in using some of these materials for teaching and post-graduate seminar work at Harvard in 1956 has, however, greatly impressed me with the high interest and value of the questions canvassed, and of the existing body of knowledge concerning them, as an introduction to advanced teaching in international law and politics. This, surely, is an area in which no labouring is required to make the consequences of theory real to the student. It is also an area of constant and fascinating interplay of publicist doctrine and diplomatic stance, encroaching constantly on the no-man's land beyond the legal order, and thus conveying admirably the special flavour which both law and politics acquire in the international sphere.

For these reasons I have added some features designed to make this book pedagogically useful as a basis for graduate seminar work in international law in law schools and departments of government and public law. The chapter organisation is in any case designed to proceed through the main branches of social and political theory involved, including the linguistic, the political, the legal and ethical, to an overall assessment of the potentialities and limits of the authority of the General Assembly in the maintenance of international peace. Much of the footnote material is designed to guide seminar groups to materials apt as a basis of discussion. The Appendix collects the texts of the main draft definitions of aggression, governmental and private, from early League days to the present. The collection is, perhaps, more comprehensive than any which has up to now been available between two covers; certainly it embraces every important definition discussed in the text.

Still, the main objects of this study remain directed to the clarification of theory essential to future progress with the problems of international aggression and peace enforcement. If my own skills and talents were to measure up to the intense topicality of the subject, this would indeed be a "popular" book; as it is, I can at least warrant the interest which its subject-matter should hold for all who have a serious and intelligent concern with the survival of mankind.

The launching of the first Soviet earth satellite as this book appears, opens new perspectives on both intra-planetary and inter-planetary aggression (or at least on aggression from inter-planetary space). The event has dramatically confirmed the present Writer's view that hopes of securing peace by inventing some precise, mechanically operating definition of aggression, are a snare and a delusion. Even if these remarkable events should in time subject humanity to a new kind of perpetual Passover of the Angel of Death, the space forces involved might fall outside the terms "land, naval or air forces" in the 1956 Soviet definition of aggression. Here, if ever, and in a literal sense, *omnis definitio periculosa.*

I owe important debts in connection with this work to Dr. Ilmar Tammelo, M.A. (Melbourne), Doctor Iuris (Marburg), sometime Privatdozent in the University of Heidelberg, and Mr. Hans J. Stieringer, M.A. (University of Illinois), LL.M. (Harvard), successively Research Fellows in the Department of International Law and Jurisprudence in the University of Sydney. Dr. Tammelo made many valuable suggestions in the initial phases of the work in 1954, when it was only an introductory paper; after I had developed it to its present broader scope in 1956 he worked intensively and imaginatively with me in combing and analysing the pre-existing literature. Mr. Stieringer was of great support to me in the final revision and reorganisation of the MS.; and he was also of great assistance in the preparation of Chapter 9, S. IV, and of the Discourse on "A United Nations Peace Force and the Authority of the General Assembly". I was often able to benefit from his advice and suggestions; and even when I was unable to adopt them, they always showed fine insight and maturity of judgment. As usual my methods of work have imposed heavy burdens on my Graduate Assistant, Miss Zena Sachs, LL.B. (Sydney); only by her knowledge and skills was the MS. brought from the very tentative shape in which it arrived in Sydney from the United States in late June, 1957, to the comparatively finished form in which I was able to send it to the Printer in mid-August. But this should not obscure my indebtedness to Mr. Milton Bordwin, LL.B. (Harvard), and to my dear wife, Reca Stone, for their equally patient and dedicated work on the earlier drafts of the MS. whilst I was working on it at Harvard. My learned friends, Professor Louis B. Sohn, and Assistant Professor Richard R. Baxter, both of the Harvard Law School, and Professor Samuel Shuman, of Wayne University, kindly read substantial parts of the MS., and saved me from some errors and many obscurities. For those that may remain, they are, of course, free of responsibility.

I must finally express appreciation to Dean Erwin N. Griswold, and to Professor Milton Katz, the Director of the International Legal Studies Programme at the Harvard Law School, as well as to the Vice-Chancellor's Research Committee of the University of Sydney, for the provision of research assistance for the completion of this study.

Faculty of Law
University of Sydney.
November 1, 1957.

JULIUS STONE.

TABLE OF CONTENTS

CHAPTER 9—AGGRESSION AND THE AUTHORITY OF THE GENERAL ASSEMBLY

A DISCOURSE ON A UNITED NATIONS PEACE FORCE AND THE AUTHORITY OF THE GENERAL ASSEMBLY

AUTHOR'S NOTE ON UNITED NATIONS DEBATES ON THE DEFINITION OF AGGRESSION, OCT.-NOV. 1957. Cabled information[1] in the final stages of printing show that the Sixth Committee debates have again failed to break the deadlock examined in the present book. They ended with a recommendation for further study of the question of defining aggression on the basis of new government comments, and for renewed General Assembly consideration not earlier than 1959.[2] The present book may thus have some additional value in contributing to the fruitfulness of this further study under United Nations auspices.

[1] I am deeply indebted to Dr. Oscar Schachter for providing, with kind efficiency, late information and documentation throughout the writing of this book.

[2] See A/C.6/SR.514-520 (Oct. 7-25, 1957) 524-529 (Nov. 1-8, 1957). The debate was briefly resumed Nov. 13, 1957, and the above resolution adopted a week later, following the failure of a U.S. proposal for indefinite postponement, as a compromise amendment of a draft sponsored by seven Latin American States and the Philippines. See A/C.6/L.403 and Corr. 1, A/C.6/L.407. For earlier phases of the debates see *infra* p. 77, and as to China's position, *infra* p. 64.

LIST OF ABBREVIATIONS

Note: See Additional List for Index of Subjects

A.B.A.Jo.	*American Bar Association Journal.*
A.J.I.L.	*American Journal of International Law.*
Ann.	Annexes.
Bourquin (ed.), *Collective Security*	M. Bourquin (ed.), *Collective Security,* A Record of the 7th and 8th International Studies Conferences, Paris, 1934—London, 1935 (International Institute of Intellectual Cooperation) (1936).
B.Y.B. Int.L.	*British Yearbook of International Law.*
Can. B.R.	*Canadian Bar Review.*
Cmd.	*Command Paper.*
Conn. Bar J.	*Connecticut Bar Journal.*
Covenant Principles	*Documents Relating to the Question of the Application of the Principles of the Covenant, L.N.O.J.* Sp. Supp. No. 154, Nov, 1936.
Eastern Q.	*Eastern Quarterly.*
F.E.S.S.	First Emergency Special Session of the United Nations General Assembly (Nov. 1-10, 1956).
Final U.N.E.F. Report	Second and Final Report of the Secretary-General on the Plan for an Emergency International United Nations Force, Nov. 6, 1956. (*G.A.O.R.* F.E.S.S., Ann., Agenda Item 5 (A/3302).
Frye	W. R. Fyre, *A United Nations Peace Force* (Carnegie Endowment for International Peace, October, 1957).
Fischer Williams, *Chapters*	Sir John Fischer Williams, *Chapters on Current International Law and the League of Nations* (1929).
Fischer Williams, *Covenant*	Sir John Fischer Williams, *Some Aspects of the Covenant of the League of Nations* (1934).
Franklin, M., *The Conception of Aggression*	M. Franklin, *The Formulation of the Conception of Aggression* (*sine anno,* probably 1952).
G.A.O.R.	*General Assembly Official Records* (followed by the number of the session in Roman capitals. Unless otherwise indicated plenary meetings are referred to.)
G.A. Resols.	General Assembly Resolutions.
Giraud	E. Giraud, *"La Theorie de la Légitime Défense"* (1934) 49 *H.R.*, pt. iii, 691-860.
Grotius Soc. Trans.	See *Trans. Grotius Soc.*
Guard Report	*Report of the Secretary-General of Sept. 28, 1948, on the Establishment of a United Nations Guard* (*U.N. Doc.* A/656).
H.R. / *Hague Recueil*	Academy of International Law (The Hague), *Recueil des Cours.*
Harvard Research, *Aggression*	Harvard Research in International Law, "Draft Convention on Rights and Duties of States in Cases of Aggression" (1939) repr. 33 *A.J.I.L.*, Supp. 826-909.
Hudson, *Int. Leg.*	M. O. Hudson (ed.), *International-Legislation* (7 vols. 1931—onwards covering treaties 1919—onwards).
I.L.C.	*International Law Commission.*
Int. and Comp. L.Q.	*International and Comparative Law Quarterly.*
Komarnicki	W. Komarnicki, *De la Définition de l'Agresseur* (1949) 75 *Hague Recueil* 5-103.
L.N. Doc.	*League of Nations Document.*
L.N.O.J.	*League of Nations Official Journal.*
L.N. Publ.	*League of Nations Publication.*
L.N.T.S.	*League of Nations Treaty Series.*
L.R.	*Law Review.*
L.J.	*Law Journal.*

Minn. L.Rev.	*Minnesota Law Review.*
Nederlands T.Int.R.	*Nederlands Tijdschrift voor Internationaal Recht.* (*Netherlands International Law Review.*)
N.Y.T. (or *N.Y. Times*)	*New York Times.*
PAL, R. B., *International Military Tribunal*	R. B. PAL, *International Military Tribunal for the Far East* (1953) (Dissentient Judgment).
PELLA, V. V., *La Guerre-Crime*	V. V. PELLA, *La Guerre-Crime et les Criminels de Guerre* (1946).
Pol.Sci.Qu.	*Political Science Quarterly.*
POMPE, C. A., *Aggressive War*	C. A. POMPE, *Aggressive War an International Crime* (1953).
Proc.Am.Ac.Arts and Sciences	*Proceedings of the American Academy of Arts and Sciences.*
Rep.	Report.
REP.	
R.D.I.	*Revue de Droit International.*
R.G.D.Int.P.	*Revue Générale de Droit International Public.*
S.C.O.R.	*Security Council Official Records.*
SOHN, *World Law*	L. B. SOHN, *Cases and Materials on World Law* (1950).
S.E.S.S.	Second Emergency Special Session of the United Nations General Assembly (Nov. 4-10, 1956).
Sp.Com.Rep. 1956	Report of the Special Committee on the Definition of Aggression, 1956. *G.A.O.R. XII*, Supp. No. 16 (A/3574. A/AC. 77,1.13).
Sp. Supp.	Special Supplement.
STONE, *Conflict*	JULIUS STONE, *Legal Controls of International Conflict* (1954).
STONE, *Province*	*Id., The Province and Function of Law* (1946, repr. 1950).
Supp.	Supplement.
Trans. Grotius Soc.	*Transactions of the Grotius Society.*
Trial Major War Criminals	International Military Tribunal, *Trial of the Major War Criminals* (42 vols. 1947-1949).
U.N.C.I.O. or *U.N.C.I.O. Docs.*	*Documents of the United Nations Conference on International Organisation,* San Francisco, 1945, 16 vols.
U.N. Doc. (or *Doc.* alone)	*United Nations Document.*
U.N.E.F.	United Nations Emergency Force.
U.N. Rev.	*United Nations Review.*
U.N.T.S.	*United Nations Treaty Series.*
WALTERS, *History*	F. P. WALTERS, *A History of the League of Nations* (2 vols., 1952).

INTRODUCTION

I. MIDDLE EAST CRISIS AND AGGRESSION.

Whether the notion of "aggression" is a useful concept in the development of international law and order, and if so, what might be a proper definition of the notion, are problems which have engaged almost continuous attention of international lawyers for the last thirty years.[1] The last series of efforts in this direction came to still another frustrating end in November, 1956. At its nineteenth and final meeting, the General Assembly's latest Special Committee on the definition of aggression concluded that it must report to the General Assembly that no general consensus was attainable, either as to whether definition is possible or desirable, or as to what the definition should be if it were possible or desirable. This failure is more noteworthy not only by dint of the great labours of the Committee and its predecessors, by the excellent documentary basis available for its work, including a substantial body of scholarly as well as polemical literature, but also and above all by the time context of the capitulation.

For it is to be observed that this Special Committee deliberated between October 8 and November 9, 1956, and that while it was deliberating, Israeli forces crossed the Gaza and Sinai frontiers with the avowed object of eliminating the nests of fedayeen raiders which during a period of years immediately preceding had admittedly carried on more than 400 raids into Israeli territory. While it was deliberating, too, the British and French Governments announced in advance, and partly carried out, an airborne invasion of the Suez Canal Zone with the announced object of separating Israeli and Egyptian forces, and thus preventing the involvement of the Canal in general hostilities. While it was deliberating, too, there occurred the events which led to intervention of Soviet forces to displace the Nagy regime in Hungary, and to establish the authority of the Kadar regime in its place. Such events, it might have been supposed, would have given an excellent opportunity to the various conflicting standpoints in the Special Committee to demonstrate their validity. They also provided a realistic demonstration as well of the need for definition if such could be supplied at all, as of the dubious sincerity of some of the most vigorous champions of definition. For the outstanding champion, the Soviet Union, was engaged in an operation in Hungary which was to fall squarely within the very defini-

---

1 The best historical survey is in Komarnicki. This learned author thinks (103) that the preceding thirty years of effort to 1949 had thrown much light on this problem, which "projects a lugubrious light on our epoch". I agree, and have for that reason made my own examination of the history of the search for definition, prior to any attempt at fuller critical analysis. There are full bibliographies in Harvard Research, *Aggression* 831-843, and L. Sohn, *World Law* (1950) 801-806. There is, however, much later work, cited herein.

tion of aggression which it was pressing on other nations as the greatest crime against mankind;[2] and this same State also immediately engaged in declaring Egypt to be the victim of Israeli "aggression", despite the fact that Egypt had for some years, in the view of many, been committing "aggression" against Israel under four and possibly five separate heads of the current Soviet definition.[3]

No situation could have been more cunningly contrived for impressing on the members of the Special Committee the practical importance of a successful consummation of their task, or for testing the sincerity of the proponents of definition generally or of particular definitions; or, indeed, for testing the validity and usefulness for peace enforcement purposes of the various competing definitions offered. It is of the utmost significance in these circumstances that the Committee adjourned with the admission that not even approximate consensus was attainable either on the desirability of definition, or as to what the definition should be; and that the General Assembly even postponed the consideration of the Special Committee's report, in a somewhat leisurely spirit, to its next regular session in 1957.

---

[2] See *infra* p.117, and International Commission of Jurists, "Hungary and the Soviet Definition of Aggression" (1957) 24 *Bar. Ass. of the District of Columbia Jo.*, 34-35, where it is pointed out that for the role of Soviet troops to have been justified under head 1 (d) of the Soviet definition by virtue of the Warsaw Pact of May 14, 1955, it was necessary that their presence should have been, within the terms of that Pact, "by agreement among the States, in accordance with the requirements of their (i.e., the signatories to the Warsaw Pact) mutual defence". Since it appears under Art. 4 of that Pact that the "mutual defence" envisaged covers only defence against the armed attack of another state, and does not cover the suppression of the people's rising within a signatory State, that role in "mutual defence" is, to say the least, legally dubious. (Soviet lawyers have been insistent that "armed attack" in the Soviet definition relates only to relations between States, but of course they view differently the efforts of a "capitalist" State to "suppress struggles for national liberation" within the sovereign domain. See *infra* pp.114-115.)

Apart from the tortuosities of merely political "law-speaking", therefore, the role of Soviet troops in Hungary would be "armed aggression" within the Soviet Union's own definition, unless there was *ad hoc* consent of the lawful Hungarian Government to this role, insofar as it went beyond the terms of the Warsaw Pact. That such consent was given by the Nagy Government for its own overthrow, is highly incredible. For a rather strained argument that on the Soviet definition the armed attack by Soviet troops would have been aggression even if requested by the lawful government, see D. A. Loeber, *"Die Ereignisse in Ungarn und die Sowjetische Definition der Aggression"* (1956) *Europa-Archiv* 9355, at 9358. It is not necessary for present purposes to enter into any questions of the Hungarian Constitution, Arts. 10, 20 and 25.

The Assembly Resol. A/Res/407, and A/Res/413 of Nov.21, and Dec.12,1956, asserted expressly or implicitly Soviet violation of Art 2 (4) of the Charter. Soviet legal authorities took the position that the Soviet Union was acting in collective self-defence with Hungary under Art. 51 of the Charter, and Art. 5 of the Warsaw Pact, alleging "indirect aggression" by other States against Hungary. They did not deal with the weaknesses of this position mentioned here.

The authoritative account of the events surrounding Soviet entries of Oct. 24 and Nov. 3, 1956, is in *Report of the Special Committee on the Problem of Hungary,* June 12, 1957, *U.N.Doc.* A/3592.

[3] L. M. Bloomfield, *Egypt, Israel and the Gulf of Aqaba* (1957) 58-68, indeed, particularises the charges of aggression by Egypt precisely in terms of the Soviet draft definition, and alleges such breaches under para. 1 (b), (e), and (f), and para. 2 (b) and (c) and paras. 3 and 4. *Cf. Sir Percy Spender,* on 17 Jan., 1957, Doc.A/PV. 638, pp.18ff., 26ff.

Moreover, in the numerous resolutions adopted by the Assembly in the Middle East Affair of 1956-57, no role at all is played by the concept of aggression, much less by any particular definition of it. The term "aggression" did figure, indeed, as a rhetorical weapon of political warfare between the States in conflict, and their champions in the Assembly debates, and as a loosely used embellishment of public pronouncements outside the Assembly.[4] If, nevertheless, the Assembly avoided any finding of breach of the Charter,[5] let alone of aggression, this must obviously raise doubts as to the practical importance of that notion, and as to the possibility of defining it.[6]

II. COMMUNICATION AND DEFINITION.

The factors which have contributed to failure of two world organisations to define the basic concept of international aggression are many; but the parlous condition of human communication is certainly one of them. Any scholar struggling through the debates of these decades since League of Nations efforts began, will be constantly aware that the men engaged on these matters of life and death for man, were far from dominated by any common human drive for truth and justice. Often, indeed, there was as little true community of drive among them as there was among the many States they represented.[7] Delegates spoke as delegates with special interests to press, rather than as men with a common stake in common survival; as advocates of a particular definition or stance on definition required by the situation and interests of particular States. As they vainly assaulted the ears of their colleagues, so their own ears were insensitive to the assaults of others.[8] With but few (and decreasing) exceptions, right through into the

---

4 On the use of the term "aggression" by particular delegates see *infra* Ch.9, n.16.

5 So *cf.* among the clearest recognitions of this by delegates not immediately involved, Mr. Carabajal-Victorica (Uruguay): "We do not condemn either one side or the other. It would be absurd to regard General Assembly decisions as judgments—for they do not have that character. We have studied the problem, and we have taken provisional measures which, so far, have been effective." (A/PV.651, 11th Session, Feb. 2, 1957, p.37); Mr. Pearson (Canada) (A/PV.660, 11th Session, Feb. 26, 1957, p.21.)

The nearest approach to any collective suggestion of breach of the Charter is a statement in the Secretary-General's Report of 24 Jan., 1957 (*Doc.* A/3511), para. 5 (a), of what he regards as a "non-controversial" point implied from "principle" governing "United Nations actions". It was that "the United Nations cannot condone a change of the *status iuris* resulting from military action contrary to the provisions of the Charter". While this long report, as a whole, was noted with approval by the General Assembly, there is no evidence that the Members addressed themselves to the accuracy of the implied legal judgment, nor to whether it was *intra vires* the Secretary-General to make such a judgment on behalf of the General Assembly.

6 On the dangers arising if questions involved in judging the merits of the Parties' causes are begged, instead of inquired into, see *infra* Ch. 9, nn.15,16,27.

7 It was, therefore, rather an understatement of Mr. Sanders (A/AC.77/SR.5, pp.3-4) that "the members of the Committee were not serving in an individual capacity; they had been appointed to represent the views of their Governments", but that this "still allowed them freedom to explore and debate the matter in its entirety".

8 *Cf.* during the recent Middle East crisis Lester Pearson's observations that the speeches of many Soviet *bloc* delegates "constituted a kind of verbal aggression against the truth in which, I am afraid, we shall never be able to bring about a cease-fire". (*G.A.O.R. XI,* 592d Plenary Meeting, Nov. 23, 1956, p.267, para. 56); and Mr. Krishna Menon's concern, at one point, to stress that he was addressing the General Assembly, and not "the gallery" (*G.A.O.R.* S.E.S.S., 571st Plenary Meeting, Nov. 9, 1956, p.75, para. 195).

work of the nineteen States represented on the General Assembly's 1956 Committee on the Question of Defining Aggression, the standpoint was ever placed before the issue, and despite the frequent invocation of truth and justice the final interests of mankind as a whole played but a lesser role. Nor were fruitful results brought nearer by the ready resort to mere debating points in support of or against particular stances; too often they merely succeeded in confusing even the grounds of dissension.

Whether or not other efforts will follow the failure of the 1956 Special Committee it is safe to predict that such efforts must also fail unless the conditions of human communication on this matter can be improved. Nor can we with any confidence predict such improvement; for it is possible that the increasing trauma of fear of war fought with modern weapons of mass destruction will benumb, rather than stimulate, the interest and sensibility of peoples and their leaders, and their willingness to face the real issues. Yet it remains a duty of all of us to attempt to improve these conditions. Certainly it seems worth inquiring whether scholarly discussion not geared to particular diplomatic stances of the final issues which these stances throw up, can offer any hope of escape from the *cordon insanitaire* with which the stalemate of the debate on the definition of aggression has invested United Nations peace enforcement. Assuredly, even scholarly discussion remains vulnerable to the distorting and insulating activities of the State entity on human communication; yet since the duty remains, we must fulfil it as best we can.

III. VIOLENCE = WAR; WAR = AGGRESSION?

Inevitably the following pages will be critical of the reasoning of many predecessors in this area, diplomatic and doctrinal; and I must perforce order my criticism according to my own convictions as to the interrelations of the problems involved. It is fitting, therefore, that I should at the outset put before the reader, as fairly as possible, the overall position from which I shall have to dissent on numerous points. I mean the position of those who assert that an advance definition of aggression, capable of yielding certainty of application in future contingencies is indispensable to human survival; and that what is thus indispensable must also be within our reach. Such assertions have been made with more or less sincerity and independence of the interests of particular States;[9] and I shall later have to examine them in these modalities. At this prefatory stage, however, I wish to present this

---

Though this is not always so, the same debates also suggest a correlation between lack of communication and resort to ambiguities in the formulation of conclusions, thus avoiding confrontation of the conflicts involved. *Cf.* Mr. Serrano (Philippines) (*G.A.O.R. XV,* 593d Plenary Meeting, Nov. 24, 1956, p.285, para. 42).

[9] Even so articulate and distinguished a critic of all aspects of the "aggressive war" count as Mr. Justice Pal, of the Tokyo Tribunal, still seems to indulge hope that the main grounds of criticism could be removed if States would only carry out their "duty of definition" in advance, and that this "would not only make the matter clear but would also give it its true place in the scheme of knowledge showing its origin and connection with other cognate facts and determining its essentials". (*International Military Tribunal* 112.)

type of position, with the fullest strength which its exponents, among whom Professor Scelle is only the most distinguished, have brought to it. I shall, indeed, take Georges Scelle's position as one whose account is clearly relevant to the definitional problem in the United Nations context, and who combines high ability with a clear devotion to the cause of peace and the advance of knowledge.

When Georges Scelle declared in 1954[10] that under positive international law, with all its deficiencies, recourse to force constitutes the crime of aggression, he did not wholly neglect the difficulties confronting his position.[11] If this assertion as to the state of the positive law is correct his position and consequential arguments are clear and courageous. International law has (on his view) moved away from recognition of any *"compétence de guerre"* of States, depriving them of all such competence except in legitimate self-defence. Self-defence apart, all "aggression" whether *"légitime"* or *"illégitime"* has become illegal, and an international offence.[12]

He recognises that this "normative revolution" has not hindered States from building up national armaments to a hitherto unparalleled level for professedly defensive purposes. The level of armaments and the danger of their use are for him *"une contingence notable"*, which cannot affect the clarity of the legal position. He recognises also that the prohibition of recourse to force leaves a wide range of legal rights and legitimate interests of States unprotected. He is concerned, indeed, rather proudly to stress that "henceforward the use of force to secure recognition of the legality of an established but contested situation, to modify existing norms, or even to demand the execution of a judicial decision", is wholly forbidden. *La compétence de guerre,* the license to use force, "even in the case of a just war" for vindication of legal rights, is henceforth the first of the international crimes now listed by the International Law Commission. For while he insists that there should be sanctions for the redress of violated international legal rights, he also insists that the power of imposing sanctions *(la compétence sanctionnaire)* no longer belongs to individual States, but only to the international organisation itself, to the Security Council of the United Nations, or its supplementary regional organisations.

Professor Scelle's idealism thus leads him to acknowledge the dependence of the tolerability of his main theme on the growth of effective means of collective redress for the violation of the rights of States generally. It leads him, indeed, also to recognise that the legal order of the United Nations (to which he has relegated redress of the violated rights of States) is "unfor-

---

10 *"Quelques Réflexions sur l'Abolition de la Compétence de Guerre"* (1954) 58 *R.G.D.Int.P.* 5,13. He does not think it necessary even to argue the legal issues, simply asserting (p.5) that "all use of force or threat of force" except for "legitimate defence" and collective action are prohibited under the Charter, citing Preamble, paras. 6,7; Arts. 1 and 2 (3) (4) and 5, and Arts. 24,25,33ff., and Chapters VII-VIII.

11 Whether he gave adequate weight to them, including the difficulty of sustaining his proposed version of positive international law on this matter, will be considered hereafter.

12 Article cited, 11.

tunately lacking in effectiveness";[13] that the United Nations Charter seems to envisage an international police only for the maintenance of peace and security;[14] that it has not in fact been possible to establish a standing international force even for that limited purpose, and that such a police authority, if it became possible in the future, would lack any legal power to act against the Permanent Members of the Security Council. He admits, in short, that "a legal order which does not import the possibility of *eliminating* litigious situations, is a notoriously imperfect legal order, for no *material security* is imaginable if it is not preceded by legal security, that is by *the ineluctable establishment* of binding judgment".[15]

Do these hard facts require us to modify the supposed unqualified prohibition of forceful individual self-redress by States, which he has asserted to be the rule of positive international law? Professor Scelle admits a natural anxiety as to whether we can regard as "a real step forward in the legal order a state of things which permits any government to flout with impunity the claims of another Government based on law, and even on unquestionable title, so long as its illegal resistance and abuse of law do not manifest itself in 'aggression' or in conduct giving the injured party the right of self-defence". He is willing to ask, in short, whether "in prohibiting all recourse to force or threat of force, before having institutionalised compulsory third party settlement as well as the collective policing power, the international legal order has not put the cart before the horse".[16]

It will be apparent as this work proceeds that I more than join in these anxious questions of Professor Scelle and that I feel compelled to answer them in a very much less optimistic sense, challenging his own basic premise and reasoning. I am here concerned, however, to state rather than criticise these; and I must therefore add that alongside his premises that contemporary positive law prohibits all individual forceful self-redress by States, Professor Scelle places an assumed axiom of legal history. "Every legal order, whatsoever", he says, "tends to become effective, that is, to realise itself in the facts. Every norm bears in itself a sanction. That is why a developed legal order enounces, side by side with the normative rules which are its substantive content, institutional and procedural norms aimed to secure the efficacy of its norms of substance".[17]

For Professor Scelle his axioms seem to dictate that we can overcome the difficulty of having "the cart before the horse", by now seeking to ensure that some United Nations organ shall be able rapidly to determine the fact that an aggression has taken place, and which State is the aggressor; that an International Criminal Court shall be instituted to determine the guilt of individuals, and the sanctions to be applied; and that these sanctions be applied effectively. All this (he would agree) presupposes the constitution of a supra-national *"force"* superior to any national *"force"* and to any com-

---

13 Article cited, 11-12.

14 For some questions as to this, see *infra* pp.95ff. And *cf.* Giraud 722-734, 788-798.

15 Article cited, 12. Translations of this article are by the present Writer; italics are in the original.

16 Article cited, 12.

17 Article cited, 7.

bination of national *"forces"*, and most of it (he also agrees) is still in the realm of the *"irréel"* despite aspirations going back to President Wilson. But he sees parts of this necessary *"régime gouvernemental mondial"* as already in sight;[18] and he appears to think that agreement among States on the definition of aggression, whereby they abandon any *arrière-pensée* such as might lead them to resort to violence by evasive and equivocal means, as the essential next step. He is mindful of the truism that "the establishment of a juridical norm in any society requires a union of ethics and power", and that we are in a revolutionary era in which we cannot derive a sense of security even from the emergence of the principles of the future. He is confident, however, that the directions for effort he has given are correct since "the history of juridical formations appears to have shown the final (though often distant) triumph of ethics over power", even for an anarchical period like ours in which "power has not succeeded in finding that single centre of concentration without which essential ethical principles cannot be made effective".[19]

Professor Scelle's position on these matters had remained unshaken by the traumatic generation which preceded his declaration of 1954. It was clearly taken nearly twenty years before[20] and in a context of the League Covenant very different from that of the United Nations Charter.[21] Then, too, though admitting that resort to individual self-redress of rights must be greater as social organisation is weaker, and therefore reflected in a more extensive right of legitimate self-defence of States in a legal order which each member is strong enough to challenge, than the corresponding right of individuals under municipal law, he nevertheless argued as if these differences were transient.[22] It is his final position that the same "juridical techniques" regulate the relations of members in the international and municipal orders, these techniques being everywhere the same. He finds singular proof of this in the evolution of law precisely in this matter of aggression,[23] and legitimate self-defence, asserting that in this regard these two juridical disciplines tend exactly to correspond; though clearly he can only have meant by this that in view of the successful emergence of the public monopoly of force in *municipal* legal orders, *we are entitled to assume* that similar success is within reach for the international order.

He affirmed therefore in 1936, as he reaffirmed in 1954, that international law adopted a "purely objective" criterion of war, "assimilating every use of force to aggression. . . . The sense of evolution also leads to this double equation: 'Every recourse to violence = War; Every War = Aggression'."

---

18 I have given the most restrained interpretation here. Literally he says that these parts of the regime *"ont été posées"* (10,13).

19 Article cited, 22.

20 G. Scelle, *"l'Agression et la Légitime Défense dans les Rapports Internationaux"* (1936) 16 *L'Esprit International* 372-393. See also *infra* Ch. 5, n.7.

21 See *infra* Chs. 2 and 3.

22 1936 article at 373.

23 On the fallacy of the assumption that municipal orders work with the notion of "aggression" at all see *infra* pp.117ff.

> Every recourse to violence is a war. If we introduce here any subjective elements, notably the will to make war, there is no longer . . . any security. What must be forbidden is precisely the will to do justice for oneself *(se faire justice à soi-même)*. . . . The only criterion of war is that of the materiality of the facts, namely use of force to support a national claim. There is no middle term: if we wish to proscribe war, and consequently aggression which is the initiative in war, we must wholly remove from international law the possibility of taking justice into one's own hands. The criterion of war and the criterion of aggression are one.[24]

Many estimable and noble arguments surround this fundamental position: the need to save our world from anarchy, and for an agreed precise definition of aggression as essential to this end; the threat to the physical survival of mankind from any breach of the peace which modern thermonuclear weapons may move uncontrollably into general world conflagration;[25] the resounding declaration that "aggressive" war must be criminal by "the very nature of international law, including its basis, end and sources", and as "an obvious negation of the ideas which are the very essence of law, such as the ideas of justice, morality and solidarity",[26] and of "natural law" and the general principles of law.[27]

Though none of these arguments self-evidently leads to the conclusion that in existing international law all forceful self-redress is "aggression" and criminal, some of them sufficed in the 'thirties to build among French jurists a deep attachment to Soviet offered draft definitions. Even as Europe moved after 1933 into its decade of agony, Paul Bastid was seeing the Soviet draft and the abortive Draft Treaty on the Definition of Aggression which embodied it, as one "of inestimable value",[28] and de la Brière was simultaneously calling, as an indispensable next step, for "a *clear,* precise, certain rule (which) permits us to recognise, *immediately* and *effectively,* in the case of any armed incursion, which is the *unjust and guilty* aggressor".[29]

Numerous other illustrations of these approaches to our problem will emerge later.[29a] We seek here primarily to display them fairly preparatory to

---

[24] 1936 article at 377-379.

[25] See e.g. H. Thirring, *"Was ist Aggression"* (1952-53) 5 *Oesterreichische Z für öff. R. (N.F.)* 226-242, who builds on it the need to accept (with a rather circuitous initial general formula) the Soviet definition of 1950. For my own contrary indications from the same perils, see *infra* Ch. 9, s.I, F.-K.

[26] *Id.* 541ff., 548ff.

[27] See e.g. S. Glaser, *"Constituye un Crimen la Guerra de Agresion"* (1953) 6 *Revista Española de Derecho Internacional* 539-562, at 542. This writer's position, however, avoids assuming, by the ambiguity of its terms "unprovoked attack" and "act of violence", the extreme range of Professor Scelle's position.

[28] M. A. F. Frangulis 3 *Dictionnaire Diplomatique* (no date), *sub voce "Agresseur"*. See on this Draft, Le Fur, in 11 *R.D.I.* 179.

[29] M. A. F. Frangulis, id., *sub voce "Agresseur"* (italics supplied). See *infra* Ch. 9, on the internal self-contradiction involved, on a full analysis, between the desiderata of those key words we have italicised. *Cf.* C. Jordan, R. Cassin, J. Limburg, H. J. W. Verzijl, and W. Komarnicki, all in Bourquin (ed.), *Collective Security* 313; the last mentioned asking for "a rigorous objective criterion" with "instantaneous", "automatic" guarantees.

[29a] So *cf.* after this volume went to press the general thesis of Professor Jaroslav Zourek of the Charles University, Prague (in his Hague Lectures, on "The Definition of Aggression

our own critique of them. Even at this point, however, it is illuminating to mention the still more ambitious structure of ideas put forward in various contemporary forms by Professor V. V. Pella, R. J. Alfaro and the late Mr. Justice Jackson. Professor Pella building enthusiastically on Georges Scelle's position[30] declared, almost at the birth of the United Nations, that many of the difficulties confronting the Security Council could only be solved by an adequate definition of aggression.[31] To this end the "justness" of the causes of war must become legally irrelevant, and "the elements of the crime of war be fixed in advance by a precise test of international law"[32] in accordance with "contemporary juridical consciousness". He called, therefore, for the adoption of the Draft Convention on the Definition of the Aggressor of 1933,[33] based on the earlier Soviet draft, with certain *"précisions"* arising from the experience of World War II.[34] This definition should operate in law "absolutely, automatically, on the basis of material facts easily ascertainable", creating a sort of presumption *juris et de jure* in international relations.[35] "Aggression" would thus be central in M. Pella's conception of international criminality, embracing any

> action or inaction internationally dangerous by reason of the fact that it has contributed to the preparation or execution of an international war; or to the violation of the laws and customs of war, or to the creation of situations of such a nature as to trouble the peaceful relations of States, or finally to a national policy offending the universality of human sentiments.[36]

Many basic components of contemporary United Nations debates arise from the matrix of such ideas. R. J. Alfaro proceeded on Professor Scelle's formula that "All recourse to violence = War; All war = Aggression"[37] in sounding one of the contrasting themes in the International Law Commission in 1950.[38] On this basis, rejecting definitions of the enumerative type, he was to propose (and in turn to have rejected) a general and abstract definition of aggression[39] as embracing all use of force or threat of force against another State except for (1) legitimate individual or collective defence against an armed aggression, and (2) action by the United Nations itself.

---

and International Law: Recent Developments of the Problem") that aggression is any "first" use of force by one State against another. His position is somewhat less simple, however, insofar as he insists that "force" is wider than "armed force". Only a brief summary has been available to us; but this indicates that the present Writer's views on Professor Zourek's main positions will be clear from the present work as it stands.

30 See *supra* pp.5ff.

31 V.V. Pella, *La Guerre-Crime* 35, 43.

32 *Op.cit.* 44.

33 See *infra* pp.35-36.

34 *Op.cit.* 44. As to the fate of certain of the States which entered into non-aggression treaties with the Soviet Union on the basis of these definitions, see *infra* Ch. 2, n.52.

35 *Id.* 45.

36 *Id.* 35.

37 And *cf.* the authorities cited *supra* n.29, and *infra* pp.94ff. *Cf.* Professor Scelle himself in A/CN.4/SR.109, paras. 22, 30: "He wondered how a meeting of jurists could overlook the opportunity to emphasise the enormous progress represented by the absolute prohibition of resort to force in order to change a legal situation, even if the change were legitimate." And *cf.* Giraud's critique of such views, Giraud, 788ff.

38 See in the next year, R. J. Alfaro, *"La Cuestion de la Definicion de la Agresion"* (1951) 59 *Revista de Derecho Internacional* 361-380, esp. 378; in French in (1951) 29 *Revue de Droit International* 367-381.

39 Article first cited *supra* n.38 at 372.

The late Mr. Justice Jackson in his arguments before and in and on the Nuremberg Trials[40] echoed the French advocacy in the 'thirties of the Soviet enumerative definition. So far as relevant to that case, he suggested, that State was the aggressor which is the first to commit any of the listed actions of declaration of war, invasion, etc., enumerated in the Soviet draft of 1933. And as with the Soviet draft and with M. Scelle's account of 1936, he would also incorporate the Soviet proviso, excluding as justification any "political, military, economic, or other considerations", except only for defence against an act of aggression. "Whatever grievance a nation may have, however objectionable it finds the *status quo* . . ., warfare is an illegal means for settling these grievances or altering these conditions".[41] He thought we need not trouble ourselves about the many "abstract" difficulties that might be conjured up about doubtful cases.

IV. PUSH-BUTTON DEFINITION.

We have, it is trusted, been sufficiently just to the logic of thought, and generosity of vision which asserts the primacy among the tasks of peace and security of finding a definition of aggression clear and precise enough for certain and automatic applications to all future situations. I have tried to mute at this point the earnest questionings which such proposals raise, for the body of this work is dedicated to them. Yet a certain core of these questions is self-raised by the proposals themselves. Professor Pella himself is constrained to qualify his institutional proposals by the admission that peace depends finally on man, that whatever the tests of aggression we devise human survival still pre-requires that "the national man become the world man, that the competitive man become the cooperative man", that "equality of moral principles" prevail between States, and that the Great Powers prefer such principles to "political considerations".[42] And if this is so the question what is a feasible priority of tasks as between the lawyer's constructs and the psychological, political and military forces to be regulated, is inevitably raised. Insofar as such proposals aspire to find salvation in a mechanical test of aggression, insulated from the merits of the situations in which States act, they have the flavour of a Utopia of the coming age of automation.

It may be that as we move from the old-fashioned production line *à la Detroit,* through the mechanical brain, to the self-correcting servile mecha-

---

[40] Robert H. Jackson, *The Nürnberg Case* (1947) 15, 86ff., 127. [41] *Op.cit.* 87.

[42] *Op.cit.* 46, quoting Politis (*La Morale Internationale* (1943))48. *Cf.* Komarnicki, 101, who traces the difficulties back to problems of international organisation, which can only be solved "on a universal plan and by juridical methods". He then adds (somewhat inconsistently, it might seem) that these problems spring from the "absence of real international spirit", which in turn is explained by the lack of any *"base sociale internationale",* so that the social conditions for the formation of a public opinion among peoples and the constitution of an international government are still non-existent. "In the problem of aggression, we find ourselves at the heart of the problem of international life. War is a manifestation of international anarchy. Peace among nations is a function of respect for international law." (103.)

While agreeing with these generalisations, we regard them rather as the starting-points than as conclusions for the present study.

nism, some push-button will be invented that will press back and make us feel wanted, and thus save our societies for humanity. It is difficult to believe, however, that such a development is yet upon us, or that such a push-button solution of the problems of peace under just law between States will be its final triumph. If, in this work, we differ much from the type positions just sketched, we would beg the reader to believe that this difference does not extend to any doubting of the grave perils with which any breach of the peace now threatens mankind, nor of the urgency of doing whatever is possible by the improvement or elaboration of international law to reduce these perils. But since we do not believe that any juristic push-button device can seriously advance this purpose, we can also give no high priority to the effort to invent one. By that we do not deny the problem; we rather assert that the problem is too urgent to permit the diversion of so much of our limited resources of intellect and energy to illusory solutions.

Certainly the cruel fact of the contemporary breakdown of the whole enterprise of definition of aggression should suggest to us the need for earnest re-examination of theories which would make human survival depend upon agreed advance tests of "aggression", capable of operating immediately and automatically and with certainty of result in any future crises. This study is such a re-examination; and we have entered on it in awareness of the constructive significance of any findings either way for the human situation. For even insofar as we have to reject such theories the result should increase rather than diminish our sense of urgent anxiety, and thus stimulate us to seek more promising paths for its abatement.

V. AWARENESS AND CYNICISM.

It should scarcely be necessary to add that scepticism of this sort toward the enterprise of precise definition of aggression springs from no condonation of aggression. With all men of good will, we give full assent to the denunciation of aggression as the gravest international crime. But this in no way excludes the possibility that it is nevertheless a crime which it may be often impossible, except in the concrete context of its alleged occurrence, to characterise as such. We do not render the notion determinate out of such context merely by characterising it as "the gravest of all crimes": we may even have to consider the possibility that, in the present state of the international order, it will be only so long as the notion is left indeterminate that there will be any humanity-wide consensus that it *is* the gravest of crimes. Nor should this paradox surprise us too much. It is also found elsewhere in man's moral and political preoccupations. Justice itself is ever praised by all our generations as the highest social virtue, and the *summum bonum* extolled as the highest goal of human endeavour. This stature would quickly fade if either were made to depend on some precise authoritatively formulated criterion for all future cases, regardless of the demands of unforeseen and unforeseeable situations.

Each of us, no doubt, as we join in denouncing this grave crime against mankind, has in his mind a more or less clear intuition of what aggression means, sufficient to make denunciation meaningful for us. But when we seek to formulate criteria which may be applied by others *independently of our own* intuitions, we are confronted not only by the distrust of the adequacy of present formulations for the unknown future, but often also by awareness that even for a present concrete situation the intuitions which seem compulsive to us may go quite unfelt by our fellows. Certainly, this is often so when we are the representatives of different States on a Committee charged with formulating criteria of aggression. Even if "aggression" as used in our debates refers to something definite in each of our respective minds, the *designata* will as often as not be not the same for all of us. Even when similar thoughts *seem* to be expressed quite different things may often nevertheless be being talked about, and the end result but a vain polyphony of voices, echoing across the chasms separating the *designata* without really bridging them. Certainly, in studying the now massive international committee work on the definition of "aggression", we have often felt as if we were attending some strange kind of Lateran Council summoned to settle with final authority the realms of "good" and "evil", and wondered whether diplomatic conferences could be an apt forum for wielding this authority. Yet even if the urgent campaign of many delegates to promote an agreed formulation of the precise criteria of aggression were always inspired by sincere conviction, it would be at best no more convincing than the view of other delegates that the objective was not feasible even if it were desirable. In fact the urgent campaign to define, as well as the definitions offered and the resistance to these, may often have to be explained in less generous terms; and from that, too, our enquiries must not shrink.

Certainly any advance in understanding requires us to face the facts that the General Assembly's Special Committee on the Definition of Aggression of 1956 failed to produce an approach to consensus either on such a definition, or as to the "possibility" or "desirability" of such a definition; and also that it manifested a real failure of human communication, leaving the whole problem not only at large, but surrounded by an ever-deepening hedge of cynicism and disillusionment. To such cynicism none of us, whether scholar or statesman, can afford to yield so far as to dismiss the question altogether. For the present study seems to show that some of the most intractable problems of justice in a shrinking and everchanging world lie deep at the core of this problem of defining aggression. The failures of States, international organs and individual thinkers, to reach consensus may have to be explained (at least in part) in terms of the impossibility of containing the unceasing struggle for a minimal justice in international relations within the straitjacket of precise formulae for the definition of aggression. The fact that the main formulae proposed have no clear warrant in existing law is of minor import by comparison.

All this is a matter for regret and dismay, in view of the implications of failure in a world in which the penalty for failure may well be the destruction of all of us by thermo-nuclear weapons. But it is important also to say that this is the possible penalty, *not of our understanding* of the failure, but of the *failure* itself. For us to face courageously the obstacles to success even when they terrify us by their insurmountability may, in the long run, be more fruitful of results. The shorter the time which may be left to us all, the less time we have to waste; at the least, by identifying and facing these obstacles we may avoid still more waste of time, frustration of intellect and desolation of spirit along certain lines of past efforts. Even if full awareness of the futility of those efforts, and of the plight in which they have left us, seems to lead to near-hopelessness, this awareness may still be an essential if traumatic precondition for our proper orientation in this complex, disappointing and menacing world. It may be an essential basis on which to reassess other approaches and techniques, besides the aggression notion, for seeking collective security. Certainly it must help us to a due appreciation of the indispensable role of justice as well as "law" (or its stand-in of wishful logic) in humanity's flight before the pursuing Nemesis. Lethe, the God of Forgetfulness, was an adversary of Dike, the Goddess of Justice,[43] as indeed Alethea, the Goddess of Truth, was an ally. Awareness and truth together may not alone suffice as foundations of justice between States; but they must at least be essential parts of these foundations.

---

[43] See Ch.1, n.31.

CHAPTER 1

THE QUEST FOR DEFINITION OF AGGRESSION

I. IMPLICATIONS FOR ACTION OF LEGAL DEFINITION.

"Aggression" between States does, of course, occur. The term "aggression" has, in this sense, indeed, as a moral characterisation of behaviour, had a reasonably well-settled (if imprecise) meaning in common usage; and this common usage has undoubtedly played a part in the international lawyer's efforts towards *legal* definition. As a term of *legal* characterisation, however, the term could scarcely be meaningful before the attempts, beginning with the League, to limit the customary licence to go to war.

It is essential, moreover, to realise that the international lawyer's problems in this area far transcend that of uncovering and clarifying the existing meaning of "aggression" as found in common usage. The lawyer's task is to provide such a definition of the concept as will simultaneously prohibit what is sought to be branded and punished as the greatest crime against mankind, while yet also leaving to States sufficient freedom of action to allow them to survive at a tolerable level of security and opportunity. What is sought, in other words, is the verbal means of distinguishing in advance between that use of coercion which may be justified (as, for example, in "legitimate self-defence"), or as otherwise free of the "aggressive" taint (e.g., as in mere "frontier incidents"), from that use of force which is to be condemned and repressed as the supreme crime of aggression.

Such a delimitation is not always easy to make, even as between individuals within a municipal society, who can usually call upon overwhelmingly powerful executive, judicial, and legislative organs to ensure the minimum conditions of survival and tolerable existence without the use by each man of his strong right arm.[1] In the international legal order there are no criteria in common usage capable of guiding us with certainty in making this discrimination in yet unforeseen circumstances. The term "aggression"[2]

---

[1] On the need in general for caution in drawing analogies from the municipal to the international order see J. Stone, "International Law and International Society" (1952) 30 *Can.B.R.* 164-174, Stone, *Conflict* liii-lv, 41-45, and literature there cited.

[2] Not desiring to encumber the text with etymological indications, nor believing these to be more than at best suggestive, a note may here be ventured on the word "aggression", *"Aggredior"* (*"adgredior"*) has a common root with *gradum,* and originally indicated approach, taking the accusative case (as in *aggredior aliquem*), and was used in the context of going or approaching someone for the purpose of conversing or advising with, asking counsel of, entreating or soliciting something of; or applying to, addressing, or soliciting, or going to or setting about or undertaking, or initiating. Even when it came to mean going to or against the other in a hostile manner, or falling on, attacking, or assaulting him, the reference was rather to the openness or directness of the attack in contrast to the secret, unexpectedness of the approach denoted by the verb *adorior.* See C. T. Lewis and C. Short, *A New Latin Dictionary, sub voce "aggredior"* (*"adgredior"*) and usage there cited.

The etymological evolution of the term, though it scarcely casts any blinding light on present problems, does suggest that the general trend has been a late injection of negative moral value into a term originally having a morally neutral reference either to

itself is one which (unless we are careful) begs the very questions we seek to use it to answer. Yet the escape from this question-begging notion, by the

---

motion in space, or to initiative in time. On early usage generally see K. Reichhelm, *Der Angriff* (1934) 2-14, who as late as 1934 thought it might be necessary to make certain whether the term was used in a particular treaty in merely a "factual" as distinct from a moral or legal sense. Reichhelm distinguishes early references to *faktischer Angriff* (17-32) in which illegality or wrongful intent is not necessarily implied, but merely an initiative in acts of force. He points out that in this older sense an aggression in fact may nevertheless be a legally justified use of force, to which the term "aggression" *in its modern sense* could not be applied.

We do not consider here the unsuccessful Grotian attempt to limit or prohibit resort to war for "unjust" causes, though the relation of the idea to modern problems will later emerge. See *infra* pp.92ff., 132 *Cf.* on the main point, R. Redslob, *Théorie dé la Société des Nations* (1927) 60; R. Théry, *La Notion d'Agression en Droit International* (1937) 22-27. The term is found almost with its present moral over-tones early in the nineteenth century. See e.g. the secret Anglo-French-Austrian Treaty of Alliance, Jan. 3, 1815, Preamble, and Art. 1, and the Franco-Belgian Convention of Nov. 10, 1832 (13 Martens, *N.R.* 57) Art. 6. And see other nineteenth century treaties referred to in E. Serra, *L'Aggressione Internazionale* (1946) 25-29, and W. Steinlein, *Der Begriff des nichtherausgeforderten Angriffs in Bündnisverträgen seit* 1870 *und insbesondere im Locarno-Vertrag* (1927) 75ff.,83ff., 105ff.

The historical account in R. Théry, *op.cit.* 19-40, asserts that the notion had no juridical meaning before 1914, though it already had a long literary history relevant to morals and politics, and that the nearest approach to its modern international sense was as a factual description of "offensive military operations", free of moral stigma. M. Théry finds its earliest use as applied to *war* in certain theological and canonical writers of the sixteenth century who, interestingly enough, use the term *"bellum offensivum"* and *"bellum aggressivum"* interchangeably, including under these just wars for the vindication of rights or punishment of wrongs. *Cf.* Komarnicki 5, 12. As late as the Napoleonic wars we find the term "aggression" being regularly prefaced by the adjective "unjust" (Théry, *op.cit.* 21, n.25). M. Théry well pointed out, however, that the injection of a moral characterisation into the notion was facilitated by the consideration that the very initiative involved in the moral notion of aggression, tends inevitably to put on the "aggressor" a burden of moral justification which is not borne by the State which is in the defensive posture; and that this position becomes readily formulated, politically and morally speaking, in the terms of the doctrine of "unprovoked attack" (see 20). *Cf.* also on the former absence of moral stigma in the term "aggression", C. A. Pompe, *Aggressive War*, 65. And see G. Piotrowski, ". . . *L'Aggression"* (1957) 35 *R.D.I.* 169.

Among French writers of the 'thirties, seeking to fix as aggression every resort to force which is not in self-defence against such a resort, the distinction between "just" and "unjust" aggression is frequently made for the precise purpose of driving home that even "just aggression" is, in their view, unlawful and a crime. Here the *moral* stigma again disappears from the term aggression; only a legal stigma is necessary. See e.g. P. Bastid, cited *supra* p.8; G. Scelle, *Droit International Public* (1944) 638; *cf.* even more recently, *id., "Quelques Réflexions"* (1954) 58 *R.G.D.Int.P.* 5, 11. The matter is further complicated when writers of this view then proceed to use the term "unjust" aggression to mean aggression that is so (i.e. is illegal or criminal) within their own definition, regardless of whether it would meet the Grotian test of "just war". See e.g. Y. de la Brière, cited *supra* Introd., n.27.

The full entry of this concept from the moral into the legal arena is not really traceable further back than the League Covenant, and Arts. 239 and 429 of the Treaty of Versailles. It would now be difficult to use the term in a neutral sense, whether for legal or political purposes. See, however, as to the morally colourless uses of the term which are still important in contemporary psychological, anthropological and sociological work, a convenient short account in M. Sharp, "Aggression: A Study of Values and Law" (1947) 57 *Ethics* Supp., esp. 2ff., 39. And see *infra* Ch. 6, n.7.

It may be interesting, even if somewhat fanciful, to see in the etymological evolution of the term reasons for the prominence of transgression of frontiers, and of "the first act" in many modern proposed tests of aggression. See *infra* pp.68ff., 114. So also in terms of the etymological history the Canadian criticism of the current Soviet definition, that it implied that "aggression" could sometimes be "justified" (see *infra* p.47), would be ill-chosen. Since, however, the term was used by the Soviet definition in the contemporary sense, involving the moral judgment, the criticism was warranted.

establishment of objectively identifiable criteria, is also extremely difficult.

The question-begging aspects of the term "aggression" as a proposed central concept of the international legal order, is clear, though by no means obvious. The fact is that no developed legal system has ever succeeded in taking the notion of "aggression" as the central point of its regulation of the use of force.[3] Municipal legal systems work rather with notions such as "assault and battery", "trespass", "taking with intent to deprive the true owner thereof", "rape", "assault with intent to do grievous bodily harm", "murder", "killing with malice aforethought", "treason" and the like. There is this critical difference between such notions and that of "aggression" as a proposed cornerstone of the international law and order. Most municipal law notions, even when some of them may have twilight fringes of discretional application ("treason"), embody an authoritative community judgment that a particular kind of external conduct (indicable by ostensive definition) of assaulting, or taking, or raping, or killing or the like, is legally culpable. The municipal law may, and often does, provide grounds of self-exculpation, such as self-defence, or *bona fide* claim of right; but such grounds too, represent authoritative community judgments establishing reasonably objective indications for distinguishing innocent and even commendable conduct from what the law condemns.

In the notion of "aggression" between States, however, no such objective criteria authoritatively settled by the community are explicit. The notion asks us, rather than tells us, what these criteria are. The call to define the notion by spelling out these criteria, therefore, is far more than a mere call to clarify the meaning of a word in common usage. It is rather a concealed demand for international legislation on a formidable scale. The legislation it demands, moreover, is of critical import, setting out (as it would by definition have to do) the limits where each State's liberty of self-assertion of its rights and interests ends, and where its duty to submit without resistance to invasion or destruction of these rights and interests by others begin. It may thus be a demand to formulate here and now, and once and for all, the rules of *meum* and *tuum* which States ought to observe in many of the most critical future situations with which they may be confronted. Here certainly is a clue to the intractability of the problem of definition which has defeated two generations, though we shall later have to refer to other very serious difficulties arising from hazardous analogies between the municipal and international legal orders.

When we seek to escape from the self-questioning indeterminacy of the notion of aggression by establishing objective criteria of conduct which is to be deemed innocent rather than "aggressive", other difficulties press. This discrimination is, as we have just seen, tantamount to concretising the rules of law by which the relations of States ought to be governed in all the as yet

[3] See *infra* Ch. 3, n.52 on the weakness of certain British arguments which fail to take account of this fact. There is a converse difficulty in G. Scelle's argument *"L'Agression et la Légitime Défence"* (1936) 10 *L'Esprit International* 372, 374, which seems to assume that "aggression" is a concept playing a similar role in municipal and international legal systems.

unforeseeable situations in which States may have to decide *whether they may assert and defend, or whether they must surrender and abandon* their rights and interests. Here precisely is a clue to the contemporary paradox in which the United States delegate was able to observe, in the recent Special Committee debates, that the very acts which the Soviet Union's draft definition offered (when "first" committed by any State) as the criteria of "aggression" might often, in the full context of action, constitute acts of "self-defence".[4] The United States position has here a deeper theoretical foundation than is obvious at first sight, or emerged in the Committee discussions.

The point is that insofar as the objective criterion offered by a definition can be sufficient only if its operation does not outrage minimal levels of justice as between the contending Parties, that criterion must allow consideration of the full socio-political context of the conduct under judgment.[5] Vital differences between international and municipal orders here again bear down. A municipal court can convict a defendant of "assault" without embarking on a judgment of justice in the full context of the relations *inter partes*. But that is because the municipal order, through its active legislative, judicial and executive institutions, generally provides other effective and compulsive means of doing final justice *inter partes*. It is with these other means at hand that the municipal order is able to use a simple notion of "assault" dispensing judgment from entering upon questions of final justice between them. And it is precisely because, as between States, no such other effective and compulsive means of doing justice *inter partes* exist, whether by adjudication, execution or legislation,[6] that the imperatives of justice remain necessarily embedded in the very notion of "aggression".[7] No

---

[4] See A/AC.77/SR.13, p.7, and *infra* pp.70-71. *Cf.* Giraud, 754-760.

[5] G. G. Fitzmaurice came near the heart of the matter when he observed in 1952 that "an enumerative definition could, after all, do little more than list a number of acts which are fairly obvious cases of aggression *if committed without adequate justification*. . . . The whole problem is to determine when certain acts are justified and, therefore, are not aggressive, and when they are not justified and therefore are aggressive. This determination is one which can only be carried out in each particular case in the light of the facts and the situation as it exists at the time, and cannot be achieved by *a priori* rules laid down in advance." (In the Sixth Committee, *G.A.O.R. VI* Sixth Committee, 292nd Meeting, para. 45, repr. (1952) 1 *Int. and Comp. L.Q.* 137, 141).

[6] *Cf.* Lord Davies, *The Seven Pillars of Peace* (1945) 26, and esp. on the last point, his *Problem of the Twentieth Century* (1930): "Change is the essence of life. This is true in the realm of nation-States as in every other sphere. . . . The problem of peace may be most realistically interpreted as the establishment of an international regime which can bring about in a peaceful manner the adjustments vital to the world's growth."

[7] Mr. Hsueh (China) came very near to the insight when he observed that definability of crimes in municipal systems was not conclusive for the international problem. For the latter "the political element was perhaps even more important than the juridical one, since the international society had not acquired such a high degree of efficiency in the maintenance of peace and order as normally obtained in a domestic society". (See A/AC.77/SR.3, pp-3-4).

On the above reasoning, also, it is rather beside the point to protest, as did M. Alvarez Aybar (Dominican Republic), that "the punishment of an offence had never been made contingent on the drafting of a perfect definition of a crime". (A/AC.77/SR.7, p.9.) The issue is not really the *perfection* of the definition, but its usefulness.

Nor does it in any way demonstrate the value of defining aggression to point out that "a definition of murder may be useful even though it would not restrain a homicidal

verbal magic can exorcise it thence: and, by the same token, any criterion of "aggression" whose operation is to be acceptable must allow to be taken into account whatever factors in those concrete situations are relevant to the doing of at least minimal justice to the Parties.

This is a core difficulty which explains the futility hitherto of so many efforts to define international "aggression" in terms of simple criteria. The simplicity of the notion of "aggression" in its vulgar version dissolves, as we approach it closely, into a welter of many-faced and multi-dimensional problems of international law and politics. It is seen to raise most of the problems of an inchoate international criminal law and criminology, and of barely formed branches of the international law of torts, and property. The solutions to many of these problems presuppose standards of ethical judgment and of sociological knowledge concerning the nature, destiny and survival of State entities which we have barely begun to explore. As soon as discussion moves from partisan debate and political warfare to the plane of intellectual examination, we are confronted by all the perplexities of the ethical judgment, as well as by the uncertainties of knowledge concerning State conduct as a manifestation of human claims and needs, at a time and in a field in which the mature perspectives of sociological inquiries are still unavailable.[8]

What has just been said does not mean that there are no rules of international law relevant to the problem of defining aggression; but it does help to explain why the search for simple objective criteria (such as armed crossing of a frontier) without reference to the complexities of ethical evaluation, and of economic, political and strategic facts, has so abjectly failed. It suggests that the very nature of the enterprise of defining aggression, at the present phase of human life, necessarily embroils the inquirer in problems of ultimate values, and in the imperfections of our present knowledge. What seemed mere practical questions, are seen as philosophical questions of the first magnitude; and though philosophers may not succeed where lawyers and diplomats have failed, they may at least help us to understand the failure.

II. AGGRESSION DETERMINATION AND DEFINITION.

It must, of course, be added immediately that the meaning of "aggression" is also more than an issue of international law merely *de lege ferenda*: the notion already figures to some extent as an operative notion of international law *de lege lata*. In the Italo-Ethiopian Affair, on the usual view,[9] as well as in the Russo-Finnish Affair, Italy and Russia were respectively branded as "aggressors", and legal action taken against

maniac". (A/AC.77/SR.7, p.12, M. Serrano, the Philippines.) What is in debate is not the value of definition in general, but the value of definition of this particular notion in the present state of the international community.

8 *Cf.* my Lectures on "Problems Confronting Sociological Inquiries Concerning International Law" in the forthcoming *Hague Recueil* (1956), Introductory, and Lectures 2 (end), and 4 (beginning).

9 But see *infra* pp.36-37 for an important reservation as to this.

them on that basis;[10] and in the Nuremberg and Tokyo Trials of Major War Criminals a number of the accused were convicted on the count of aggressive war-making. And by the U.N. General Assembly Declaration of February 1, 1951, the People's Republic of China was declared an aggressor in respect of assistance to North Korea in the Korean Affair.[11] Insofar as most people would agree that some (at least) of these determinations were correct, the notion of aggression would appear to contain a rather determinate nucleus within its otherwise indeterminate range and outline. And it may well be possible to seize and embody this nucleus in words.

Yet such a core definition would really be beside the point of the real debate about definition; and this in two respects. First, the judgment of "aggression" in each of those cases was given on the basis of the full context of impugned action, without the mediation of precise advance criteria. Judgment was not only *ad hoc* but even *post hoc*.[12] Second, such clear cases were *ex hypothesi* cases where the varied intuitions of States were able to converge *ad hoc*, and where therefore criteria are unnecessary.[13] It is pre-

---

10 On League steps in peace enforcement in the Italo-Ethiopian affair, see Stone, *Conflict* 176-184; Wright, "The Tests of Aggression in the Italo-Ethiopian War" (1936) 30 *A.J.I.L.* 45, esp. 53, who observes on the flagrancy of the Italian attitude that ". . . the Italian representative was able to say almost nothing relevant in defence of his country's acts". The application of sanctions to Italy under Art. 16 was accepted by all members of the Council, except Italy. And see the works cited *infra* Ch. 2, n.45.

In the Finnish-Soviet affair, the Assembly of the League in its resolution of Dec. 14, 1939, condemned the action of the Soviet Union against Finland. The Council taking cognisance of this resolution associated itself with the condemnation and found that "by its act, the Union of Soviet Socialist Republics has placed itself outside the League of Nations. It follows that the Union of Soviet Socialist Republic is no longer a Member of the League". For the Assembly resolution see *L.N.O.J.*, Nov.-Dec. 1939, Ann. 1756, p.540. Part I of the resolution read:

> Whereas, by the aggression which it has committed against Finland, the Union of Soviet Socialist Republics has failed to observe not only its special political agreements with Finland but also Article 12 of the Covenant of the League of Nations and the Pact of Paris;
>
> And Whereas, immediately before committing that aggression, it denounced, without legal justification, the Treaty of Non-Aggression which it had concluded with Finland in 1932, and which was to remain in force until the end of 1945; . . .
>
> Solemnly condemns the action taken by the Union of Soviet Socialist Republics against the State of Finland; . . .

The reversal of the initiating roles of the Council and Assembly, though interesting from other standpoints, is not material for present purposes.

11 C. A. Pompe (*Aggressive War* 65) points out that this was the first example of a State being declared an aggressor on account of its intervention on the side of the original aggressor State. *Cf.*, however, the analogous grounds taken by the British retaliatory orders against Japan in World War II. See U.K. Order-in-Council of Dec. 12, 1941 (S.R. & O. 1941, No. 2136).

12. *Cf.* on such determinations without definition, Sir J. Fischer Williams (*et al.*), *International Sanctions* (1938) 178, 186. M. Bourquin in *id.* (ed.), *Collective Security* 329. The argument of C. A. Pompe (*op. cit.* 94) that since the practice of the League and the United Nations and of the Nuremberg Tribunal has held determinations of aggression within the limits of declaration of war, invasion and armed attack, this forms some basis for the feasibility of binding rules for determination by way of a definition of aggression, ignores the above considerations. The fact that these organs "have never recognized the existence of a case of aggression in any of those unforeseeable situations on account of which a definition of aggression has systematically been rejected" is not, as Mr. Pompe thinks decisive, but is better understood by reference to the basic considerations canvassed in these pages touching the state of the international community.

13 Neither the Nuremberg nor Tokyo Tribunals formulated any precise criteria of

cisely for the wider areas, *where intuitions do not converge,* that the establishment of objective criteria in advance of action and judgment are so earnestly sought.[14]. Nor is there any assured way of moving rapidly from converging intuitions in a few *ad hoc* decisions into these wider areas. We might conceivably, as the growth of the common law shows, build up criteria on the basis of such decisions even of so difficult a notion as "aggression". This kind of building, however, is a slow and laborious process, even for the relatively simple notions of municipal law. For a notion with the kind of built-in complexities which there is reason to believe the notion of "aggression" contains,[15] such a process would require a lapse of time vastly greater than the advocates of the definition of aggression say we can afford.[16]

III. IS DEFINITION IMPORTANT UNDER THE CHARTER?

As we now approach our subject more closely in the United Nations context, two other questions stand at the threshold.

The first, and more easily answered, is why the virtually unlimited power of the United Nations Security Council under Article 39 of the Charter to determine which State is an "aggressor", should not have quieted the demand for precise advance criteria. One answer, of course, is that the paralysis of this function of the Security Council by the Great Power veto has blocked the way to such a case by case elaboration of the notion of aggression. Another is that even if this way to institutional elaboration

---

aggression. See *infra* pp.134-37.

14 It is thus curious to find Mr. Pompe (*op.cit.* 95) so confident that lack of advance definition "enabled" international organs to ignore "classic" cases of "aggression", e.g. of Japan in China, when he has complained on the previous page that determinations of aggression have been made in such cases without the aid of definition.

15 Unrestrained advocacy from various standpoints simply ignores these complexities. See e.g. M. Franklin, *The Conception of Aggression,* advocating the Soviet draft, and imputing unwillingness to accept it with alacrity either to conservative refusal to generalise (9), to the "sophism" of the International Law Commission (16-17), to an unnecessary distrust of analogising (*ibid.*), to Western "subjectivistic" disregard of law (p.12), (somewhat inconsistently with the preceding point), to "imperialism" and capitalism (pp.6ff.), and arguing that the state of international tension makes acceptance imperative (p.9). Nor, with the most earnest will to do so, can we see that Mr. Franklin's imputation to opponents of definition of adherence to "Kant's obscurantist idea of 'the thing in itself'" (*op.cit.* 14-15, *à propos* of M. Spiropoulos) affects the main question here raised, even if (as we do not believe) M. Spiropoulos was using the term "notion *per se*" in the Kantian sense. *Cf.* from less politically tendentious, but no less over-simple standpoints, V. V. Pella, *La Guerre Crime* (1946) 43, arguing (as if argument were necessary) that adequate definition of "aggression" and "legitimate self-defence" would help the Security Council (43), that we cannot refuse this definition to humanity (43), and that a slightly modified form of the Soviet draft of 1933 should do (40). The answer to the question whether we can refuse to grant a definition to humanity, does not tell us whether it lies in our power to grant it. And *cf. inter alia* the vehemence on this point of G. Scelle, *supra* pp.5-6.

16 Professor Wright ("The Concept of Aggression . . ." (1935) 29 *A.J.I.L.* 373, at 389) has well pointed out that while "the accumulation of precedents by international courts, commissions or institutions competent to deal with [international claims involving responsibility for injuries arising from hostilities] would in itself act as a deterrent to aggression", the circumstances pointed to by these precedents would be useless in a crisis for purposes of preventing or stopping hostilities, since time is not then available for ascertaining them.

remained possible, distrust among the Powers as to how they might respectively vote on future issues has provoked the hope that agreement on precise criteria in advance of the particular crisis may afford guarantees of impartial and passionless determination of future decisions. Certainly unless such a hope can be fulfilled, determinations by the Council, even when it can reach them, are likely to have a sporadic and uneven appearance somewhat repugnant to a judgment involving justice. We shall later see the special meaning of this hope in relation to the General Assembly.[17]

The second question is why the notion of aggression, whether with or without precise advance criteria, should be regarded at all as an essential foundation of the system of peace enforcement under the Charter. For it is clear that under the Charter the vast legal powers of the Security Council, as well as any legal powers that the General Assembly may have, can be activated under Chapter VII and the Uniting for Peace Resolutions respectively, by any threat to the peace, or breach of the peace", as well as by an "act of aggression". Insofar as an aggression can rarely (if ever) occur unaccompanied by either "a threat to the peace" or "a breach of the peace", collective peace enforcement would seem legally possible without the use of the notion of aggression at all. Any supposed "aggression" could be far more easily brought under control as a "threat to" or "breach of the peace". This truth seems, for the most part, rather submerged in the mass of contemporary controversy.[18] Quincy Wright, however, well pointed out in his account in 1956, that a finding of "aggression" (at any rate, of armed aggression)[19] almost certainly presupposes a finding either of a threat or use of force across frontiers, and therefore, presumably, either a threat to the peace or a breach of the peace under Article 39.[20] And his own argument that agreement on a satisfactory definition of aggression is an essential prerequisite for a collective security system has to be framed on the assumption, to which we shall return in the concluding Chapter, that "collective security" does not depend on decisions of the Security Council, but on voluntary action by Members in response to recommendations of the General Assembly.[21]

---

17 See *infra* Chs. 3 and 9.

18 It does, however, occasionally break through even there. See e.g., the Swedish Government's comment on the Report of the 1953 Special Committee (*G.A.O.R. IX* Ann., Item 51, p.5), that since the Security Council's full powers extend to "threat to the peace without aggression . . . a comprehensive and precise definition [of aggression] would be . . . unnecessary." It seems inconsistent with both the *travaux préparatoires* and common sense to say that the terminology of Art. 39 indicates that "breach of the peace" and "threat to the peace" are not included within the notion of "aggression". The term "aggression" can and often will embrace them, the debate as to definition is largely an effort to draw the line. *Cf.* on this point Professor Zourek's recent lectures *supra* Intro. n.29a.

19 On the question whether the term is to be given an extended meaning beyond this, see *infra* pp.58,67-68. And see the not very convincing argument in "The Meaning of Aggression . . ." (1954) 33 *Nebraska L.R.* 606, 611, that since in at least one article of the Charter (Art. 53) the word "aggression" appears without any reference to "threat to the peace" or "breach of the peace", these latter two phrases are illustrative, rather than exhaustive, ways in which an aggression may take place.

20 Q. Wright, "The Prevention of Aggression" (1956) 50 *A.J.I.L.* 514, 526. We agree with his inference of this from the close relation of "act of aggression" to "breach of the peace" or a "threat to the peace", in the context of Art. 39.

21 See article cited (1956) 50 *A.J.I.L.* 514, 518.

Obviously, the difficulties of bringing home a charge of aggression (however defined) are far graver than those involved in proof merely of "a threat to the peace" or "a breach of the peace". Either of these more modest holdings would give ample powers to the Security Council, and impose ample duties on Members under Articles 2 (5) and 25, for collective enforcement of peace. It would also, as we shall see, base any such legal powers as the General Assembly may have in this area. Why then do not the lawyers and the organs and Members of the United Nations rest content with the easier task? Why has the problem of definition of a conception whose very use at all is dispensable endlessly agitated the writers, the International Law Commission, the General Assembly and its Committees, including two Special Committees on the Definition of Aggression, which have vainly held over 100 meetings on this matter in the last six years?

The United Nations Secretary-General, following in 1952 some thoughts of M. Politis in the 'thirties, has suggested five reasons why aggression must be defined. First, so that governments should not commit aggression unawares (as it were); second, to assist the Security Council in determining the aggressor; third, to guide Members in exercising self-defence or other action in default of Security Council action; fourth, to guide public opinion; fifth, for courts trying persons charged with aggressive war-making.[22] We beg to doubt whether the first (avoidance of inadvertent aggression) is a serious problem; whether the third (guiding individual Members in default of collective United Nations action) could make much difference to their attitudes at the moment of crisis. As to the fourth, we also doubt whether the refinements inevitably involved in an advance definition of aggression would much assist public opinion at moments of crisis. We are left therefore with two alleged reasons[23] for the urgency of defining aggression, namely the guidance of the Security Council and General Assembly in determining the aggressor, and the judicial trial of certain war criminals. We shall return to the latter in Chapter 8; the issues are separate and different from those which concern us at this point.

As to the former, we have just pointed out that the Security Council has ample peace enforcement powers based on mere threat or breach of peace, without even invoking, let alone defining, the troubled concept of

---

22 *Cf.* the summation of views of the Sixth Committee of the Ninth General Assembly (*G.A.O.R. IX*, Ann., Item 51, p.10), omitting some of these but adding that: "In a world that lived in fear of aggression, the existence of a definition of aggression would do something to ease men's minds," and that "it would promote the development of international law". *Sed quaere.* Professor Zourek's account in August 1957 (see *supra* Intro. n.29a) does not seriously add to these reasons, nor does he (in the present view) confront the basic difficulties obstructing definition herein discussed.

23 It is not necessary for present purposes to do more than mention the more technical legal reason urged by Professor Wright (article cited (1956) 50 *A.J.I.L.* 514, 524) that "the competence of the General Assembly under the Uniting for Peace Resolution depends, in case the matter is on the agenda of the Security Council, on general acceptance of a definition of the terms in Article 39 so precise that a failure of the Security Council to function will in fact be self-evident". It will sufficiently appear that we regard the hope of such advance precision, in any definition which is also acceptable to most States, as quite chimerical.

aggression;[24] and that this is also the case *mutatis mutandis* for the General Assembly. Even in terms of differentiating between breaches of the peace, so as to proportion enforcement measures to guilt (which though unmentioned by the Secretary-General, seems to have been one preoccupation at San Francisco), the problem also seems rather unreal at the present stage. To assert that collective peace enforcement is impossible except on the basis of the aggression notion, and even on agreed advance criteria of it, is to add unnecessary[25] complications to the already difficult tasks of making Chapter VII of the Charter work, or giving substance to any supposed powers of the General Assembly. Whatever be the speculative attractions of "quasi-punitive" measures against "aggressors", they should scarcely be allowed to supplant, embarrass or confuse the primary tasks of maintaining and restoring peace.

This view receives some support from the negligible number of crises in which the aggression concept has been a necessary base for peace enforcement action either by the League (for instance, in the Soviet-Finnish Affair of 1939) or the United Nations (for instance, as against Communist China in relation to Korea), and by the slightness of any results which appear to have flown from its invocation. We shall show later that though different considerations apply to General Assembly action under the Uniting for Peace Resolutions, the conclusion to be reached may be substantially the same.[26]

IV. NO DEFINITION SELF-APPLYING.

It may be added that even ardent advocates of the need to establish advance criteria of aggression, must admit that such criteria cannot take the applying organ more than a part of the way towards determining whether, in a particular situation, aggression has indeed occurred. There are thus introduced into the process of determination additional elements of uncertainty of interpretation of the criteria themselves.[27] Insofar as these criteria

---

[24] We need not go so far as to say, with Professor Röling ("On Aggression . . ." (1955) 2 *Nederlands T.Int.R* 167-168), that "in the history of the Security Council, no instance can be mentioned in which the Security Council was in need of a definition", nor indeed as to say with him and a number of other delegates that definition would be dangerous insofar as it would *compel* the Security Council to brand specific acts as aggression, or prohibit it from so branding specific acts. We shall later explore the degree of truth in these last propositions.

[25] Professor Pella has suggested that the reason for demanding that the Security Council be provided with a binding definition is that otherwise the Council is left to determine the question of aggression and the measures to be taken in each case. He thinks that "humanity" is entitled to know of what this gravest of all crimes consists: that if the Security Council acts flexibly for the maintenance of peace in each case, the Security Council will be making law in each case, and that this would be a denial of "the permanent existence of an international morality and of certain fundamental principles of the common life of States". See V. V. Pella, *La Guerre-Crime"* (1946) 43-44. That humanity may be entitled to know does not (as already seen, *supra* n.15) necessarily mean that anyone can tell it at this stage.

[26] See *infra passim* and especially the Conclusions.

[27] *Cf.* as regards general definitions the governmental views reported in *G.A.O.R. X,*

are intended as permanent bridges across the gaps between the notion of aggression and the concrete situations to be judged, the assistance they give can be no greater than their own length and strength.

This is not to say that this kind of bridge of subsumption is not often valuable, especially when used within municipal legal systems by stable judicial institutions, in relation to the simpler concepts of such systems, such as "rape", "larceny" or "murder". In use by political organs like the Security Council or even the General Assembly, however, in connection with a notion such as "aggression" which usually involves the vital interests of the very States which man the applying organs, such bridges are likely to render the leap to judgment even more hazardous. In such an area and before such an organ, the more words, the more doubts and disputations. The deeper obstacle to peace enforcement by the Security Council is the *Willkuer* of the veto, not the indeterminacy of the notion of aggression.[28]

The desire to control determinations to be made when passions are aflame by advance criteria agreed upon before national passions were embroiled in the situation now to be judged, is a natural one. But even if that were always the sincere intent of advocates of definition, the desire does not prove its own feasibility in this particular area of human endeavour. To stake so much on a verbal formulation which still has to be interpreted and applied by the very organs whose unreliability is the reason for the formulation, is to seek salvation in shadows. No normative formulae that have the slightest chance of even wide minority approval can hope to deprive the applying organ of ample leeways to decide a particular case according to its arbitrary will. This is inevitable in a problem as critical to State survival as that of controlling "aggression" in a world as confused and divided as our own. To hope that some ingenious definition of aggression can produce an automatic or near-automatic judgment in future conflicts by any political organ, be it Security Council or General Assembly, is to imagine that we can somehow immunise this segment of international life from the acknowledged principles of social and political life generally.[29]

We return, however, to the main point. To say that other States on or off the Security Council must be convinced, before peace enforcement action can be initiated, that the State whose conduct is impugned is both a lawbreaker *and* a political menace, seems to be a radical and unnecessary emasculation of the existing legal powers of the Security Council. As

---

Ann., Item 51, p.10 (Sixth Committee); but the point may be equally, or even more applicable, to some "enumerative definitions".

28 See Stone, *Conflict* 221-23. *Cf.* on the present point that no formula can be self-applying, Sir J. Fischer Williams (*et al.*), *International Sanctions* (1938) 178, A. Forster, in Bourquin (ed.), *Collective Security* 308, M. Bourquin, *id.* 329, R. Forges-Davanzanti, *id.* 334, who point out that of course a definition may still be valuable as a guide.

29 *Cf.* Sir J. Fischer Williams, *Chapters* 236ff., esp. 238: "These discussions of 'aggression' and 'self-defence' often seem to be based on a rather simple view of international affairs. Those who take part in them seem often to be under the illusion that there can exist, either at Geneva or in Foreign Offices, a sort of carefully classified card-index of events or, better still, 'situations'. . . ."

It seems difficult, once the complexities of these issues are realised, to believe that

regards action initiated by the General Assembly, which depends on voluntary cooperation of Members (and therefore on psychological persuasion rather than legal power)[30] other considerations arise. And it is in connection with such Assembly initiated action that there arise some of the main questions with which the present work is concerned. Among them are: (1) Is the notion of aggression, whether defined or not, an essential notion for ensuring peace and security? (2) Is a definition fulfilling this function capable of being drafted at all? (3) Is it possible to draft a definition which would perform the functions for which the definition is needed ("feasible" definition)? (4) If such a "feasible" definition were drafted, would the product have any real chance of acceptance by States generally in the world as it is ("acceptable" definition)? (5) If such a definition were found and accepted (which thirty odd years of effort suggest to be a fantastic hope) would the gains arising from trying to use it outweigh the dangers? Would it, in short, be a "desirable" definition? (6) Assuming it might in these senses be "possible", "feasible" and desirable to have a definition framed and accepted, what form and contents should the definition take? In due course we shall approach the many distinctions involved in exploring this last question; but since our analysis leads to negative answers to all except the second of the preceding questions, the question what would be the contents of a definition *that was feasible, desirable and acceptable* to most States, is an illusory one.

Certainly we face the unpleasant fact that two generations of effort and the experience of two world security organisations have not seriously advanced the search for such a definition. It is perhaps time for us to consider whether failure may not have been due in part to the very vigour and directness of our search, without careful enough survey of the surrounding and underlying terrain. This, at any rate, is the hypothesis on which we here proceed. If in this we seem too sceptical and hesitant in our approach to a human situation which seems to cry out for deep convictions and precipitate action, we would observe that a "sceptic" (in the fuller meaning of that term) is one who seeks to penetrate beyond appearances to the hidden features of a situation.[31] Such a mood may well be both wise and responsible as we observe the Twelfth General Assembly's discussion in 1957 of the meagre results of its latest Special Committee on the Definition of Aggression.

---

the efforts at definition can be warranted by any realistic hope of thereby "fortify[ing] the moral conviction of individual men in a world of power politics of individual States". (B.V.A. Röling, "On Aggression . . ." (1955) 2 *Nederlands T. Int. R.* 167, 178). On such issues definitions are more likely to confuse and beguile him who runs and reads. And I find it particularly difficult to conceive of any *tour de force* of definition which would be decisive in preventing "a wicked government" from "luring its subjects into an aggressive policy". (See *id.* 177-78.)

30 See *infra* Ch. 9.

31 So the Greek root, "*skeptomai*". It is perhaps not unduly fanciful to see this attitude of circumspection as appropriate to Dike, the Greek goddess of justice. For among the adversaries with which the mythology surrounded her were Lethe, the deity of forgetfulness and concealment (*Vergessenheit und Verborgenheit*, Erik Wolf's terms) *Amphilogiai* (*Logoi pseudeis*), the deities of deceitful and disruptive words, and Hybris, the deity of excess. See generally on Dike and her relations of affinity and tension to other Greek deities, E. Wolf, *Griechisches Rechtsdenken* (1951), 22-165, esp. 49ff.

CHAPTER 2

LEAGUE OF NATIONS QUEST[1]

I. AGGRESSION AND THE COVENANT.

The only explicit reference[2] to "aggression" in the scheme of the League of Nations Covenant was in Article 10, though inferential references were later to be spelled out of other Articles, such as Articles 11, 12, 15 and 16 of the Covenant. Article 10 provided:

> The Members of the League undertake to respect and preserve as against external aggression the territorial integrity and existing political independence of all Members of the League. In case of any such aggression or in case of any threat or danger of such aggression the Council shall advise upon the means by which this obligation shall be fulfilled.

Between the two world wars, a number of cases actually occurred which were generally thought to involve aggression, and the notions of "aggression" and "aggressive war" were certainly much discussed. Discussion, however, was more in the course of attempts to make good certain notorious deficiencies of the Covenant, than in the actual exercise by League organs of peace enforcement powers under that instrument.

It is an irony, from which we shall later have to draw some significance, that though Article 10 was the one in which the term "aggression" appeared, that article tended to be shunned by most League Members as a focus for the sought-for criteria of aggression. This is the more striking because, insofar as Article 10 ceased to be central, the peace enforcement provisions did not in terms turn on the notion of "aggression" at all, but on those of "war", "threat of war", "resort to war in breach of the Covenant", including of course (though *inter multa alia*) the undertaking of Article 10. Clearly the Covenant did not prohibit all wars. War was not prohibited, in particular, if the procedures and delays required by Article 12 had been followed, or if the Council had failed to reach a unanimous report under Article 15, or if it were waged against a State which had not accepted the unanimous report of the Council. In part, the introduction of the notion of aggression, and the agitation for more precise criteria of it, were an attempt to rationalise (or perhaps "moralise") these quasi-procedural limitations. In part, they were an attempt to supplement the obvious deficiencies and to close the so-called "gaps" in the Covenant, by discriminating still further among the non-prohibited wars between those wars which were tolerable and those which were not. Contrary to the beliefs of many, the League Covenant did

---

1 On the context of customary law see *infra* Ch. 5, and see for a balanced account of the historical background of early debates on definition, Komarnicki, esp. 7-16. On the aggression notion in relation to League collective security efforts, see *id.*, 29-37.

2 In particular, the operation of the "sanctions" Art. 16 was not conditioned on "aggression" at all. And see *infra* pp.38-40 as to practice.

not embody the Grotian doctrine of "just" and "unjust" wars: rather was the agitation around the notion of "aggression" part of an attempt to inject that notion *ex post nativitate*.

One point of injection was *via* Article 11 of the Covenant which, without in itself imposing obligations on any State, empowered the Council to intervene in the event of war, threat of war, or rupture of the friendly relations between States. Regardless of breach of Covenant, the League Council under Article 11 skilfully exercised various kinds and degrees of economic, political and moral persuasion to induce the contestants to agree to Council action aimed at removing the threat of war, or to bring a cease-fire to hostilities already started. In the course of these procedures the idea arose that the refusal of a party to comply with directions of the Council, particularly as to cease-fire, might serve as a criterion of moral or legal culpability, and even of "aggression". It must be observed immediately, however, that this was certainly not a legal conclusion ever reached by the League in the sense of attaching legal sanctions to such culpability. This, indeed, was not really conceivable under Article 11, for under that Article both contestant States were entitled to be present and vote on the Council, and the Council had to be unanimous. A culprit State would scarcely vote sanctions against itself.[3] And it is also to be observed that insofar as there was here any determination even on "quasi-aggression", the Council did not in any case adopt any advance criteria which limited its discretion. Before the Council's orders could be disobeyed, the Council had to decide to issue them: and in *that* decision it was free to consider the full context of the conflict without inhibition by any precise criteria.[4]

II. FROM THE DRAFT TREATY OF MUTUAL ASSISTANCE TO THE KELLOGG-BRIAND PACT.

League theorising concerning "aggression" and its definition in connection with new collective security proposals and disarmament discussion of the 'twenties and 'thirties, proceeded side by side with the above practical political approach of the Council under Article 11, and in the main independently of it. The applications of any theory of aggression proper in

---

[3] Lest our generation despise such "nonsense", attention is drawn to the proceedings of Commission II, Committee I at San Francisco (8 *U.N.C.I.O. Docs.* 375): "The Committee discussed a proposal submitted by the Delegation of Costa Rica that Members to whom acts of aggression were attributed should not vote in their own cases." This principle was rejected by a vote of 20 to 5.

[4] It is believed, with respect, that Quincy Wright's devoted glosses on League practice in this regard involved some oversimplifications and rationalisations. See generally, Q. Wright, "The Test of Aggression in the Italo-Ethiopian War" (1936) 30 *A.J.I.L.* 45-62. He there describes (at 52; and see his earlier article "The Concept of Aggression" (1935) 29 *A.J.I.L.* 373, at 381ff.) three "tests" of "aggression", as "discussed" by the League: (1) Which State was responsible for the first act of war, especially by invasion of foreign territory? (2) Which State was under the least defensive necessity at the time hostilities began, as the aggressor? and (3) Which State has refused to accept an armistice proposed in accordance with a procedure which it has accepted to implement its no-force obligation. Obviously the first two of these tests are as regards precision of application open at both the inculpating and exculpating ends. As to the third,

League peace enforcement are, indeed, both exiguous and slight in their consequences.

On August 28, 1921, the International Blockade Committee of the League Assembly, considering the conditions under which sanctions under Article 16 should be applied against a Covenant-breaking resort to war in breach of Covenant, interpreted[5] "resort to war" as the *"undertaking of armed action"*.[6] The abortive Draft Treaty of Mutual Assistance, elaborated by the Assembly's Third Committee,[7] and communicated to the Governments on September 29, 1923,[8] contained proposed criteria of aggression which were much discussed. The Third Committee rejected the idea of formulating criteria of "aggression", and thought that "Governments can only judge by an impression based upon the most various factors, such as the political attitude of the possible aggressor; his propaganda; the attitude of his press and population; his policy on the international market, etc". The opinions of the Belgian, Brazilian, French, and Swedish delegations in the Permanent Advisory Commission,[9] and in what is the first official League "Commentary on the Definition of a Case of Aggression", drawn up by a Special Committee of the Temporary Mixed Commission.[10] were even more emphatic. The former doubted the possibility of "accurately defining *a priori* in a treaty the expression 'cases of aggression' ". The latter declared it impossible "under the conditions of modern warfare . . . to decide even in theory what constitutes a case of aggression", and with no less emphasis that "the test of violation of a frontier has also lost its value". It affords somewhat ironic support for such scepticism that of the seven signs of an "impending" aggression which the former opinion was nevertheless rash enough to list, all except the seventh (actual hostilities) are now regarded by the Great Powers as elementary precautions for self-defence.[11]

The Draft Treaty itself abstained from defining aggression, although

---

he noted in 1936, that it was not regarded as seriously relevant to League action in the Italo-Ethiopian conflict. (*Op.cit.* 53) And see *infra* pp.36-37.

[5] Report of the International Blockade Committee of Aug. 28, 1921. See *L.N. Doc.* A.14. 1927, V, pp.15ff.

[6] The omission of any reference to the shunned Art. 10 (the only one using the term "aggression"), in the enumerated Arts. 11, 12, 13 and 15 is to be noted. See *infra* Ch. 6, s.IV. It seems to misinterpret this view of the 1921 Committee for the Secretary-General's Report (A/2211) flatly to assert that in that Committee's view "the use by a State of its armed forces against another State constitutes aggression". In the first place that Committee was addressing itself not to "aggression" but to "resort to war in breach of Covenant". Second, and more seriously, the words underlined in the text were by way of definition of "resort to war", not of "in breach of Covenant".

[7] See *L.N.O.J.* Sp. Supp. No. 16 (1923), Annex 10 (Part I) pp.203-09.

[8] For a general account of the place of negotiations on this and other instruments here considered in League history, see 1, F. P. Walters, *A History of the League of Nations* (1952) 226ff., 383, and *passim.*

[9] This Commission convened at Geneva on 16-22 April, 1923, to examine the Assembly Resols. XIV and XV relating to treaties of mutual guarantee. The report of the Commission is to be found in *L.N.O.J.*, Sp.Supp. No. 16 (1923) 114-124. On the problem of aggression, see 116-118.

[10] See *L.N.O.J.*, Sp. Supp. No. 16 (1923), Ann. 4, pp.183-184.

[11] "1. Organisation on paper of industrial mobilization. 2. Actual organization of industrial mobilization. 3. Collection of stocks of raw materials. 4. Setting-on-foot of war industries. 5. Preparation for military mobilization. 6. Actual military mobilization. 7. Hostilities."

Article 1 declared aggressive war to be "an international crime" from which the Parties agreed to abstain. While the same article provided that certain wars to enforce third-party decision against the non-complying State were *not* aggressive wars, it did not base any inference that all other wars *were* aggressive. Indeed, the deepest doubts as to the feasibility of precise criteria pervaded the observations of twenty-eight governments on the Draft Treaty,[12] ranging from the Italian view that it is "not easy" to define either "in law or in fact" what constitutes aggression,[13] to the more optimistic French view that "though it is difficult to define specifically all cases of aggression, it is undoubtedly possible to specify the most flagrant cases".[14]

The problem was again discussed in connection with the draft Geneva Protocol[15] adopted on October 2, 1924, by the League Assembly. Article 10 defined aggression as resort "to war in violation of the undertakings contained in the Covenant or in the present Protocol"; and Article 2 prohibited recourse to war "except in case of resistance to acts of aggression or when acting in agreement with the Council or the Assembly of the League of Nations in accordance with the provisions of the Covenant and of the present Protocol". It was in the course of these discussions that the able M. Politis made the classical observation[16] that while it was "a relatively easy matter" to define aggression, it was a very difficult one to "ascertain the existence of aggression" in a concrete case, since this tends to be a "question of fact concerning which opinions may differ".

The Locarno Treaty of Mutual Guarantee[17] concluded under League auspices on October 16, 1925, between Belgium, France, Great Britain and Italy, was one of the few relevant texts of this period which went beyond abortive drafts. Designed as an integral part of a regional security system, including a network of non-aggression treaties, it contained in Article 2 the undertaking that the Contracting Parties ". . . will in no case attack or invade each other or resort to war against each other". This stipulation, however, was not to prohibit: (1) The exercise of the right of "legitimate defence";[18] (2) Action in pursuance of Article 16 of the Covenant; (3) Action as a result of a decision taken by the Assembly or the Council of the League of Nations or in pursuance of Article 15, paragraph 7, of the Covenant, as directed, however, only against a State which was the first to attack.[19] In his report on the Treaty to the League Council[20] on December 1, 1926, M. de Brouckère mentioned among the difficulties of advance definition, that while self-defence still remained permissible, disproportion of the

---

12 See *L.N.O.J.*, Sp. Supp. No. 26 (1924), Ann. 3, pp.131-168.

13 *Id.* 162.

14 *Id.* 160.

15 *L.N.O.J.*, Sp. Supp. No. 24 (1924) Ann. 18, pp.136-140; 2 Hudson, *Int.Leg.* 1378. (The Protocol was abandoned a few months after its adoption.)

16 *Id.*, Ann. 16, p.127.

17 54 *L.N.T.S.* 289.

18 "The exercise of the right of legitimate self-defence." On this concept see Giraud.

19 By Art. 15 (7) the Members in case of failure of unanimity of recommendation in the Council in effect reserved their liberty of action "for the maintenance of right and justice". The effect of the Locarno provision was to maintain the Covenant inhibitions in favour of the victim of such a "first attack".

20 *L.N. Doc.* A.14. 1927. V, pp.60-72.

reaction to the initial violence and danger would prevent the self-defence being "legitimate". A *"flagrantly"* excessive reaction to "some incident of little intrinsic importance", would (he thought) turn the reacting State into "the real aggressor",[21] but his proposition would obviously help little in most cases where disproportion was not so monstrous. Nor does the latter history of the Locarno system help the present inquiry very much.

III. THE ANTI-WAR PACT AND AFTER.

As late as 1927, when the League Assembly adopted [22] a declaration "that all wars of aggression are, and shall always be prohibited", and "that every pacific means must be employed" to settle all international disputes; and when the Preparatory Commission for the Disarmament Conference established[23] the Committee on Arbitration and Security, no serious advance in our enterprise was evident. The Rutgers report[24] on Articles 10, 11 and 16, presented to the Assembly by this last-mentioned body on September 26, 1928, aptly summarises the first half-decade of the enterprise of definition. The Dutch jurist drew attention to the dangers of any hard-and-fast definition either of "aggression" within Article 10, or of "resort to war" within Article 16. Not only might this lead Members of the League to apply sanctions when other methods of handling the breach might be more effective; it might also "lead to a State which was not in reality responsible for hostilities being described as an aggressor".[25] We shall see that these dangers have haunted Committee discussion and reports ever since.

Certainly, as the world approached the Kellogg-Briand Pact of 1928 League efforts had produced little advance towards State consensus on the criteria of aggression. The value of provisions describing aggression in terms of resort to war in violation of treaty undertakings, was necessarily subject, even if the instruments had become operative, to the degree of precision of the undertakings; in practice they did little more than attach the label "aggression" to resorts to war already caught by Article 16. The Locarno test of "attack or invade", for example, lost much of its precision when limited by reference to a notion of "legitimate defence" which itself remained unclarified except at the extreme ends, where advance criteria were in any case unnecessary for *ad hoc* application. And while the development of techniques of pressure for obedience to cease-fire orders was an important development, we remain unconvinced by Professor Wright's thesis that this ever produced in a substantial sense a criterion of *aggression,* as distinct from a basis of Council discrimination as to where pressure should next be

---

[21] He admitted, however, that "it is not so easy as it may seem at first sight to determine when a country 'resorts to war' " (*id.* 69).

[22] On Sept. 24, 1927. (*L.N.O.J.*, Sp. Supp. No. 53, p.22).

[23] On Nov. 30, 1927.

[24] *L.N. Doc.* C.165. N.50. 1928. IX, pp.142ff.

[25] M. Rutgers did not reject outright the possibility of defining aggression. He considered that "it would be . . . practical to enumerate some of the facts which, *according to circumstances* (italics supplied), may serve as evidence that aggression has taken place". He enumerated an illustrative series of acts of force, or preparatory to the use of force.

applied.[26] Cease-fire techniques and Council action generally under Article 11, were directed to *forestalling* questions of "aggression" and "sanctions" under Articles 10 and 16. It was precisely in this light, and significantly at this point in League history, that the Assembly, on September 20, 1928, resolved[27] "without detracting from the value of the other Articles of the Covenant", that the League's "first task is to forestall war . . . to prevent hostilities or to stop hostilities which have already begun", that is to act under Article 11. Action under this Article presupposed only "war", "threat of war", or "circumstances threatening to disturb international peace . . .", all of them concepts free of the penal connotations of "aggression", and even of "breach of Covenant".

The Pact of Paris (Briand-Kellogg Pact) for the Renunciation of War as an Instrument of National Policy on August 27, 1928,[28] did not by its terms centre on the notion of "aggression", much less define that notion precisely; though much play is often centred on it in the present context.

It is possible, of course, to argue that the outlawry of war "as an instrument of national policy" impliedly equivalated such a war with "aggression"; or alternatively, that insofar as the gist of "aggression" is resort to war in breach of treaty undertaking to refrain, the effect of the Pact was to bring all wars of the stated kind within the motion. And certainly the attempts from 1929 onwards to "close the gaps in the Covenant" by bringing the Covenant into harmony with the Pact, bring the latter into the stream of thought which is the subject of our inquiry. But even when all this is admitted, any contribution of the Pact is subject not only to the vagueness of the terms "as an instrument of national policy", but also to the serious reservations and limitations attached to the apparently unqualified terms of its two articles by the exchange of diplomatic correspondence accompanying the conclusion of the Pact. It was generally agreed among the Signatories that the Pact did not preclude the rights of legitimate defence, or resort to war against a State which violated the Pact; and the reservations of some important Signatories were even more striking.[29] Nor was it possible by establishing agreed criteria of aggression to harmonise the Covenant with

[26] See Q. Wright, "The Test of Aggression in the Italo-Ethiopian Affair" (1936) 30 *A.J.I.L.* 45, at 52ff.; *id.*, "The Prevention of Aggression" (1956) 50 *A.J.I.L.* 514, at 520ff.

[27] *L.N.O.J.*, Sp. Supp. No. 63 (1928) p.16. [28] 94 *L.N.T.S.* 57.

[29] See Mr. Kellogg's Note to the Signatory Governments of June 23, 1928, confirming that the Treaty did not "restrict or impair . . . the right of self-defence. That right is inherent in every sovereign State and is implicit in every treaty. Every nation is free at all times and regardless of treaty provisions to defend its territory from attack or invasion and *it alone is competent to decide whether circumstances require recourse to war in self-defence.*" (Italics supplied.) And he went on to say that, as with the notion of aggression, it was both difficult and dangerous to attempt a legal definition of "self-defence".

The preceding British Note of May 19, 1928, had recalled that "there are certain regions of the world the welfare and integrity of which constitute a special and vital interest for our peace and safety. His Majesty's Government have been at pains to make it clear in the past that interference with these regions cannot be suffered. Their protection against attack is to the British Empire a measure of self-defence. It must be clearly understood that His Majesty's Government in Great Britain accept the new treaty upon the distinct understanding that it does not prejudice their freedom of action in this respect." The Note extended to the United States concurrence in the assumed

the Pact. Some Governments and Members of the Committee of Jurists, for instance, would have held it *not* aggression for a State to resort to war to enforce a decision in its favour;[30] and that the contestant State refusing arbitration or judicial settlement would be an aggressor.[31]

It is at any rate clear that the League Assembly's First Committee, at the end of the first decade of search, did not believe that they had found sufficient criteria of aggression even after the Paris Pact. M. Rolin came in his relevant report for that Committee in 1931 to the conclusion that neither the Pact nor the Covenant excluded the right of "legitimate self-defence", and that "the satisfactory enumeration of the distinctive characteristics either of aggression or of legitimate self-defence appears difficult and even impossible".[32] This conclusion was also implicit in the further abortive draft General Convention to Improve the Means of Preventing War, approved by the Assembly on September 26, 1931.[33] This draft openly gave up any attempt to involve the process of peace enforcement with the determination of the aggressor; the latter was to be left to *post mortem* inquiries after attempts to safeguard or restore peace had failed.[34] We shall later have to refer to the importance of this approach for the contemporary scene.[35]

---

reciprocal position. See *Cmd.* 3153, 2ff., esp. 9-10, and other texts in J. T. Shotwell, *War as an Instrument of National Policy* (1929) 293ff. See also Mr. Kellogg's explanation to the U.S. Senate Committee on Foreign Relations, Dec. 7, 1928: "I knew that this Government, at least, would never agree to submit to a tribunal the question of self-defence, and I do not think any of them would." (Quoted in L. Sohn, *Cases on United Nations Law* (1956) 935.

In the Tokyo Tribunal the dissents of Judges Pal and Röling based very drastic inferences on this position. Judge Pal (*International Military Tribunal* (1953) 37) said that as a result of the reservation of this right of self-determined self-defence "the Pact did not in any way change the existing international law", since it did not bind States "independently of their will", its obligation remaining "always . . . *dependent on the will of the States* . . ." (42). He also denied, for the same reason that the Pact had even the effect of placing on the Party resorting to war any special burden of justifying the resort, so that the resort "still remains without the province of any law requiring justification . . ." (50). So Judge Röling (quoted Sohn, *op.cit.* 935) thought, for similar reasons, that it was even a begging of the question for the Nuremberg Tribunal to have asserted that justification of a resort to war as self-defensive must ultimately be subject to adjudication "if international law is ever to be enforced".

30 Such a view would have clearly warranted Israeli action against Egypt to enforce the Security Council decision of 1951.

31 This would also have operated against Egypt in the recent crisis.

32 *L.N.O.J.*, Sp. Supp. No. 94 (1931) p.146.

33 Prepared by the Committee on Arbitration and Security. (*L.N.O.J.*, Sp. Supp., No. 92, p.24.)

34 *Cf.* F. P. Walters' observation (I *History* 383) that "the 1928 Assembly marks, for practical purposes, the end of the long attempt made by the organs of the League, under the pressure of France and her European allies, to build up a security system as those countries conceived it—that is to say, a system providing, in terms more precise and binding than those of the Covenant, first, that all disputes without exception should be submitted to peaceful processes of settlement; secondly, that any State which rejected such peaceful processes and resorted to war should be assured of automatic, swift, and effective assistance from the rest of the world." It may be argued that the wane of interest in the definition of aggresssion in some way *caused* the failure of the search for collective security; or, on the contrary, that the attempt to tie collective security schemes to a mechanically operating definition of aggression contributed to this failure. In fact both phenomena are more likely to have sprung from factors extraneous to either of them.

35 See the general conclusions in Ch. 9.

IV. THE SOVIET DRAFT DEFINITION OF 1933.

Only in the League's later years, from 1932 onwards, and in the quite different context of the attempt by the Disarmament Conference and its organs to distinguish offensive from defensive armaments,[36] was there any apparent advance in elaborating proposed criteria. In this context, on February 6, 1933, the Soviet delegation offered a draft definition which (with variations and additions) has run the gauntlet of a quarter of a century and of two world security organisations, without achieving either assured life or certain death. According to this proposal:[37]

> 1. The aggressor in an international conflict shall be considered that State which is the first to take any of the following actions:
>
> (a) Declaration of war against another State;
>
> (b) The invasion by its armed forces of the territory of another State without declaration of war;
>
> (c) Bombarding the territory of another State by its land, naval, or air forces or knowingly attacking the naval or air forces of another State;
>
> (d) The landing in, or introduction within the frontiers of another State of land, naval or air forces without the permission of the government of such a State, or the infringement of the condition of such permission, particularly as regards the duration of sojourn or extension of area;
>
> (e) The establishment of a naval blockade of the coast or ports of another State.
>
> 2. No considerations whatsoever of a political, strategical, or economic nature, including the desire to exploit natural riches or to obtain any sort of advantages or privileges on the territory of another State, no references to considerable capital investments or other special interests in a given State, or to the alleged absence of certain attributes of State organization in the case of a given country, shall be accepted as justification of aggression as defined in Clause 1.
>
> In particular, justification for attack cannot be based upon:
>
> A. *The internal situation in a given State,* as for instance:
>
> (a) Political, economic or cultural backwardness of a given country;
>
> (b) Alleged maladministration;
>
> (c) Possible danger to life or property of foreign residents;
>
> (d) Revolutionary or counter-revolutionary movements, civil war, disorders or strikes;

---

[36] On the earlier linkage between disarmament planning and the debate on definition of aggression, see 1 Walters, *History* 226.

[37] See L.N., *Records of the Conference for the Reduction and Limitation of Armaments,* Series D., vol. 5, p.11. For a convenient text see the Secretary-General's Report, *G.A.O.R. VII,* Ann., Agenda Item 54, pp.34ff.

(e) The establishment or maintenance in any State of any political, economic or social order.

B. *Any acts, laws or regulations of a given State,* as for instance:

(a) The infringement of international agreements;

(b) The infringement of the commercial, concessional or other economic rights or interests of a given State or its citizens;

(c) The rupture of diplomatic or economic relations;

(d) Economic or financial boycott;

(e) Repudiation of debts;

(f) Non-admission or limitation of immigration, or restriction of rights or privileges of foreign residents;

(g) The infringement of the privileges of official representatives of other States;

(h) The refusal to allow armed forces transit to the territory of a third State;

(i) Religious or anti-religious measures;

(j) Frontier incidents.

3. In the case of the mobilisation or concentration of armed forces to a considerable extent in the vicinity of its frontiers, the State which such activities threaten may have recourse to diplomatic or other means for the peaceful solution of international controversies. It may at the same time take steps of a military nature, analogous to those described above, without, however, crossing the frontier.

Following the Soviet proposals the Committee on Security Questions drew up, on instructions by the Political Committee of March 10, 1933, a draft Act relating to the Definition of the Aggressor.[38] This Act, in general, reproduced the substance of the Soviet proposals, adding in the inculpating acts that of supporting armed bands, and omitting the Soviet paragraph 1 (d) dealing with the landing or introduction of forces into the territory of another State.[39] The added sub-paragraph designated as aggression "provision of support to armed bands formed in its territory which have invaded the territory of another State, or refusal, notwithstanding the request of the invaded State, to take in its own territory all the measures in its power to deprive those bands of all assistance or protection". The draft Act also reproduced in Article 2 the Soviet proposal that no political, military, economic or other considerations might serve as "an excuse or justification" for aggression, and reproduced in a Protocol the substance of the Soviet's

---

38 For a convenient text of relevant provisions see the Secretary-General's Report in *G.A.O.R. VII,* Ann., Agenda Item 54, p.35.

As revised by Conference's Political Commission (Chairman, N. Politis), the draft was embodied in the provisional text of the Draft Disarmament Convention, 1933. Text in *L.N. Publ.* 1935, IX. 4, pp.683ff.; and see *L.N. Publ.* 1936 IX. 3, p.154. It also figures in a series of Soviet-sponsored non-aggression treaties. See *infra* pp.37-38.

39 There is a strangely sounding introduction of the italicised phrase into the opening para. of Art. 1: "The aggressor . . . shall *subject to the agreements in force between the Parties to the dispute,* be considered to be that State" *etc.* Probably intended as a substitute for the detailed Soviet para. 1 (a), the words suggest pleasing possibilities in cooperative mutuality of aggression.

proposed list of illegalities by the victim of "aggression" to be immunised from the listed kinds of self-redress by the wronged State. The draft Act added the judicious if wishful proviso that "the present Protocol can never legitimate any violations of international law that may be implied in the circumstances comprised in the above list".

The draft Act relating to the Definition of Aggression of 1933, based in substance on the Soviet proposals, can scarcely be said ever to have become more than a draft drawn by one subordinate committee for consideration by another, though the substance of its criteria was in turn embodied in various bilateral treaties promoted by the Soviet Union.[40] It is doubtful whether it had even the non-binding persuasive force of a *voeu* of the League Assembly or Council.[41] These very years were to witness the stream of expansive adventures which opened with Japan's seizure of Manchuria and closed with the German and Japanese initiatives in the Second World War; and it may not be without significance that as opportunities for testing the value of debated criteria thus presented themselves, the interest of States in the definitional problem waned,[42] and feeling grew that the whole enterprise was a "trap for the innocent and signpost to the guilty".[43] All this does not prove, of course, that if (for example) the Soviet criteria had been formally accepted by States, they might not have influenced the course of events. Yet it seems ludicrous to suppose, even if they had been accepted by all States, that either Japan and Italy or their fellow-Members would have been any less in doubt than they actually were that the relevant conduct of Japan and Italy constituted "aggression".

V. THE ITALO-ETHIOPIAN AND SOVIET-FINNISH AFFAIRS.

The League Council's proceedings of October 7, 1935, in the Italo-Ethiopian affair[44] are often treated as one of the two League instances of concrete application of the notion of aggression. Yet it is important to observe that the tenour of the decisions of League Members in that case avoided the necessity for resort to the *legal* notion of "aggression", and that this avoidance almost certainly facilitated the nearest League approach to peace enforcement against a major Power. What the action of Council Members of October 7, 1935, and the later action of Assembly Members did, was to affirm their judgments that "the Italian Government had resorted to

---

40 See *infra* pp.37-38, and Appendix, pt. v.

41 See J. Stone, "The Rule of Unanimity" (1933) 14 *B.Y.B.Int.L.* 18.

42 *Cf.* the somewhat similar paradox in 1956-57.

43 *L.N. Doc.* C.166.M.50.128.IX, p.176. This famous phrase was first used by Sir Austen Chamberlain in the House of Commons on Nov. 24, 1927. When Komarnicki observes (6) upon "the real progress" achieved in this period, this must be understood with the qualification he immediately adds that always *"le progrès n'est pas achevé, il se poursuit"*, and in a literally reflexive sense. The Writer would make a similar comment as to Professor Zourek's recent optimism (*supra* Intro. n.29a) in asserting that later debate is clarifying the task of definition, and that the slow progress is due merely to obstruction by governments, the complexity of the problems, and the present stage of transition from war to collective security.

44 *L.N.O.J.*, Nov. 1935 (89th Session) pp.1209-1229.

war in disregard of its covenants under Article 12 of the Covenant".[45] It was not necessary under the League Covenant, any more than it now is under the United Nations Charter,[46] to embroil the maintenance of peace with the notion of "aggression" at all, much less to make the maintenance of peace dependent on advance criteria of aggression capable of precise application.

Neither can it be said, in the other main case of concrete League application of the "aggression" concept, that its use by the Assembly seriously enhanced the moral or practical effectiveness of Assembly action. In the Soviet-Finnish affair the League Assembly resolved on December 14, 1939, that "the attitude and acts of the Government of the Union of Soviet Socialist Republics . . . have been incompatible with the commitments entered into by that country"; that "the Soviet Government has violated, not only its special political agreements with Finland, but also Article 12 of the Covenant of the League of Nations and the Pact of Paris"; and that it had therefore committed an "aggression" against Finland, which action was solemnly condemned.[47] The expulsion of the Soviet Union from the League followed.[48] The League, however, was already *in extremis,* and the consequential policies of all States were already dominated by the outbreak of World War II; so that few solid inferences can be drawn as to whether resort to the notion of "aggression" made any decisive difference, or as to whether the Soviet criteria of aggression really added to the ease of characterising the Soviet action as such.

VI. REGIONAL AND BILATERAL TREATIES.

About seventy regional or bilateral security or non-aggression treaties of the late 'twenties and 'thirties rang the expected verbal changes on the notions of aggression, and its related notions. Many of them—about thirty —did not use the "aggression" notion, but referred merely to "attack" or "invasion" or "use of force", or some variant of these; about forty spoke in terms of the aggression concept and its variants, usually without any clarifying definition. In six treaties, however, there was an enumeration of aggressive acts, mostly based[49] on the Soviet formula as adapted by the 1933 Committee on Security;[50] and in another four cases there was a brief general definition of aggression (also Soviet-inspired) in terms of "any act of violence attacking . . . the integrity and inviolability of the territory or the political

[45] See for a brief account Stone, *Conflict* 176-184, 278-281.
For fuller analyses see Sir J. Fischer Williams (*et al.*), *International Sanctions* (1938); A. J. Toynbee, *Survey of International Affairs 1935: Abyssinia and Italy* (vol. ii, 1936). And see the last cited at 215 on the non-corporate nature of the League finding in this case.

[46] See *infra* pp.92ff.

[47] *L.N.O.J.,* Nov.-Dec. 1939, Ann. 1756, p.540.

[48] *Id.* p.506.

[49] The main variants are in the Iraq-Afghan-Iran-Turkish Treaty of July 8, 1937 (190 *L.N.T.S.* 4402, Art. 4), and the Iraq-Transjordan Treaty of April 14, 1947 (*U.N.T.S.* No. 345).

[50] For listings of these treaties with references see *U.N. Doc.* A/2211, pp.47-50.

independence of the H.C.P. . . . even if committed without warlike manifestations",[51] (It may be noted, with no desire to be tendentious, that a number of States which benefited from either the short or the long Soviet definition were later overrun and absorbed by the Soviet Union.) [52]

Nor do regional or other security treaties between 1945 and 1950, when the matter of definition of aggression emerged into debate in the United Nations General Assembly, add any new features to the alternatives offering except perhaps a certain concentration, of Latin-American inspiration, on armed invasion "trespassing boundaries" established by treaty or third party decision,[53] as a criterion of "aggression". Apart from invasions directed to asserting territorial claims, the Rio Treaty reimported into post-World War II treaties the exculpating notion of "provocation" as a limit on the notion of aggression, which had also been very common in League Days.[54]

VII. LEAGUE LESSONS.

Clearly League efforts to find precise advance criteria, though they produced certain proposals, produced no final consensus as to these proposals. In our later pages, we shall return to evaluate the main Soviet proposal, but we can observe immediately that League experience seems to show that adequate enumerative tests of aggression were probably impossible to find,

---

[51] For relevant texts see Treaties of Non-Aggression, Lithuania-U.S.S.R. 28 Sept., 1926, 60 *L.N.T.S.,* No. 1410; Latvia-U.S.S.R. 5 Feb., 1932, 148 *L.N.T.S.* No. 3408; Estonia-U.S.S.R. 4 May, 1932, 131 *L.N.T.S.* No. 3020; Poland-U.S.S.R. 25 July 1932, 136 *L.N.T.S.* No. 3124; Treaty of Neutrality and Mutual Non-Aggression, Turkey-U.S.S.R. 17 Dec., 1925, 157 *L.N.T.S.* No. 3610; Treaty of Guarantee and of Neutrality, Persia-U.S.S.R. 1 Oct., 1927, 112 *L.N.T.S.* No. 2620. Up to 1932 Soviet treaties did not seriously attempt to define aggression nor did her 1939 Treaty with Nazi Germany. For convenient documentation on many of these matters see V. Bruns (ed.), *Politische Verträge* (2 vols. 1936-1942); and see *infra* Ch. 6, on the political aspects of this course of treaty making.

For an examination of the inter-war regional guarantee treaties with a view to ascertaining whether they manifest any *opinio juris sive necessitatis* sufficient to base a customary rule as to the definition of aggression, see E. Serra, *L'Aggressione Internazionale* (1946) 129-174. That work reaches a negative conclusion, with which the present Writer agrees.

[52] L. Schultz, *"Der Sowjetische Begriff der Aggression"* (1956) 2 *Osteuropa Recht* 274, 279, cruelly calculates that by 1950 seven of the eleven States bound by non-aggression treaties with the Soviet Union had experienced Soviet aggression. It would be wrong not to make the comment that Mr. Schultz is of course using his own definition of aggression, at any rate in some of the cases. And *cf.* M. Röling in the Sixth Committee (*U.N. Doc.* A/C.6/SR. 289, p.12) who observed that such facts did not recommend acceptance of the Soviet definition.

[53] See, e.g., the Act of Chapultepec of Mar. 8, 1945 (9 Hudson, *Int. Leg.* 286ff.), of which pt. I, 3 provides that aggression includes "every attack of a State against the integrity or the inviolability of the territory, or against the sovereignty or the political independence of an American State", and in any case, "invasion" and the "trespassing of boundaries".

The Inter-American Treaty of Reciprocal Assistance of Sept. 2, 1947 (21 *U.N.T.S.* No. 324) Arts. 3 and 9, while leaving the Organ of Consultation free to characterise other acts as "aggression" declared to be aggression "unprovoked armed attack by a State against the territory, the people, or the land, sea or air forces of another State" and armed invasion "affecting a region under the effective jurisdiction of another State", or "trespassing of boundaries demarcated, etc."

[54] No less than 24 treaties between the two wars employed such formulas as "attacked without giving provocation", "unprovoked attack". See the examples in U.N. Doc. A/2211, p.51.

though the search was not wholly abandoned. On the level of action, League experience raised doubts[55] to which I shall also have to refer in connection with the United Nations, as to whether there was much to be said for making the system of peace enforcement hinge on the notion of aggression at all.[56]

I have already referred to the well-known assessment by the League Assembly itself in 1928[57] of Article 11 of the Covenant, as the Article which "without detracting from the value of the other articles of the Covenant", best expressed the fact "that the League's first task is to forestall war, and that in all cases of armed conflict or of threats of armed conflict, of whatever nature, it must take action to prevent hostilities or to stop hostilities which have already begun . . .".[58] This recommendation followed a report by N. Politis, in which he emphasised that in relation to the essential purpose of the League, namely the prevention of war, Article 11 was of special significance from three points of view, even as compared with the famous Article 16 on sanctions. "First", he said, "as regards chronological order, since the Council, in dealing with an international crisis, must apply Article 11 before Article 16; secondly, Article 11 is important because it is undeniably far better to prevent war than to stop it"; and finally because resort to Article 11 played a vital role preliminary to invocation of Article 16, by permitting observation of the disputants and their attitudes towards the Council's task, thus aiding in the collection of information for determining later, in case of need, which party is the aggressor.

The outstanding unofficial study of the League Council's functions in maintaining peace by T. P. Conwell-Evans,[59] based on the more successful decade of the Council's activity, confirms the inferences which might be drawn from the attitude of the League organs themselves. His close examination of seventeen cases likely to lead to a rupture, which were successfully dealt with during the period, satisfied him that success depended not on "complicated formulae" or on any agreed definition of aggression or

55 See T. P. Conwell-Evans, *op.cit. infra* n.59, at 59, 156, 255.

56 Professor Wright, "The Concept of Aggression" (1935) 29 *A.J.I.L.* 382ff., thought that the League "moved towards" the three tests of aggression summarised *supra* n.4. It will be apparent from the above account that Members steadily resisted the first, as an advance test, and that the second was scarcely a precise test, merely transferring the indeterminacy (as it does) to "the least defensive necessity". As to the third, see *infra* Ch. 5, s.1. For that learned writer's history of these supposed tests see *op.cit.* 382-389.

57 See *L.N.O.J.* Sp. Sup. No. 63, p.16.

58 The U.N. Secretary-General (*G.A.O.R.* VII, Ann., Item 54, A/2211, p.30) accurately restated the gist as being that "prevention is better than punishment" and that the first duty of an international body is to take the most effective action to prevent the outbreak of hostilities or to bring about the cessation of hostilities which have already begun.

Cf. also the assumption of the abortive General Convention to Improve the Means of Preventing War of 26 Sept. 1931, of which Art. 2 contemplated measures to ensure evacuation of forces after invasion without determining the aggressor or applying sanctions. This solicitude is sometimes carried to the point of saying that even where an aggression is clear the priority of the tasks may "make it politic to refrain from actually naming the State concerned" if that State seems willing to desist. See G. G. Fitzmaurice, *G.A.O.R. VI,* 281st Meeting, para. 12. And see A/2211, para. 264.

59 T. P. Conwell-Evans, *The League Council in Action* (1929) 35ff. The 1936 official

self-defence, nor on use of the sanctions article, but on diligent attention to the simpler tasks under Article 11 of arresting hostilities and removing a probable cause of war, and the use to these ends of the Council's "moral and political authority, supported by world public opinion".[60] The mere fact of war or threat of war, as a matter of concern to the whole League under Article 11, was the main and a sufficient basis of this activity. And that writer observed, in connection with what he obviously regarded as a model case:

> The wide competence enjoyed by the Council under Article XI enabled it to act without its being first obliged to establish facts or prove charges, as it would be forced to do were it a question of applying Article XVI. Its primary task being to separate the combatants, it addressed itself to both disputants, as if each were equally at fault.
>
> This example gives further emphasis to the comment . . . that when it is a question of ending hostilities, the need for a ready-made definition of an aggressor—which has aroused so much controversy at conferences on "security and arbitration"—does not necessarily arise.[61]

The main task which seemed to be opened up by experience, as distinct from speculative theories and plans, was thus in his view not "to make war on an aggressor—but to improve and develop the means of prevention, of separating the combatants, of bringing about an armistice";[62] and above all, the immediate use of Article 11 to restrain hostilities as such, in conjunction with positive continuing pressure on the parties under Article 16 to some conciliatory adjustment of the merits of a dispute. There were, of course, a number of factors in the League Council's work of the 'twenties which may render its experience inconclusive for the United Nations in the 'fifties. The outstanding of these is undoubtedly the fact that neither Russia nor the United States were in the League, and that the remaining Great Powers were usually of one mind and interest towards threat of hostilities between minor States.[63] Yet, some other aspects, namely the absence of compulsive power of the Council over the peace-threatening States under Article 11,[64] and the need therefore to exploit to the maximum techniques of persuasion and moral pressure, accompanied by assurance of fair adjustment on the merits, render its experience most pertinent to the tasks of the General Assembly which we shall later have to examine.[65]

---

study after the Ethiopian Affair (*Covenant Principles*, c.x,s.vi, paras, 3-4 pp.87-89) scarcely illuminates the present issues, though a few State comments favoured inclusion of a definition of aggression in the Covenant, or at least the use of that notion to base sanctions.

60 *Op.cit.* 254. But see the Chinese and Argentine insistence in 1936 (*Covenant Principles* 88) that the "aggressor" must be determined as a prerequisite to sanctions.

61 *Id.* 51. He is referring to the Greco-Bulgarian hostilities of October 1925, in which despite the fact that Greece had invaded Bulgarian territory, the Council carefully refrained from attempting to allot responsibility until the hostilities had been brought under control. The charge of breach of Covenant, said Mr. Conwell-Evans, had to be investigated, but "that would have required time, and there was no time to spare when the task was immediately to bring hostilities to an end."

62 *Id.* 259.

63 There were, however, some cases handled which did involve major Powers.

64 Since these were entitled to be represented on the Council with a right of vote under Art. 4 (5), and the Council had to be unanimous for decision under Art. 5 (1).

65 See *infra* esp. Ch. 9.

CHAPTER 3

UNITED NATIONS QUEST

I. WHAT THE CHARTER DRAFTSMEN MEANT.

The wane of interest and hope in the task of fixing criteria of aggression which marked the dying days of the League continued into the prenatal and infant life of the United Nations. It is true that at San Francisco both Bolivia[1] and the Philippines[2] submitted to the Third Committee of the Third Commission definitions of the enumerative type of the Soviet model of the 'thirties, the former laying particular emphasis on refusal to submit the dispute for settlement to "the peaceful means provided",[3] or to comply with "a judicial decision pronounced by an International Court".[4] In the Bolivian view it was essential to define "aggression", even though the Security Council's full powers were to arise on a mere threat to the peace or breach of the peace, because as against aggression enforcement measures "should be applied immediately by collective action", that is, should be automatic.

The majority of the San Francisco Committee, however, regarded any preliminary definition of aggression as beyond both the possibilities of the Conference and the purposes of the Charter. M. Paul Boncour in his report[5] stressed the difficulties of definition arising from techniques of modern warfare, the danger that a necessarily incomplete list of criteria would encourage ingenious aggressors to proceed by methods not clearly branded, thus obstructing Security Council action; as well as the danger of requiring "premature" sanctions and thus restricting the Council's discretion in the listed cases to decide that measures short of peace enforcement would be more effective.[6] The text of Article 39 of the Charter thus left "aggression"

---

[1] See "Proposals of the Delegation of the Republic of Bolivia for the Organisation of a System of Peace and Security", 3 *U.N.C.I.O. Docs.* 577, 579. The proposal repeated the main heads of the Soviet 1933 draft (without making the priority principle explicit), adding: (e) intervention in another State's policy; (f) Refusal to submit the cause of belligerence to the procedures of peaceful solution; (g) Refusal to comply with a decision pronounced by a court of international justice; and also urging that armed invasion "should dictate the adoption of immediate sanctions without the need of previous consultation." And see *id.* 585, 586. And for Czechoslovak support of definition, *id.* 468.

[2] See "Proposed Amendments to the Dumbarton Oaks Proposals submitted by the Philippine Delegation", 3 *U.N.C.I.O. Docs.* 535-42, esp. 538, adopting in substance the Soviet 1933 draft omitting the aid to armed bands provision but with a new head (4) concerning interference with the internal affairs of another nation by various means embracing *inter alia* support of any armed band.

[3] A curiously indeterminate formula—"provided" by whom?

[4] But what about an arbitral decision, or a decision of the Security Council?

[5] 12 *U.N.C.I.O. Docs.* 505.

[6] Paul Boncour stressed the similarity of the rejected proposals to the drafts of the inter-war period. See 12 *U.N.C.I.O. Docs.* 505. He also dealt (*ibid.*) with the New Zealand proposal for automatic sanctions in case of "aggression". New Zealand had proposed in Commission I (see 6 *id.* 81) that "when the Security Council has decided that an act of aggression against one of the members . . . has taken place, there will

undefined, and gave equal weight to the "threat to the peace, breach of the peace, or act of aggression", as regards the legal powers which the Security Council's determinations conferred. It was left to the Security Council, in the light of all the circumstances and antecedents of a particular affair, *after it has arisen,* to make the appropriate determination, and to decide what if anything should be done about it.

Other provisions of the United Nations Charter relevant to our problem are Article 51 reserving the liberty of self-defence against armed attack on a Member, Article 2 (3) providing that "All Members shall settle their international disputes by peaceful means in such a manner that international peace and security, and justice,[7] are not endangered", and the still more critical Article 2 (4), prohibiting "the threat or use of force against the territorial integrity or political independence of any State, or in any other manner inconsistent with the Purposes of the United Nations".[8] None

---

immediately result a clear and unmistakable duty on every member of the Organisation, great or small, to resist and defeat that aggression by the means laid down by the Security Council". This proposal received 26 votes against 18 which was not a sufficient majority. In Paul Boncour's view, apparently accepted without demur, the New Zealand proposal fell with the adoption of the view that aggression should not be defined.

"The Committee", he said, "therefore decided to adhere to the text drawn up at Dumbarton Oaks and to leave to the Council the entire decision as to what constitutes a threat to peace, a breach of the peace, or an act of aggression." And see generally *id.* 502-14.

It adds nothing, for present purposes, to refer to the Committee's "conviction" that the Security Council's discretion should not retard or weaken its action, or to its picture (which now reads very sadly) of the firm obligations of Members after due decision to provide the Council with a force in being for use against a persistent aggressor. See 12 *U.N.C.I.O. Docs.* 507, and 1 *id.* 668 (Paul Boncour's Report).

Cf. E. Serra, *L'Aggressione Internazionale* (1946) 194ff.

[7] See 3 *U.N.C.I.O.* 582 and 6 *U.N.C.I.O.* 333 for the Committee's adoption by 27 votes to 11 of the Bolivian proposal to insert the words "and justice" in the last line of para. 3. The full Conference, indeed, recognised in the Statement of June 22, 1945, that Members might withdraw, and dissolution become "inevitable", if the U.N. could only "maintain peace . . . at the expense of law and justice". (7 *U.N.C.I.O.* 310, rev. *Doc.* 1178 I/2/76 (2), in 16 *id.*, approved in the Plenary, 1 *id.* 620.)

And see also on the history of the words "and justice", 3 *U.N.C.I.O.* 25, reproducing "Chinese Proposals on Dumbarton Oaks Proposals", envisaging *inter alia* that "the Charter should provide specifically that adjustment or settlement of international disputes should be achieved with due regard for principles of justice and international law"; 6 *id.* 23, where the Egyptian delegate suggests "that after the words 'to maintain international peace and security' we should add the words, 'in conformity with the principles of justice and international law' "; 6 *id.* 70, where the Egyptian representative said "force will be used by the International Organization only to apply law and achieve justice"; 6 *id.* 27, where the Panama representative answered the question, "How are peace and security to be maintained?" by invoking "justice"; and he said that along with Bolivia, Ecuador, Egypt, France, Greece, Iran, Mexico, the Netherlands, Panama, and Uruguay, his State wanted "a peace founded upon justice and nothing but justice, a peace that will be on no occasion a peace of expediency, a peace of force, a peace of appeasement. It must be a peace of justice."

So *cf.* the U.K. representative (*id.* 25): "The placing of these words as proposed by the Committee does . . . in fact secure that settlements and adjustments of any disputes should be in conformity with justice". The U.S. representative said (6 *id.* 30): ". . . when you begin to function as a jury you must do so in conformity with justice and international law". So also *cf.* the Uruguayan statement (6 *id.* 32), and Report of the Rapporteur of Sub-Committee I/I/A (Farid Zeineddine, Syria) (6 *id.* 318) indicating awareness of the difficulties which might arise from vagueness of the concept.

[8] On the by no means clear history of Art. 2 (4) see *infra* Ch. 5. And see the New Zealand proposed amendment that: "All members of the Organization undertake collectively to resist every act of aggression against any member." (6 *U.N.C.I.O.* 334.) The

of these latter provisions refer to "aggression" in terms, though they were later to become central in the definitional debate. As we shall later show more fully, it is far from certain that the obligations to refrain from the threat or use of force, stand unqualified either on the texts themselves, or in the light of the *travaux préparatoires*.[9] Article 2 (3) as a *general* provision on peaceful settlement must, in any case, be read by reference to the *special* provisions of Article 2 (4), and of Chapter VII, concerning the prohibition of resort to force. Indeed, unless this is done, Article 2 (4) becomes largely redundant.

We will later submit that when Article 2 (4) and its drafting are looked at with care, the qualifications on its prohibition must be taken seriously. What it prohibits is not use of force as such, but as used against the "territorial integrity or political independence of any State",[10] or "in any other manner inconsistent with the Purposes of the United Nations". These "purposes" may properly extend beyond Article 1 (devoted to "the Purposes of the United Nations"), to include *(inter alia)* the preambulatory references to the saving of the world from the scourge of war, to fundamental human rights, and maintenance of the conditions assuring justice, respect for the obligations arising from treaties, and general international law. The purposes expressed in Article 1 itself, moreover, embrace not only collective measures against threats to the peace, breaches of the peace and acts of aggression, but also (and coordinately) the bringing about "by peaceful means, and in conformity with the principles of justice and international law, adjustment or settlement" of peace-endangering disputes.[11]

It is, we shall submit, far from impossible to argue that a threat or use of force employed consistently with *these* purposes, and not directed against the "territorial integrity or political independence of any state", may be commendable rather than necessarily forbidden by the Charter. Nor is it inconceivable that situations may arise in which attempts to settle disputes by peaceful means may be so delayed, and prospects of success so fantastically remote, that a minimal regard for law and justice in inter-State relations might require the use of force in due time to vindicate these standards, and avoid even more catastrophic resort to force at a later stage. There is, at any rate, no clear legal warrant for reading the Charter and the *travaux préparatoires,* as is sometimes done, as if Article 2 (4) excluded all resort to force except in self-defence or under the authority of the United Nations, thus excluding these other possibilities.[12]

Moreover, neither the text nor the *travaux,* nor as will be suggested,

---

U.S. representative opposed the New Zealand amendment on the ground that "paragraph 4 as adopted was adequate. It seemed undesirable to include too narrow a concept of aggression in the Charter. He pointed out that in the future there would be many kinds of aggression and that these would be covered in the Charter by the words 'threat to the peace' ". (344.) The New Zealand amendment failed to receive a two-thirds majority and the motion was lost (346). All this gives, at best, very hazardous support to the extreme view, for Art. 2 (4) uses neither the term "aggression" nor the term "threat to the peace".

[9] Thus the words "and justice" were certainly not inserted in Art. 2 (3) by mere inadvertence. See *supra* n.7.

[10] Dubious aspects of the use of "or" instead of "and" here need not detain us.

[11] *Cf. supra* n.7.

[12] See also *supra* pp.21ff., and *infra* pp.94ff.

the underlying policies of the Charter, make it sensible to assume that Article 51 was intended to set the outer limits of self-defence for all purposes. In reserving a licence limited to the case of "armed attack against a Member" the draftsmen were delimiting the reserved powers of Members as against United Nations organs. For other purposes, for instance where the Security Council is not acting, the broader licence of self-defence and self-redress under customary international law[13] must surely continue to exist so far as the positive prohibitions of the Charter do not exclude it. Article 51 itself, in reserving as against the Security Council's powers a narrow range of self-defence, can surely not have destroyed the broader area of the licence of self-defence and self-redress where the Security Council is not acting, and there is no inconsistency with the purposes of the United Nations.[14]

Nor did the Charter draftsmen lay down any clear criteria for delimiting "aggression", as against such obviously related notions as "justice", the "self-defence" referred to in Article 51, or the "legitimate self-defence" clearly intended to be reserved by the draftsmen.[15] Nor was this restraint by any means fortuitous. First, some of the ablest and most experienced among them, like M. Paul Boncour, were very familiar with the long vain search for such criteria under League auspices. Second, we have seen that Article 39 was drafted so as to avoid the need for determination of "aggression", granting the full plenitude of powers to the Security Council on a mere threat to the peace, or breach of the peace, and thus making resort to the aggression notion unnecessary. The suggestion that "aggression" should work different results was explicitly rejected. Third, the clear design was to give the Security Council full freedom to examine all relevant circumstances in determining whether a particular conflict did involve a "threat to the peace, breach of the peace, or act of aggression". Then, as now, it was apparent that if use of the Great Power veto paralysed Security Council action, none of these terms could be given meaning in the particular case, and that means other than legal coercion under the Charter would have to be used.[16]

---

[13] The main limiting concept to Art. 2 (4) used in the *travaux* was not "self-defence against armed attack" in the sense of Art. 51, but the broader traditional concept of "legitimate self-defence". Thus, in Commission I, Committee I, the term "legitimate self-defence" was used by the Brazilian delegate in discussions on Art. 2 (4), though the delegate of Norway in the same discussions spoke of "individual and collective self-defence". See 6 *U.N.C.I.O.* 334. In the Report of the Rapporteur of Committee I to Commission I, the phrase "legitimate self-defence" occurs in relation to Art. 2 (4), namely: "The use of arms in legitimate self-defence remains admitted and unimpaired". (6 *U.N.C.I.O.* 459.) And see also *infra* p.98. The continued vigour as well as indeterminacy of the traditional concept, even after 1928, are well recalled in Mr. Kellogg's Note of June 23, 1928, to the Signatories of the Kellogg-Briand Pact: "Express recognition by treaty of this inalienable right, however, gives rise to the same difficulty encountered in any effort to define aggression. It is the identical question approached from the other side. Inasmuch as no treaty provision can add to the natural right of self-defence, it is not in the interest of peace that a treaty should stipulate a juristic conception of self-defence since it is far too easy for the unscrupulous to mold events to accord with an agreed definition." (See Shotwell, *op.cit.* 297.)

[14] Any inference based on *inclusio unius exclusio alterius* is neutralised by the clear reference of what is included to the situation where the Security Council is acting.

[15] See *supra* nn.8, 13. [16] See Stone, *Conflict* 218-223, and documents there cited.

It is, we believe, in the light of the draftsmen's deliberate refusal to formulate advance criteria of "aggression", and of the breakdown of Security Council action to determine existence of a "threat to the peace, breach of the peace or act of aggression" in the circumstances of a particular case, that the contemporary drive in the General Assembly to formulate advance criteria is to be understood.[17] In this light it is easy to understand the hope that the Assembly, lacking as it does the legal powers of binding determination and action vested in the Security Council, should attempt to build up by the emotive effects of the verbal symbol of "aggression" a psychological foundation for securing voluntary compliance by Member States with its hortatory resolutions. Only in this sense, can there be any serious truth in the frequent contemporary assertion that the "aggression" concept is the keystone of United Nations peace enforcement.[18] Certainly this was not so in the original design of the United Nations; but this does not mean that it could not be made so in the future. The question is, *can* it be made so? The present search for criteria precise enough to brand future situations, has been one way of seeking to make it true. But this way can succeed only if there is a sufficiently wide and deep consensus among States as to the criteria proposed. Such a consensus presupposes that States are willing to commit themselves both to the absolute liability, whatever the circumstances, to be suppressed themselves if they should engage in the conduct impugned by the criterion, and to unquestioning cooperation in the task of suppressing such conduct by other States. It has become obvious by 1957 that this consensus is not within reach.

This does not exclude the possibility that the General Assembly may, without any advance criteria, nevertheless apply the aggression notion *ad hoc* to conflicts as they arise with a degree of righteousness, impartiality and freedom from the national or *bloc*-interests of its Members, which wins the approval from the majority of its Members for each particular finding of aggression and consequential recommendations. It is probably true that the very constitution and voting rules of the Assembly, and the chronic divisions among its Members on such issues as "colonialism" and "totalitarianism", make success on this basis also unlikely. Certainly, as will be later more fully shown, the emotional impulse to voluntary cooperation of Members could not be expected to arise even from an *ad hoc* finding of "aggression", unless the Assembly were able and willing to review fully as well as fairly the merits of the conflict before it.

If, as our later analysis suggests, [18a] this way too is unpromising, the entire assumption that the "aggression" notion is a possible basis of General

---

17 *Cf.* among many writers, Q. Wright, "The Prevention of Aggression" (1956) 50 *A.J.I.L.* 514, 518; W. W. Kulski, "The Soviet System of Collective Security Compared with the Western System" (1950) 44 *A.J.I.L.* 453, who observes that "the United Nations cannot guarantee collective security against aggression, because any Permanent Member of the Security Council may prevent, by its single veto, the application of sanctions against itself or any other state guilty of aggression"; and see Stone, *Conflict* 217.

18 See, for instance, among the more solid authorities, Professor Quincy Wright's work, cited *supra* n.17.

18a See Ch. 9 *infra*.

Assembly peace enforcement action may have to be reviewed. We shall, for example, find that there is much to be said for the view that in an age of thermo-nuclear weapons, the morally neutral and less emotionally charged concept of "breach of the peace" may still provide a stimulus to voluntary action by Members. Certainly such stimulus seemed to suffice in the recent Middle East crisis, where no formal determination of "aggression" was found necessary.[19]

II. QUIET ON THE DEFINITIONAL FRONT.

Inter arma silent definitiones might be a significant maxim for the decade of muted debate on the definition of aggression from 1935 to 1945. And the interlude was to continue until 1950, even through the polemical period of the war crimes trials. On the face of the United Nations Charter, as we have now seen, the "aggression" concept was not an essential basis of peace enforcement, and the draftsmen made clear their assumption that the Security Council, insofar as it applied it, would determine its limits *ad hoc* in each affair.

It is thus no mere chance that the war of definitions did not resume till the full paralysis of the Security Council after August, 1950, and the move in the Uniting For Peace Resolutions to assert compensatory powers in the General Assembly. The Assembly having no powers of legal compulsion in this area[20] and thus depending on voluntary cooperation of Members, the emotive force of the aggression concept was sought to be harnessed by advance consensus as to its definition to ensuring that cooperation. This, and the older themes of the 'thirties, were also reinforced by certain new strains deriving from controversies surrounding the trial and punishment of the major war criminals on the count of aggressive war-making. It will later be seen[21] that the latter function holds different directives as to definition from the function of politico-military peace enforcement; and the contemporary attempt to frame definitions without regard to these differences has increased the attendant confusions.

III. THE INTERNATIONAL LAW COMMISSION AND THE SOVIET DEFINITION.

In the First Committee of the General Assembly on November 6, 1950, the Soviet Union revived, under the item "Duties of States in the Event of the Outbreak of Hostilities", the substance of its draft definition of 1933, and this with related matters was submitted in due course to the International Law Commission for its views.[22] Following another Soviet initiative[23] in the First Committee of the Fifth General Assembly, the Assembly also adopted a resolution[24] which, after condemning "the intervention of a

[19] See *infra*, esp. Ch. 9.
[20] See Stone, *Conflict* 234-237, 266-284, and the authorities cited *infra* Ch. 9, n.4.
[21] See *infra* Ch. 8.
[22] *G.A.O.R. VII*, 308th Plenary Meeting, Nov. 17, 1950, Resol. 378B (V).
[23] To include in the Agenda an item entitled, "Declaration on the removal of the threat of a new war . . .".
[24] Resol. 380 (V).

State in the internal affairs of another State for the purpose of changing its legally established government by the threat or use of force", reaffirmed that "any aggression, whether committed openly, or by fomenting civil strife in the interest of a foreign power, or otherwise, is the gravest of all crimes against peace and security throughout the world . . .".

The International Law Commission studied the Soviet-proposed definition of aggression[25] through eleven meetings.[26] That definition, like its earlier prototype of 1933, enumerated five main acts of State violence, the first commission of any of which would render the State concerned an "attacker".[27] There is here a curious change from the 1933 form, in that the term "attacker" is substituted for the term "aggressor". A possible interpretation of the change might have been that whether an "attacker" is also an "aggressor" may still depend on whether circumstances of justification can be shown.[28] And it might support this that the Soviet formulation in paragraph 2 continued also its earlier proposal that such "attacks . . . may not be justified by any arguments of a political, strategic or economic nature, or by the desire to exploit natural riches in the territory of the State attacked or to derive any other kind of advantages or privileges, or by reference to the amount of capital invested in the State attacked or to any other particular interests in its territory, or by the affirmation that the State attacked lacks the distinguishing marks of statehood".[29] But since the new wording was still preceded by a preamble asserting that the purpose of all the provisions was to determine "which party is guilty of aggression", and since the whole definition was expressed in grounds of exculpation, it would appear on the whole that the word "attacker" in paragraph 1 was merely a synonym for "aggressor by armed violence".

The illustrative list of non-justifying acts again made clear, as in 1933, that in the Soviet view even the gravest and most blatant violations of the rights of the "attacker" State were not to justify "attack" by way of self-redress against the violator, so long as they were held short of "attack" on the injured State. Even when the "victim" took the initiative in mobilising and concentrating its armed forces on the frontier, the State threatened was permitted only to seek "peaceful settlement" (which, of course, the other side would normally have rejected already), or at most to obey the maxim, "Go thou and do likewise". The inadequacy of such a precept

---

25 *G.A.O.R. V*, Ann. 2, Item 72, p.5, 1950.

26 *G.A.O.R. VI*, Supp. No. 9, C.3 (A/1858).

27 See *supra* pp.34-35. In summary the acts were (a) Declaration of war; (b) Armed invasion; (c) Bombardment of another State's territory, ships or aircraft; (d) Unlicensed landing, leading or maintaining of forces on another State's territory; (e) Naval blockade.

28 The Soviet definition maintained this change also in 1956 as regards "armed aggression". The reasoning is obscure unless it was thought that this change would meet the objection raised in the 1956 Committee that since to call an act "aggression" was in itself a legal judgment, it was contradictory to speak of "justification" for "aggression". It will be clear from the text that it does not in fact meet this objection.

29 It went on to give the extended list (in substance identical with that of 1933, though with verbal changes) of examples of acts of provocation by the alleged victim which were *not* justifications for attacks. See also *infra* pp.88ff. as to the provision that the Security Council might declare unlisted acts to be aggression.

where the concentration is at a frontier so near to the capital and main resources of the threatened State as to make the latter's survival dubious in case of an assault, was ignored by the Soviet draft. Under paragraph 3 the latter would still be the "attacker" if it crossed the frontier first, even if this was essential in the circumstances to avoid its own destruction. And this result was rendered even stranger by paragraph 2 which laid down that "frontier incidents" did not justify the State threatened by the concentration crossing the frontier. The threatened State must not treat frontier crossing by the threatening State as an "attack"; but if the threatened State reacted to such a penetration by itself crossing the frontier, it was itself to become "the attacker" (and presumably "the aggressor").

The International Law Commission reported to the Assembly that "it was undesirable to define aggression by a detailed enumeration of aggressive acts, since no enumeration could be exhaustive", and that it was inadvisable unduly to "limit the freedom of judgment" of the competent organs by a "rigid and necessarily incomplete" list of acts of "aggression". It preferred, therefore, to seek "a general and abstract definition".[30] The contrast thus made is between, on the one hand, a list of concrete acts, each of which is to constitute (either conclusively or presumptively) an "act of aggression"; and on the other, a description of the "elements" which if present in any concrete acts turn those acts (either conclusively or presumptively) into "acts of aggression". M. Alfaro's proposal for a "general and abstract" definition was as follows:

> Aggression is the threat or use of force by a State or government against another State, in any manner, whatever the weapons employed and whether openly or otherwise, for any reason or for any purpose other than individual or collective self-defence or in pursuance of a decision or recommendation by a competent organ of the United Nations.[31]

In a report at the same session M. Spiropoulos, Special Rapporteur on the Draft Code of Offences Against the Peace and Security of Mankind, concluded that any " 'legal' definition of aggression would be an artificial construction" which could never, in view of the steady expansion of methods of aggression, be comprehensive enough for all future uses.[32] He thought that this difficulty affected "general and abstract" definition, as well as the Soviet type of enumerative definition. The general and abstract elements

---

[30] I.L.C. Report covering the . . . Third Session 16 May-27 July, 1951, c.III, p.9, A/C. 1/108.

[31] See *supra* pp.9-10. For a full statement of M. Alfaro's position see R. J. Alfaro, "*La Question de la Définition de la l'Agression*" (1951) 29 *R.D.I.* 367, esp. 378ff. In his view prior failures were due to use of enumerative definitions. But, of course, unless he had accepted the drastic premises of Professor Scelle (see Introd. *supra* pp.5ff.) he could not have framed so apparently simple a general definition; while the fact that he accepted such drastic premises made it certain that his definition could never have won general acceptance. The legislative experience which he says (367) leads to the rejection of enumeration as a means of reaching future eventualities, equally rejects all-embracing general definitions unless relieved by *Fluchtklauseln* at necessary points.

[32] The Report was entitled "The Possibility and Desirability of a Definition of Aggression" (A/CN.4/44, c.ii.). Summarised in the Commission's Report (16 May-27 July, 1951), (*G.A.O.R. VI,* Supp. No. 9 (A/1858) p.8.)

of the notion of "aggression" which governments in fact apply *ad hoc* to frame a judgment in a particular case,[33] were, he thought, at least twofold: The "objective" element of external State conduct, and the "subjective" element of the *animus aggressionis,* or *mens rea,* or intent behind that conduct.[33a] He thought that the requisite kinds or degrees of direct or indirect violence could not be determined in advance, apart from the circumstances of the particular case; and that the notion of "aggression" was therefore an undefinable "concept *per se*".[34]

Insofar as the Commission rejected even M. Alfaro's very attractive proposed "general and abstract" definition,[35] and proposed no other, it appears to have supported M. Spiropoulos' conclusion. This is confirmed by the grounds given for rejecting the Alfaro formula, namely, that it did not comprehend all conceivable acts of aggression and "might prove . . . dangerously restrictive of the necessary freedom of action of the organs of the United Nation in specific cases", and (in the view of some Members) it might, by its over-stringency brand as "aggression" conduct which should *not* be so branded.[36] The Commission even rejected[37] a proposal to continue its efforts to define aggression on the basis of new texts. It should be noted, for later discussion, that though the main focus of the Commission's task was that of criminal liability of individuals, the reasons it gave for rejecting definition were inspired by the different function of politico-military peace enforcement. Little awareness was shown that the diverse functions might require diverse answers.[38] Nor was the position of the Commission radically changed, when, after reconsideration in connection with various proposed definitions having reference to the Draft Code of Offences against the Peace and Security of Mankind,[39] it formulated the following para-

33 "The 'natural', so to speak, notion of aggression . . ." (*ibid.*) M. Spiropoulos' meaning should not be concealed by this hazardous use of the term "natural".

33a So *cf.* a number of delegations in the Sixth Committee who thought it impossible to define aggression solely by describing objective acts, and favoured the inclusion of a provision concerning the intent with which the acts were committed. See Sixth Committee Report, *G.A.O.R. VI,* Agenda Item 49, p.16. And see the fuller discussion *infra* pp.139-142.

34 For a Marxist critique of the position on the ground that M. Spiropoulous was merely reviving "Kant's obscurantist idea of the thing-in-itself", see M. Franklin, *The Conception of Aggression* 14-15, relying on Hegel's well-known critique of the Kantian notion, on the ground that things have properties, which produce effects. (Hegel, *Science of Logic* (transl. Johnston and Struther, 1929), vol. ii, p.116ff.) I beg to doubt, however, that M. Spiropoulous' position has any more than a mere verbal relation to Kant's conception of "the thing-in-itself". A notion may defy adequate definition for the practical purposes of a particular political function even if it refers to a phenomenon and not a noumenon. The Soviet acts which have led from time to time to the absorption into itself of minor States (with some of which it had concluded treaties incorporating the Soviet definition of aggression) may display the phenomenon of aggression, even though (or indeed precisely because) that phenomenon was not and could not be adequately defined in general terms in advance of the events in which it was manifest. A main purpose of this study is to show why this is so.

35 By 7 votes to 3, with one abstention.

36 See A/C. 1/108, pp.9ff. See *infra* 72ff., 94ff., as to the legal problems arising on Arts. 2 (4) and 51.

37 By 6 votes to 4.

38 See *infra* Ch. 8 generally, and for this unawareness among the writers, *id.* nn.30ff. and Q. Wright, "The Concept of Aggression . . ." (1935) 29 *A.J.I.L.* 373, 376.

39 On the request of M. Scelle who had been absent on the previous vote.

graphs for the consideration of the General Assembly;

> Article 2: The following acts are offences against peace and security of mankind:
>
> (1) Any act of aggression, including the employment by authorities of a State of armed force against another State for any purpose other than national or collective self-defence or in pursuance of a decision or recommendation by a competent organ of the United Nations.
>
> (2) Any threat by the authorities of a State to resort to an act of aggression against another State.[40]

This was regarded by the Commission as consonant to the above quoted Resolution 380 (V) of the General Assembly of November 17, 1950, declaring the gravity of the crime of aggression, as well as with the aggressive war count of the Article 6 of the Charter of the Nuremberg International Military Tribunal. But the important point, from the present aspect, is that Article 2 (1) though it superficially resembles M. Alfaro's proposal, does not purport to be a definition. It affirms that aggression "includes" certain uses of force, but left open what else it might include. It is open at the inculpating end. It is, moreover (as indeed also was M. Alfaro's proposal), open at the exculpating end, insofar as it is left uncertain whether the licensed "national or collective self-defence" may not in a particular case be broader than the self-defence against "armed attack" within Article 51 of the Charter, and if so how much broader.[41]

IV. THE GENERAL ASSEMBLY MOVES IN: THE OVERTURE.

On November 13, 1951, the General Assembly, having placed the Report of the International Law Commission's Third Session on its agenda, referred to its Sixth Committee the question of defining aggression.[42] After eighteen meetings,[43] in which the questions whether any definition at all was possible or desirable figured prominently, the Committee, on January 21, 1952, took a position opposed on the whole to that of the International Law Commission, based on the view that it would be advantageous to provide "directives" for international bodies which "may be called on to determine the aggressor".[44] It will be observed that the interest in definition has at this point clearly shifted to the function of peace enforcement, even though the item under discussion arose from work on the criminal liability of individuals.[45] The Committee considered that

---

40 Report of the I.L.C. covering the . . . Third Session, 16 May-27 July, 1951, *G.A.O.R. VI*, Supp. No. 9, c.iv, pp.11ff. These articles remained unchanged in the draft of 1954. See Report of I.L.C. covering the . . . Sixth Session, 3 June-28 July, 1954, *G.A.O.R. IX*, Supp. No. 9, c.III, p.11.

41 *Cf.* the apt comment of the Bolivian Government, *infra* p.52. There is also possibly some room for manoeuvre in determining which "organs" of the United Nations may be regarded as "competent" to make this kind of recommendation. See Stone, *Conflict* 228-237, 266-284; and *infra* pp.88-89, and the Discourse to this book, *infra* p.185.

42 341st and 342nd Plenary Meetings, *G.A.O.R. VI*, Supp. No. 9 and Supp. No. 20, p.xvii.

43 From Jan. 5-22, 1952, *G.A.O.R. VI*, Ann., Item 49, pp.12ff.

44 See *id.* p.15.

45 See *infra* pp.137ff.

> although the existence of the crime of aggression may be inferred from the circumstances peculiar to each particular case, it is nevertheless possible and desirable, with a view to ensuring international peace and security and to developing international criminal law, to define aggression by reference to the elements which constitute it.[46]

This seemed to propose an "abstract or general" definition, as distinct from enumerating concrete "aggression-situations".

The General Assembly, in adopting the Sixth Committee's proposal, instructed the Secretary-General to submit to its seventh session a report on the problem of defining aggression in the light of views expressed in the Sixth Committee, and the draft resolutions and amendments submitted on the matter; and it requested Members to give particular attention to the same matter in their comments on the Draft Code of Offences against the Peace and Security of Mankind.[47] Of the fourteen States who so commented, a number including Costa Rica, Denmark, and the United Kingdom doubted both the possibility and desirability of seeking further definition.[48] Costa Rica thought the word "aggression" had a definite meaning in all languages and should be applied in its "simple and current meaning";[49] and Denmark distrusted all currently proposed definitions.[50] The United Kingdom's reasoning[51] had a somewhat mixed value which will later call for examination. Its sounder basis was that "in practice it will never be possible to establish aggression except in the light of particular circumstances in which the act concerned takes place".[52]

Egypt, France, Iraq, the Netherlands, and Yugoslavia took the general position that it was, or should be,[53] possible to frame a definition to guide the appropriate organs, and that, if possible, it would be desirable to do so.

---

[46] For a statement of the main U.K. arguments contrary to this view of the Sixth Committee, see G. G. Fitzmaurice, "The Definition of Aggression" (1952) 1 *Int. and Comp. L.Q.* 137-144. (extracts from speech of Jan. 9, 1952).

[47] *G.A.O.R. VI,* Supp. No. 20, pp.84ff., Resol. 599 (VI).

[48] *G.A.O.R. VII,* Ann., Item 54, p.3. The United States did not comment.

[49] *Id.* 4. [50] *Id.* 5. [51] *Id.* 14.

[52] More questionable was its argument that a municipal system of law does not attempt "to specify or define what particular acts constitute the crime of murder, since one and the same act may be murder or may be excusable or even justifiable homicide". This analogy, however, bases an argument merely against definition by the "enumeration of aggressive situations"; in fact, municipal systems invariably do define murder in "general" or "abstract" terms by setting out the elements necessary and sufficient to constitute murder or defences thereto. This is not to say that the United Kingdom's main conclusion may not be sound: but its soundness depends not on the assumed analogy between aggression and murder, but precisely on certain differences which will emerge later in these pages. So, conversely, it does not necessarily advance the cause of definition to argue (see e.g. the Yugoslav delegate in 1956, A/AC.77/SR.7, p.7) that since definitions of municipal law crimes have not aided criminality, definitions of aggression internationally could not assist aggressors. This may or may not be so, but *non sequitur* from his argument.

A similar fallacy has long been indulged even by most thoughtful and distinguished writers. See e.g. H. Lauterpacht, "The Pact of Paris . . ." (1935) 20 *Trans. Grotius Soc.* 178, 200-201, who to base an argument for requiring definition observes: "In the sphere of municipal law we do not usually object to defining murder or manslaughter for the reason that a definition may on occasions prove insufficient or unjust. We put our trust in the skill of the draftsmen and the wisdom of the Courts."

[53] France introduced this cautionary clause. See *G.A.O.R. VII,* Ann., Item 54, p.7.

In the hopeful Yugoslav view existence of a definition "would make it possible for States and for competent United Nations bodies to ascertain clearly, and without hesitation, the occurrence of acts of pressure and, especially, of acts of aggression".[54] Among these States two main positions are detectable: one favouring some variation of mixed definition, the other a form of "abstract or general" definition only. These positions may be summarised as follows:

(1) The definition should be "mixed", i.e., it should include: (a) a statement of the "constituent elements" of aggression. (Egypt, France, Indonesia, Yugoslavia) ;[55]

AND EITHER (b) a "precise list of the acts treated as 'acts of aggression' ", but drafted to allow other non-enumerated acts to be held to be aggression in particular cases with the evolution of new methods of aggression (that is, open at the inculpating end). (Egypt, Indonesia) ;[56]

OR (bb) a mere illustrative list of "the most characteristic cases of aggressive circumstances". (France.)[57] While France seemed, like Egypt, to stress that the purpose was to keep the text open at the inculpating end, its reasoning suggested openness also at the exculpating end.

Both alternatives, (b) and (bb), proceeded on the view that if "enumerative definition" that is "complete and limitative" is sought, the effect might paralyse the competent organ in face of unforeseen forms of aggression.

(2) The definition should include only an "abstract" or "general" statement of the constituent elements of aggression. This seems the assumption of the Netherlands proposed draft definition as follows:

> Aggression is the threat or use of force by a State or government against the territorial integrity or political independence of another State or against a territory under international regime in any manner, whatever the weapons employed and whether openly or otherwise, for any reason or for any purpose other than individual or collective self-defence against such a threat or use of force or in pursuance of a decision or recommendation by a competent organ of the United Nations.

The essentially indeterminate nature of such a definition was made clear by the concurrent Bolivian comment[58] that the main need for a definition was in order to define and clarify the conditions which would base "national and collective self-defence" as a justification. Clearly, the Netherlands draft would not have limited "self-defence" to "self-defence against armed attack" on a Member within Article 51. Its main apparent effect would have been to enlarge the self-defence licence under Article 51 by whatever measures are necessary to repel *the threat or use* of force against a State's territorial

---

[54] *Id.* p.12. [55] *Id.* pp.5,7,8 and 12 respectively. [56] *Id.* pp.5,7.

[57] *Id.* p.7. France used the term "synthetic" to refer to definition by "elements", and "analytic" to refer to enumerated concrete situations. This use of the latter term for the enumeration of concrete aggression situations seems misleading. So does the similar Iraqi use of the term "pragmatic", *id.* p.8.

Yugoslavia used the term "flexible" to refer to the definition by elements i.e. subpoint (a) above in the text. On this see *infra* pp.88-90.

[58] *Id.* p.3.

integrity or political independence within Article 2 (4) of the Charter.

The historical compilation of data by the Secretary-General in the Report[59] prepared in compliance with the Resolution 599 (VI) might conceivably have formed a useful *point de départ* in the search for consensus in this critical area of contemporary thought and policy. The document covers, in its first part, the search for definition from the foundation of the League of Nations up to the General Assembly's Session of 1951-52; in its second part, it compiles the main views expressed for and against defining aggression, and presents the various types of definitions under the headings "enumerative", "general", and "combined".[60] The striking fact that this Report still presents itself as the summation of failure, rather than as the *point de départ* for success, sharpens a main theme of these pages. This is that the mere compilation, arrangement, analysis, and manipulation of legal formulae are simply not enough in this area of human effort: for the real difficulties lie outside the present scope both of the Charter, and of international law generally.

They lie, as we shall later show, in the cardinal facts that the international community lacks any collective means of vindication of violated legal rights, as well as any collective means of legislative adjustment of new conflicting claims, or even of existing legal rights. In a community of this sort, all attempts to define "aggression" with a precision sufficient to marshal collective force automatically for its suppression, inevitably brings down onto the head of the unfortunate draftsman all the unsolved problems of law enforcement between sovereign States, along with the even more intractable problems of justice between States, and between the human beings who make up their peoples.

V. FIRST *MÊLÉE,* 1952-53.

At its seventh session, on October 17, 1952, the General Assembly referred the question of defining aggression, together with the Report of the Secretary-General, to the Sixth Committee. This Committee's discussion ranging over seventeen meetings from November 19 to December 9, 1952,[61] focussed largely on the above-mentioned Soviet draft,[62] and on a joint draft resolution of Afghanistan, Bolivia, Chile, China, Dominican Republic, El Salvador, Iran, Netherlands, Peru, and Yugoslavia,[63] and proposed amendments thereto.[64]

---

59 *G.A.O.R. VII,* Ann., Item 54, pp.17-86, Doc. A/2211.

60 His discussion of the formal mechanics of putting a definition into effect, if and when achieved, and its legal value and authority when so put in effect, does not affect the present subject.

61 *G.A.O.R. VII,* Sixth Committee, pp.141-233.

62 Substantially in the form *supra* pp.34-35,46-47.

63 *G.A.O.R. VII,* Ann., Item 54, p.82.

64 The joint draft resolution and its amendment were the basis for the resolution which the Sixth Committee recommended to the General Assembly for adoption. This was the resolution by which the Special Committee of 15 members was established "to study all the problems . . . on the assumption of a definition being adopted by a resolution of the General Assembly".

Few new insights emerged.[65] There was the expected division between delegations which (along with those of the above States) favoured defining aggression, and those which opposed it. The former urged the importance of making widely known the meaning of so grave a crime, and that even if lists of aggression situations could not be exhaustive, a partial list was better than none for discouraging potential aggressors, especially in the present state of international tension. It would, in particular, it was thought, guide public opinion, and promote "the development of international law". Those of the opposed view, argued that the experience necessary for codification was here lacking; that a "flexible" definition would permit different States to interpret it differently, and thus defeat the main purpose; while "rigid" definition could not cope with changing techniques of aggression, and would, far from aiding the responsible organs, delay and impede them in following the adequate Charter procedures for determination of the aggressor. One novelty, however, interesting for our later analysis, did emerge from these 1952 discussions. This was the pressure of certain Latin American States, shortly to be espoused by the Soviet Union,[66] for the inclusion within any definition adopted of reference to "economic", "cultural" and "ideological" aggression.[67]

On the Sixth Committee's recommendation the General Assembly duly appointed its first Special Committee of fifteen Members of 1953 on the "Question of Defining Aggression"[68] with the mandate to produce "draft definitions or draft statements of the notion of aggression", and study the problems arising "on the assumption of a definition being adopted" by Assembly resolution. The Special Committee's report was to come before the Ninth Session with Member States' comments thereon.

---

65 See generally the Report of the Sixth Committee, *G.A.O.R. VII,* Ann., Item 54, pp.86-91.

66 In 1953. Until then, with one notable exception in the proposed Three Power Pact with Britain and France in 1939 (on which see the perhaps disputable interpretation in L. Schultz, *"Der Sowjetische Begriff der Aggression"* (1956) 2 *Osteuropa Recht* 274, 282), the Soviet Union had not accepted the idea of embracing "indirect aggression" within its definition. If this were deemed to be dictated by the importance of subversive techniques in Soviet strategy, the quick change of front in 1953 calls for explanation. One possible explanation is that Soviet tactics as to definition belatedly caught up with changes in the relative situations of the Great Powers, and in particular the fact that the disintegration of the colonial empires left Western interests increasingly exposed in the newly emergent States, so that definitions forbidding even non-forcible pressure would increasingly cripple Western means of protecting them. It may be recalled that Stalin's death in 1953 was a signal for major reviews of policy on many heads.

Incidentally, and by the same token, the inclusion of indirect aggression had political appeal as favouring Soviet influences with Arab and African States, as well as with the Central and South American sponsors. Ancillary, though clearly subordinate to this, may have been the feeling that a show of flexibility might be seen as conforming to the general "Geneva spirit" of relaxing tensions. It will be seen *infra* that while, up to 1953, Soviet spokesmen condemned resistance to the rigidity of the exhaustive listing of acts of aggression in its definition of 1950 as proof of Western aggressive intent, it also itself abandoned the exhaustive form in 1953.

67 See the Bolivian view in the Sixth Committee, *G.A.O.R. VI,* Sixth Committee, 293rd Meeting, para. 30. And see the fuller discussion in the text and notes *infra* pp.58-60,66-68.

68 Resol. 688 (VII) *G.A.O.R. VII,* Supp. 20 (A/2361), p.63.

VI. FIRST SPECIAL COMMITTEE FOR DEFINING AGGRESSION, 1953.

Besides the existing stock of official documents the meetings of the Special Committee from August 24 to September 21, 1953, had before it five main *ad hoc* submissions.[69] (1) A Soviet revision of its earlier draft, supplemented by new paragraphs on economic and ideological aggression. M. Morozov made clear that his Government sought by these additions to satisfy the Asian and Latin American pressure to brand and condemn "economic, ideological and indirect aggression".[70] We shall later deal with the less obvious political meaning of this proposal.[71] (2) A Chinese working paper presenting a general definition of aggression, with attached illustrative list of typical acts of aggression—a variation of the so-called "mixed" definition. (3) Another Chinese working paper setting out certain principles to be recommended to the Security Council and Members as non-exhaustive guides in determining aggression—presumably a "statement" rather than a "definition" of the notion.[72] (4) A Mexican proposal for certain changes in the Soviet proposal.[73] (5) A Bolivian proposal for definition by enumeration, open at the inculpating end—that is, listing certain situations deemed to be aggression, but allowing the competent organs to designate other particular situations as aggressive even if not listed.[74] The Committee sent on these submissions to Member States and the General Assembly without voting on them. And even its Report[75] consolidated the growing fashion of compensating for the basic lack of agreed conclusions by a balanced summary of the conflicting views.

In its deliberations disagreement persisted as to the "possibility" and "desirability" of defining aggression. Bolivia, France,[76] Iran, Mexico, Poland, the Dominican Republic, Syria, and the Soviet Union[77] gave an affirmative answer, while other States thought it was not possible, and that if possible it would be of no value and even dangerous to the maintenance of international peace and security.[78] The reality of the consensus even among the protagonists of definition was marred by continuing disagreements as to what particular definitions might be acceptable to them.

The three supposed main types of definition detected and popularised

---

69 *G.A.O.R. IX,* Supp. 11, pp.13-15.

70 *G.A.O.R. IX,* Supp. 11, p.9. See *infra* pp.66ff.

71 See *infra* pp.66ff., 111ff. 72 Both *G.A.O.R. IX,* Supp. 11, p.14.

73 *Id.* pp.14ff. 74 *Id.* p.15. 75 *Id.* pp.1-12.

76 *Cf.* the later comments on the 1953 Committee's Report, *G.A.O.R. IX,* Ann., Item 51, p.2, stressing the "feasibility" and "desirability" both for purposes of peace enforcement, and in the code of crimes against peace, indicating however that the two tasks "would not be a duplication".

77 The Soviet *bloc* countries have steadily led the pressure for definition. *Cf.* the Comments of Governments on the Report of the 1953 Special Committee, *G.A.O.R. IX,* Ann., Item 51, pp.2ff. (Soviet Union, Poland, Byelo-Russia and Ukraine.)

78 *Id.* p. 11. *Cf.* the Greek Government's comment on the Report, *G.A.O.R. IX,* Ann., Item 51, p.3, on its "sceptical view"; and the U.K. comment, *id.* p.2, that "H.M.'s

by the Secretary-General's Report,[79] namely, "general definitions", "enumerative definitions", and "mixed or combined definitions", established themselves thoroughly in the 1953 Committee as rallying points and points of attack for conflicting views. The Soviet delegate Morozov led the attack on "general" definitions as valueless, insofar as they always approximated to saying that "aggression was aggression".[80] On the other hand the Soviet plan for an "enumerative definition" was the main target of criticism, especially from the United Kingdom,[81] as not really a definition at all, but merely an incomplete catalogue of acts thought to constitute aggression,[82] which would by its incompleteness imply a licence to commit aggression by other acts, thus providing, in the old phrase of Sir Austen Chamberlain, a signpost for the guilty.[83] The Soviet delegate thought his draft free of this criticism, since it was "both synthetic and analytical", meaning presumably that its list of aggression-situations was now left open at the inculpatory end, so that the competent organs may hold that non-listed situations are

---

Government have always doubted whether it is possible to evolve an entirely satisfactory definition which would not oversimplify the issue . . .", and the Argentine comment, *id.* p.2.

79 Doc. A/2211. For a critique of this classification, see *infra* pp.80ff., 88ff.

80 *Id.* p.4. *Cf.* the development of this in the Sixth Committee's Report, *G.A.O.R. IX*, Ann., Item 51, p.10. While there was little support for a "general" definition in the 1953 Committee itself, Sweden in its comment on the Report (*G.A.O.R. IX*, Ann., Item 51, p.5) favoured such a definition in terms of "first resort to armed force . . . provided that armed force has not been expressly declared as legal", conceding only that the competent organ might be provided with a number of "examples of modes of aggression to serve . . . as guides without prejudice to its discretion". It referred to examples in the Disarmament Conference's project of 1933.

81 *Cf.* also M. Hsueh (China), *G.A.O.R. IX*, Supp. 11, p.4. Other criticisms which fully emerged later in the Sixth Committee (*G.A.O.R. IX*, Ann., Item 51, p.11) were that (1) the rigidity of such definitions is incompatible with Arts. 2 (1), 24, and 39 of the Charter, the sovereignty of States and the principle of unanimity in the Security Council; (2) that it would leave loopholes for aggressors; (3) that it might catch acts which were not really "aggression". See e.g. on points (2) and (3), G. G. Fitzmaurice's observations, repr. (1952) 1 *Int. and Comp. L.Q.* 137, 140.

82 *Ibid.* Much of this earlier criticism seemed directed only at the possibility that some acts of aggression would not be inculpated by the list; but by the time of the 1956 Committee (see *infra* p.62) the criticism had become more general that the effect of the list would be to inculpate acts which should, on a correct view of the context of action, be *exculpated.*

83 See for the British position in the Sixth Committee in 1952, "The Definition of Aggression" (1952) 1 *Int. and Comp. L.Q.* 137, 138. G. G. Fitzmaurice there observed that such an incomplete list "may point the way to a country which is in fact desirous of embarking . . . on . . . an aggressive policy, and may indicate to it by what means it can achieve its object without incurring the liability to be branded as an aggressor." He referred to the analogy of the skilled lawyer in municipal law being assisted in avoiding legal pitfalls by the existence of precise and rigid legal definitions in the code. With respect, more careful analogising is required if the argument is not to prove far too much, i.e. that definitions generally are not useful and even necessary in municipal law. The truer analogy is the narrower one of the refusal of courts of equity to provide an advance definition of "equitable fraud" on this same ground. The point is that in "aggression" as in "equitable fraud", the ethical components are crucial, and advance definition tends to thwart or distort ethical judgment at the critical moment. See Lord Hardwicke's well-known statement (quoted Parkes, *History of the Court of Chancery* (1828) 508): "Were a Court of Equity once to lay down rules, how far they would go, and no further, in extending their relief against it, or to define strictly the species or evidence of it, the jurisdiction would be cramped and perpetually eluded by new schemes which the fertility of man's invention would contrive."

also "aggression".[84]

It is to be observed, however, that the merely "open-ended" enumeration differs from the "mixed" or "combined" definition proper, in an important respect. In the former the residual power of the competent organ to inculpate non-listed acts or (as the case may be) to exculpate listed acts, is exercised without the aid of any additional guide by way of an additional "general" or "abstract" definition. In the latter, however, such an additional "general" or "abstract" definition is provided to supplement the "open ended" list of aggression situations.[85] But the "mixed" type even in this precise sense, though the trend was already strong in 1953 among governments favouring definition to prefer it to either of the pure types,[86] still received substantial criticism. The United Kingdom, for example, thought it combined the evil potentialities of both the "general" and the "enumerative" types, for instance of causing delay and uncertainty and multiplying the points of controversy in application,[87] and conversely of prematurely rendering formal condemnation necessary in situations which might be more effectively handled by other means.[88]

A quite different type of approach from any of these had been suggested by the General Assembly's inclusion in the Committee's terms of reference of an alternative request for a "draft statement" of the notion of aggression. The Chinese proposal for the formulation of principles to guide the appropriate organ seems to have been of this type; and it was clearly the gist of the American proposal, which had other support, to draw up, for the competent organs, a list of factors to be considered in deciding a given case.[89] But this was immediately recognised by the protagonists of definition as a "circumvention" of their objectives rather than a mode of implementing them.[90]

---

[84] It was not so of course, in its earlier form; see *supra* pp.34-35. See *infra* pp.88ff.

[85] See the 1953 Special Committee discussion *G.A.O.R. IX,* Supp. 11, pp.4-5. By the above test the Soviet reply to the Philippine delegate that the Soviet definition was not enumerative but "analytical and synthetic", requires close scrutiny. It was that the Soviet definition contained more than an enumeration, in its adoption of (1) the priority principle, (2) the principle of the non-justification of the use of armed force in the specified circumstances, and (3) the principle that a State might never use armed force in response to a threat of force. (See A/AC.77/SR.3, p.11, where Professor Scelle's view (see *supra* p.5) is cited in support.) Heads (2) and (3), however, would seem to be merely enumerations of non-exculpatory elements serving but to close more firmly the list of acts of aggression. See *infra* p.88. *Cf.* on the priority principle, the Czech and Polish views, A/AC.77/SR.6, p.5 and SR.7, p.3. The priority principle might, indeed, be regarded as an element of an abstract definition, if it were practicable. On this, however, see *infra* pp.69ff., 143-44.

[86] *Cf.* the Sixth Committee's Report on the 1953 Committee's Report, *G.A.O.R. IX,* Ann., Item 51, p.10, and the French Government's comment, *id.* p.2 calling for "a mixed definition" as "an act of cooperation".

[87] *Cf.* the view of some Members of the Sixth Committee summarised (Report *G.A.O.R. IX,* Ann., Item 51, pp.9ff.

[88] See e.g. G. G. Fitzmaurice, repr. (1952) 1 *Int. and Comp. L.Q.* 137, 140-141.

[89] *G.A.O.R. IX,* Supp. 11, p.5. It is in this sense only of definition that I understand G. A. Podrea, *"L'Agression . . ."* (1952) 30 *R.D.I.* 367, 370, when he simultaneously rejects any test of "first commission" of a limited number of designated acts (369), and asserts a certain freedom of *"appréciation"* as inevitable in the applying organ, and the need for definition as "a means of orientation" and "a guide in appreciation". Unless this is so, his whole thesis seems self-contradictory.

[90] *G.A.O.R. IX,* Supp. 11, p.5. *Cf.* also the Swedish Government's position, *supra* n.80.

VII. ARMED AND OTHER AGGRESSION.

The relation of the General Assembly's search for a definition of aggression to the existing obligations of Members of the United Nations under the Charter had already been given a certain focus in the Secretary-General's Report of 1952.[91] Insofar as a proposed definition would prohibit conduct not otherwise prohibited by the Charter, the legal power of the General Assembly to make it binding on Members or on the Security Council was obviously dubious, a conclusion which was to become ever clearer in later discussions. On the other hand, insofar as definition did not go beyond basic elements found in the Charter, Soviet and similar views would reject it as a useless "general" definition. "It was just because the Charter confined itself to dealing with the question in general terms" that (on this view) further definition was being sought by the Assembly.[92]

The Asian-Latin American-Soviet drive for a definition embracing "economic" and "ideological" aggression, now thrust to the fore this question of the relation of definition to existing Charter provisions. While (as we shall see) [93] the question is perplexing even as to the conventional "armed aggression", the difficulties are more dramatic with these newer proposed forms of aggression; and the 1953 Committee's pioneering discussion is the more noteworthy.

While a majority of the Committee conceived their mandate to be limited to defining aggression "in the sense of the Charter",[94] disputation was keen as to whether this sense extended beyond "armed" aggression.[95] The Bolivian delegate sought to infer a Charter prohibition of "economic aggression",[96] from the three Charter principles of "political independence", "sovereign equality" and "non-interference in the domestic affairs" of States.

---

91 *G.A.O.R. VII*, Ann., Item 54, Doc. A/2211.

92 The point emerged clearly in these terms in the following Sixth Committee Report, *G.A.O.R. IX*, Ann., Item 51, pp.10ff.

93 See *infra* pp.66ff., 72ff.

94 *G.A.O.R. IX*, Supp. 11, pp.5ff.

95 For an attempt to formulate an abstract definition of "aggression" under the Charter not tied to armed aggression see Note: "Meaning of 'Aggression' in the United Nations Charter" (1954) 33 *Nebraska L.R.* 606-612 (Results of a Short Seminar at the College of Law, University of Nebraska). The proposal is (6-7): "An act of State A which is intended to and which in fact does contribute to or result in a substantial encroachment upon the independence of State B or the security of the people of State B in their right to be free from political repression is an act of aggression within the meaning of the Charter of the United Nations." The indeterminacy of such phrases as "contribute to", "substantial", "independence", "security", "free from political repression" means that, whatever its other merits, the definition does not seriously promote certainty of determination in future crises. See at 611 for an exegetical argument for such an extended meaning of the Charter.

96 For a good if somewhat over-enthusiastic account of the nature and historical background of the demand as to "economic" aggression, see R. P. Gonzalez Muñoz, *Doctrine Grau* (1948) *passim*. The doctrine is named after Ramon Grau San Martin who, as President of Cuba, expounded it to the Rio de Janeiro Conference which adopted the Inter-American Treaty of Mutual Assistance. In its intra-American context, of course, the doctrine was not free of anti-United States innuendo. The 1948 Conference declined to bring this kind of aggression within the orbit of the security system, or the power of its organs, only four nations supporting it in this original context. (See

On this view, insofar as "political independence was closely linked with economic independence", a threat to the latter was "as much an act of aggression as was armed aggression".[97] M. Adamiyat (Iran), too, classing "economic aggression" as an important form of "indirect" aggression, saw its essence as "coercive economic and political measures taken against a State . . . designed to impede the exercise of its sovereignty over its natural resources or its efforts towards economic development". He thought that the Charter tacitly included them under "acts of aggression".[98] The United States delegate, Mr. Maktos, pointed out some of the *non sequiturs* involved in this torture of the Charter,[99] as well as the danger that such extensions of the notion of aggression, and the equivalation of "economic" with "armed aggression" would "weaken the whole concept of aggression" in its primary application to armed aggression. And at least one State, the Argentine, which thought that a definition to be of value must cover "economic" and "ideological" aggression, nevertheless regarded definition as undesirable in part because of this very fact.[100]

Similar differences affected the proposal as to "ideological aggression",

---

op. cit. 83-84, 89, 90-91.) It was, however, approved by the Fifth Inter-American Federation of Lawyers at Lima in 1947.

M. Muñoz presents the doctrine as complementary to the Monroe and Drago Doctrines, and the non-intervention doctrines (24, 75) as necessary to protect a range of State interests not covered by armed aggression (23), especially in a Latin America far from the European and Asiatic centers of armed conflicts, where armed warfare is of less practical importance than economic struggles (67).

And see *id.* 75ff., on the earlier Colombian draft at the Eighth International American Conference, in Lima in 1938, (*"Tratado de Liberación del Comercio Interamericano y de No Agresión Económica"*); and the draft Article V submitted by a Mixed Commission to that Conference, condemning economic aggression in the Parties' mutual relations, and renouncing the use of coercive methods of economic character in disputes, except as a collective instrument.

This draft was not adopted but only referred to the Pan-American Union for study and co-ordination with other similar instruments.

For suggestions in League days for including indirect aggression in the definition of aggression, see A. Derying, in Bourquin (ed.), *Collective Security* 325. Distinguish the problems of economic preparation for armed aggression discussed e.g., in connection with the Draft Treaty of Mutual Assistance, 1923. See *L.N.O.J.*, Sp. Supp. 16, pp.116-117.

97 *G.A.O.R. IX,* Supp. 11, pp.8ff. *Cf.* in the Sixth Committee *G.A.O.R. IX,* Ann., Item 51, p.11, where Preamble, para. 4, and Art. 55 were vouched in support.

So *cf.* recently Professor Zourek (*supra* Introd., n.29a) who points out that Art. 2(4) prohibits not merely armed force, but "force" as such.

98 *Id.* p.9.

99 *G.A.O.R. IX,* Supp. 11 (A/2638) (Report of the Special Committee on the Question of Defining Aggression, 24 August-21 September, 1953) p.9, paras. 76, 77.

100 See the comment on the 1953 Committee's Report, *G.A.O.R. IX,* Ann., Item 51, p.2. *Cf.* C. A. Pompe, *Aggressive War* 50-51, 97, who dubs these proposals as "inflation" of the notion of aggression. "Dilution" might be a better term for the purpose of his argument that by this extension "the military element—the nucleus of the concept of aggression—has been completely lost". We may well agree with this, and yet add (see *infra* pp.69ff., 104ff.) that the core concept, as generally understood, has itself proved unworkable without the reference to the concomitant non-military components. Mr. Pompe indeed seems later to admit this (see at 57) where he points out that insofar as there may be "provocation" which may justify military attack, and thus qualify the notion of military aggression, that provocation itself can never consist in a military attack. His conclusion that, however grave the provocation, the provoking State is acting in self-defence when it reacts to the military measures which it had itself provoked, while the provoked State has on the other hand, under a non-aggression treaty formulated in these terms, not violated its obligations, should put us on notice of the inadequacy of current analyses. *Cf.* the Secretary-General's remarks, Doc. A/2211, p.74.

pressed by Soviet delegate Morozov, as including particularly "war propaganda", propaganda for the use of atomic, bacterial, chemical and other types of weapons of mass destruction, and "also the promotion of the propaganda of fascist-nazi views, racial and national exclusiveness, hatred and contempt for other peoples".[101] M. Adamiyat (Iran), as well as others, saw "ideological aggression" as a form of "indirect aggression",[102] of intervention in another State's internal or foreign affairs, including "direct or indirect incitement to civil war, threats to internal security, and incitement to revolt by the supply of arms or by other means".[103] The United States representative again stressed the danger that to extend the notion of aggression thus would weaken its application to "armed aggression", and he also pointed to certain collateral dangers to freedom of the press, and freedom of opinion.

On one of the few points of general agreement, it is difficult to think that the Committee meant quite what it said. It was well pointed out by M. Röling (Netherlands) that while the influence of any definition adopted by the Assembly upon the action of competent organs might be great if most States including the Permanent Members concurred in it, adoption by only a narrow majority, or without such concurrence, would have little value. This is clear enough. But the Committee was also substantially agreed that any definition adopted by General Assembly resolution could have only the status of a recommendation, and would not have a binding character.[104] M. Röling (Netherlands) even thought that a definition "could play only a negligible part in the maintenance of international peace and security, since it would bind neither the Security Council nor the General Assembly of the United Nations."[105] Insofar, however, as a definition merely brands as "aggression" what is already so branded by the Charter (as its proponents claimed, for example, that "economic aggression" was) the definition would surely be legally binding on competent organs for that reason. It seems fair to infer, therefore, that whatever their argumentation, most of the champions of the inclusion of "indirect", "economic" and "ideological" aggression were aware that their formulations went beyond what interpretation of the Charter could sustain.

The problem of defining aggression for the purpose of enforcing liability of individuals for the crime of "aggression" is free of some of these problems, insofar as the definition chosen may be incorporated in the new instruments

---

101 *Id.*, 9-10.

102 For a brief recent summary of particular cases of indirect aggression, such as prolonged presence of foreign troops in a territory, the use of fraud and duress to achieve aggressive aims, the setting up of puppet governments, infiltration by subversive agents, and incursions of armed bands from an adjoining State, see S. Sucharitkul, *The Problem of Defining Indirect Aggression* (1955-56) (Harvard Law School Library).

103 *Id.*, 10.

104 *Id.*, 11. This view was also taken with apparent unanimity in the following Sixth Committee's Report (*G.A.O.R. IX*, Ann., Item 51, p.10) subject to the qualification that "a definition solemnly adopted by the General Assembly might become a general principle of law recognised by civilised nations and so might in future become an integral part of international law", binding on the Security Council.

105 *Cf.* the view of many delegations in the Sixth Committee reported *G.A.O.R. IX*, Ann., Item 51, p.10, that no definition "would be really useful unless it was accepted by a large majority of Member States".

which would in any case be necessary to create an International Criminal Court, and lay down the offences which it may try. Indirectly, however, insofar as there must be some correspondence between the legality of State action, and the criminality of the action of individuals acting on behalf of that State, many of the difficulties must also be transmitted.[106] And still other problems also arise here from the difference in function.[107]

In this connection a critical difference may lie in the widely accepted view that individual criminal responsibility requires *mens rea,* that is, proof of guilty intention. The question, however, whether reference to "aggressive intention" must be contained in the definition of aggression has been discussed,[108] and States have divided in their views thereon, without adequate reference to the very different functions of definition involved. It may be true that the need to prove aggressive intention would invite subjective arguments by possible aggressors and hinder peace enforcement; but criminal (and possible capital) punishment of individuals without such proof may still be unthinkable.[109]

VIII. SECOND MÊLÉE, 1954.

The Report of the 1953 Special Committee was commented on by eleven Member States before its consideration by the Sixth Committee.[110] Not many new matters were raised either in the comments or in the Sixth Committee discussion and Report.[111] An argument was canvassed, which was later much to occupy the 1956 Special Committee, that the question whether it was "possible and desirable" to define aggression has already been foreclosed in the affirmative by the General Assembly's adoption by a small majority of Resolutions 599 (VI) and 688 (VII).[112] So far as the "possibility" of this enterprise was concerned, this raised the entrancing question whether the General Assembly could by resolution, by whatever majority, render that "possible" which otherwise would be impossible, particularly if possibility were taken to embrace not merely "draftability", but feasibility and general acceptability to States of whatever might be drafted.[113] The Sixth

106 With some additional ones, arising from incompatibility between the objectives sought respectively in peace enforcement and the punishment of war criminals.

107 *Cf.* the Swedish Government's careful distinction between the peace enforcement function where it opposed precise definition, and the question of criminal jurisdiction where it said "a precise definition would naturally be required" (*G.A.O.R. IX,* Ann., Item 51, p.5). The Swedish Government doubted, however, the desirability of creating an international criminal jurisdiction for the crime of aggression (*ibid.*).

108 See e.g., in the Sixth Committee, *G.A.O.R. IX,* Ann., Item 51, p.11.

109 See the fuller discussion hereafter in Ch. 8. Professor Zourek, as late as 1957, seems so far unaware of some of these problems as to deny that there can or should be any differentiation of definition for these different purposes. See *supra* Introd. n.29a.

110 After circulation in accordance with the G.A. Resol. 688 (VII).

111 See *G.A.O.R. IX,* Ann., Item 51, pp.2-12 (Doc. A/2806) for the Comments and Report. The Sixth Committee devoted 18 meetings to the item, from October 14 to November 10, 1954. References on particular points raising no new issues have already been incorporated *supra.*

112 See *supra* pp.53,54.

113 See *G.A.O.R. IX,* Ann., Item 51, pp.9ff. On the meaning of "feasibility" and "acceptability" see *infra* pp.78-79.

Committee discussions on this matter were also notable for the introduction of a number of other drafts,[114] including a Soviet draft, embracing provisions as to "economic", and "ideological" aggression, conformable to the Latin American suggestions above mentioned. These additions will be considered later.[115]

Without substantially altering this state of the matter, the Ninth Session of the General Assembly on December 4, 1954,[116] adopted a resolution drafted by the Sixth Committee appointing a further "Special Committee on the Question of Aggression", this time of nineteen States.[117] This Special Committee was to prepare for the Eleventh Session in 1956 "a detailed report followed by a draft definition of aggression, having regard to the ideas expressed at the Ninth Session of the General Assembly"[118] and to "the need to coordinate the views expressed" by Members as revealed at the Ninth Session. The form of this mandate by its terms invited further controversies, which duly occupied the 1956 Committee, as to whether the Assembly had not indeed intended to determine affirmatively that definition was both "possible" and "desirable", and what would be the effect of that intention if it existed.

IX. SECOND SPECIAL COMMITTEE, 1956: THE SETTING AND THE TASK.

The new Special Committee on the Definition of Aggression, which we may term for brevity and clarity "the 1956 Special Committee", held nineteen meetings from October 8, to November 9, 1956.

Rarely can the exponents of a theory of human salvation have had so dramatic a setting for its discussion than was provided by the outbreak of the Middle East crisis of October-November, 1956, during the deliberations of the 1956 Special Committee. It is for this setting, indeed, and against it the display of the deadlock on the major theoretical and practical issues,

114 A Paraguayan draft offered a general statement with illustrations of some typical aggression situations, not extending to ideological and economic aggression. (*G.A.O.R. IX*, Ann., Item 51, pp.9ff.) A joint Iran-Panama draft was also similarly limited and of a "mixed" nature, declaring the enumerated situations "to constitute aggression . . . in all cases". A Chinese draft offered another kind of "mixture". First, it defined "aggression" as "the unlawful use of force by a State against another State, whether directly or indirectly". Second, it illustrated this by "(a) Attack or invasion by armed forces; (b) organisation or support of incursion of armed bands; (c) promotion or support of organised activities in another State aiming at the overthrow by violence of its political or social institutions." Third, it declared the use of force lawful (1) when in pursuance of a decision or recommendation by a competent United Nations organ; (2) when in self-defence against armed attack until a competent United Nations organ has acted to maintain international peace and security; and (3) when consisting of "measures, other than armed attack" necessary to remove the danger arising from an indirect use of force, until a competent United Nations organ has acted to remove the danger. (While this is not express, such measures *might* include the use of force, short of armed attack.)

115 See *infra* p.66ff. 116 *G.A.O.R. IX*, Ann., Item 51, p.12, Resol. 895 (IX).

117 China, Czechoslovakia, Dominican Republic, France, Iraq, Israel, Mexico, Netherlands, Norway, Panama, Paraguay, Peru, the Philippines, Poland, Syria, U.S.S.R., the United Kingdom and the United States. In fact Panama did not send a representative to the Committee.

118 For the desultory remarks of three delegations in the plenary session, see *G.A.O.R. IX*, Plenary Meetings, 504th Meeting, pp.361ff.

rather than for the emergence of any new ideas, that the 1956 Special Committee will be remembered.

At the outset the Committee was baulked by discord as to what its mandate really was. The Philippine and Iraqi proposed working plans[119] stressed the duty to prepare a draft definition, coordinating views and reducing controversies by finding the common denominator ". . . acceptable to a substantial majority of Member States".[120] The Netherlands plan was that the Committee must "first examine the possibilities of coordinating the views expressed by Member States, and thereafter proceed to the drafting of a definition of aggression if this preliminary study indicated that a useful and widely acceptable definition could be achieved".[121]

This conflict reflected the general position among Members of the United Nations, at this stage, on the preliminary question of "the possibility and desirability of a definition". This manifested a lack of communication among them at least as grave as any lack of consensus.[122] While statistics could suggest that 14 Members either denied or doubted either the possibility or desirability or both,[123] while 26 affirmed that definition was possible and desirable,[124] not even a majority consensus could spring from such statistics. For the majority of twenty-six were not only divided among themselves as to the function, the content and the form of a definition, but the views of a number of them depended on the extraordinary belief, or at any rate profession, that the General Assembly had ruled on "possibility" and "desirability", and that this foreclosed these issues.[125]

Members ranged themselves on both sides of the debate, intermingling with their views as to whether this question of "possibility and desirability" was already foreclosed, arguments both ways on the merits of it, in case it was not foreclosed.[126] Among States favouring [127] definition the variety of

---

119 See *1956 Sp.Com.Rep.* p.4, para. 20. See also A/AC.77/SR.1, pp.9-11, SR.2, pp.3-4, and SR.4, pp.3-4. *Cf.* the viewpoint of the French delegate who said that "the Committee, unlike its predecessors, was now expressly required to arrive at a single definition". A/AC.77/SR.1, p.6.

120 See the 1956 Committee's Report, *1956 Sp.Com.Rep.* 4 (para. 20).

121 See *loc.cit.* So *cf.* the view of Mr. Sanders (U.S.) (A/AC.77/SR.5, p.3) that "neither the establishment of the Committee by the General Assembly nor the acceptance of membership in it by the Governments implied in any way that the basic issues of substance and method had been resolved".

122 See *supra* Introd.

123 Of which 8 denied and 6 doubted.

124 *Cf. 1956 Sp.Com.Rep.* 5.

125 By Resol. 599(VI), see *supra* p.53. The extraordinary formalistic nature of this passage is not seriously improved by the distinction offered by some delegates between "legal" possibility (assumed to be settled as above), and "political" possibility (assumed still to be open). See *1956 Sp.Com.Rep.* 5. For no mere assertion of possibility of either sort by the General Assembly could make the enterprise "possible"; and whether more could be done was still to be seen. And see *infra* n.147.

126 It must be said that both the negative and the positive views advanced exhibit in some of their exponents too much zeal in pressing their points to the limits of plausibility, to sustain a quality of intellection which so important a subject warrants We have already referred (*supra* p.61) to the nonsensical aspect of the "possibility" debate. So also the argument that a definition of aggression would leave concepts like "self-defence" unelaborated, while valid enough as against particular drafts, e.g. the Soviet, are certainly no objection to definition of aggression generally, since an adequate definition would necessarily have to elaborate this ground of exculpation. See *1956 Sp.Com.Rep.* 5, 6.

127 The delegations of China, Czechoslovakia, Dominican Republic, France, Iraq,

grounds and definitions desired was such as to make the appearance of agreement quite deceptive.[128] Against "possibility and desirability" were urged the unpropitious nature of the existing international situation, especially as regards disagreement of the Permanent Members of the Security Council; the dangers of wrongful inculpation of a State exercising mere self-defence as well as of wrongful exculpation of an ingenious aggressor taking advantage of loopholes in the definition, and generally the danger of automatic application of a definition without due regard to the particular circumstances, and of inadequate regard for the needs of self-defence;[129] the delays in action of the competent organ at the crisis of action due to the need to interpret definitions; the danger from enumerative definitions of over-concentration on certain kinds of aggression; and the non-binding nature, in any case, upon Members and upon the Security Council of any definition adopted by a mere majority of the Assembly.

Even when delegations were agreed that the problem of definition of aggression was urgently relevant to current international developments, the indications they drew were opposed. For some the state of international tension negatived the "possibility and desirability", for others, it proved it.[130] For some, the current disarmament negotiations were a reason for not defining, since a definition might have unfortunate repercussions; for others

---

Mexico, the Netherlands, Paraguay, Peru, the Philippines, Poland, Syria, U.S.S.R. and Yugoslavia favoured definition as furthering the maintenance of international peace and security. See *1956 Sp.Com.Rep.* 11, and for the discussion, see e.g. U.S.S.R. A/AC.77/SR.3, pp.9ff., Czechoslovakia, A/AC.77/SR.6, p.4, and Mexico A/AC.77/SR.7, pp.4-6. And see *infra* n.128 and *passim* as to the variety of grounds for various groups of convergent views.

128 *Cf.* the U.S. delegate's more general comment, that "the impression that there existed a large measure of agreement among Members of the United Nations on the possibility of drafting an acceptable definition of aggression" was inaccurate. See A/AC.77/SR.13, p.3, and *cf. 1956 Sp.Com.Rep.* 1. It will be seen that the outcome of the 1956 Committee's work supported this observation.

China, though generally favouring definition, thought the times inauspicious since the "present" international community might be compared with a community where everyone freely carried arms, everyone freely produced arms, and where no police force or courts with compulsory powers existed." See Mr. Hsueh, A/AC.77/SR. 18, p.6, and *1956 Sp.Com.Rep.* 12. So *cf.* the U.S. point that the enumerations of aggressive acts in the Act of Chapultepec of 8 Mar., 1945, and the Inter-American Treaty of Reciprocal Assistance signed at Rio de Janeiro on 2 Sept., 1947, could not serve as precedents since the signatories of those instruments were situated in the same geographical area and were united by many bonds, including a feeling of solidarity, which were not found to the same degree among the Members of the United Nations. (A/AC.77/SR. 5, p.7, and *1956 Sp.Com.Rep.* 12-13.) In Oct. 1957 in the Sixth Committee China squarely joined those who regarded the search for definition as futile.

129 Contrast on this narrow point the diametrically opposed view of other delegations that a definition would prevent an aggressor from using the pretext of acting in self-defence, U.S.S.R. (A/AC.77/SR. 3, pp.9, 11), the Netherlands (A/AC.77/SR. 3, pp.6-8), Czechoslovakia (A/AC.77/SR.6, p.4), and Norway (A/AC.77/SR.6, p.10).

The Syrian delegate observed that "it was of vital importance to avoid over-defining the concept of self-defence for it was a natural right of self-preservation based on the duty of each State to ensure its own protection". (A/AC.77/SR. 13, pp.9ff. and *1956 Sp.Com.Rep.* 15.) But for the Soviet delegate a main function of definition was to ensure "that the aggressor could not follow the familiar pattern and invoke the right of self-defence". (A/AC.77/SR. 3, p.11, and *1956 Sp.Com.Rep.* 16.)

130 Thus Mr. Sanders (U.S.) said that events in the immediate post-war period had made plain the technical difficulties of drafting a definition of aggression and the dangers inherent in an inadequate definition (A/AC.77/SR. 1, p.11). Mr. Asha (Syria)

"a definition was all the more needed since the concept of aggression appeared to be connected with the prevention of atomic warfare".[131] And even among delegations which all favoured definition there was a startling variety of views concerning the precise functions which definition should serve, as well as concerning the question whether it would be sought to make the same definition serve all functions. Though all these delegations seemed to give prime importance to the function of guiding United Nations organs, for example, some were critical of the Soviet insistence[132] that only the Security Council was competent to deal with aggression, pointing out that under Resolution 377A (V) the General Assembly had also declared itself competent in cases where the Council was unable to act. There was no clear appreciation of the senses in which both of these views can be correct as well as incorrect.[133] And though all agreed that another main function of definition was for the purpose of the creation and administration of an international criminal law, and that the policy *nulla poena sine lege* was therefore relevant, there was disagreement as to whether, and how far, this imported any extra need for definition or any need for different definitions for these respective purposes,[134] and as to how far definition for one purpose might be easier than for the other. On this matter of function, too, dissension even among the majority of States favouring definition *in abstracto* gave little encouragement to the hopes of fuller consensus.[135]

After no less than seven meetings had failed to resolve these preliminary

---

said that to look for unanimous support in the present state of international relations appeared to be a vain hope (A/AC.77/SR. 4, p.6). Mr. Vennemoe (Norway) said that he had serious doubts concerning the possibility and desirability of preparing any general definition at the present time. In contrast to them, Mr. Röling felt that the question of definition of aggression was now more topical than ever (A/AC/SR. 3, p.7); and Mr. Michalowski (Poland) said that a definition of aggression would contribute to a further relaxation of international tension (A/AC.77/SR. 7, p.4).

131 See *1956 Sp.Com.Rep.* 6, 13 and M. Röling's own definite earlier view in "On Aggression . . ." (1955) 2 *Nederlands T. Int.R.* 167, 169, that "the introduction of the concept of aggression in disarmament discussions has no bearing—either favourably or unfavourably—on our problem of defining aggression". So *cf.* Mr. Hsueh (China) who with an apparently similar reference felt that "the definition of aggression should be deferred . . ." (A/AC.77/SR. 1, p.10).

On one aspect of this point we agree wholeheartedly with Judge Lauterpacht ("Limits . . . of the Law of War" (1953) 30 *B.Y.B. Int.L.* 206, 221), namely in rejecting the relevance of the aggression finding to the question whether the victim should thereby "be entitled to resort to weapons the use of which may otherwise be illegal". We also agree with both of his reasons: (1) that it would thus be made easy in the heat of impending conflict for the actual aggressor to engineer an appearance of being the victim of aggression, and thus free himself to use the weapons; and (2) that in many cases where such weapons are available to the actual aggressor, he will certainly not tolerate passively the use of prohibited weapons against himself.

132 See A/C.6/L.332/Rev./1. *Cf.* the Polish delegate, sharing the Soviet view A/AC. 77/SR. 7, pp.3-4. See also *1956 Sp.Com.Rep.* 6.

133 See the further discussion of the matter, *supra* p.45, *infra* Ch. 9 and Discourse.

134 Contrast e.g. the Iraqi view (A/AC.77/SR. 4, p.3 and *1956 Sp.Com.Rep.* 6) that the municipal rule that offences must be expressly defined also applied to international law, with the Netherlands view that the post-war trials showed that a definition was not a *conditio sine qua non* for a code. (A/AC.77/SR. 8, p.6.)

135 A fair sampling of the facile thought on functions may here be given. The Netherlands thought that definition would serve (1) the peace enforcement organs under Art. 39 of the Charter; (2) in determining in what cases States might act in individual or collective self-defence, by defining "armed attack" under Art. 51; (3) to

questions, the Committee decided to adopt none of the working plans, but to have "a general exchange of views" followed by "a study and discussion of the various draft definitions before it", and only thereafter to "decide on its further procedure".[136]

X. SOME MAIN PROBLEMS AT THE 1956 COMMITTEE.

For its deliberations the Special Committee had available, of course, the ever increasing earlier documentation, as well as an *ad hoc* working paper by the Secretariat[137] reproducing a number of draft definitions selected from this documentation. Soviet, Iranian, Panamanian and Paraguayan definitions dating from the Ninth General Assembly were reintroduced, as well as a Mexican working paper embodying a Mexican proposal to the 1953 Special Committee, other drafts from Iraq, and jointly from the Dominican Republic, Mexico, Paraguay and Peru,[138] and a "tentative formulation" from the Netherlands.[139]

We may perhaps summarise that part of the Committee's contributions which advanced the analysis of our problem under four main subheads: A. Indirect, Economic and Ideological Aggression; B. Frontier Incidents; C. The Priority Principle as a Criterion; and D. The Attempted Approach to Definition through the Notion of "Armed Attack".

A. *Indirect, Economic and Ideological Aggression.*

On the supposed indirect, economic and ideological heads of aggression introduced into the Soviet draft during the 1953 Special Committee, and retained in 1956,[140] the 1956 Committee's discussions, besides illuminating the earlier objections to the introduction of these notions,[141] also exposed the relation of these proposals to some of the deepest obstacles to the definitional drive. Insofar as such non-violent invasions of the interests of other States were now to be characterised as "aggression", logic as well as the emotive and value components in that term seemed to require that the State victim of indirect or economic or ideological aggression be allowed to defend itself by force against that aggression without itself being branded as an "aggressor".[142]

Here delegation standpoints splintered off still further. Opinion which objected to the extension of the meaning of aggression argued precisely that the extension "might suggest the right to go to war in self-defence

assist in working out disarmament arrangements; and (4) in relation to the draft code of offences against the peace and security of mankind. (See A/AC.77/SR. 8, pp.5,6 and *1956 Sp.Com.Rep.* 6.)

136 A/AC.77/SR.8, pp.3-5, and *1956 Sp.Com.Rep.* 4.

137 Doc. A/AC.77/L.6.

138 See *1956 Sp.Com.Rep.* Ann. II.

139 *1956 Sp.Com.Rep.* 25. See also A/AC.77/SR.13, p.17.

140 A/C.6/L.332/Rev.1. *Cf.* also the Paraguayan (A/C.6/L.334/Rev.1), Iran-Panama (A/C.6/L.335/Rev.1.), and Chinese (A/C.6/L.332/Rev.1), proposals.

141 See *supra* p.58ff., and *1956 Sp.Com.Rep.* 8.

142 It will be recalled that in earlier debates, see e.g. as to the Kellogg-Briand Pact, *supra* p.32, and as to the U.S. Proposal to the London Conference on the Nuremberg Charter, *infra* p.134, such a reaction of the victim of "aggression" was assumed to be permitted, in the context, however, of an armed aggression only.

against acts of economic and ideological aggression",[143] and thus extend the legitimacy of the use of force under the Charter.[144] But even delegates supporting the extension of the scope of the aggression notion also rejected the implied extension of the self-defence notion, asserting that "economic or ideological aggression did not entitle individual States to the same defensive action as did armed attack". This exchange was most revealing. On the one hand, it made patent that the emotive and value components of the term "aggression" do not permit any clean-cut demarcation between armed and other aggression,[145] and that in the minds of many delegations the degree of "unjustifiable" invasion of another State's "legitimate" interests or rights was as central to the felt notion of aggression as the element of physical force. But as soon as this is asserted against the alleged "aggressor", the very nature of the notions "justifiable" and "legitimate" requires that there be brought into account not only the invasion of the alleged victim's "legitimate" interests or rights, but also any "legitimate" interests and rights of the alleged "aggressor" which it may have acted to protect.

A large part therefore, of the problem of legislative demarcation of a just international legal order is here seen to be hidden within the aggression debate.[146] If a distinction is to be made between "armed aggression" on the one hand, and "indirect", "economic" and "ideological" aggression on the other,[147] for instance as to whether an armed reaction to the latter is permitted or is itself to be regarded as "armed aggression",[148] it must turn on

---

143 *1956 Sp.Com.Rep.* 8. *Cf.* H. Thirring, *"Was ist Aggression?"* (1952-53) 5 *Oesterreichische Z. für öff. R. (N.F.)* 238-240.

144 A view squarely taken in 1954 by Professor Röling ("On Aggression . . ." (1955) 2 *Nederlands T.Int.R.* 167, 171).

145 The more revealing in the Soviet draft which substituted the term "attack" for "aggression" as to armed aggression, but preserved "aggression" for "economic" and "ideological" aggression. The Chinese representative pointed out that "armed attack" was the most obvious form of aggression, which stood least in need of definition (A/AC. 77/SR.3, p.5), while subversion was far more dangerous. A definition limited to armed attack would, therefore, only create an illusion of definition. (A/AC.77/SR.14, pp.4-5, and *1956 Sp.Com.Rep.* 25).

At the other extreme, the primary Soviet solicitude for her own political and territorial interests led her to insist that the branding of armed attack was the principal task, and that disagreement about indirect economic and ideological forms of aggression (even though the Soviet Union supported the Asian and South American demand for their inclusion) should not be allowed to prevent agreement as to armed attack. (See A/AC.77/SR.3, pp.10ff.; and see *infra* p.68.) And see *infra* Ch. 6, *passim.*

146 It is important to add this observation to the conclusion of Mr. Pompe (*Aggressive War* 57) that "the mixture of military and non-military criteria makes the problem of the determination of the aggressor in case of provoked aggression equal to that of the finding of a *Zirkelquadratur* to which Bismarck reduced the whole problem of aggression in a war". (The quotation is in 6 Lepsius *et al.* (ed.), *Die grosse Politik der europäischen Kabinette 1871-1914: "Eine Zirkelquadratur, definitiv nicht klar zu stellen und durch keinen Vertragstext theoretisch lösbar, sobald man nicht der bona fides des Verbündeten mehr vertraut als dem Wortlaut der Klauseln."*)

147 On the distinctions in Soviet usage between "indirect", "ideological" and "economic aggression", "indirect aggression" denoting generally "subversion", while "economic aggression" is censured as a form of "direct aggression", and "ideological aggression" as an "aggression *sui generis*", see L. Schultz, *"Der Sowjetische Begriff der Aggression"* (1956) 2 *Osteuropa* 274, 284. This writer observes that Soviet lawyers have characterised the Marshall Plan as "economic aggression".

148 See *supra* n.145, as to the Soviet use of "attack" as equivalent to this.

some other judgment than the weighing of the respective "legitimate" interests and rights that have been invaded.[149] For so far as the "legitimate" interests of States are concerned, there may obviously be an "armed attack" within the Soviet draft the effects of which are negligible as compared with some imaginable forms of indirect economic and ideological aggression.[150] This raises the question, which will later be fully discussed, whether the special treatment of resort to armed force is not really a matter distinct from the problem of defining "aggression", and is not better examined as a function of the special dangers of a chain reaction leading to thermonuclear war in our present age. Conceivably, as we shall suggest, more progress might be likely if these questions were clearly separated out.[151]

The valuable service of the 1956 Committee in raising these and other problems[152] did not extend to the advance of any solutions. Clearly, for example, no State was really asserting that every degree of propaganda and economic pressure would constitute aggression: but little light was cast on *the degree* which would. Confusion was compounded by the bland Soviet assertion, side by side, of the propositions (on the one hand) that economic blockade against another State constitutes "economic aggression", and (on the other) that such "economic aggression" may not be justified *inter alia* by the fact that it is a defensive response to the violation by the "victim" of "the rights and interests" of the "aggressor" in the sphere of "trade, concessions, or any other kind of economic activity acquired by another State or its citizens", or to "rupture" by the "victim" of "economic relations" with the "aggressor", or to violation of any treaties by the "victim".

B. *Frontier Incidents.*

We have already mentioned earlier in this Chapter some of the problems raised by the Soviet draft's assertions that invasion by armed forces of

---

149 R. P. Gonzalez Muñoz, *Doctrina Grau* (1948) 23ff., is therefore correct in stressing the importance for the notion of "economic" aggression of the nature of the value attacked, as distinct from exclusive concentration on the form or motive of the attack.

150 Insofar as Professor Wright (article cited (1956) 50 *A.J.I.L.* 514, 526-27) implies the contrary we must disagree with his view. Insofar as he is saying that "aggression" in Art. 39 must mean only "armed aggression" because the Security Council may use military means of repression, it must be observed that much of Chapter VII also deals with non-military means of repression. It seems far preferable, in any case, to cut through to the real motivation of differential treatment of the use of armed force discussed in the text, and *infra* Ch. 9. That writer's inadvertence to these perplexities persists in his "Intervention, 1956" (1957) 51 *A.J.I.L.* 257, 268ff. See *infra* Ch. 5, n.23.

Cf. this point in R. P. Gonzalez Muñoz, *op.cit.* 67.

151 See *infra* Ch. 9. Professor Röling in 1954 ("On Aggression . . ." (1955) 2 *Nederlands T.Int.R.* 167, 170) made a related observation (falling short however of the present point) that the anxiety behind the desire to define aggression arises from "hatred" of war, while "the supporters of the inclusion of . . . 'economic aggression' wish to eliminate foreign interference by economic measures, and . . . are motivated by the love of their country. . . . [E]conomic measures have tremendous effects. . . . But we are not discussing the means to protect the political independence of a State, we are discussing the possibilities of eliminating war. . . . Other evils, other remedies; other vices, other dooms." (Röling, 171.)

152 See also on the active or passive capacity for aggression of non-State entities the Iraqi draft (A/AC.77/L.8/rev.) and the Netherlands and Chinese comments in A/AC. 77/SR.13, p.15, and SR.14, pp.4-5, and *1956 Sp.Com.Rep.* 22, 23.

another State is culpable "armed attack", while "frontier incidents" even if initiated by the "victim" to which the armed invasion was a response, should not be such culpable "armed attack". The distinction here intended (which, of course, goes back into League debates), turns either on some element of intent or of degree or "seriousness" of the force used, or its geographical range.[153] Here again, though the questions raised were scarcely given even provisional answers, the emergence of questions of degree and of the just weighing of conflicting claims illuminates the nature of the general problem. What is even more important is some proper ground of suspicion that answers may often not be available at all, in the present state of the international community, and of our knowledge concerning it, to the questions as they are formulated in the debates.[154]

C. *The Principle of "The First Act".*

"The principle of priority" or of "the first (guilty) act" as central in the notion of aggression, had of course long been central in the Soviet draft,[155] which purported to determine who was the attacker or armed

---

[153] *1956 Sp.Com.Rep.* 7, 18, 19, and see A/AC.77/SR.13, p.14. M. Röling well pointed out the intractability of the questions, what use of force constituted a frontier incident, and what constitutes an attack, and that in League practice when both parties had used force the priority principle was not decisive.

The problems here are not substantially changed from those arising in the early Politis definition, and the de Brouckère Report, cited *supra* Ch. 2, n.20. The latter well pointed up these problems, the solutions to which are no nearer today. See Mr. Eden in the General Commission of the Disarmament Conference, Series B, vol. ii, p.514, and the more contemporary views of MM. François, Hsu, and Cordova in *U.N. Doc.* A/CN. 4/SR.93, paras. 19, 30, 40. And see other views collected by the Secretary-General, *U.N.Doc.* A/2211, paras. 301-305, 382-85.

[154] But it may not be mere delight in debate which led the Netherlands representative to criticise the Iran-Panama draft for failing to exculpate mere "frontier-incidents", and simultaneously to criticise the inclusion of incursions of "armed bands" in the inculpated list, on the ground that this suggested that an initial aggression may occur even before any incursion had taken place, thus allowing a potential aggressor the pretext of self-defence. (A/AC.77/SR.17, p.6, and *1956 Sp.Com.Rep.* 20.) If "frontier incidents" are exculpated, "legitimate self-defence" is imperilled in some sense; if they are inculpated, aggressors are afforded easy pretexts. The problem lies neither in the various formulae of definition, nor even in the use or not of definitions. It lies in the deeper considerations affecting the state of the international community, and the absence of effective organs already referred to, and further discussed in the conclusions. A similar observation is to be made on the question whether definition should embrace subversion, as to which British delegates have aptly observed on the danger both of its inclusion and its exclusion from the definition; "the moral was not to try to define . . . at all." (A/AC. 77/SR.16, p.5.)

It scarcely solves these perplexities for Professor Zourek to tell us (see *supra* Introd. n.29a) that repelling a border incident does not justify an invasion. If he means merely that self-defence under Art. 51 must be proportionate to the attack, this may be so; but this still does not tell us when such an incident comes to involve an act of aggression. Nor is Professor Zourek very convincing as to the distinction between encouragement and aid to armed bands rebelling against the victim State, which are not "aggression" because (he thinks) this is in the natural order of evolution; and intervention in the political affairs of another State, even by propaganda, which (he thinks) is aggression. The relation of these enigmas to Soviet policy and ideology and political techniques is scarcely concealed. And see *infra* Ch. 6.

[155] A/C.6/L.332/Rev.1.

aggressor not according to which State *committed* any of the listed acts, but rather according to which State *first* committed any of them.[156] This priority element was pressed as essential in order simultaneously to allow as self-defence acts of violence otherwise prohibited, while not allowing such acts to forestall merely anticipated dangers of the commission of such acts by the victim, that is, without sanctioning preventive war.[157] It was pressed, in short, as drawing a line between *permissible* self-defence and *prohibited* "preventive war". It was urged with much less persuasiveness[158] also that this principle of priority was a long-recognised principle of international law, which was also embodied in Article 51 of the Charter.[159] Other delegates denied that any such principle of international law existed, and also denied the basic relevance of the question who was the "first" to commit any of the acts enumerated in the Soviet definition since "everything depended essentially upon the circumstances".[160] It was also pointed out that it might often be difficult to decide who acted first, especially when many States were in conflict and for different objects, and that in any case a State that initiated a process was not necessarily responsible for *all* the acts which followed.

The import for the whole question of definition of the test of first commission of the acts designated by the Soviet Union was admirably and dramatically stated by the United States representative, Mr. Sanders. He squarely rejected the principle of priority on the ground that even the first commission of the acts concerned might, according to the circumstances, be either "aggression" or "self-defence".[161] Here again it became apparent that there were involved in the judgment of "aggression", tasks of evaluation, and in particular of justice,[162] which simply cannot be performed by limit-

---

156 A/AC.77/SR.3, p.11; SR.14, p.9; SR.18, p.4.

157 *Ibid.*

158 As to the former, since before the League Covenant the licence to resort to war under customary international law was certainly not inhibited; and after the League Covenant because it is doubtful whether any principle so defined can be extracted with any confidence from the tangled and amorphous history sketched, *supra* pp.27-40. As to the latter, since such an interpretation begs one of the very questions in issue as to Art. 51, namely whether that article must be taken to describe the entire scope of the customary law licence of self-defence as existing after the Charter. On this see Stone, *Conflict* 234-37, 243-46, 272-78 and *infra* Ch. 5 *passim.*

159 G. Scelle's position as regards the priority principle as between "aggression" and "self-defence" (article (1936) cited *supra* p.17 at 374) may, however, be referred to.

160 See *1956 Sp.Com.Rep.* 9, 19. See the United Kingdom criticism (A/AC.77/SR.16, p.4), that of Iraq at SR.14, p.7, SR.4, pp.3-4; and the Dutch criticism of the concessions sought to be made by the Soviet delegate in order to meet the difficulties. (A/AC. 77/SR.13, pp.14ff., SR.16, p.8 and SR.17, p.5.)

161 It is the crucial artificial closing of the list of legally culpable acts which is the Achilles' heel of the priority test, and it is important to focus attention on the heel. Once this vice is forgotten the test has apparent self-evidence; but when this vice is observed, the self-evidence is seen as illusory. *Cf.* G. A. Podrea, *"L'Agression . . ."* (1952) 30 *R.D.I.* 367, 369, who observes that unless some artificial step is established by law, we cannot ascertain in final analysis which is the first act of aggression without going back further into its historical, political and other antecedents, the special circumstances of its commission, its degree of intensity of violence, and the general attitude accompanying it. *"Tous ces éléments, en effet, jouent un rôle primordial dans l'acte lui-même et par conséquent deviennent autant de facteurs essentiels d'une juste détermination de l'agression." Cf.* also *infra* pp.143-144.

And see *supra* (Ch. 1, n.9) the similar Soviet view of 1924, now abandoned.

162 Professor Röling's mode of rejection of the priority principle was thus illuminating in respects other than those which he may have intended. "In the case of real armed

ing consideration to the occurrence of a precisely defined act, at a particular moment, in insulation from the broader context of the relations of the States concerned.[163]

This difficulty was increased to the point of caricature by the express provision in the Soviet draft that virtually no considerations whatsoever "political, strategic, or economic", nor in particular any of a rather exhaustive list of provocative invasions by the "victim" of the "attacker's" legal rights and legitimate interests, could justify the attack. In a state of the world in which there is usually no other possible means of vindicating rights and interests, this is rather like proposing a municipal legal order in which the only law which is enforced is a law forbidding physical trespass against the realty or person of another.[164] If common sense here rebels, it is not

attack within the meaning of Article 51," he said, "the concept of priority in time was superfluous, since, as the State attacked was entitled to take up arms immediately in its own defence, the aggressor would be the one which attacked first." The proposed priority rule diverted attention from the major factor, which was, as he had shown, the nature and magnitude of the act of aggression. (A/AC.77/SR.8, pp.8-9.) But when Professor Röling came to formulate his view of a "real armed attack" analysis shows that it involved in major part an examination of the position of the Parties in terms of justice. Professor Röling, indeed, virtually recognised this when he attacked the Soviet enumeration of acts of "armed attack" as purporting to be objectively observable since "it was not . . . enough to prove the use of force. Qualitative and quantitative considerations had to be taken into account besides the use of force. . . . The crux of the matter was really the nature of the armed intervention rather than the intervention itself." (A/AC.77/SR.8, p.8.)

Cf. G. A. Podrea, "*L'Agression . . .*" (1952) 30 *R.D.I.* 367, 369, who observes that the value of the priority test is dubious, since that test certainly cannot produce "*à travers le prisme des notions connexes de la provocation et de la légitime défense, un éclaircissement péremptoire à même de constituer une preuve indiscutable de l'agression.*"

[163] The recent Israeli-Egyptian struggle is a classical illustration of the indeterminacy of the priority principle. See e.g., Sir Pierson Dixon (U.K.): "It would be a profitless task to attempt to apportion the blame between Israel and the Arab States." He went on to say that while it was arguable whether Israel was more at fault as to border incidents, they could not ignore Egypt's declared plan for hegemony after eliminating Israel (*G.A.O.R.* F.E.S.S., 561st Plenary Meeting, Nov. 1, 1956, p.6, para. 82). So M. Cañas (Costa Rica) observed that "Israel violated the terms of an armistice but it did not really commit aggression. The initial aggression occurred eight years ago, and peace has still not been established. . . ." (*G.A.O.R.* F.E.S.S., 563rd Plenary Meeting, Nov. 3, 1956, p.64, para. 199); and the remark of Mr. Casey (Australia) that to call prior events "provocative" to Israel was to use a word of studied moderation. He suggested that the term "slow motion aggression" would better describe prior Egyptian conduct. (*G.A.O.R. XI*, 595th Plenary Session, Nov. 26, 1956, p.398, para. 119.) And see the penetrating legal analysis in L. Gross, "Passage Through the Suez Canal" (1957) 51 *A.J.I.L.* 530, esp. 568.

And see, from an opposed standpoint, Mr. Rifa'i (Jordan): "The Palestine question is so wide and deep-rooted that no one can start discussion of it from any recent date. And see *id.*, A/PV. 664, Feb. 28, 1957, p.22. *Cf.* also Sir Percy Spender (Australia) (*G.A.O.R. XI*, Nov. 1-2, 1957, p.883, paras. 64-67); Mr. Eban (Israel) (*G.A.O.R. XI*, Jan. 19, 1957, p.955, para. 102); Mr. Gunewardene (Ceylon) (*G.A.O.R. XI*, Jan. 28, 1957, p.973, para. 48).

It would follow logically from this point that the determination of "priority" in time may often be a *conclusion from* the judgment of moral responsibility, *rather than an easy method of reaching this judgment.* Thus we find M. Jamali (Iraq) appealing to the Assembly to consider Israel as "the *prime* aggressor in the Middle East with expansionist aims" (*G.A.O.R. XI*, 596th Plenary Session, Nov. 26, 1956, p.342, para. 211).

[164] It should be added to savour the full absurdity that we would also have to suppose that in this fabulous municipal legal order, one half of its worthy citizens were bailees holding on their realty a substantial portion of the worldly resources and means of livelihood of the other. (See *infra* Ch. 9, s.II.) And also, of course, that in this municipal society no means whatever existed for changing the law except with the consent of every individual member of the society.

only because the proposal lacks humour, but also because it empties the aggression notion of that reference to minimal justice which is at least one main source of men's impulse to suppress aggression.[165] At this point, in the view of many delegations, as probably of most men who approach this problem without political *arrière pensée,* the Grotian *bellum justum* dons its knightly armour to do battle with the pretensions of those who would mechanically outlaw, as "the gravest crime against mankind",[166] what may in some circumstances be the only escape from perpetual wrong and tyranny.

D. *The Attempted Approach to Definition through Armed Attack.*

The 1956 discussions made clear that no major escape from the substantive ethical and socio-political issues involved in the notion of aggression could be found by shifting attention to the limits of the victim's permitted icence of self-defence against "armed attack" under Article 51.[167] This proposal, though not new in 1956, was pressed with special vigour and acumen by the Netherlands delegate, M. Röling, as a way of breaking the voting deadlock on the main issue;[168] it received, in view of its promise of a ready solution, remarkably little State support. After much reflection, the Writer is convinced that the promise of the proposal becomes in any case illusory, as soon as certain ambiguities in it are clarified.

If States generally really accepted the view that all forceful self-redress by individual Members is forbidden by the Charter except in "self-defence against armed attack against a Member" within Article 51, they should certainly have rallied immediately to the thesis that nothing more was necessary to denote "aggression", than to define "self-defence against armed attack". For the concept of "self-defence" would then not have its vague customary law outlines, but be more precisely limited by reference to "armed attack" as an observable phenomenon against which it reacts. Some problems would remain, of course, for instance of distinguishing what degree of violence "armed attack" must involve.[169] and as to the proportionality requirements for "self-defence".[170] Yet the more intractable problems raised by invasion of rights by illegal measures other than "armed attack", would have been resolved clearly (if arbitrarily, and probably intolerably in the long run) by exposing them to the tender mercies of the State which has them within its territorial domain. If States really accepted this view of the Charter, indeed, the question of "aggression" itself would become irrele-

---

165 See *infra* Chs. 7, 9 *passim*. 166 See *infra* pp.131-35.

167 For a modest recent study of American views on the notion of "armed attack" in general and in relation to Art. 51, see J. H. Quinn, *"Armed Attack" as Interpreted Chiefly by the United States* (1954) (MS., Harvard Law School Library).

168 He contended that the notion of aggression in Art. 36 was "useless", "dangerous" and "impossible" to define (*1956 Sp.Com.Rep.* 24), and (if it could be defined) required a wide and flexible definition; and also that a "lowest common denominator" definition proposed by the Four Power Joint Draft would be unacceptable. (On this last draft see A/AC.77/L.11, and SR.16, pp.6ff.) Art. 51, he thought, on the other hand, "required as rigid a definition as possible, designed to ensure that no aggressor could fraudulently plead to be acting in self-defence". (See A/AC.77/SR.3, p.8, and SR.13, p.15.)

169 See *supra* 68-69 especially as to frontier incidents.

170 See *infra* pp.74-76.

vant;[171] the question what is "armed attack" would have been substituted for it. Reasonable force to repel such "armed attack" would be lawful; any other force would be unlawful and the United States' objection that an unlawful use of force was not necessarily "aggression" would become practically irrelevant.[172]

The fate of the Netherlands' proposal, however, made it certain that, whatever casual generalisations were made from time to time, there was no consensus favouring that extreme view of Charter inhibitions on the use of force.[173] Indeed in the final analysis even the Dutch proposal itself drew back at accepting it.[174] For that proposal,[175] after opening *as if* it were merely defining "armed attack",[176] went on also to provide that "the definition may never be construed to comprise *(inter alia)* acts of *legitimate* individual or collective self-defence". Insofar as meaning must be given to this emphatic proviso, it obviously subjects the test of aggression afforded by the definition of what "armed attack" justifies forceful self-defence, to whatever qualification may be read into the formula of "legitimate individual or collective self-defence".[177] This last formula is obviously looser than M. Röling's purported definition of "armed attack" in at least the respects that the "legitimacy" of measures of self-defence (whatever that may mean) is

---

171 That is, so far as armed aggression is concerned. And see the Chinese objection (A/AC.77/SR.14, p.4) to M. Röling's proposal that it "might create an illusion that aggression had been defined", and thus leave "subversion" and other "aggression" unbranded.

172 See *infra* p.94.

173 When M. Röling emphasises that "a definition of armed attack within the meaning of Art. 51 would not . . . cover the concept of aggression within the meaning of Art. 39", he seems, insofar as we can follow him, to be proceeding on this view. See A/AC.77/SR.8, p.6. But as we shall shortly show the proviso in his offered definition is a repudiation of it.

174 Indeed, as between the views of Quincy Wright (cited *infra* n.181) and C. A. Pompe, M. Röling embodied in his definition the view that not all illegal force was to be deemed an armed attack, but only such force as left no alternative to the victim but forceful self-defence. He thus adopted a qualifying formula on this point similar to that in C. A. Pompe (*Aggressive War* 113).

175 See *infra* Ch. 4, n.22. We reproduce the short text here for convenience: "Armed attack as this term is used in Art. 51 is any use of armed force which leaves the State against which it is directed no means other than military means to preserve its territorial integrity or political independence; it being understood that the definition may never be construed to comprise acts of legitimate individual or collective self-defence or any act in pursuance of a decision or recommendation by a competent organ of the United Nations." (*1956 Sp.Com.Rep.* 25. See also A/AC.77/SR.8, pp.5-10 and SR.13, pp.14-18, esp. 17.)

176 Even this part of the definition has in it elements which by extending or contracting the bounds of "armed attack" in the ordinary sense, may be regarded as qualifying by reference to value elements the inference which the extreme view above would draw from Art. 51. What use of armed force would leave the victim State no means other than military to preserve its "territorial integrity or political independence", is scarcely so rigidly plain as to exclude the fraudulent pleas of self-defence by aggressors which M. Röling appears to believe he is excluding. It was this element, no doubt, as well as the proviso, which led the U.S. representative to contend that the Netherlands formula was "initially as much dependent on subjective evaluation by a State . . . as any determination that State might make under the language of Art. 51 itself, . . . and that it might seriously prejudice the right to resort to self-defence, as recognized under Art. 51, [and] . . . do more harm than good". (A/AC.77/SR.13, pp.4-5, and *1956 Sp.Com.Rep.* 25.)

177 No doubt M. Röling was conscious, in adding the proviso, that it was important not to leave NATO (predicated as it is on any "armed attack" on a Member, even if

a sufficient justification, and that it is a justification even if the measures are not made necessary by such an "armed attack" as he has previously defined. The apparent escape from the intractable value elements in the notion of aggression as used in Article 39 by defining precisely what kind and degree of "armed attack" a State may react against by force, is thus rendered nugatory by the introduction of the very same intractable elements in an over-riding proviso to the definition.

Thus qualified the definition comes to have the basic structure that any use of armed force is an "armed attack" giving rise to the right of self-defence under Article 51, if it leaves the victim only the military means of preserving its territorial integrity and political independence, *unless that use of armed force is an "act of legitimate individual or collective self-defence"*.[178] And it finally emerges as a division of the whole class of acts of "use of armed force", from the present standpoint, into (1) acts of "legitimate self-defence" which are permitted,[179] and (2) other such acts which are forbidden. And Mr. Röling's brave efforts have thus merely reproduced in the sphere of "armed attack" under Article 51 the problem of determining the line between the resort to force which is just, and that which is unjust, which we have seen to be a central difficulty of defining "aggression" generally. "Legitimate self-defence" is thus seen presented as one limiting notion on "armed attack", just as it is on "aggression"; and the hope for escape via the "armed attack" notion is barred.[180] So far as the central difficulty is concerned it seems no easier to say what makes a "legitimate self-defence" justifiable, than it is to say what makes an "armed attack" or an "aggression" unjustifiable.[181]

The entire expedition of escape from the jungle of ethical and socio-political judgment on alleged aggression, so courageously led by M. Röling

---

not such a one as fell within his definition) open to the risk of impeachment as an "aggressive" organization. Soviet comments of 1936 (*Covenant Principles* 88) indicated keen awareness of the danger of definitions of aggression catching acts of collective self-defence or mutual assistance.

178 We omit, to avoid encumbering the argument, the qualifications for acts pursuant to decision and recommendation of competent U.N. organs.

179 It should scarcely be necessary to point out that the notion "legitimate self-defence" must both in ordinary usage, and by the gloss of history of the '20s and '30s, refer us on further to norms of valuation, legal or moral, outside M. Röling's formula. "Self-defence" alone may be characterisable by merely physical tokens. A criminal shooting at the police to avoid arrest may be said to be acting in self-defence; but he is not acting in legitimate self-defence. Here the norms are legal, supplied by the municipal law. As between States, they are not yet fully given by international law: indeed the search for a definition of aggression is an attempt to find them and make them law. Until they are made law, they must be norms of morality or of some like non-legal system of norms. E. Giraud's massive 1934 study of "legitimate self defence" certainly negates any simple identity of that concept with "defence against armed attack". See *id.* *"La Théorie de la Légitime Défense"* (1934) 49 *H.R.* (pt. iii) 691-860.

180 This truth is underlined, rather than otherwise, by the Rapporteur's recognition that "it was logically impossible to talk of a justification of aggression. If aggression could be justified, it would cease to be aggression." (A/AC.77/SR.19, p.6.) It is precisely because "justification" (in this case "legitimate self-defence") is in ordinary usage a limiting notion *vis-à-vis* "aggression", that the logical contradiction which he detects arises.

181 Professor Wright well stated this point ("The Concept of Aggression . . ." (1935) 29 *A.J.I.L.* at 387) in observing that "the term defence has tended to be used

through the seemingly well-cleared route of definition of "armed attack", thus finds itself finally back in the very same jungle from which it started. The notion of "aggression", as Judge Lauterpacht long ago pointed out, and many before him, is complementary to the notion of "self-defence".[182] To reassert this in 1957 even by an excursus on "armed attack", is only to restate the problems for the solution of which a definition of aggression is

---

to cover all the unnamed circumstances which should extenuate the strict application of the rule against force". And of course, where self-defence is conceived as "a fundamental right" to which "the whole of the duties of States are normally subordinate" (see e.g. R. B. Pal, *International Military Tribunal* 43), its purported use as a delimiting concept for "armed attack" or "aggression" becomes even more unhelpful.

It is no answer to this crucial point for Professor Röling to say ("On Aggression . . ." (1955) 2 *Nederlands T.Int.R.* 167, 173): "The duty to refrain from the threat or use of force covers more cases than the right to use force", since under Art. 51 force may only be used as a provisional measure so long as resort to the United Nations organs is not possible. Even if this be accepted, discounting the chronic paralysis of the Security Council in these matters, it does not resolve the main difficulty. This is that for those cases of alleged self-defence (almost certainly the majority) where such resort is not possible, the same problems are still met whether we frame the issue in either the form (1) Was the alleged act of self-defence a reaction to an "armed attack" or "aggression"? or in the form (2) Was the reaction to the alleged "armed attack" or "aggression" an act of "self-defence"?

So *cf.* Sir J. Fischer Williams, *Chapters* (1934) 236, who observed that "the absolute prohibition of war has to be qualified by an exception for self-defence", and that "it is no less difficult to characterise the war which is forbidden, 'aggressive war', or the war which is allowed, 'war in self-defence' ". Just as "aggression" could not be given an advance definition capable of automatic application, so (said this writer) it seems equally impracticable to give an exhaustive or adequate verbal "definition" or explanation beforehand of the conception complementary to that of "aggression"—"self-defence". For the list must cover the different forms of attack—that is, we are brought back to defining "aggression". Yet, he added, no right was more certain or inalienable than that of self-defence. (*Op.cit.* 237-238.) *Cf.* generally C. A. Pompe, *Aggressive War* 39.

Cf. also the belief in "The Meaning of Aggression . . ." (1954) 33 *Nebraska L.R.* 606, 611, that the Seminar had been able to define aggression without defining either self-defence or legitimate self-defence. Insofar as it had, this was because the requisite qualifications were already built into the indeterminacies of its definition of aggression, *supra* n.95. We thus go echoing back to the old doctrinal debates on the just war doctrine. See also J. L. Kunz, "*Bellum Justum . . .*" (1951) 45 *A.J.I.L.* 528, 531: "There are no objective criteria between 'just' and 'unjust' wars. If the just war is one of self defence, it is just if directed against a present or imminent unjust attack. When is an attack in a concrete case unjust? . . . In a war of execution to enforce a right, the right and its violation need definition."

The difficulty is basically similar in proposals such as that of H. Thirring ("*Was ist Aggression?*" (1952-53) 5 *Oesterreichische Z. für öff.R.* (*N.F.*) 226) which would make a State an aggressor if it carries on military operations on another's territory unless it "proves" to "the United Nations" that the latter State had itself first committed, and threatens to continue, an "act of war-like aggression . . . against which only military operations across the border were an effective defence". Unless "act of war-like aggression" means simply armed attack, the crucial questions of justifiability have shifted back to it. And what is "proof", and what is "the United Nations" for these admirable purposes?

182 H. Lauterpacht, "The Pact of Paris . . ." (1935) 20 *Trans. Grotius Soc.* 178, at 199. This position is very widely acknowledged and is, we believe, a correct one, subject to minor variations of the complementary areas by specific treaty provisions. See among numerous examples, Robert H. Jackson, Address of March 27, 1941 (1941) 35 *A.J.I.L.* 348-350, 357; G. Scelle, "*L'Agression et la Légitime Défense . . .*" (1936) 10 *L'Esprit International* 372, 373, in whose view the correspondence of the questions is exact, since (matters of proportionality apart) only when aggression occurs does the right of self-defence arise. Indeed, on his view, all that distinguishes self-defence from aggression is that the former takes place first. So, he pointed out, when there was no legal restraint on the licence to go to war, there was also no restraint on the right of self-defence. (376.) He said indeed that it is because "*la notion de légitime défence se*

being sought; it is certainly not to advance the solution of these problems.[183] Nor does it in any way help the case for M. Röling to admit[184] that the notion of "self-defence" in his "definition" could not be applied automatically, and yet to insist at the same time that the definition did indicate "very clearly in which cases a country would not be entitled to use armed force".[185] For, after the above analysis, it must be clear that the latter cannot really be much clearer than the former.[186]

XI. ADVICE TO THE GENERAL ASSEMBLY.

The fate of all the draft definitions, old and new, in the Committee was no happier than that of the proposed working plans. When after eighteen meetings which spanned the most intense period of the Middle East crisis, the Committee "decided on its further procedure after its long exchange of views, and its study and discussion", it had no alternative but to decide "not to put the draft definitions before it to a vote". It transmitted them with the report prepared by its Rapporteur, M. Röling (Netherlands), to the General Assembly, expressing the trust that its work would contribute to the problem of defining aggression.[187] Many representatives on the Committee expressed at this point the interesting "hope that the development of friendly international relations will make possible in the

---

définit par l'agression", that this latter notion must be defined (374).

Professor Röling's fruitless journey is the more remarkable since that learned jurist made it very clear in his views before the Legal Committee in 1954 ("On Aggression . . ." (1955) 2 *Nederlands T. Int. R.* 181) that he was well aware that by framing an exception in terms of "legitimate self-defense" rather than in the words of Article 51 the effect is to "leave it to later statesmen and scholars" to decide e.g. whether force used against an immediate threat of attack was to be deemed "aggression".

Cf. as to the related pair "provocation" and "legitimate self-defence", and their indeterminacy of application, G. A. Podrea, *"L'Agression* . . . (1952) 30 *R.D.I.* 367, 368-69. We find scarcely any warrant save Professor Scelle's own authority (which though high can scarcely be decisive on such a matter) for his appropriation of the term "legitimate self-defence" to the much more restricted and determinate sphere which he asserts it to have. See Introd. *supra* pp.5ff.

183 Insofar as Judge Lauterpacht's cited article of 1935 similarly suggests (see e.g. at 200) that we can reduce the difficulties of defining "aggression", by choosing rather to define "self-defence", it is open to a similar observation. And so is the converse sanguineness of V. V. Pella (in Bourquin (ed.), *Collective Security* 318) that a "precise" definition of "legitimate self-defence" can be reached by defining "the aggressor", though this has somewhat more to be said for it. See Giraud, 704, 857ff.

184 A/AC.77/SR.8, p.9. And see A/AC.77/SR.13, p.18 where he asserted that his proposal would provide "an authentic interpretation of the Charter and define the limits of the right of self-defence."

185 His argument that his proposal was different in nature from that rejected by M. Paul Boncour's report at San Francisco also lacks any persuasiveness, in this light. (See A/AC.77/SR.8, pp.6-7.)

186 Both the U.K. and U.S.S.R. representatives, at odds on most other points, united in their attack on this aspect. The U.K. representative insisted that "armed attack" in Art. 51 could not be satisfactorily defined without defining self-defence, and that the latter could not be effectively passed on, except in the light of the particular circumstances. (A/AC.77/SR.16, p.5ff.) And the U.S.S.R., as well as the Czech representative, "considered it inconsistent with the Charter to argue that the notion of armed aggression in Art. 39 was different in principle from the notion of armed attack in Art. 51. [They] . . . formed a single concept . . .". (A/AC.77/SR.10, pp.5ff., and see *1956 Sp.Com.Rep.* 25.)

And for a more sanguine, but scarcely thought out, reaction to the Dutch view on this point, see the Norwegian representative at A/AC.77/SR.6, pp.9-10.

187 M. Stavropoulos, the Legal Counsel, had stated (A/AC.77/SR.1, p.5) at the

future the formulation of a generally acceptable definition".[188] And as to its mandate to "coordinate" the views of Members, the Philippines representative made the somewhat humourless suggestion that "in case the General Assembly would meet the same difficulties as the Committee in coordinating the views regarding the definition of aggression", it could, instead of a "definition" or "statement" of the notion of aggression, at any rate "concentrate on drawing up a declaration" about it.[189]

On October 7, 1957, the Twelfth General Assembly's Sixth Committee at its 514th Meeting began discussion of the Report of the 1956 Special Committee, some draft definitions including the Soviet being formally re-submitted. No major change in the situation above described has emerged in these further proceedings, nor has the access of new Members created such a change. Absence of new arguments does not necessarily imply lack of open-mindedness; it may also spring from growing recognition of the obstacles to agreed definition. The renewed discussions thus underline the need for thorough examination of these obstacles to which the present work is devoted. And they reinforce the view, which will here emerge, that among the tasks vital for man's survival and welfare in a world of nuclear and interplanetary dimensions, the finding of an authoritative definition of aggression is among the least constructive.

---

opening of the 1956 Committee's work that, unlike the 1953 Special Committee, the 1956 Special Committee "had been asked to formulate and adopt a single draft definition of aggression", and that insofar as it could not reconcile the preceding divergent views, it was instructed "to choose between them by vote". It was emphasised also by M. Chaumont (France) that ". . . the Committee, unlike its predecessors, was now expressly required to arrive at a single definition". (SR.1, p.6.) And see *infra* Ch. 9, s.I, *passim.*

188 *1956 Sp.Com.Rep.* 5.

189 A/AC.77/SR.19, p.4. M. Serrano termed this "a realistic solution" which "might enable the Assembly to avoid the purely legal difficulties (such as the scope of a definition and whether it was consistent with the Charter) which had hampered progress for six years . . .".

CHAPTER 4

AGGRESSION AND WORDS

Logical Definition and Legal Definition

Though the search for a definition of aggression has produced few operative instruments save some transient non-aggression treaties,[1] and few other results whether under the League or the United Nations, its course may yet hold important insights for scholars (and even for statesmen) who believe in the relevance of historical experience. These efforts have at least articulated the advantages and dangers of various kinds of definition, and have made some kind of classification of definitional possibilities. Above all, they have provided, in the behaviour of the participants, materials for juristic and sociological analysis of the nature of the road block on this supposed highway to human salvation. With these insights we shall be concerned throughout the balance of this work; we may here open with certain preliminary observations as to language and logical structure in the search for definition.

I. "POSSIBILITY" AND "DESIRABILITY" OF DEFINITION.

One unnecessary contribution to the conflict of opinion as to "the possibility" of defining aggression, lies in the ambiguity of the word "possibility". If this is taken to mean merely "logical conceivability", the debate is largely vain; there may obviously be definitions that are "possible" in the sense of some *mundus fabulosus,* and yet quite irrelevant to present human problems.[1a] But even when this sense is dismissed, two meanings of "possible" still remain. First, that the draftsmen could devise a definition which would serve the purposes which most Governments would wish to see fulfilled in our actual world, a sense which may be rendered by the most "feasible". Second, however, insofar as the object of definition is to marshall support of Members to the recommendations of international political organs, a definition is only "possible" if (as the 1956 Committee seemed to agree)[2] an overwhelming proportion of Members (including the Great Powers) were willing to accept it as a standard of conduct for all Members, them-

[1] See *supra* Ch. 2, s.VI.

[1a] It is with respect only for such a *mundus fabulosus,* that Professor Zourek can assert as he did in his 1957 Hague lectures (see Introd., n.29a) that the "legal possibility and technical possibility" are "admitted today".

[2] It was one of the few points of near consensus. Among the expressions there may be instanced notably that of France, that "a definition would be of real value only if it were acceptable to all the great Powers primarily responsible for the maintenance of international peace and security as well as to the great majority of Member States" (A/AC.77/SR.2, p.3); and of the Netherlands, that the definition should be "acceptable to the great majority of the Member States and to all, or nearly all, the Permanent Members of the Security Council . . ." (A/AC.77/SR.13, p.15). And *cf.* the *1956 Sp.Com.Rep.* 11ff.

selves as well as others.[3] We may render this meaning perhaps as "acceptable". The poor prospects of the enterprise of definition arise, in the present view, on the levels not of "conceivability" but of "feasibility" and "acceptability". "Possibility" in these latter senses cannot be asserted merely *a priori,* but requires empirical determination;[4] and no assertion in any General Assembly resolution can foreclose the answer, any more than it could arrest the law of gravity, or cause elephants to grow wings and fly.

Similar confusions affect the debate as to the "desirability" of defining aggression.[5] Since human desires have no necessary rational limits, and the Assembly's question whether a definition is "possible and desirable" must be taken as requesting a rational answer, we must take the question to be whether definition is "possible, and insofar as possible, also desirable". And given the above meanings of "possible", the question must be whether any definition such as would be "feasible" in the above sense, as serving the purposes which most States wish fulfilled, and such as could be made "acceptable" to most States, would be "desirable". This makes clear that the term "desirable" here has reference not to the logical or even empirical *possibility* of being desired, but to whether such a definition as is feasible and acceptable in the above sense *ought to be* desired. It asks, in other words, whether the adoption of such a definition would in fact improve peace enforcement, deter potential aggressors, and generally strengthen international law and order. Seen in this light, the British point that "possibility" and "desirability" are not separate questions, is well taken.[6] It is obviously not possible to say whether any definition at all of aggression is desirable, until we are given for testing at least the range of definitions which might be "feasible" and "acceptable".[7]

---

3 *Cf.* Professor Röling's formulations in the Legal Committee of the General Assembly, Ninth Session, repr. in "On Aggression, on International Criminal Law, on International Criminal Jurisdiction—1" (1955) 2 *Nederlands T.Int.R.* 167-196. "It would be a remarkable and astonishing thing: to find a generally acceptable definition of aggression." (Oct. 28, 1954); and see *id.* 168: "'Generally acceptable' indicates an overwhelming support, not a unanimous support", but "a qualified 2/3 majority would be sufficient."

4 The question of "desirability" is thus an additional one, even though, as the Chinese delegate observed in 1956, the immediate problem was not so much to determine whether it was desirable to define aggression, but whether a definition acceptable to States could be found at all. See A/AC.77/SR.3, p.4. It seems better to make the distinction in the text than to mix up "desirability" with acceptability to the majority of States. A definition might be "desired" by States which was not a "desirable" one. See A/AC.77/SR.6, pp.6-7, where Mr. Bushe-Fox's final view seems to agree with this.

5 See also *supra* pp.55,61-62,63-66.

6 The U.K. delegate remarked in the 1956 Committee that whether, considered as an abstract proposition, a definition was desirable depended on whether any satisfactory definition was possible. The desirability of adopting a particular definition depended on whether it was a satisfactory one or not. (*1956 Sp.Com.Rep.* 12, and A/AC.77/SR.6, p.7.) Nor, in abstraction from particular definitions offered, is it more than mere rhetoric to say with the Yugoslav (A/AC.77/SR.7, p.8) and other delegates that the adoption of a definition would "demonstrate that the international community was determined to prevent aggression". So *cf.* Mr. Hsueh (China) who observed that "his delegation could not subscribe to the view that the adoption of an imperfect definition of aggression was better than the adoption of no definition at all". (A/AC.77/SR.14, p.5.)

7 After more than thirty years of effort, the joint draft of the Dominican Republic, Mexico, Paraguay and Peru (A/AC.77/L.11), drawn late in the 1956 discussions especially with an eye to acceptability "to the greatest possible number of States", and making

II. "GENERAL AND ABSTRACT", "ENUMERATIVE" AND "MIXED" DEFINITIONS.

Certain comments are also invited by the insufficient analysis in the discussions of the distinctions adopted between "general and abstract", "enumerative" and "mixed" (or "combined") definitions.[8] We do not here stick in the bark of the classical view requiring *definitio per genus proximum et differentiam specificam,* so that enumerative definitions would strictly not be definitions at all; though certain comments arising from the theory of definition are made in the next section. But even if we were to accept ostensive definition as definition, it would still be most doubtful whether the ostentation of "aggression-situations" could proceed in the manner of: "This and this and this are chairs". For the "aggression-situations" or "acts of aggression" which purport to be pointed to are not cognisable in the sense in which the presence of a chair is cognisable, for the basic reason, shortly to be elaborated, that "aggression" refers to a relation, which must not be confused with the terms whose relation is involved. The pretended concrete acts or situations, moreover, which figure in the enumerative part of definitions, often have a latent reference to universals, which in turn still demand "general and abstract" definitions—only more of them. The multiplication of universals provides no escape from the fact that a relation cannot be defined merely by identifying some or even all of its terms. The relatively minor perplexities of distinguishing excusable "frontier incidents", from the "armed attack across the frontier" which would be "the gravest crime against mankind", are an old and well-known example.[9] The thought behind the so-called "mixed" or "combined" definitions is that they offer a "general and abstract" definition in a general clause,[10] along with a list of concrete "aggression-situations" or "acts of aggression" to assist understanding or application of the general formula. If the abstract definition in the general clause could be self-applying, the list of acts or situations would be unnecessary; and it is not, in any case, really a part of the definition. Its inclusion manifests doubt as to the adequacy of the definition in the general clause[11] and seeks to ensure that it shall at least extend to the list of acts or situations.[12]

---

substantial sacrifices of viewpoints to that end, got little support. See A/AC.77/SR.16, pp.6ff., and *1956 Sp.Com.Rep.* 23. For the Soviet and U.S. criticisms see A/AC.77/SR.16, pp.9-10, and SR.17, p.3, and *1956 Sp.Com.Rep.* 23ff. The U.S. delegate observed that the effort at compromise had produced merely a patchwork combination of so-called "common elements" which it would be inadvisable to lay before the General Assembly. (A/AC.77/SR.17, p.3.)

[8] For convenient summary of the usage see the Secretary-General's Report, *G.A.O.R. VII,* Ann., Item 54, A/2211, pp.59-78, and the *1956 Sp.Com.Rep.* 8ff., 17.

[9] See *supra* pp.68ff. *Cf.* in relation to the Soviet draft Professor Röling's comment in 1956 in Doc.A/AC.77/SR.8, p.7.

[10] Of the drafts submitted to the 1956 Special Committee, only the Iraqi revised draft resolution (A/AC.77/L.8/Rev. 1; text also in Ann. II, pp.31-32 to *1956 Sp.Com.Rep.*) contains a definition which is strictly of an abstract or general character.

[11] *Cf.* the Mexican delegate's view, A/AC.77/SR.7, p.5, that though strictly no definition at all, a mixed definition may serve as a "guide".

[12] It is therefore not quite adequate to say, as did the United Kingdom (A/AC.

Conceivably there might be a mixed or combined "definition" in which the abstract definition, and the list of acts or situations, were, together, final and complete. This would require that to the extent that the list of acts or situations went beyond the abstract or general formula, it should be conclusive in all circumstances. Acts or situations listed would be caught under all circumstances; acts or situations not listed would only be caught if they fell within the abstract definition, but would then always be caught. If draftsmanship were perfect in both the general definition and the list, this could yield a fully exhaustive and rigid definition; that is, one that is closed at both the inculpating and exculpating ends. We know of no offer of official mixed definition which has really aspired to this, much less achieved it; and we also know of no merely enumerative drafts of official origin, since the early Soviet efforts of the 'thirties, which purport to be "exhaustive" and "rigid" in the same sense.[13] Nor is there much support in the current debates for merely abstract or general definitions.[14]

A main motive behind the so-called "mixed" definitions now most in favour is concerned not so much with the problem of definition, but rather with limiting the discretion of whatever organ is to apply the definition. The "abstract or general" part of a mixed definition leaves the organ comparatively uninhibited in its choice of fact situations to subsume thereunder; the enumerative part of the definition seeks to exclude freedom of manoeuvre by the organ in the enumerated fact situations. We should consequently not be surprised to find, as we have done, that particular States tend to include in their proposed enumerations of "acts of aggression", those activities which they regard as particularly menacing to their own special interests.

Granted (as is generally agreed) that no such enumeration can exhaust the concept, and thus provide a definition *stricto sensu,* it may be argued that it may still be possible to enumerate a list of *indicia* or criteria of aggression, as guides to the applying organ, just as we may list some *indicia* or criteria by recourse to which the truth or justice of given assertions or situations can be evaluated for practical purposes. Fairness, therefore, seems to require us to reinterpret enumerative definitions, and the enumerative parts of mixed definitions, as efforts to provide *indicia* or criteria of aggression. This view of the matter, moreover, draws attention sharply to the probability, which is central to our whole subject, that the referent of the notion of aggression is not a mere genus of *fact situations,* but includes a judgment of value, and in particular of justice. And this hypothesis is supported by the observed fact that we find it very difficult to apply the term "aggression" to conduct for which we cannot feel an emotion of condemnation.[15]

.77/SR.16, p.4), that all mixed definitions "must stand or fall by their introductory general formula".

[13] *Cf.* the Yugoslav delegate at the 1956 Committee: "A purely enumerative definition was now rejected by all the Member States." See A/AC.77/SR.7, p.6.

[14] In the 1956 Committee the delegates of France (A/AC.77/SR.2, p.3), Iraq (A/AC.77/SR.4, p.4), and the Netherlands (A/AC.77/SR.8, pp.5ff.) were in principle in favor of a general definition setting out the basic elements of aggression.

[15] Mr. Sanders (U.S.) was right on the point when he observed: "The problem of

The question raised is, in short, whether it is sensible to search for criteria consisting of simple fact elements such as the armed crossing of the frontier, declaration of war, bombardment of land or vessels, or threat or use of force. Such criteria could only be valid on the assumption that each such fact element will *always* and *only* be found within a context which will also guarantee the presence of the negative value element (i.e., "lack of justification", "injustice" or the like) of the aggression notion.[16] Particular contexts are, of course, imaginable in which particular criteria consisting of simple fact elements would be accompanied by the presence of the requisite negative value elements. Yet there is surely no way of guaranteeing, for any list of simple fact criteria, that each such fact will only occur in all future situations when the context necessarily entails the presence also of the negative value element. Nor is it easy to imagine, in view of the marvellous forevision and draftsmanship which would be required, that any such list will ever be devised. It follows that unless we are willing to reconcile ourselves to branding as aggression situations in which such a judgment will revolt our sense of justice, we must be satisfied to grant leeways, that is discretion, to some arbiter or other in applying the criteria to later situations unforeseen or unforeseeable when the criteria were framed.

It is often thought that the freedom of action of an applying organ must inevitably be more restricted in an enumerative, as distinct from an "abstract" or "general" definition; and that the former must be more rigid and less flexible than the latter. And since a great deal of argument in this field turns on the respective merits and demerits of "flexibility" and "rigidity", it is important to envisage this matter correctly. In the first place, we must observe that either in enumerative or in general and abstract definition, problems of further definition of terms used in the definition are still bound to arise.[17] Neither kind of "definition", nor any combination or mixture of them, can really be self-applying.[18] In the second place,

---

defining aggression had been pursued because we wanted peace with justice. Any definition had to be tested in the light of the occasions when it was likely to be invoked." (A/AC.77/SR.5, p.4.)

16 We are concerned here, not with the practicality of such criteria (as to which see Ch. 9, s.I(E) and (F), but with their theoretical conceivability, in terms of criteria of value which themselves may not be values. *Cf.* 2 N. Hartmann *Ethics* (transl. S. Coit, 1932) 70: "Just as the principle of motion need not itself be motion, of life not itself life, just as the principles of knowledge are evidently far from being knowledge, so the universally ruling principle of the domain of value could very well be something else than value." *Cf.* S. E. Toulmin, *The Place of Reason in Ethics* (1950) 11ff. (on tests to recognise qualities which are not directly perceivable), and W. M. Urban, *Valuation, Its Nature and Laws* (1909) 129ff. (on the sufficient reason of valuation).

17 *Cf.* Mr. Sanders' comment in the 1956 Committee that the Soviet draft definition created more definitional problems than it solved. This was the inevitable effect of defining a term in other terms no more precise than itself. (A/AC.77/SR.13, pp.6-7, and *1956 Sp.Com.Rep.*21.)

18 We do not linger on the difficulty of finding the facts which are clear, honest, and capable in Sir J. Fischer Williams' terms (*Chapters* . . . (1934) 235). His further words are, however, still worth quoting: "To suppose that men can get something which is in any way an automatic definition, that is to say, a definition which will act without an application of human judgment to the facts of a particular case, is a vain imagination. . . . Men cannot expect to have something in the nature of a mechanical guillotine which will do automatic execution." We have given some important additional reasons for

other things being equal, an enumerative definition is likely, by the very number of concepts it uses, to have more need for further definition of terms, than an abstract or general one.[19] The more *definientes* the more *definienda*. Moreover, the more *definienda*, the more terms to be defined, the more arenas are available in which political passions can manipulate the main definition to suit the drives of particular interests.

In the third place, however, there is dangerous generalisation even in the preceding paradox; for clearly not all *definientes*, or defining terms, leave their own further definition equally at large. "Armed attack on territory, ships or aircraft" leaves little[20] at large; notions like "subversion", "hostile propaganda", "economic pressure", "legitimate self-defence", "unprovoked attack" leave a great deal. A definition, whether enumerative, or general or abstract, which makes enough use of indeterminate terms such as these latter, may leave the applying organ as much or even more[21] at large, than if it were required to apply merely the simple undefined notion of "aggression". And by the same token, a definition of any sort, whether enumerative, general or abstract, or mixed, which is qualified by such terms as "national or collective self-defence", or "legitimate self-defence",[22] or "unprovoked", without further precise delimitation of these terms, leaves to the applying organs much the same freedom of appreciation as if the notion of aggression were not defined at all.[23]

---

this in the present study, arising from the specific structure of the aggression notion, as it appears at the present state of the international community.

19 *Cf.* the U.S. view of the Dutch proposal. (A/AC.77/SR.13, p.5 and *1956 Sp.Com.Rep.* 12.)

20 Even these words, however, may be very deceptive in their apparent precision. As Professor Röling observed on the Soviet draft in 1956, that draft sought to fix responsibility by reference to the first act of invasion of the territory of another State, attacks on ships and aircraft, support of armed bands etc. Yet acts of this enumerated kind were characteristic of most frontier incidents, which the Soviet draft specifically provided should *not* ground any justification of the use of force in self-defence. Professor Röling would meet this difficulty by requiring a certain magnitude of the act to turn it into armed attack. But of course certainty is thereby largely reduced.

21 Since the very multiplicity of "weasel" words leading to cross-purposed controversy may decrease the chances of working out consistent principles by reasoned elaboration in a succession of instances.

22 The point is exquisitely illustrated by the Netherlands proposal in the 1956 Committee to approach the problems of clarifying the meaning of "aggression" under Art. 34, by defining the kind of "armed attack" which, under Art. 51, would permit the victim to react by force. M. Röling proposed defining it to mean:

> . . . Any use of armed force which leaves the State against which it is directed no means other than military means to preserve its territorial integrity or political independence; it being understood that the definition may never be construed to comprise acts of legitimate individual or collective self-defence or any act in pursuance of a decision or recommendation by a competent organ of the United Nations. (A/AC.77/SR.8, pp.5-10 and SR.13, pp.14-18; and see *1956 Sp.Com.Rep.* 25.)

The effect of thus substituting the exculpating formula "legitimate . . . self-defence" for "self-defence against armed attack on a Member" (in Art. 51), was as M. Röling admitted, to require an evaluation of all circumstances, and thus admit divergent viewpoints. Yet he still curiously insisted that "it implied clearly enough in what cases a State might not go to war in self-defence". We are quite unable to follow. See *1956 Sp.Com.Rep.* 25, and *supra* Ch. 3, s.XD.

23 So, on the Paraguayan draft (A/AC.77/L.7) the U.S. representative pointed out that the phrases "provokes a breach or disturbance of international peace and security", and "against the . . . sovereignty or political independence of another State", are so

III. FUNCTIONS OF "LOGICAL" AND "LEGAL" DEFINITIONS.

We have thus far taken at their face value the tangled arguments and counter-arguments of this long debate. Yet, if understanding in this area is to be advanced at all, it would be quite wrong to leave the matter in those terms. It is necessary, first, to recognise the cardinal distinction so constantly overlooked between logical and legal definition, and to make sure that the argument does not move treacherously from the one to the other. The former is a matter of epistemology, the latter of statecraft.

Logical definition is directed to placing the subject of knowledge at its proper point in the matrix of knowledge. But knowledge may be had without defining, as we know a dog without defining it. To assign an object to its genus with adequate differentia results in classification, which is useful as a mnemonic device, and harmless as long as *genera* in adequate and systematic distribution are available. From definition in this sense, applicable to substantive objects, there must be sharply distinguished, for reasons clear since Plato's time, both the mere enumeration of characteristics (which is a way of knowing, but not of defining), and attempts at definition through the statement of relations between terms whose definition is being sought. Where what is sought to be defined is not the terms as substantive objects, but a relation between these, the above theory of definition is irrelevant. In a complex situation where knowledge is sought of the relation between parts or processes, knowledge does not proceed by definition, even though the relation concerned may often have undergone hypostasis, and received a name to confound and torture the taxonomists. In such a situation, the relationship between a number of terms can be sought only by identifying the various distinct terms, and fixing their positions or movements in space and time. Identification of the terms is here in no sense a definition of the relation between them. It is only a preliminary step to seeking that definition. And that search is usually very long and complicated in social processes where the terms of the relation are themselves usually variables, which may have to be allowed for in a range descending to zero.

---

vague as to force the Security Council's inquiry back into the procedure it would follow in the absence of definition, of considering all the circumstances of the case. (A/AC. 77/SR.13, pp.5ff., and *1956 Sp.Com.Rep.* 19-20.) And *cf.* the similar U.K. (A/AC.77/SR.16, p.4) and Netherlands criticisms (A/AC.77/SR.17, p.5).

Cf. the discussion of precisely this aspect of these terms, bringing out their inter-relations, in G. A. Podrea, *"L'Agression. Ses Critères Déterminatifs et Sa Définition"* (1952) 30 *R.D.I.* 367-383. Mr. Podrea well points out that "provocation" is rather a complementary concept to "legitimate defence" (369). *Cf. supra* Ch. 3 as to the similar relation of "aggression" and "legitimate defence". Mr. Podrea may perhaps go too far in concluding that in these notions *"le terrain reste manifestement libre à toutes les interprétations"*, but his main point scarcely seems impeachable for such historically given concepts of "legitimate self-defence". I therefore find it difficult to follow Quincy Wright when he asserts that a clear concept of aggression was developed in the War Crimes Trials after World War II simply because the main tribunal considered and rejected the pleas that the German Government was acting in necessary self-defence, or with the consent of the Government concerned. Unless "necessary self-defence" is more closely tied down, this method cannot yield the kind of definition which that author purports to base on it. See his "The Prevention of Aggression" (1956) 50 *A.J.I.L.* 514, at 521-522.

Aggression between States is, at any rate, a complex relation of this nature involving a number of variables; its definition should therefore never be discussed as if it were a substantive object such as a horse, or a spade. To defy this precept is to encumber with intellectual confusion the already hard tasks of formulating the basis of mutual accommodation of power centres which is at the heart of the problem of *legal* as distinct from *logical* definition. The problem of legal definition of "aggression" pertains to the regulation of the relations between States, and not (as does logical definition) to the classification of knowledge. Its task is to find a formula which, if resorted to as a basis of decision in crisis, will produce the harmonious deployment of sufficient social and political forces to constrain other forces (those deemed "aggressive") from operating in a manner unacceptable to those agreeing on the formula. This may seem, in terms of current thought, an unduly complex way of referring to that deployment of a force, usually military, which is to be regarded as the constant term in aggression situations. But this objection can but remind us of the importance of two other basic truths.

First, there is not, and never has been, any society or group of societies in which force has not operated. (Basically a political force is an organisation of demands, and differs from a military force mainly in equipment and logistic.) The endless problem of civilisation is to equilibrate the forces operating at a given time, and we count a generation adequate and happy if the equilibration is in terms of an ethos inspired with intelligible and accepted social objectives. This means that for a legal definition of aggression to serve its function, it must be operable in terms of this theory of social forces. Any such definition must therefore attend not only to the variable fact ingredients of any situation, but also to the techniques of equilibration, their ethos, power, and flexibility; the League and United Nations struggle for definition is strewn with the casualties arising from lack of this attention.

Second, we should recall the methodologically basic problem of social theory arising from the fact that the delimitation of a problem (here that of defining aggression) is an act of abstraction. While abstraction is dictated by the need for solution, abstraction beyond a certain point may also create conditions making solution impossible. The intellectual limits set up by the very act of isolating the problem, may block the mind's approach to it. If in a given supposed "aggression-situation", the "facts" as so isolated are taken to be a geographical milieu, a political context and the movement of a force, it is as tempting as it is common to try to define aggression by reference to two or three of the variable terms of the whole relationship of aggression, usually by reference to some act or movement of force in the historical process. Yet, obviously such an abstraction if really acted on would commit us to the absurd proposition that no social force of a physical kind is entitled to move in any circumstance. In short, the purported "definition" of aggression by reference merely to the acts of the putative aggressor, destroys by its intellectual stage-rigging the very possibility of intellection concerning aggression.

At the level of practice, definition in terms *merely* of resort to force must obviously abort. But as soon as even the simplest qualification is introduced, for instance, for "self-defence" against armed attack, we are outside the context of definition *merely in terms of acts of the putative aggressor. A fortiori* as the qualification moves out to "legitimate self-defence", "defence of rights", "just cause of war" and the like. At the level of socio-juristic theory we may have only the alternatives—either to recognise that the theory of aggression is not the whole theory of force, but only a part of it; or to cease altogether from intellectual troubling concerning aggression. And if we choose the path of intellectual viability, as this Writer must, we may be compelled to recognise that legal definition pre-requires a theory which shall comprehend a larger context than the acts of putative aggressors, wide enough, in particular, to embrace men's "legitimate aspirations", meaning their demands and the norms whereby these are to be judged and legitimised. There can, in other words, be no theory of aggression except as part of the theory of the "rights" of States *de lege ferenda* as well as *lata;* and no operable definition of it save one which is based on a minimum of mutual acceptance of such "rights". A theory of international aggression must be a theory of social force, physical as well as other.

IV. DISCRETION OF THE APPLYING AUTHORITY.

Nor do we escape this by seeking to use the notion of *animus aggressionis* in order to distinguish "aggression" from these other limiting concepts. For, as will later be stressed, this notion of the *animus aggressionis* itself refers us back to "aggression", as if we knew what aggression was.[24] The term *animus aggressionis* is thus circuitous, at any rate in relation to any situation on which there can be a division of opinion as to whether aggression has taken place.[25] If a State declared on invading another that the latter had no right to exist, that the purpose of the invasion was "to drive the other State into the sea", or annex its whole territory, and made no claim of provocation or other claim of right, this would certainly manifest an *animus aggressionis* in the given situation. Yet such an example is little to the point, for when a State is found to make its purpose and lack of claim of right so clear, no dispute is likely as to whether the attack constitutes "aggression". No one doubts that there are core situations of aggression as to which no debate is possible. The great search for precise definition is inspired, not by difficulties with this core, but rather by those of the penumbra of doubt with which it is surrounded. It is precisely in this penumbral area that definition has appeared neither feasible nor acceptable in the senses

---

24 This is constantly overlooked by the writers. See e.g. R. Théry, *La Notion d'Agression* (1937) 226-27, who insisted that without use of this animus, we cannot identify either "aggression" or the "aggressor", that the very notion of the "criminality" of aggression is dependent on the possibility of finding *"l'intention agressive"*. He thought, however (227), that no corresponding intent was necessary for "legitimate self-defence."

25 See *supra* pp.19-21, and *infra* Ch. 7 as to the very limited area in which there is a core of determinacy in the aggression notion.

above indicated, producing inevitable frustration.

In all cases falling within this penumbral area neither the undefined concept of aggression itself nor any definitions offered, can exclude the need for application by human agents, individual and collective. The freedom of appreciation thus inevitably left to such agents extends beyond that which is always involved in saying whether a given set of facts falls within the terms of a rule. In the case of these penumbral areas of the aggression notion (which *ex hypothesi* have not been illuminated by applicable definition or criteria) the organ concerned cannot avoid a quasi-legislative drawing of the boundaries of the aggression,[26] or self-defence (or similar complementary notions, as the case may be), in the course of its *ad hoc* determinations. This, as we shall later show,[27] is not dissimilar from the well-known process in American constitutional decisions of fixing the line between what is not, and what is, due process. And I shall later suggest that this similarity is not coincidental, but turns on the "ethical" or "justice" or "value" element which is built into the respective notions.[28]

Even in municipal systems the power thus given to mere human beings can be the subject of suspicion and even challenge, as recent racial integration controversies in the United States show. But even stable municipal societies with strong legal traditions must finally on many critical questions still rely on the creative choices made by "right-minded men of the community",[29] guided to some degree but not wholly controlled by the duty of rationalising the decision within the body of traditionally received authorities and the received ideals of the legal system. Despite restlessness and even occasional crises, and with the moderating and corrective power of legislative and constitutional amendment when judicial *Rechtsgefuehl* strays too far from what is felt generally to be tolerable, the men and women of municipal societies learn to live with and even respect and bless the exercise of this power.

In the relations of States, however, it is difficult if not impossible to find men who can be said to be "right-minded men" *of the international community* to play an analogous role, and if we could find them we would still have grave difficulties of securing their appointment to the arbiter's role by the States concerned. Nor, in an area such as that of the determination of aggression, is it easy to find any authorities or ideas which can as yet be

---

26 The terms of the abstract definition which is a starting-point for the legislative task need not, if it is drawn in appropriate terms, refer expressly to self-defence. See e.g. "The Meaning of Aggression . . ." (1954) 33 *Nebraska L.R.* 606, 611; but that will only leave the self-defence concept to be drawn out legislatively from the flexible terms used in defining "aggression".

27 See *infra* esp. Chs. 5 and 7.

28 It is essential if either theoretical or practical progress is to be made that these matters be pressed beyond such formulations as those of the U.K. delegate, when he urged in 1952 that ". . . the concept of aggression is . . . incapable of definition. Alternatively, [it] is not a purely legal matter capable of being established by ordinary juridical methods. . . . [It] is also to a large extent a military, and political matter . . .". ("The Definition of Aggression" (1952) 1 *Int. and Comp. L.Q.* 137, 138.)

29 *Cf.* the recent perhaps oversimple formulation in A. Denning, *The Road to Justice* (1955) 4. And see H. Isay, *Rechtsnorm und Entscheidung* (1929). And *cf.* J. Stone, *The Province and Function of Law* (1950) 368.

said to be "traditionally received" to guide and check judgment.[30] It is not surprising, therefore, to find both a reluctance to recognise the extent of the power necessarily implied in the attempt to make "aggression" a central concept of peace enforcement; as well as a feeling that this power should be hemmed in and guarded as far as possible from subjective or morally outrageous exercise by giving precise directives to the organ concerned. This is undoubtedly one motive, especially among smaller States, of the desire for "definition" of aggression; and it is a motive with which, if it were only practicable, all of us should have the deepest sympathy.

V. FORMAL STRUCTURING BY INCULPATION AND EXCULPATION.

If efforts are to proceed in the future to make it practical, it seems important at any rate to clear the analytical decks. In the first place, it is important to recognise that the feasibility and acceptability of a definition depend on the conformity to minimal justice not only of what the definition inculpates, but also of what it exculpates. Power may become tyrannous not only by sanctifying and protecting what should be branded as "aggression", but also by branding as "aggression" what moral judgment denies to be such. Using these as poles of reference, the following seems a rational account of the alternatives analytically available.

First, definition may provide exhaustively inculpating determinations, declaring certain precisely defined acts, and only them, to be aggression, open neither at the inculpating or the exculpating end. Such, as we understand it, was the original Soviet draft of 1933. No State known to the writer now favours definition of this kind. Second, a definition may include inculpating determinations of the above nature which do not purport to be exhaustive, that is which are still left open at the inculpating end, for the responsible organ to characterise as "aggression" new forms of activity not enumerated. This is the form which Soviet drafts have recently assumed; though it is to be added that insofar as the Soviet draft was intended only for the Security Council, the Great Power veto would make the inculpation of new activities impossible unless it suited the interest of each Great Power, including, of course, the Soviet Union.[31] This form of definition, in short,

30 These difficulties are rather lightly ignored by M. Morozov (U.S.S.R.) when he insists that "in the sphere of municipal law people did not usually object to defining murder or manslaughter for the reason that a definition might on occasions prove insufficient or unjust; they put their trust in the skill of the draftsmen and the wisdom of the courts". (A/AC.77/SR.10, p.4.)

31 With great clarity, though with the sincere unconsciousness with which we must credit a colleague, Mitchell Franklin . (. . . The Conception of Aggression (*sine anno*, apparently 1952) displays the ulterior motivations which may lie behind the Soviet definitional campaign. While denouncing all and sundry who do not accept the Soviet plan of definition, he is no less hostile to conferring any power to apply the definition on any organ except the Security Council, where, of course, the Soviet veto is available. The supposed clear Soviet definition would be subject to Soviet interpretation, both as to what it excluded and what it included. The greater inhibitions of the Western Permanent Members in relation to the interpretation of their obligations would also be likely to work to Soviet advantage. It would be the plainest folly to leave out of these debates this differential effect of the same definition on the freedom of action of

is especially likely to be motivated by the self-regarding political interests of a Great Power proponent.[32] Third, a definition may include exhaustively inculpating determinations as well as (non-exhaustively) exculpating determinations.[33] In all these three cases, the more precision there is in the inculpating determinations, the less power is left to the organ, and the more chance there is that innocent acts in uncontemplated situations will *prima facie* be unjustly branded as aggression.[34] The more precision there is in the exculpating determinations, the less power in the organ, and this time the more likely that ingenious aggressors will use them as a cover for new forms of aggression.[35]

It is these considerations which suggest, fourth, a kind of "definition" in which both the inculpating and the exculpation determinations are inex-

---

opinion, and to that supposed entity which President Eisenhower has termed "the decent opinions of mankind". See on this aspect, the thesis (even if it is somewhat overstated) of J. Poniatowski, "War and Aggression in Western Eyes" (1953) 6 *Eastern Q.* 27ff. And see *supra* pp.2-3,21,38,67, and *infra* Chs. 5,6 esp. p.114, on the overt double talk involved even in Soviet legal use of such terms as "aggression", "peace-loving", etc.

Cf. also Professor Franklin's enthusiasm for the Soviet definition (17 and *passim*) with his apology (9) for the Soviet refusal to supply the Nuremberg Tribunal with its definition (see *infra* Ch. 8, s.I), and with his absolute insistence on the exclusive competence of the Security Council, and on the Great Power veto (22-23).

Contrast also his somewhat unrestrained criticism of the thesis of Professor M. S. McDougal and Dr. Oscar Schachter as to the need for flexibility in application of the United Nations Charter (M. S. McDougal and R. Gardner, "The Veto and the Charter . . ." (1951) 60 *Yale L.J.* 258, 263; and O. Schachter, Book Review, *id.* 189, 193), with his own rather inconsistent defence of the Soviet definition against the charge of overrigidity, on the ground that any shortcomings in the definition could be made good by "analogical" development (17) of the definition by the Security Council, proceeding on "the richest history of legal method" of "Romanist training". (19-20.)

32 This may be the correct light in which to understand the sharp Soviet reaction to the Philippine suggestion (A/AC.77/SR.1, p.10, and SR.2, p.4) that "nothing in the definition would prevent the Security Council from dealing with the cases enumerated in the relevant provisions of the Charter in the manner it deemed proper in the circumstances". The Soviet representative retorted that there would be no point in working out a definition if its efficacy was to be destroyed by such a reservation. (A/AC.77/SR.3, p.9, and *1956 Sp.Com.Rep.* 14.) The veto power still permits the Soviet Union to prevent any addition in a given situation to the list of acts of aggression which it has initially selected. If State A reacts by one of the listed acts to a provocation by State B, then even though all other members of the Security Council were agreed that in the given situation it was State B that had committed the first "act of aggression", State A would still be left under the Soviet definition guilty of aggression. This is why, as the U.S. delegation has pointed out, the Soviet definition might make it impossible in a given case to brand the real aggressor as an aggressor, and involve branding the State acting in self-defence as an aggressor. *Cf.* the warning of M. Mufti (Syria) in A/AC.77/SR.13, p.9 against the effect of "over-defining the concept of self-defence". At the least, all this would put powerful weapons of political warfare in Soviet hands; and possibly more serious weapons as well. The Soviet Union's comparative lack of any inhibitions in use of the veto scarcely needs underlining in this regard; and it can certainly be assumed that any discretion left to the Security Council could never be used in a way which the Soviet Union disapproved.

33 The exculpating determinations may of course be either exhaustive or not. Logically this is merely the first category above, with matters of exculpation allowed for. On the meaning of "inculpating" and "exculpating" see *supra* Ch. 4, s.V.

34 *Cf.* Mr. Sanders (U.S.) (A/AC.77/SR.5, p.6). ". . . A definition . . . which had the effect of impairing the right of self-defence . . . by handicapping the Member State which might be the object of an armed attack, might even be an incentive to aggression. . . ." A definition of aggression, he added, should not be such as to encourage governments to ignore certain elements of the situation.

35 *Cf.* the U.S. representative's stress on the difficulty of putting into words something that was so dependent on circumstances, and that it did not escape this difficulty

haustive, leaving room for the law-applying organs to declare facts to constitute aggression which do not *prima facie* fall within the definition, as well as to declare facts to be not aggression which *prima facie* fall within it. In this type, discretional power is left to the organ concerned at both the inculpating and exculpating ends, additional to the power of subsumption, to condemn or exonerate in the light of all the circumstances of the particular affair.[36]

It must be stressed, however, that the scope of free appreciation left to the organ is not a function merely of which of these types of formulation is adopted; it is equally and concurrently a function of the degree of precision and determinacy of the terms used in the respective definitions. The more precision and determinacy in these, the greater the danger of guilty acts being exonerated, and the greater the danger of innocent acts being branded. Draftsmen must calculate on both levels. Moreover, *mutatis mutandis* all of the above observations apply equally to "general and abstract" as well as to "enumerative"[37] or "mixed" or "combined" definition, or to what I have above termed definition by "elements" as well as by enumerative "criteria".

The further distinction should perhaps be added that where definition is left open at the inculpating or exculpating ends or at both, provision may be made or may already exist for some person or organ to exercise the resultant power to inculpate or exculpate in the area left open. On the other hand where in such a definition no provision is made for such a competence, there will necessarily exist *"rechtsfreier Raum"*[38] in relation to the question of aggression in many cases.

VI. CENTRAL DIFFICULTIES OF "LEGAL" DEFINITION.

So far as the exigencies of logical structure are concerned, nothing im-

---

to say that any definition must, of course, be interpreted and applied in the light of the circumstances as a whole. Since each threat of aggression varied in its history and its facts in an infinite number of ways, it taxed human ingenuity and wisdom beyond reasonable limits to evolve a formula which would anticipate events and provide useful guidance. (See generally A/AC.77/SR.13, pp.3-8, and *1956 Sp.Com.Rep.* 12.

[36] The discretion here in question relates to the fixing of the conditions of legal liability not to subsumption of facts under these conditions. It is what Karl Engisch calls a *Tatbestandsermessen* (see K. Engisch, *Einführung in das juristische Denken* (1956) 116ff.). Thus, Mr. Serrano (Philippines) (A/AC.77/SR.2, p.4) thought that: "A saving clause explicitly giving the Security Council a free hand in dealing with each particular case on its merits would eliminate the dangers seen by some delegations in the enumeration of types and examples of aggression, and should be acceptable even to those who questioned the desirability of a definition."

This theoretical openness at either end is still affected, as the U.S. delegate pointed out in 1956, by psychological hazards that what was included or left out of the enumerations would create in the applying organs a false impression of hierarchy of importance which might produce delay or error in decision. (A/AC.77/SR.13, p.7, and SR.17, pp.3-4). *Cf.* the virtually identical U.K. view, A/AC.77/SR.6, pp.7-8, and SR.16, p.3, and *1956 Sp.Com.Rep.* 18.

So also *cf.* as to the Iran-Panama proposal (A/AC.77/L.9), the U.S. delegate's comments at A/AC.77/SR.13, p.6 and *1956 Sp.Com.Rep.* 20-21.

[37] It may be pointed out that if determinations are made by way of exhaustive enumeration, it follows *ex contrario* that any situations not listed (whatever appearance they may present in the full context of crisis) do not constitute aggresssion.

[38] Karl Engisch, *op.cit.* 24, 136, 138.

pedes the successful definition of aggression. Much current and future discussion might, we venture to believe, gain in clarity and purposiveness by reference to the discriminations above indicated, and by a more careful use of terms by reference to them. Yet we should still hasten to remind ourselves that what hinder the achievement of a "feasible" and "acceptable" definition are considerations of quite a different and more intractable order than those of language and logical structure. These graver obstacles arise from the compulsive need to build into a "feasible", "acceptable" and "desirable" definition of aggression, by way of a limiting concept, some kind of minimal substitute for the frequent lack in international law of any effective non-forcible redress for violations of legal rights, as well as of any means of legislative adjustment of the deepest conflicts of interests. The difficulties, in short, are primarily ethical, political and sociological, not logical.[39] For facing these difficulties the logical features of various offered definitions of aggression are merely instrumental; they may help or hinder solutions, or they may do neither. If, however, we do not remain conscious of these more basic difficulties, the search for a definition which is logically structured, as well as "feasible", "acceptable" and "desirable", will but continue its vain and endless course.[40]

---

[39] H. Lauterpacht's view ("The Pact of Paris and the Budapest Articles of Interpretation" (1935) 20 *Trans. Grotius Soc.* 178, at 200ff.) that international lawyers should pay less attention to somewhat ingeniously devised possibilities showing the difficulties of a definition, and rather help to frame a definition of aggression "so as to provide, as far as the nature of that task permits, for unforeseen contingencies, including the unavoidable residuum of discretion for the adjudicating agency", involves for this reason over-simplification of the problem. The "nature of the task" may not permit *any* progress with merely lawyers' tools. And see the Soviet endorsement of Professor Lauterpacht's position, in A/AC.77/SR.10, pp.3-4. So also it is far less than half the truth to say with M. de la Colina (Mexico) (A/AC.77/SR.16, p.11) "that the confusion and the tragic errors which the world was witnessing were in part due to the absence of such a definition", and that countries which lacked substantial economic and military means placed their only hope in the triumph of law. The lack of definition may proceed from the very same source as do "the confusion and tragic errors", rather than *be that* source. "The triumph of law" thus hoped for can probably only come from changes in the relations of States far transcending the devising of even the most ingenious definition of "aggression". See *infra* Chs. 7 and 9 *passim*.

So *cf.* H. Lauterpacht, article cited at 190: "The inconsistencies and shortcomings of international law cannot be removed by juristic effort, however well-meaning. They are the manifestations of the will of the still paramount power of State sovereignty. Only this will, aided by such assistance as lawyers can legitimately give it, can provide the remedy." We would respectfully add, however, that if we are to make progress in thought we must push analysis behind the symbol of sovereign will to the ethical and sociological components of the notion which dictate the obstinacy of that will. Failure in this led Professor Lauterpacht in the very same article (20) to suggest that, on this very matter of the definition of aggression, "the piling up of objections by international lawyers", and their failure to "help" in forming a definition, were the reason for lack of progress. Twenty-two years have now passed without serious advance, and we doubt whether it could be said that the lawyers have failed to contribute what they could. Is it not time to face the facts?

[40] While therefore it solves no problems to conclude as does R. Théry, *"La Notion d'Agression . . ."* (1937) 239, that "aggression is a constraint *unduly* exercised by one State on the person of another", it does, at any rate, prevent us from overlooking the main problem.

CHAPTER 5

AGGRESSION AND THE CHARTER

THE LEGAL SETTING

I. PROHIBITION OF FORCE IN THE CHARTER.

We have lingered somewhat on the history of our subject because of a profound conviction that on the great issues of men's social and political lives we break, only at our peril, the continuity of human experience — whether experience of failure or experience of success.

In the League of Nations, as in the United Nations, the projected system of peace enforcement did not centre on the concept of aggression. The failure of this concept, despite the great attention devoted to it, to assume this role under the League or to attain the clear definition deemed necessary for this purpose, was a lesson open for the draftsmen of the United Nations Charter to read. They did in fact read the lesson; and as the Charter came from their hands the full plenitude of peace enforcement powers of the Security Council arose on any threat to the peace or breach of the peace, whether or not aggression was present. The Charter scheme of security did not require for its working even the invocation, let alone the definition, of the long-troubled concept of aggression; its possible value for the subsidiary purpose of graduation of measures has also proved quite unreal in the existing state of collective security. The view here held, that the attempt at advance definition of "aggression" is a gratuitous embarrassment of the immediate tasks of collective peace enforcement, has also been seen to receive some support from the negligible number of crises in which the concept has ever been of real assistance to peace enforcement organs either of the League or the United Nations.[1]

Persistence of demands to centre peace enforcement on the notion of aggression, and in the search for precise advance criteria of aggression, seems to have been mainly inspired by the attempt after 1950 to substitute for the Charter scheme of the Security Council's binding legal powers of peace enforcement, a system of voluntary cooperation of Members under the Uniting for Peace Resolutions of the General Assembly.[2] This is how we should understand, it is believed, the view expressed by Quincy Wright that peace enforcement may depend on giving to the "aggression" notion such agreed criteria as will reassure the great majority of States that any State declared to be an "aggressor" will be not only a "law-breaker", but also a "political menace". Only as it were, on such a basis, could there be aroused the sense of injustice and indignation necessary to ensure that voluntary cooperation

---

[1] See *supra* Ch. 1, s.IV, and Chs. 2-3 *passim*.

[2] We assume here the analysis of the status of this action in Stone, *Conflict* 266-281. And see also *supra* and *infra* Ch. 9, s.IV, and the Discourse.

of Members necessary to make the General Assembly system work in time of crisis. And it is here, of course, that the central difficulty arises. Assurance that the desired sense of indignation will be aroused among States generally presupposes that a judgment of "aggression" in the particular case would not conflict with a judgment of at least minimal justice as between the States in conflict. Such consistency could only be fully assured if account is taken of the *causes* of resort to force in the instant case, by reference to some standard such as justice or legitimate defence or defence of rights. Obviously, to apply such standards, all kinds of relevant factors, legal, military, psychological, procedural or other would have to be weighed in the full context of the crisis. Yet the long tortuous story of efforts to define aggression is that of a search for simple tests which will avoid this need to judge the justice of the *casus belli* of the respective States.

Many of the old debates have continued inconclusively into the General Assembly's search of the present day for advance criteria that are *both* morally convincing, *and* capable of quasi-automatic future application. The limited success of this search for short cuts still seems to bring our generation back to the longer and more arduous judgment calling for the weighing of all the facts of the situation as it appeared or reasonably should have appeared at the moment of crisis, involving inquiries as broad as the "justice" of the respective causes, and therefore leaving the notion of aggression undefined for unique application to each case.

The most powerful *legal* argument which is offered in support of the desire to insulate the question of aggression, from this critical question of the justice or injustice of the *casus belli* of the Parties, is that international law, as developed in the Charter of the United Nations, prohibits the threat of force, or resort to force with only two present exceptions, namely, force used in self-defence against armed attack under Article 51, or under authority of the United Nations.[3]

---

[3] It scarcely needs observation in the text that it is in any case not the incidental breach of any obligation which can give rise to a charge of aggression, but only breach of an obligation not to resort to force; at the very least (though the least may not be sufficient) there cannot be an aggression unless there is an antecedent obligation not to resort to force. So *cf.* Q. Wright, "The Concept of Aggression in International Law" (1935) 29 *A.J.I.L.* 373, 375, who points out that "A State's refusal to submit a dispute to arbitration or to carry out an arbitral award in the teeth of an explicit treaty obligation, while a breach of international law, is not necessarily a case of aggression", and that even resort to force thereafter would not be aggression unless there was such an applicable antecedent legal obligation to refrain from force. (See *id.* 376.) This is also the only contribution of Harvard Research, *Aggression,* to the precise problem of *definition* of aggression. See Art. 1 (c) and pp.871,876, putting aside all other issues. *Cf.* as to the irrelevance of degree of military efficiency, or respect for the laws of war, by each party, Q. Wright, *op.cit.* 381.

C. A. Pompe (*Aggressive War* 97, 113) would make a further distinction within this criterion, of resort to force in violation of an obligation not to do so, by saying that even such resort to force will be "aggression" only when it leaves the victim State no choice except military means to preserve its territorial integrity or political independence, or has a corresponding effect on an international territorial regime. Other resorts to force against territory or independence would be merely "illegal" and not "aggression". This type of test continues, in the present view, to overlook the really intransigent elements in the problem of definition. It was attempted, in vain, to be adapted by M. Röling into the definition of "armed attack" which he offered at the 1956 Special

According to this argument the Charter imposes upon a wronged State, be its wrongs ever so grave and threatening to its survival, so long as it is not actually subject to armed attack, the absolute duty to refrain from threat or use of force. It is argued that, except as against an actual armed attack, the State is forbidden to resort to force for the vindication of its rights and interests, and this even though neither international law nor the Charter offer it any alternative effective means of vindication. Theoretically, on some views, the Security Council might by due decision secure adjustment necessary to remedy grievances; and if this were also the actual position an absolute prohibition of resort to forceful self-help by individual States would make sense. In fact, of course, for reasons too notorious to retail, this theoretical process of the collective righting of wrongs does not work.

This, surely, is an essential if dispiriting approach to the tangled questions of Charter interpretation touching the scope of the prohibition of threat or use of force. But before taking it, we must interpose this further preliminary point: Even if the view of Article 2 paragraph 4, most restrictive of the use of force for the righting of wrongs is correct, it does not follow that a prohibited resort to force would necessarily constitute "aggression", as that notion has been under discussion since the 1920's. Whether a particular resort would be "aggression" (as the United States delegate, Mr. Sanders, recently pointed out to the Special Committee) would be still a different question, the answer to which would depend on the still unclear results of the debate on that notion.[4]

II. TEXTUAL BASIS OF THE PROHIBITION.

The extreme view of the scope of the prohibition of legal resort to force under the Charter is centred on Article 2 (3) and Article 2 (4), and asserts that those provisions, in their relation with other parts of the Charter, forbid all such resort with only two exceptions. One is for collective or individual self-defence against armed attack on a Member within Article 51

Committee. See *supra* Ch. 3. It is agreed, however, that "illegal" war and "aggressive" war are not the same thing.

It may be added that Mr. Pompe's assertion (113) that even "all non-violent actions against the territory or independence of a State" are illegal under the Charter is a dubious variation of the extreme view criticised in the text.

[4] And see further *supra* n.3, *infra* n.13 on this distinction. With respect, a similar comment is to be made on Professor Lauterpacht's unusual impatience (see *infra* Ch. 8, n.53) with those of his colleagues who have refused to say that all illegal war is a crime by the State and its human agents. His condemnation of his colleagues as worse even than *Begriffsjuristen,* because they will not take this step in sweeping deduction, is the more notable since he himself observes three pages later in the very same article, that in a "defective legal system" like international law "the maxim *ex injuria jus non oritur* often yields to the rival principle, *ex factis jus oritur.*" See *op.cit.* at 212.

For a recent straight assertion of the extreme view see the position of Soviet delegate M. Morozov on the 1956 Committee (A/AC.77/SR.10, pp.3ff.) who asserted that there was in this regard a "fundamental difference" from the League of Nations. A view no different, however, was taken by G. Scelle under the League Covenant, as under the United Nations Charter. See the citations to his views and those of M. Pella, M. Alfaro, and other exponents of the extreme view, in some form or other, in the Introd., *supra.* And see also *infra* nn.10,17, on M. Scelle's position, and on that of the U.S. delegate, Mr. Sanders, *infra* n.13. On Q. Wright's recent position see *infra* n.23.

of the Charter; the other is for collective action pursuant to competent decisions of the United Nations organs. These apart, the extreme view asserts that resort to force by a Member is unlawful, regardless of any wrongs or dangers which provoked it, and that if no collective United Nations relief is available, the Member may still have to submit indefinitely without redress to the continuance of these wrongs and dangers.

The first observation called for by this extreme view is that it does not spring self-evidently from the relevant provisions of the Charter. Article 2 (4) does *not* forbid "the threat or use of force" *simpliciter;* it forbids it only when directed "against the territorial integrity or political independence of any State, or in any other manner inconsistent with the purposes of the United Nations".[5] By the preceding paragraph 3 of Article 2, Members also undertook to "settle their international disputes by peaceful means in such a manner that international peace and security, and justice, are not endangered". But the suggestion that this positive injunction of Article 2 (3) to settle disputes by peaceful means carries with it so revolutionary a negative implication as the absolute prohibition of the use of force for the vindication of rights, even when no other means exists, is also dubious. For, in the first place, if Article 2 (3) really imported such a blanket prohibition of the use of force, why should the draftsmen have felt it necessary to follow it immediately with a very much more limited prohibition, in Article 2 (4), of the use of force against the "territorial integrity and political independence of any State, etc."?[6] Moreover, in the second place, it is not easy to reconcile the blanket prohibition with the words "and justice" in Article 2 (3).

Other provisions of the Charter, often vouched for the extreme view, also seem to us to leave the matter in debate. In the Preamble, for instance, the determination "to save succeeding generations from the scourge of war" is coupled with that of establishing "conditions under which justice and respect for the obligations" arising under international law can be maintained.[7] The hope of assuring "by the acceptance of principles and the institution of

---

[5] It is a matter of surprise that the precise provisions of Art. 2 (4) are so often quite overlooked by learned advocates of the extreme view. See e.g. R. J. Alfaro, *"La Question de la Définition de l'Agression"* (1951) 29 *R.D.I.* 367, 374, following G. Scelle, article cited (1954) 63 *R.G.D.Int.P.* 5-22, *passim.* There is frequently a similar chronic inadvertence to the exact terms of and reservations to the Kellogg-Briand Pact, and other relevant instruments. See *supra* pp.32-33. Yet if the position of these writers (see e.g. Alfaro, at 380 and Scelle, *passim*) be correct, that the licence to make war under customary international law no longer exists, this must turn on the operative terms of instruments or related acts which have (in part or in whole) abolished it. No omnibus inference can be drawn from the judgment of the Nuremberg Tribunal except as to "aggressive" war. And the very question still under debate is precisely the penumbral extent of that notion. Unless such questions are begged it is impossible to assert positively as does M. Alfaro (375) that "legitimate defence" can today only arise in answer to armed attack, i.e. under Art. 51. Art. 51 saves self-defence when inconsistent with other Charter provisions: it says nothing about self-defence when no breach of other Charter provisions is involved. See for fuller discussion of this basic matter, Stone, *Conflict* 243-46. And see *infra* n.11.

[6] Many writers who rely on this negative implication from Art. 2 (3) show but little awareness of this difficulty. See R. J. Alfaro, article cited, at 374.

[7] So *cf.* for some curiously parallel problems under the League of Nations Covenant, Sir John Fischer Williams, *Some Aspects of the Covenant of the League of Nations*

methods, that armed force shall not be used, save in the common interest", still leaves to be answered what is in "the common interest", and in particular, what is to be the position of wronged States when the collective means of determining and assuring this common interest do not work.[8] It again reinforces, moreover, the organic dependence of any renunciation of individual force in the Charter, on the effective establishment of collective institutions and methods; and this has not, of course, occurred.

As to the Purposes of the United Nations with which resort to force must not under Article 2 (4) conflict, these are of course expressed in Article 1. But when we look at Article 1, it is by no means certain that it imports legal obligations for Member States at all, as distinct from setting out the purposes of the United Nations as an Organisation. But even if that Article did clearly import obligations on Members, what are those obligations? So far as relevant they are to take effective collective measures for the prevention and removal of threats to peace and for suppression of acts of aggression and other breaches of the peace, and to bring about by peaceful means, and in conformity with the principles of justice and international law, adjustment or settlement of international disputes or situations, etc. Here again any implied prohibition on Members to use force seems conditioned on the assumption that effective collective measures can be taken under the Charter to bring about adjustment or settlement "in conformity with the principles of justice and international law".[7a] It is certainly not self-evident what obligations (if any) are imported where *no* such effective collective measures are available for the remedy of just grievances.

Moreover, the relation of the generalities of the Preamble and of Articles 1-2 to the more specific provisions of Chapters 6 and 7, raises still other doubts as to the extreme view of Article 2 (4).[8] The powers of recommenda-

---

(1934) 118ff., where it is observed that "aggression implies a moral stigma", and that in the light of the Covenant Preamble "aggression" must in some way or other be contrary either to the "maintenance of justice" or to "a scrupulous respect for all treaty obligations", and that the really difficult cases arose where one desideratum involved, in the particular case, the denial of the other.

The more extreme view of the League Covenant, opposed to this, has been considered at length in Introduction *passim*. And see also the similar views of the Covenant taken by MM. Politis and Litvinov quoted in the Secretary-General's Report, *U.N.Doc.* A/2211, pp.65-66. Notice especially the relentless logicism of the Politis position.

7a For clear evidence of this conditioning, see *supra* p.42, n.7.

8 The questions both of the legal effect of phrases from the Preamble taken out of context and of the meaning of "the common interest", are occasionally nicely begged in the recent General Assembly discussions on the Middle East. M. Carabajal-Victorica (Uruguay), for example, said that the preambulatory words that "armed force shall not be used, save in the common interest" was "the spiritual key" to the interpretation of the Charter, "except when it is in contradiction with legal criteria". The delegate seemed to assume that by rejecting as "barbarous" the idea that force can override legal commitments, he automatically established that all force for self-redress must be prohibited. Nor did he clearly distinguish self-redress from self-defence. But international law proceeds on the *tertium quid,* namely that the scope of the prohibition turns on the operative words of the Charter in their context. (A/PV.651, Feb. 2, 1957, p.21.) The *non sequitur* is similar to that in G. Scelle, *"Quelques Réflexions sur l'Abolition de la Compétence de Guerre"* (1954) 58 *R.G.D.Int.P.*5, at 11, and Mr. Walker (Australia) *G.A.O.R.* F.E.S.S., 567th Plenary Meeting, Nov. 3, 1956, p.114, para. 116. Contrast the view of M. Schurmann (Netherlands) *G.A.O.R.* F.E.S.S., 563rd Plenary Meeting, Nov. 3, 1956, p.49, para. 47.

tion, determination and decision of the Security Council under Chapters 6 and 7, and the obligations of Members to accept and carry out these decisions under Articles 2 (5) and 25, are the theoretical means of remedying injustices by that proper collective adjustment which would make feasible the extreme view of the prohibition of use of force under Article 2 (4). To assume that this extreme view can be constructed on the early generalities of the Charter *regardless* of whether the machinery for adjustment works or has any prospect of working, is to leave the so-called community of States in a very odd position. Members would be required to submit abjectly and without respite to any and all wrongs which do not involve "armed attack on a Member" within Article 51. Before Italy became a Member of the United Nations, for example, this extreme view (if carried through) would have forbidden other Members of NATO to come to her aid if she had been subjected to armed attack by the Soviet Union.

We do not deny that, *as a matter of exegesis,* the extreme view of the prohibition of force in Article 2 (4) is possible.[8a] We *do* question whether, even in terms of exegesis, it is the *only possible,* or even the more likely view; and whether in the light of the absurdities and injustice to which it would lead, it must not be regarded as an incorrect one. We are also concerned to point out that if such an extraordinary effect is sought to be given to some generalities in the Charter, the inconsistency of this effect with other generalities should be recognised. We refer, in particular, to the steady and repeated stress on the requirements of justice, on respect for the obligations of treaties and international law, and on the principle of "the sovereign equality of all its Members". It would be a strange application of such principles to require law-abiding Members of the Organisation to submit indefinitely to admitted and persistent violations of rights.

We are aware, of course, of the very substantial support thought to be drawn by the holders of the more extreme view from the *travaux préparatoires* of the San Francisco Conference relating to Article 2 (4).[9] It is clear that in the Report of Committee I to Commission I it was affirmed that under Article 2 (4) "the unilateral use of force or similar coercive measures is not authorised or admitted", and that "the use of force . . . remains legitimate only to back up the decisions of the Organisation, etc.". Even here, however, inferences must be drawn with care. For, first, the Committee itself reported that "the use of arms in legitimate self-defence remains admitted and unimpaired", using a formula which, in debates of the 'thirties,[10]

[8a] For other examples both of the invocation and rejection of the extreme view by States supporting the Assembly recommendations during the recent crisis, see *infra* Ch. 9, nn.16ff.

[9] See 6 *U.N.C.I.O. Docs.* 304, 334, 459.

[10] And (we may add) in continuing current usage; see e.g., G. A. Podrea, *"L'Agression . . ."* (1952) 30 *R.D.I.* 367, 368-69, B.V.A. Röling, "On Aggression . . ." (1955) 2 *Nederlands T.Int.R.* 167, 181. And see Podrea's article also on the relation of the self-defence to the provocation concept. For an illustration of the awareness of a sophisticated mind of the inextricable value element which links both these concepts with the exigencies of minimal justice see K. Tanaka, "Peace and Justice" (1952) 2 *Catholic University of America Law Review* 70-74; "To neglect self-defence . . . amounts to passive cooperation with the forces operating to destroy the order of the whole world. . . . Peace must essentially be founded on justice and common weal." (Mr. Tanaka

certainly has a meaning wider than the limited notion of defence against "armed attack against a Member" now embodied in Article 51.[11] And, second, the Committee Report itself obviously proceeded on the assumption (which has thus far proved vain) that the Organisation would be in a position to take effective action for the relief of serious grievances.[12]

III. ABSURDITIES OF THE EXTREME INTERPRETATION.

It has been submitted, therefore, that the extreme view of Article 2 (4) prohibiting resort to force by States for the vindication of their rights, save in reaction to armed attack or pursuant to collective decisions, is neither self-evident nor even beyond reasonable doubt in the whole context of the Charter.[13] These doubts on grounds of exegesis are (as we have shown) powerfully reinforced by the persistent illegality and injustice which the

---

is Chief Justice of the Supreme Court of Japan.)

The effort of Professor Scelle, and other writers (see e.g. *supra* Introd., *passim*) to divert the term "legitimate self-defence" to the more precisely defined area of self-defence which they seek to have established as law, is noted. History does not, however, support this usage, nor (as has been several times observed) does the sincere idealism and rigid logicism of their position establish it as international law. See *supra* pp.74-76.

[11] Due recollection of this historical truism in interpreting the *travaux* would avoid much perplexity. See e.g. the thesis of J. H. Quinn, *"Armed Attack" as Interpreted Chiefly by the United States* (1954) (MS. Paper, Harvard Law School Library) esp. at 5-6, that "if a State is in immediately impending danger of battery, should not the law as well as reason say that the State may resort to armed force to ward off the blow? It is difficult to believe that nations at San Francisco intended to give up this right". (20, and see 33 and *passim* on the relation of this to United States official views.) But he has difficulty in reconciling this with his recognition that "the draftsmen of the Charter wanted to avoid (in Art. 51) using a word with such ambiguous inferences as aggression in defining the circumstances under which a state has the right of self-defence" (6). But the point is that Art. 51 is only intended to save that part of the right of self-defence which would otherwise conflict with the Charter. As to the remaining range of the historically given licence of legitimate self-defence at customary international law, the *travaux* indicate that it was intended to be preserved so far as consistent with other provisions of the Charter. On this historically given range, see Giraud's capital survey of 1934. And see *supra* n.5.

[12] This torture of history by verbalism and logicism involved in the extreme view becomes even more extraordinary when it is argued (see e.g. D. W. Bowett, "Collective Self-Defence . . ." (1955-56) 32 *B.Y.B. Int.L.* 130, esp. 138, 159, 160) that the licence for "collective" self-defence does not arise even in case of armed attack on a Member, except for States which are themselves put under immediate self-defensive necessity by the attack—presumably have been "attacked" themselves (see 152-153), or after decision of the competent organ of the United Nations authorising it. It is perhaps characteristic that Mr. Bowett acknowledges (161) that even if his exegesis produces an impossible situation in the world as it is, we have still the alternatives of either depriving all States of their nuclear weapons, or creating a world federation.

[13] We leave aside the question which may well be one of mere terminology whether every resort to force in violation of an obligation to refrain therefrom is necessarily "aggression". See, on the one hand, Professor Wright, article cited (1935) 29 *A.J.I.L.* 373, who insists not only that "war resulting from the violation of an anti-war treaty is one form of aggression" but also that war contrary to obligations not to resort to force short of war, "as well as the use of armed violence contrary to such treaties" would be "aggression". (376.) And see *supra* nn.3-4.

See, on the other hand, the U.S. representative's criticism of the Chinese draft that it made explicit an assumption, which was also implicit in other definitions, which "equated aggression with illegality". It was not true that under the Charter everything illegal was, therefore, aggression, and the assumption that it was might be one reason for definitional difficulties. It was also, moreover, dangerous to suggest that what was not aggression was therefore not illegal. See A/AC.77/SR.13, pp. 6-7.

extreme view would require States to tolerate indefinitely. The only *legal* certainty in this area is, in the present opinion, that States have an obligation to desist from threat of war, breach of the peace, or act of aggression, once their conduct has been so characterised by the Security Council and decisions have been taken to bring an end thereto, and to carry out such decisions.[14] It is significant that, in the recent Suez crisis, there was neither a decision of the Security Council to this effect, nor did the General Assembly in its Resolution of November 1, 1956, seek to give any moral or legal characterisation *in terms of the Charter,* much less in terms of "aggression", to the conduct of either Israel or of Great Britain or France in the concrete circumstances in which they acted. And this is quite apart from the fact, as was shown in the writer's work on *Legal Controls of International Conflict,* that the binding force of General Assembly resolutions on Members who do not voluntarily accept them is in any case open within this whole area to the gravest doubt.[15]

The General Assembly's restraint, at any rate, seems eloquent of the soundness of the present thesis. Indeed, whatever view we take of the technical legal question, it is well to pause and consider how it would be if States were committed by Membership in the United Nations to submit in default of collective action, to all kinds of illegality, injustice and inhumanity as long as these do not take the specific form of an "armed attack" under Article 51. Suppose, for example, that a Great Power decided that the only way it could continue to control a satellite State was to wipe out the satellite's entire population and recolonise the area with "reliable" people. Suppose the satellite government agreed to this measure and established the necessary mass extermination apparatus for carrying out the plan. Would the rest of the Members of the United Nations be compelled to stand by and watch this operation merely because requisite decision of United Nations organs was blocked, and the operation did not involve an "armed attack" on any Member of the United Nations?[16] Or again suppose military intelligence at the Pentagon received indisputable evidence that a hostile State was poised to launch intercontinental ballistic missiles, at a fixed zero hour only 24 hours ahead, against New York, Boston and Washington, would it be an aggressor under the Charter if it refused to wait until those cities had received the missiles before it reacted by the use of force? We assume of course that it should exhaust its means of defence, and all means of aborting

---

14 *Cf.* H. Lauterpacht ("Limits . . . of the Law of War" (1953) 30 *B.Y.B. Int. L.* 206, 220) who points out that in view of the exclusive power of the Security Council to make a binding determination, "there may be no means, so long as the war lasts, by which an authoritative judgment can be arrived at on the question as to which belligerent side is the aggressor", and that where there is Great Power unanimity, extensive hostilities are in any case unlikely.

15 See citations *infra* Ch. 9.

16 *Cf.* the implications of W. E. Rappard, *The Quest for Peace . . .* (1954) 38, B. V. A. Röling ("On Aggression . . ." (1955) 2 *Nederlands T.Int.R.* 167, 176-77, that a main reason for questioning the extreme view of the prohibition of force under the Charter is that it would exclude the historical role of intervention on grounds of humanity in international law. We are not clear, however, that we understand the analogy to "*force majeure*" in this connection.

the attack by non-violent means: but *at a pinch,* if these cannot give it assurance, is it *bound by law to wait for its own destruction?* Such questions, we know, raise horrifying thoughts of preventive war, and its perils in our age: but the perils are there even if we do not ask the questions.[17]

Even if the grand design of the United Nations *was* to substitute collective peace enforcement and peaceful change for the traditional role of war as a means (in part at least) of vindicating rights, and effecting adjustment of the *status quo* so as to secure a tolerable level of justice, are we to say that resort to force has been completely outlawed, even when no substitute means of relief is available?[18] It is not believed that such a position makes either moral, political or even legal sense.[19] To take it would require us to say, even if the Egyptian nationalisation of the Canal were clearly illegal, and even if Egypt had deliberately barred all Western ships from passage through the Canal, and the Security Council had called on her in vain to desist, and even if enforcement action was blocked by the veto, and the requisite General Assembly authority not obtainable, it would still require

---

17 See *infra* Ch. 6, s.II. *Cf.* the question of Messrs. Maktos (U.S.) and van Glabbeke (Belgium) (quoted U.N.Doc.A/2211, paras. 392-93), whether the U.S., if it had had prior notice of an impending Japanese attack on Pearl Harbour, would have been an aggressor if it had first destroyed the Japanese forces destined to make the attack. And see *ibid.* for various positions on this matter. It is easy enough to assert with G. Scelle, as at 1936 (article cited *supra* p.000 at 387) that no threat or danger can possibly ground legitimate self-defence until "actual aggression" occurs, because preventive war cannot be legitimate. But under modern conditions we may yet have to distinguish between legitimate and illegitimate anticipatory self-defence. Contrast with Professor Scelle's position that of Professor Röling ("On Aggression . . ." (1955) 2 *Nederlands T.Int.R.* 167, 180-81). *Cf.* J. H. Quinn, *"Armed Attack" as Interpreted Chiefly by the United States* (1954), (MS. Paper, Harvard Law School Library). The Soviet Union has consistently denounced any suggestion that forceful measures taken against threatened attack could be self-defence (or conversely that threat of attack could constitute aggression). This view, even if it is based on principle, is also remarkably consistent with the Soviet's own interests—both as leaving it freer to engage in pressures such as those exerted from time to time against the satellites, and also as a means of discrediting the small but vocal body of American advocates of "preventive" action against the Soviet Union during the early post-war years.

18 We readily admit that it is *possible* to interpret these and similar references in the Charter to "justice", and "respect for the obligations" arising under international law, as meaning that these *should* be brought about by peaceful means, just as resort to force to bring them about *should not* be used. On all heads, however, the *legal* prescription of what is to be done in case the assumed obligations were not respected was left by the Charter to the vast powers conferred on the Security Council. The present problem arises because that legal prescription does not work; and the present view is that no dogmatic answer can be given to the question, What does the Charter prescribe *as a matter of legal obligation* when the collective legal powers for securing justice and respect for the obligations of international law, as well as for suppressing the use of force, simply do not work.

It is easy, of course, to adduce numerous speeches of delegates which in a rhetorical sense, or in support of a particular political position, express the view that the use of forceful self-redress, whatever the wrongs, is always forbidden, except under United Nations authority or by way of self-defence against armed attack. From a legal point of view they can scarcely be decisive. In the recent Middle East crisis no corporate action of the Assembly turned on any explicit finding that the use of force by Britain, France, and Israel violated any Charter obligation, much less that it constituted "aggression". We are aware, in saying this, that the Israeli position was easier to justify in terms of self-defence than that of Britain and France, but the restraint of the General Assembly on this point is the more significant by this fact.

19 Even writers who advocate the Scellian formula (see *supra* p.7) that "all resort

us to say—despite all this—that the States injured would nevertheless be violating the law, and even on some views were "aggressors" if they used force to vindicate their rights. In the current Soviet draft definition, indeed, they would be aggressors even if they used merely economic pressures. No international organisation based on such principles could long possibly survive in the world as it is, and as it is likely to be (we fear) for some considerable time. For such an organisation could only become a protective shield for those States whose predatory and imperial interests could sufficiently realise themselves without the need for "armed attack" upon other Members, and whose plaintive motto of self-assertion is, "This is a very wicked animal; when we attack it, it defends itself."[20] Such a principle would also be a denial of that essential reciprocity between States, without which the supposed rule of law and the principle of sovereign equality can be but the merest mockeries. Only if unredressed wrongs were exceptional between States, and could not threaten their very survival, and if the use of the decisive surprise thermo-nuclear attack were *effectively* proscribed, would the view make sense that military initiative is always the grave crime of aggression, and military passivity always righteous.[21]

IV. CONSEQUENCES OF ERRONEOUS BASIS OF GENERAL ASSEMBLY ACTION.

It may still, of course, be said that even if all this be granted on the strictly legal level, there have arisen since the Charter over-riding considerations in a time of thermo-nuclear weapons and international tension, requiring us to maintain the maximum barrier against armed action. And there is little doubt that the resultant fear of a chain reaction leading to world conflagration was (for example) the main factor in the catalysis of Assembly reaction to the Anglo-French intervention in the Canal Zone, as well as in the reaction to the Israeli action in Sinai. Nor does the present Writer disapprove of such catalysis of Assembly activity as such.

What is questioned is not the freedom and indeed duty of the General Assembly to make all efforts to stop any resort to force by seeking to rally the cooperation of its Members towards a peaceful adjustment of the conflict. It is rather the assumption that every such resort to force is necessarily illegal or even constitutes aggression, or that it must be so characterised if Members of the United Nations are to be given a sufficiently strong motivation for cooperative action to end the resort to force, under

to force equals war and that all war equals aggression", explicitly or implicitly recognise this truth (except as to the legal sense), but they do not draw the consequences in relation to their views about aggression. See e.g., V. V. Pella, *La Guerre-Crime* (1946) 46; P. Bastid in M. A. F. Frangulis, 3 *Dictionnaire Diplomatique, sub voce "Agresseur"*; Y. de la Brière, *ibid.;* R. J. Alfaro, *"La Question de la Définition de l'Agression"* (1951) 29 *R.D.I.* 367, 374; G. Scelle, *Quelques Réflexions . . .* (1954) 63 *R.G.D. Int.P.* 5, esp. 11-12. And see the Introd., *supra.*

20 Paul Bastid thus vastly understates the point when he admits that the extreme view which he adopts "protects . . . the existing *status quo*". See M. A. F. Frangulis, *op.cit. sub voce "Agression"*.

21 Professor Scelle admits (G. Scelle, *"Quelques Réflexions sur l'Abolition de la Compétence de Guerre"* (1954) 58 *R.G.D.Int.P.* 5 esp. 11-13) the deficiencies which would thus produce quite different effects in international society from those produced by the

guidance of General Assembly resolutions. We are in an age when, as recent events have shown, and as we shall later stress, general and intense anxiety concerning the spread of hostilities into thermo-nuclear war provides quite adequate motivation, without continuing on the hazardous and up to now barren quest to make salvation depend on an agreed and detailed advance definition of aggression. And, under present conditions, we may also have to question the wisdom of making even the *undefined* notion the basic concept in law enforcement.

Moreover, the difference between stating the Assembly's function in terms of ending a threat to or breach of the peace (on the one hand), and stating it (on the other) in terms of the suppression of aggression, is crucial in practice. It may make the difference between long term success or failure of the Assembly's work.

If the resort to force is always regarded as *per se* unlawful, or even as aggression, then the action taken by the Members to restore peace takes on automatically the aspect of punitive sanctions against the supposed culprit State, and protective action towards its supposed victim. The supposed culprit may be deemed legally bound to submit to the sanctions; and neither the General Assembly, nor the Members need go behind the resort to force to ask where, in reality, the responsibility lies for the rupture. Misled by this illusory notion they may feel a misplaced compulsion to recreate (under the slogan of "not rewarding an aggression") the very conditions which are widely acknowledged to have created the breach of the peace; under cover of restoring a *status iuris* they may restore a *status iniuriae*. On the other hand, if the resort to force is not to be regarded as always *per se* illegal, but as requiring cooperation to deal with a breach of the peace *simpliciter,* while the freedom of the General Assembly to rally the cooperation of Members to bring it to an end still exists, and the overriding motive of Members to cooperate also sufficiently arises, certain radically different implications also follow. For this basis of cooperative action implies also a clear freedom and duty on the part of States uniting for peace to ascertain where, in reality, the responsibility for the rupture lies, and to direct the pressure for corrective measures and undertakings simultaneously to both parties in proportion to the merits of their position, so as to minimise the risks of recurrence. This is very different from demanding unconditional obedience by one side to its recommendations, even when the almost certain effect will be to rekindle the flames of threat to the peace or breach of the peace.[22] And

---

public monopoly of force in stable municipal societies. He feels entitled, nevertheless, to ignore this difference on the theory that "positive international law" requires it. He has not, however, established any such rule of international law to a point of certainty on the texts which entitle him to choose an interpretation compelling such extraordinary results. Certainly the list of crimes drawn up by the International Law Commission which he invokes (11) gives no warrant for such a procedure. Nor can it improve this result that Professor Scelle is careful to say that his view implies that certain other conditions will come into existence, when these (e.g. general compulsory jurisdiction (12), and the creation of an effective supra-national force (13)) are unlikely to become feasible in any foreseeable future.

[22] The difference is even more dramatic where as in the Israel-Egypt affair of 1956-57 what is done is to demand that State A hand back to State B the precise localised

in the even longer range, we should remain intensely aware of the likelihood, if the minimal requirements of justice are thus overridden, that the mere repression of forceful self-redress will not avert an explosion but merely render it more inevitable and more disastrous when it comes.[23]

---

bases from which State B has for years carried on with impunity belligerent activities against the first State, and that it do so unconditionally without any undertaking being required from State B not to resume such belligerent activities.

Such a course could only be warranted on the assumption that the mere resort to force by Israel across the frontier constituted "aggression". The moral as well as the legal bases of this assumption remain, in the present view, dubious. Even our own well-tried criminal law imposes on the victim of violence (as Israel had admittedly been at Egypt's hand) neither the legal duty to let the attacker take good aim before he defends himself; nor the duty, if he succeeds in seizing the attacker's gun, to return it except to the police, or to the Court, or after the attacker has been bound over not to resume his deadly assault.

Washington's contrary stand on this point was the more puzzling since, at the very time when the Israeli-Egyptian hostilities were in progress, its representative on the 1956 Special Committee on the Definition of Aggression, was squarely rejecting a Soviet proposal which would *inter alia* declare as an "aggressor" the State which first invades the territory of another State by armed force. And the reason then given by the U.S. delegate, Mr. Sanders, is central to the present point. It was that such an invasion may, according to the circumstances, be either "aggression" or "self-defence".

23 *Cf.* the more general point made by the U.S. delegate that "wrong definition could do great harm. . . . A definition might have the effect of impairing the right of self-defence, and by curtailing the freedom of action of the State attacked, might even be an incentive to aggression. On the other hand, a party might be tempted, in case events occurred constituting acts of aggression under the terms of the definition, to take up arms without waiting for a decision by the Security Council." (A/AC.77/SR.5, pp.3ff., esp. 6-7; *cf.* SR.13, pp.3ff., and *1956 Sp.Com.Rep.* 12ff.)

In the light of the above analysis the recent thesis of Q. Wright ("Intervention, 1956" (1957) 51 *A.J.I.L.* 257) seems to be questionable in the following main respects: (1) The underlying assumption that the definitions he chooses have authority warranting his confident judgments (see esp. 269-270); (2) His reliance on three distinct definitions, from at least two of which (see 266, 270ff.) opposed conclusions seem to flow for the Middle East Crisis (see *supra* pp.68n., 84n., *infra* 106ff., 109n., 131n., 155ff., 161n., 217 for the present writer's criticisms of Wright's 1956 definition, *supra* pp.28n., 31ff. and 108ff. for criticism of his "cease-fire test", and *supra* p.93n., *infra* p.215 on the Harvard Research Draft); (3) His assertion, without attending to the difficulties (see *supra* pp.45-46, *infra* 153ff., 164ff., 176), that the General Assembly has power to "bind" States by its finding of "aggression"; (4) Relation of his argument to the fact that the General Assembly in the Suez Crisis made no finding of aggression or Charter breach (see *supra* pp.99, 100n., *infra* 157n.); (5) The interpretation of Arts. 2 (3) and (4) out of the full context of the Charter and the *travaux* (see *supra* pp. 41ff. esp. 42, n.7, 94ff., 97ff.); (6) His virtual reading (269) *out of* Art. 2 (4) of the words limiting the no-force obligation while reading such words (272) *into* Art. 51, thus limiting the self-defence licence and leading, with respect, to some of the absurdities noted *supra* pp.97ff., *infra* 108ff.; (7) The argument (in effect) that a State's use of armed force against e.g. purely economic rights of other States located within its territory, is a matter of "domestic jurisdiction" not restricted by the Charter (269, 272), seems inadvertent to Art. 2 (7) which preserves the Security Council's Chapter VII powers "to maintain or restore international peace and security."

CHAPTER 6

AGGRESSION AND POWER POLITICS

The Political Setting

I. VAIN ATTEMPTS TO ABOLISH POWER.

It may well be the very fact that the Charter's prohibition of the resort to force is far less sweeping than is usually assumed, which has contributed some of the sense of urgency recently surrounding the search for precise criteria for determining which resorts to force are "aggressive". And the chronic inability of States to reach any consensus on this matter may thus be eloquent not only of the difficulty of the task, but of the wishful optimism of those who think that clear legal obligations under the Charter inaugurated a new system of international law and order in which such questions could not arise.[1]

From this aspect, the search for precise criteria of the notion of "aggression" is a further phase in the attempt to escape the much maligned nineteenth century system of the balance of power. As such, the search centres on the moral *quality* of the use of State power, as distinct from the mere *quantity* of State power. The balance of power system was (and is) essentially quantitative in its approach to power and its exercise. The excessive concentration of power is conceived as a threat whether its control be in a conservative Britain dominant at sea, or in a Napoleonic France, an imperial or dictatorial Germany, dominant on land, or, as at present, in a United States, or a Soviet Union bidding for dominance in the air, on the sea and on land. The regrouping of States, in face of such excessive concentration, the moves to counterbalance one State's seizure of additional power, by compensating accretions of power to States thereby threatened, by establishing buffer zones against the expanding State, or by intervention against it through its clients—these are not conditioned on the quality of the conduct or purposes or ideals of the expanding State. Neither its democratic nor authoritarian government, nor its peaceful nor warlike traditions, nor devotion to "the rule of the law" in its internal social life, nor even the degree of "international understanding", nor even the legality, justice or morality of the particular State conduct, are *on this older theory* and its residual strains even today, decisive for international security.[2]

This kind of view of international security corresponds, of course, to the view of war taken by customary international law, leaving States virtually uninhibited as to the grounds of recourse to war for the protection of their self-determined interests.[3] And it is clear that the earlier phases

[1] See the Introd., *supra*.

[2] *Cf.* for fairly non-controversial assessments in this controversial field, Martin Wight, *Power Politics* (1946); Q. Wright, "The Prevention of Aggression" (1956) 50 *A.J.I.L.* 514, 517.

[3] Komarnicki (10, 12) sees the evolution from the Middle Ages to the beginning of that century as one towards this lack of inhibition and away from the older natural

of the effort to hem in this liberty by treaties, from the League Covenant onwards, are designed, by one course or another, to impose inhibitions additional to those inherent in the balance of power system.[4] The new inhibitions thus sought to be imposed are, it is clear, different from those inherent in the old system in the respect that they are to be *legal* inhibitions.

But the will to escape the anarchical consequences of power politics is one thing, the dream that somehow power can be abolished from that area of human life denoted as politics, is quite another. The control of power, that is of men's ability to act, whether by law or morality, is still a function of power in the same sense, as well as of ethics; just as power itself is in important part a function of the ethical convictions of those who act and of those affected by the action.[5] And this is true for the relations of the organised communities we call States, as well as for the relations of individuals, though there are vital differences in its application to which we shall have to advert from time to time. It remains essential, therefore, in seeking to control the anarchical manifestations of power politics, not to fall into the fallacy of wholly disparaging the role of the nineteenth century system. The psychological implications of that system have, it is true, made it almost disreputable to refer to it without words of blame. Yet we should resist the fashion, modelled on the dream work of our own age, of assuming that the operations of power for good or ill can be abolished by drafting the constitution of a world security organisation. Philosophically speaking, the concept of power is ethically neutral, and it remains in any kind of society a basic principle of social cohesion. It was no doubt, in the nineteenth century, a *bête noire* of weaker States and of dependent peoples, and had many other sins. That does not, however, justify identifying problems of power merely with the illegitimate manifestations of it. For such

---

law doctrine of "the just war". This is certainly so, at least in a doctrinal sense. (In practice the just war doctrine can scarcely be said to have established itself as operative law during this period.) This view represents a singular contrast, in terms of the correct interpretation of history, to the views of some of those who would enthrone the aggression concept and its definition as an inevitable product of the long unfolding story of human society.

See generally on the "just war" doctrine A. Wanderpol, *Le Droit de la Guerre Juste d'après les Théologiens et les Canonistes du Moyen-Âge* (1911); G. Salvioli, *Il Concetto della Guerra Giusta negli Scrittori anteriori a Grotius* (1915); J. von Elbe, "The Evolution of the Concept of Just War in International Law" (1939) 33 *A.J.I.L.* 665-688; J. L. Kunz, "*Bellum Justum* and *Bellum Legale*" (1951) 45 *A.J.I.L.* 528.

As Professor Kunz points out, insofar as the early doctrinal writing assumed that its principles bound the prince, it was "wholly an ethical [doctrine]". Insofar as the later doctrinal writers tried to make the doctrine more than a merely ethical one by asking who was to decide whether the war was *justum,* they came to say that each State must decide for itself, thus "deforming" the original doctrine, and (the present Writer would add) merging it gradually into the actual practice which left war within the licensed area so far as positive law was concerned.

4 *Cf.* in this context the thesis of C. A. Pompe, *Aggressive War* 39: "The addition of 'aggression' or 'aggressive' lifts the concept of war from the neutral field of pure fact and indicates an action and a responsible actor." So also he adds, "the complementary notion of 'defensive war' or 'war of defence', indicates the legal or moral position of one of the parties in the pre-classic terminology of just and unjust war . . .". And see Komarnicki, 14-15, who observes that it is only with the League Covenant that "there was born the question of aggression so far as it touches the legal order."

5 See the Chapter on "Power and the Complexity of Law" in Stone, *Province* 705-749.

naïveté easily overlooks those elements of statecraft in the nineteenth century system which led Alfred Zimmern to observe, in the days of the League,[6] that the path indicated by history was that by which "the Great Powers" must resume the role of "the Great Responsibles". It overlooks the important fact that it was the series of equilibrations produced by the statecraft of nineteenth century leaders which made possible, without any major war for a century, the emergence of the modern politico-economic and technological structure of the world, and the rise to self-help and self-assertion of the great peoples of Asia and Africa. It is neither necessary nor possible, in order to escape from its more evil consequences, for our age to plunge into a vacuum of statecraft. The neuroses, indeed, which produce this very escapism, and manifest themselves in monolithic ideologies of our time, may well be among the most evil of these consequences which now threaten us. In a deep sense the long vain search for a precise automatically operating definition of aggression is a product of these neuroses, an escape into fantasy from the hard tasks of statecraft.

As to *the need* for additional inhibitions to escape the anarchical consequences of power politics in an era when not even such giants as the Soviet Union and the United States dare to contemplate periodic thermonuclear Great Wars to adjust the balance of power, there can be no argument.[7] The difficulty begins, when, as now, the publicists and diplomats feel driven to try and define, in advance of the event and so as to allow automatic application, that quality of State conduct which is to be deemed aggressive. Professor Wright (we have seen) [8] urges that satisfactory criteria must test all proposed definitions by two main measuring rods. First, is the defined conduct such that any State which commits it will certainly have been guilty of acts which condemn it as a lawbreaker? Second, is the defined conduct so dangerous to the vital interests of these other States that they will immediately join in action to suppress it—as a political menace? So far, so good! But this stops short of two other crucial questions which (we believe) the leaders of a major State also ask, and may even have a duty to ask. One is whether the proposed definition would stigmatise as aggression, action which that State may in some yet unforeseen but not unforeseeable future circumstances feel justified and even compelled to take.

---

[6] See his *Europe in Convalescence* (1922) 123, 129, and his *League of Nations and the Rule of Law* (1936) 83-4.

[7] The only partial shift in the *general* usage of the term "aggression", away from the notion of morally neutral struggle is well pointed out by M. Sharp, "Aggression: A Study of Values and Law" (1947) 57 *Ethics,* Supp. who observes (1-2) that "we speak with approval of an aggressive suitor, worker, competitor, or fighter, so long as the fighter is on our side. In this sense non-aggressive war (*sic*) would be a contradiction in terms, yet we condemn what we are likely to call 'aggression' in warfare." It is implied in the former usage that aggression may be either constructive or destructive, its essence being moral persistence in a coherent course of behaviour against obstacles. The latter usage may arise as an effort to deal with "the form of destructive aggression which most threatens human health and perhaps human life—modern warfare" which, this writer observes, "may require for its control an effective tradition and technique of repression and policing by military agencies" (15).

[8] See *supra* Ch. 1, s.IV; Q. Wright, "The Prevention of Aggression" (1956) 50 *A.J.I.L.* 514, 517.

Another is whether the indirect effect of the definition is such as to grant an excessive licence for illegal and predatory activities by other States, by condemning as "aggression" the only kind of vindication of violated rights which may in fact be available.

It is at the point when these further questions are asked (as they undoubtedly are asked) that most States, and certainly all major States, are thrown back on the haunches of their "vital interests". At this point passionate declarations about "the crime of aggression" dissolve into endless disagreements as to exactly what "aggression" is.

The vital interests invoked are legally undefined, and may be undefinable; and there has been a long struggle to exorcise them from some fields of international law in which they once played a prominent role. Yet it remains true that preoccupation with them continues to limit, inspire and control the major policy decisions of many, if not most, foreign offices. (How, indeed, could it be otherwise?) This is an area in which, even in our transformed world, power politics still has its residues, good and evil, and very important ones. And the determination to defend those interests is still far from being contained, as the recent conduct of several Great Powers (and we do not mean merely Britain and France) reminds us, in any collective channels of third party process.[9] This, we suggest, and not any refinements of competing drafts, is a main reason why governments have not approached consensus on any precise advance legal definition of aggres-

---

9 There have, indeed, been few more dramatic illustrations of the impotence of high-sounding repudiation of power politics to vindicate itself against the realities of that process than the course taken by the U.S. Government in the Middle East crisis of 1956-57. In President Eisenhower's speech of Oct. 31, 1956 (*N.Y.T.*, Nov. 1, 1956, p.11), declaring that there was to be one "code" for the friends of the United States as well as for those opposed to her, and the subsequent policy of subordinating American policy to the vote of the General Assembly on the assumption that that body represented "the conscience of mankind", the United States appeared to be renouncing any effort to take account of the principles of power politics. In token of the repudiation it joined in dealing severe blows at the interests and power positions of its closest allies, weakening the whole structure of NATO, and as regards Australia and New Zealand, of SEATO as well.

Yet power politics immediately had its revenge. Within weeks of this defiance of its exigencies, the U.S. administration was pronouncing the Eisenhower Doctrine, for maintaining a permanent posture of American military and logistic preparedness in the Middle East, on the frankly avowed ground that this was necessitated by the destruction of British power in that area. Whatever else that Doctrine may be, it is clearly a manifestation of the U.S. Government's determination that, after the crippling blow which it had "on principle" delivered to the power of its allies in the Middle East, the wane of that power should not be allowed to become the occasion for uncontrolled extension of Soviet power there. The Doctrine indeed is openly based on the assertion that it is as against the extension of Soviet ("international communist") power that the protection of the independence of the Middle East is a "vital" United States interest. And in the movement of the Sixth Fleet on May 25, 1957, in the Jordanian crisis, this motivation was clear and was, as was to be expected, challenged by the Soviet Union as an "aggressive" action of the United States.

In the sweep of history it is rather likely that the recent crisis will take its place in the pattern of events made up of the British victory over Napoleon, the Franco-British alliance against Russian penetration in the Crimean War, manifest in the British struggle with France in Egypt and Disraeli's purchase of the controlling shares in the Suez Canal, the U.S.-U.K.-French Tripartite Declaration of 1950, and the breakthrough of Soviet influence in Egypt and Syria in 1955-56. It is rather unlikely (however devoutly we might wish the contrary) that it will figure as a staging-post towards a millennium

sion, even when they assert the urgency of attaining it.[10] And this failure, after all, merely exposes to view the deceptive indeterminacy as well of the notion of "aggression", as of the notion of a "political menace" by which it is sought to be clarified. We have already referred to the moral dubiety even of the notion of "law-breaking" as a test of aggression in a legal order which lacks any authoritative working institutions for collective redress of grievances or orderly legal change.

II. REPUGNANCY TO JUSTICE OF SIMPLE APPROACHES.

Certainly there is no sign of contemporary readiness of States to accept for the future, and *for themselves as well as for other States,* the simple test of compliance with a cease-fire order which has sometimes been suggested as an easy way out.[11] The staunchest protagonists of such tests have to admit that there is no necessary correspondence between the doing of even minimal justice between parties in conflict and the freezing of the line of battle, or even restoration of the military *status quo*.[12] Even in terms of conventional

---

in which peace and justice reign and from which power politics have been finally expelled, under the stable and effective aegis of the United Nations. And *cf.* the U.S. Note of Mar. 11, 1957, rejecting the Soviet proposals of Feb. 11, 1957, for a regime of Four Power surveillance of the Middle East, accompanied by withdrawal of bases and forces and of the Eisenhower Doctrine.

10 It may well be (as Professor Wright asserts (". . . Aggression" (1956) 50 *A.J.I.L.* at 519)) that traditional methods of alliances, tempered by traditional methods of peaceful settlement, cannot give us collective security, and that hopes for "peaceful change", as they affect claims which States deem vital, "prove illusive under conditions of power rivalry". But the main reason why they prove illusive is also a sufficient reason why definitions of aggression which would leave such claims exposed to illicit encroachment by other States simply cannot win acceptance by States. It is precisely for this reason, among others, that definitions such as the one Professor Wright proposes (see 526) have made no headway whatever. See Chs. 1, s.I,2, s.VII, and *infra* pp.132-133. *Cf.* C. A. W. Manning in Bourquin (ed.), *Collective Security* 337: "The difficulty is not . . . of arriving at a true definition: it is the political difficulty of agreeing on a conventional definition."

11 See e.g. Q. Wright, "The Concept of Aggression" (1935) 29 *A.J.I.L.* at 382ff., for the strongest plea for recognition of the cease-fire order as the focal point of the definition of aggression. (See esp. 395.) The structure of the United Nations and the growth of modern weapons have not improved the prospects of acceptance. And see *infra* Ch. 9.

12 For an interesting discussion of the question whether under the League Covenant a State occupying portions of another State, the latter having been the first attacker, could properly claim to retain that territory consistently with the guarantee of "territorial integrity" of members under Art. 10, see Sir J. Fischer Williams. . . . *Covenant* (1934) 121. Sir John gave an affirmative answer if the retainer was "desirable, in the general interest of the peace, order, and good government of the world", the attacker not being entitled to rely on Art. 10.

In the Egyptian-Israeli Affair of 1956-57 the unacceptability of the simple cease-fire test *as a test of aggression* was very clear. On a widely canvassed, but legally dubious view, Israel was requested to evacuate Gaza and Sharm el Sheikh in order to restore the *status iuris* so as to deny a supposed "aggressor" (though this itself was never determined by the General Assembly) the fruits of his "aggression". If, however, the facts ante-dating the Israeli invasion of Sinai were considered, the conclusion might well have been reached that Egypt herself was an "aggressor" in respect not only of her maintenance of a state of war, of belligerent acts against Israeli ships, her tolerance of hundreds of raids of armed bands from Gaza, not to speak of the economic boycott. In this light, Israel might well have had to be regarded as acting in self-defence, the *status quo ante* of her measures being not a *status iuris* requiring restoration, but a *status iniuriae* urgently demanding corrective action. On this view Fischer Williams' principle,

land warfare, this is clear, but it becomes terribly and embarrassingly clear if one imagines (if one can) a cease-fire order directed to a State which has been the victim of a massive thermo-nuclear air attack, as well as to its assailant. When hostilities may be opened by a surprise thermo-nuclear attack, which may itself be decisive of the war, compliance or recalcitrance towards a *subsequent* cease-fire order becomes a pathetic basis for collective action for preventing or ending hostilities.[13] Even if there were sufficient warning of the *imminence* of attack to permit issuance of conservatory measures *in advance of hostilities,* it would still seem futile to have to wait until an act of defiance which might itself be decisive of the whole conflict.[14]

We have also seen, even under the League, the lack of usefulness of the *ex post bello* test of obedience to a cease-fire order as a test of aggression in the context of distinguishing offensive from defensive purposes of armaments, and the subsequent efforts to find acceptable criteria limiting legitimate purposes in substance to defence of a State's territory against hostile invasion or attack. What blocked progress here also were considerations of justice and power. On the one hand, there was the unwillingness of States to confine the legitimate use of force to protection of a State's *territorial* interests,[15] in a world where there often existed no other effective non-

---

if acceptable (a matter on which no opinion is here expressed), might have justified the General Assembly in considering whether there was any duty to return one or other of the territories. On some views this would be an *a fortiori* case, insofar as the Gaza and Sharm el Sheikh areas were the main bases from which the supposed prior attacks from Egypt were launched, and as Egypt had refused the Israeli demand for assurances against resumption of belligerent acts from these bases.

13 Q. Wright, "The Prevention of Aggression" (1956) 50 *A.J.I.L.* 514, at 530, still proposes reliance on this kind of test of aggression, without reference to the changed methods of warfare.

14 See for example the writers cited in the Introd., *supra.*

A similar wry light is cast on Vattel's propositions that "all States are justified in organising their forces for defence against a potential aggressor, but should not actually use those forces until an aggression had occurred". Even Vattel recognised, for his time, that the duty to refrain from acting until actual assault did not correspond to the realities of inter-State life. It is strange, therefore, that modern writers on the United Nations system should struggle, as does even Professor Wright (article cited (1956) 50 *A.J.I.L.* 514, esp. 526, and *passim*) to exclude all forceful self-defence except after an armed attack has already taken place, i.e. under Art. 51. He would indeed seem also to require some "authority of the United Nations", even after an armed attack. (It must be assumed in the context, and in the absence of contra-indication, that in his definition on 526 he is using the term "individual or collective self-defence" in the sense of Art. 51. If he is not, the above criticism would not apply, except so far as he seems in the present political climate of the United Nations to make the liberty of self-defence wait on the authority of some organ of the United Nations.)

It seems unnecessary to enter in the text into other obstacles to this test arising from frequent indeterminacy of the orders. As C. A. Pompe (*Aggressive War* 96) observes, "the endless negotiations, discussions, compromising proposals, efforts of mediation, and the repetition of recommendations and orders which usually follow and which constitute ninety-five per cent of all international interference with aggression and with the aggressors, make it difficult to speak of disobedience to Security Council orders as a test of aggression in the system of the United Nations. . . ." We would add, among these difficulties, the resort to ambiguity of directive arising from inability of the members of the organ to reach genuine agreement on the issue of ultimate moral responsibility; this was very prominent in the recent Egyptian-Israeli Affair.

15 There was a gentle unconscious irony in the view of M. Chaumont (France) in 1956 that general agreement would be impossible if States insisted on the inclusion of elements which were of particular interest to them in the present situation; followed

forcible means of securing these other interests which might be no less vital. On the other hand was their unwillingness to accept the positive implication of such tests of aggression, namely that the Versailles territorial settlement was to be eternal and immutable.[16] This kind of simple test of aggression, giving, as it did, immunity from forcible redress to all State delinquency that did not encroach on territory, had won little acceptance when it was revived as a basis of United Nations efforts to define aggression in 1950.[17]

This discrepancy between the demands of easy peace enforcement and those of justice could be removed only if one of two assurances were present: First, that a cease-fire order would always issue before the *status quo ante* had been seriously disturbed; second, that insofar as this is impossible, the peace-enforcing authority has the assured means of restoring the *status quo ante*. The Great Power veto, however, in our actual world, would usually falsify both assumptions; and where it did not the use of modern weapons would usually have a similar effect in major conflicts.

III. IMPLICATIONS OF DEFINITION FOR STATE POWER.

The final acceptability, indeed, of any precise criteria centred on protection of the *status quo* from the exercise of force between States must always depend, to a degree, on whether the *status quo* is itself within the limits of tolerable justice, or will simultaneously be brought, by the criterion, within these limits. At this point we must again stress the hazard of the analogy for inter-State relations, often drawn from the unconditional primacy of law and order over justice in most municipal societies. The acceptance by a municipal society of this primacy of law and order depends on the existence of legal organs and processes *within the effective municipal legal order* for adjudicating and enforcing legal rights, as well as for legislative

---

immediately (as it was) by his view that it would be more promising of agreement to concentrate on armed aggression, leaving more subtle forms of aggression for later. (A/AC.77/SR.2, p.3.)

Contrast Mr. Hsueh's view, quite on the contrary, that "the Security Council had been able to deal with cases of aggression [by armed force] without any definition, but it had not so far been able to deal with any other form of aggression"; and that a definition which ignored half of the elements constituting aggression would be unsatisfactory. (A/AC.77/SR, pp.3,5.) See also the related position of Mr. Asha (Syria) at A/AC.77/SR.4, pp.6-7.

16 *Cf.* as to the Covenant, Art. 10, *supra* Ch. 2, esp. s.I.

17 And it scarcely is improved in the recent Soviet draft which would simultaneously make armed invasion of territory always aggression, and mere "frontier incidents" always innocent. *Cf.* G. G. Fitzmaurice, repr. 1 *Int. and Comp. L.Q.* 137, 140: "There are frontier incidents and frontier incidents. . . . On the basis of the Soviet draft, one State could indulge in deliberate frontier incidents against another State, even of a major kind; but any military reaction to this on the part of the other State would automatically constitute aggression, so long as what the first State did could reasonably be represented as being in the nature of a frontier incident, however serious."

We would add that there are also "frontiers", and "frontiers", frontiers e.g. giving quick access to a country's vital political and economic centres, as well as frontiers far distant from them; and that it is here again to be remembered that the Soviet draft is geared to the Security Council, where the veto operates.

change of the *status quo* to accord with tolerable justice. It would be the wildest Utopianism to suggest that any comparable means have existed in the relations of States either under the League or under the United Nations.[18] Even to the extent that they exist on paper, as they did under Article 19 of the Covenant, and perhaps in the present powers of the Security Council, they do not exist as an effective living law, on which peoples who conceive their very existence to be at stake can be expected to rely. The decisive question is not whether some States are willing to order others to live and die by such a sanguine faith, but whether they are themselves ready to do so.

Operating in this situation the terms of many other current proposals for definition of aggression would have the disastrous effect of giving to some States an advance dispensation and indulgence to violate the legal rights and legitimate interests of other States, of sanctifying existing and promoting future injustices, and of marshalling such collective military and political authority as exists in the United Nations in support of such violations and injustices.[19]

The Soviet proposed definition discussed in October-November, 1956, in New York, for instance, brands as economic aggression measures of economic pressure (only vaguely qualified) or economic blockade by one State against another;[20] and asserts with studied particularity that such measures cannot be justified by any "considerations of a political, strategic or economic nature", or of "capital invested", or any other particular interests; and, with even more studied particularity, that it is no justification for such measures that the so-called victim of this so-called aggression has violated treaties,[21] concessions or other trade rights of the reacting State or

---

18 It is also a most striking procedure to acknowledge, as does Professor Scelle in the articles cited, Introd. nn.13-15, that no such means exist and then proceed with the argument concerning the human future as if they did. See esp. the 1936 article at 372 where, despite the acknowledged differences, he asserts his firm belief that the juridical analysis and technique must be the same.

19 In this light the terminological confusion in the position of some delegates, e.g. Yugoslavia, that any agreed definition however "imperfect" would be more conducive to justice than "no definition at all", becomes very clear. See e.g. A/AC.77/SR.7, p.8, and *1956 Sp.Com.Rep.* 13. *Cf.* the Peruvian views, A/AC.77/SR.18, p.9. Some "imperfect" definitions could certainly have the effect of constantly protecting the unjust and punishing the just.

Nor is it necessary to run to the extreme opposite position which at moments is suggested in the Chinese view, that "a defective definition would only have a confusing effect and would therefore be harmful and dangerous. The adoption of such a definition could only be detrimental to the prestige of the United Nations". (A/AC.77/SR.14, p.5, and *1956 Sp.Com.Rep.* 13.) Within limits imperfection of definition will be tolerable, so far as adequate arbiters and procedures for correcting its application exist. As a practical matter international law still lacks these checks; and the choice for the future lies not necessarily between authoritative definition (however imperfect), and helplessness. The need may rather be for change in the conditions which prevent more adequate application of the concept, as well as the improvement of institutions and procedures for application of it.

20 The drive of this part of the definition is indicated by the views of some Soviet lawyers that the Marshall Plan was a form of United States economic aggression.

21 "Surely," G. G. Fitzmaurice (repr. "The Definition of Aggression" (1952) 1 *Int. and Comp. L.Q.* 137, 140) has observed, "it depends on the nature of the treaty whether a violation of it justifies another State in going to war or not."

its citizens, ruptured diplomatic or economic relations, instituted economic boycotts, repudiated debts or the like. Here, indeed, would be a new "Charter", custom-made for the carefree violation of the legal rights and legitimate economic interests of the Western States throughout the Middle East, Asia and Central and South America. For in the absence of any collective means of righting such wrongs,[22] the definition would guarantee in advance to each wrongdoer virtual immunity from any effective measures of redress at all. We need scarcely spell out the relevance of this to the politics of the contemporary scene.

For any States which accept this or any other like advance definition would thereby commit themselves irrevocably in advance, *in abstracto,* and out of the context of future unforeseen circumstances, (1) to observe the set standard themselves; (2) to suffer grave penalties if they violate it, whatever their justifications; (3) to take coercive measures against other State violators, whatever *their* justifications, and (4) to assist any State victim of a violation, however unworthy. The Soviet definition would strip each State, moreover, of any liberty of redress for such grave invasions of its rights and interests, including probably even the comparatively peaceful means of redress by economic measures, by branding all such measures as "aggression". In the face of all this, it must at least be clear that unwillingness of responsible delegations (including the American and the British) to engage on such adventures in definition need not be referred to any lesser dedication to the desire for peace and security. It may be far better explicable as a recognition of the imperatives of a changing and unpredictable world situation, in which no effective alternative means of peaceful adjustment or vindication of rights has yet emerged. It is to be observed, moreover, that insofar as it has been until recently an essential part of the Soviet Union's position that the determination of aggression take place only in the Security Council, subject to the Great Power veto, it was thereby in effect reserving its own liberty of interpretation as against minor States, and even (to the extent that they may feel more inhibited by accepted texts) as against the other Permanent Members.[23]

IV. RELATION TO POWER DRIVES OF SOVIET DRAFT DEFINITIONS, 1953-56.

By the same token as the view of States which shrink from such definitions, or from any definition at all, imports no lack of love of peace and security, so also we must now stress that the zealous promotion of definitions may not always mean any great love of these ideals.[24] Demands for

---

22 This is an important point to be added to the very proper comments of G. G. Fitzmaurice, *op.cit.* 140 on this part of the Soviet proposal.

23 See Ch. 4, nn.31-32, and *cf.* the vigour of emphasis on the Security Council role in M. Franklin, *The Conception of Aggression* 22-23, chastising even any reference by the International Law Commission to "competent organs" in general terms, on the ground that "the principle of the concurrence of the Permanent Members of the Security Council . . . reflects the principle of their co-equality and co-existence."

24 *Cf.* M. Vennemoe (Norway) in A/AC.77/SR.6, p.9: "Lack of support for the idea of defining aggression did not mean, as some people seemed to suggest, a lack of appreciation of the seriousness of the crime of aggression."

definition, and for particular definitions, also have *their* objective political meaning which we will fail, only at our peril, to recognise. Some very earthy and self-regarding objectives of some States may be spectacularly advanced by even the most high-sounding principles, endorsed in the utmost good faith by others.[25] To assess the objective reality of the intense Soviet-led campaign for outlawing nuclear weapons we have to observe that it passed its zenith when the Soviet Union's stockpiling approached a level of substantial retaliation.[26] So also now with proposed definitions of aggression, Soviet or other, they must be examined not only in terms of logic, and juridical principles, but also in terms, *cui bono?* and *cui malo?*[27] Which States would benefit or be sacrified by the proposed definition, over and

---

It may be observed that in the rather different power setting of 1924, the Soviet Government took a position very near to the present position of the United States, and dramatically opposed to her present position. In commenting on the League-sponsored Draft Treaty of Mutual Assistance" (see *L.N.O.J.*, Sp. Supp. No. 26, p.138), the Soviet Government denied "the possibility of determining in the case of every international conflict which State is the aggressor and which is the victim. . . .

"[I]n the present international situation, it is impossible in most cases to say which party is the aggressor. Neither the entry into foreign territory nor the scale of war preparations can be regarded as satisfactory criteria. Hostilities generally break out after a series of mutual aggressive acts of the most varied character." It went on to point out that in its view the Japanese attack on the Russian Fleet at Port Arthur in 1904, though "aggression" from a technical point of view was "politically speaking" a reaction to Czarist aggressive policy.

So *cf.* Mr. Maktos' explanation (*G.A.O.R. VI,* Sixth Committee, 286th Meeting, para. 36) of the U.S.'s reversal of its former support (in 1945, see *infra* pp.132-33) of definition, on grounds that its hope of international cooperation had been disappointed: "Unfortunately, the state of international relations had become such as to convince the United States that a definition of aggression had become not only undesirable, but even dangerous. The United States delegation had not obeyed a whim; it had adopted a position which was diametrically opposed to the stand it had taken in 1945 and had done so in view of international developments."

25 *Cf.* the U.S. representative (J. Maktos) in the Sixth Committee on Jan. 10, 1952; and *cf.* his article, *"La Question de la Définition de l'Agression"* (1952) 30 *R.D.I.* 5, 8.: *"Je crois que cette définition est en réalité un piège destiné à servir des desseins autres que les desseins de ceux qui l'accepteraient de bonne foi. Il pourrait s'agir d'un instrument de propagande destiné à porter de fausses accusations qui causeraient d'irréparables dommages."*

26 *Cf.* even though it may be rather overstated, a main point of J. Poniatowski, "War and Aggression in Western Eyes" (1953) 6 *Eastern Q.* 27-32, esp. 29-30, as to the relation of Soviet "peace campaigns" of the late '40's and early '50's, to the time needed for military strengthening of the Soviet Union and China, to the greater susceptibility of democratic electorates to pacifist appeals, and to the special strategic advantages of surprise in warfare with the new weapons.

27 We are more likely to understand the arguments of States in these terms than in terms, e.g. of preference of code and common law countries for and against definition, of logical Latins as against case-by-case Anglo-Saxons. *Cf.* H. Lauterpacht, "The Pact of Paris . . ." (1935) 20 *Trans Grotius Soc.* 178, 190. The Soviet Union and the satellite countries are of course neither of these latter, though most of them have codes. And it is also to be noted that some code States, e.g. Norway, Germany, and the Netherlands, have usually opposed definition; and at least one State (Hungary) whose system is analogous to a common law one, has steadily (though, of course, also as a Member of the Soviet *bloc*) supported definition. Moreover, of course, even the most common-law common lawyer now accepts as inevitable in many areas the careful statutory definition of numerous municipal law offences. Finally, even if a full correlation were shown it would not negative the other influences above indicated; nor would it prove that definition would otherwise be feasible for the purposes envisaged.

This is not to deny that such factors may have some final relevance, and it is recognised that the majority of States active in support of definition are code States, and

above any common benefit or sacrifice to mankind?[28]

In Europe between the two wars, for instance, the objective political reality which lay behind the demand for criteria centred on territorial frontiers, was the desire of States which feared disturbance of the Versailles territorial settlement for its further guarantee.[29] The reluctance of States, other than France and the successor States, to stand militarily behind this

---

of those opposing definition are common law States. For the view that the common law-civil law distinction is decisive, see C. Jordan, in Bourquin (ed.), *Collective Security* 301; and for an opposed view, C. A. W. Manning, *id.* 338.

[28] We do not suggest that such self-regarding, and self-advancing motivations are always conscious. Yet in a State like the Soviet Union political thinking has long taken it as self-evident that aggression is characteristic of the Western world, as deeply rooted in the nature of capitalism; and orthodox communist doctrine excludes the possibility that any Soviet war could be a war of aggression, since it is argued aggressive attitudes contradict the inner structure of the socialist society, so that the foreign policy of the Soviet Union must always be peaceful. At the same time wars of liberation from "capitalist exploitation" and colonial "oppression" are deemed just wars which cannot be designated "aggressive" in the Soviet sense. See e.g. Stalin, *Geschichte der KPdSU(B), Kurzer Lehrgang* (1952) 210; and E. Korowin, *Die Grundprinzipien der Aussenpolitik der UDSSR.* (1953) 38, quoted L. Schultz, *"Der Sowjetische Begriff der Aggression"* (1956) 2 *Osteuropa Recht* 274. *Cf.* the formulation of Komarnicki (6) who treats the matter in more traditional terms.

So *cf.* in United Nations proceedings M. Vyshinsky's account on Nov. 3, 1950 (*G.A.O.R. V,* First Committee, 380th Meeting, p.223) of the official Leninist doctrine, as then still held, that "a just war was a war waged by people against foreign aggression or capitalist slavery, or, in the case of a country under colonial rule, for its liberation". He instanced the war of the Northern United States against the South, and World War II, as "just wars" and continued: "In the case of a liberating war, only a traitor could shirk his duty by pleading the horrors of war. . . . Only a person devoid of all culture could fail to understand the Leninist concept of the just war; the concept was also embodied in the Charter. . . ."

At the 383rd Meeting (p.242) after chastising those "who seemed unable to grasp the most elementary ideas", he pointed out that "the U.S.S.R. did believe that a war against capitalist slavery, indeed a war against any form of slavery, was a just war. But how could it be said that that opened the door to Soviet Union intervention in a struggle against the capitalist regime in any country?" He thought that the proposal to add the words "including any form of intervention in a civil war" to the "Declaration on the Removal of the Threat of a New War" (see *supra* Ch. 3, n.23) "made its conception of aggression and unjust war quite clear; any unjust war was an aggression and *vice versa;* similarly every just war was a defensive war against various forms of aggression." The present writer joins those who remain unable to grasp the "elementary idea" that this kind of *exposé* dispels all fear that the Soviet concept of aggression "made intervention in support of a rising against any capitalist regime possible".

Cf. the statement by M. Morozov, *G.A.O.R. V,* Sixth Committee, 234th Meeting, p.157; and see the views of M. Franklin, cited *infra* Ch. 7, n.45, and Krylov cited in B. Meissner, *Die Sowjetunion, die baltischen Staaten und das Völkerrecht* (1956) 166ff., and the observations of Professor Röling in A/AC.77/SR.3, p.8.

[29] It is with the utmost respect, and with no intention to question the sincerity of the scholars concerned, that attention may be drawn to the strength of the conviction among French jurists in the 'thirties in support of the sternest forms of the extreme view of the prohibition of resort to force. P. Bastid, indeed, in M. A. F. Frangulis, 3 *Dictionnaire Diplomatique* (*sine anno,* after 1933, but before World War II), *sub voce "Agression",* draws attention to the relation of this view to the protection of the *status quo.* And he interprets all opposition to the Soviet-French *rapprochement* on this basis in the London Convention of 3 July, 1933, to demands for the redistribution of territories of the advocates of dynamic change and restlessness. *Cf.* Y. de la Brière, *ibid.* So in 1936 W. Komarnicki (in Bourquin (ed.), *Collective Security* 314-16) pressed for a rigorous "territorial" criterion in which aggression = invasion, territory for this purpose being territory under *de facto* as well as *de jure* control. And on this last point see the view of N. Politis discussed by M. Amado in I.L.C. A/CN.4/L.6, p.4, in relation to the Chaco, Leticia and Vilna Affairs.

demand caused Article 10 of the Covenant, the only Article expressly referring to "aggression", to fade into the background even as efforts grew to define "aggression".[30] In the 'thirties the continuing Soviet fear of interventionism was surely part of the reason for a similar concern with collective guarantees and the definition of aggression.[31] And it is useful to examine, in the same light, the current Soviet proposed definition of aggression (presented to the Special Committee on October 23, 1956,[32] but first introduced in this precise form in 1953) viewing the world as the Soviet Union saw it at the time, when its control of the zone of satellites was not subject to the doubts at present affecting it.

The first paragraph of the Soviet proposal covers the general areas of so-called "direct" or "armed aggression". It declares:

> 1. In an international conflict that State shall be declared the attacker which first commits one of the following acts:
>
> (a) Declaration of war against another State;
>
> (b) Invasion by its armed forces, even without a declaration of war, of the territory of another State;
>
> (c) Bombardment by its land, sea or air forces of the territory of another State or the carrying out of a deliberate attack on another State or the carrying out of a deliberate attack on the ships or aircraft of the latter;
>
> (d) The landing or leading of its land, sea or air forces inside the boundaries of another State without the permission of the Government of the latter, or the violation of the conditions of such permission, particularly as regards the length of their stay or the extent of the area in which they may stay;
>
> (e) Naval blockade of the coasts or ports of another State;
>
> (f) Support of armed bands organised in its own territory which invade the territory of another State, or refusal, on being requested by the invaded State, to take in its own territory any action within its power to deny such bands any aid or protection.

Clearly, of all the Powers, the Soviet Union registered the greatest terri-

---

[30] See *supra* Ch. 2, s.I.

[31] *Cf.* on the tactical adaptability of Soviet attitudes on this matter to particular situations in world politics, L. Schultz, *"Der Sowjetische Begriff der Aggression"* (1956) 2 *Osteuropa Recht* 274, 275, and *passim*. Schultz points out that the Soviet initiative in its draft definition of 1933, was itself a swing away from the doctrine of E. Paschukanis that international law was merely an instrument of struggle against the Western world inspired by the threats of Japanese and Hitlerite expansion, and in lesser degree by a desire for economic aid to consummate the First Five Year Plan. On earlier Soviet non-aggression treaties which, as late as 1932, did not attempt to define aggression, see *supra* Chs. 1, n.9, and 3, n.9. Even at that stage the favourable propaganda effect of the Soviet initiative upon dependent nations was obviously present to Litvinov's mind when he called the Soviet draft a "Charter of Freedom of Nations". See Litvinov's 1935 publication on Soviet foreign policy, in Russian, cited by Schultz at 275. Soviet reaction to rejection of the draft followed the natural pattern of charging "reactionary" circles in the West with encouragement of aggression against the Soviet Union, and even with responsibility for World War II. (See the article by G. Tunkin, on the definition of aggression, cited Schultz, *op.cit.* 277.) So *cf.* the reversal of Soviet attitudes on the veto, *Covenant Principles,* 87.

[32] *1956 Sp.Com.Rep.*, Ann. II, pp.30-31. It was first introduced in the precise form in 1954, and has of course a long prior history. See *supra* Chs. 2, s.IV, 3, ss.III,VI.

torial gains both prior to and after the Second World War. The rights and wrongs of these gains do not now concern us; they are a fact. It does concern us, however, that the objective political meaning of a definition centred on armed invasion of territory and declaration of war, is to give an extra stamp of legitimacy and collective guarantee to these gains (including the guarantee of those States at whose expense she expanded). Such guarantees may, as Soviet delegates have urged, be implied in co-existence; the effect of the definition is still to consolidate a co-existence highly favourable to the Soviet Union.[33]

The clause of the Soviet definition covering the landing or leading of forces inside the boundaries of another State without the permission of the Government of that State, or in violation of the conditions as regards length of stay or area of deployment, is even more thought-provoking. As between movement of NATO forces in NATO countries, and of those of Warsaw Pact countries between those countries, this category of aggression seems fair and sensible on its face. We, in the West, may feel that the consent of NATO Members to such movements between their countries is genuine in a sense in which that of satellite countries, e.g., East Germany, Poland and Hungary, is not. But even if we are less suspicious, and more wide-eyed in faith, the point remains. The buffer-zone of satellites by which the Soviet Union insulated the Russian heartland from the West, was a projection of her influence and power deeper into the heart of Europe than she could have hoped to achieve. As long as she can maintain it she attains three objectives: First, she reduces her age-old fear of invading land armies from over the great European plain. The quieting of that fear, no one would wish to deny her. Second, however, by deploying her forces at will and manipulating satellite forces within that zone, she presents a sturdy *offensive* front towards West Germany, Austria, Yugoslavia and West Europe generally. (Despite the chronology of the NATO and Warsaw Pacts, NATO itself is basically a Western response to this offensive front.) Third, of course, this protective satellite zone, with its sturdy offensive posture towards Europe, is a mighty shield behind which Soviet Union has been able to advance its objectives in Asia, and later, in the Middle East, and no doubt hopes to advance them further.

This mode of analysis makes it clear, we submit, that despite the apparent Olympian impartiality of stigmatising as aggression the landing or leading of troops into a country affected without its consent, part at least of the political reality is quite otherwise. It is precisely in the satellites, so important for Soviet defensive and offensive power, where struggles are most likely to arise between two governments, one puppet, one not. As things seemed when she proposed this definition, Soviet troops would usually be present

[33] While leaving the Soviet Union with the apparent lack of inhibition which enabled her to absorb some States to whom she was bound by non-aggression treaties embodying the Soviet draft definition of 1933. See Chs. 2, n.5, and 4, nn.31-32. It is a strange experience in the light of this history, to find M. Franklin, *op.cit., supra* n.23 at 25, complaining that "another serious weakness of the *project* of the International Law Commission is that it does not seem to recognize as war crimes the violation of particular treaties of non-aggression, such as the U.S.S.R. made before the Second World War".

with the permission of the Government concerned, that Government being acceptable to, if not dominated by, the Soviet Union. By swallowing this part of the Soviet definition, therefore, the Powers would not only give their blessing to Soviet military domination of these countries. They would also brand in advance as the crime of aggression, the only recourse that might some day be open to themselves for assisting peoples held down by Soviet forces, after the clear overthrow by the people concerned of the Soviet-supported regime. We do not here speak of a Western military initiative for European "liberation". But why should Western countries condemn themselves in advance as aggressors if they should ever decide to aid peoples who have clearly rejected a Government, which then is kept in office by the naked power of Soviet arms?[34] Nor is the self-interested political import removed by the mere fact that in Hungary in 1956[35] the Soviet Union committed some grave miscalculations, which would have led to her being hoist

[34] So also it is significant that (by an extraordinary omission) the Soviet draft definition fails to make any exception to its enumerated list of culpable attacks for collective security measures, possibly even if these are at the behest of the Security Council, and certainly if pursuant to Art. 51. Exemption for Security Council action may be implied insofar as the acts involved might be deemed to be done not by States but by the Security Council. As to collective self-defence by States other than the one attacked, the exemption is most dubious under the present draft. A definition without the latter exemption would of course cripple the NATO system. *Cf.* Mr. Sanders A/AC.77/SR.13, p.7. And see D. W. Bowett, "Collective Self-Defence . . ." (1955-56) 32 *B.Y.B.Int.L.* 130, 137ff., 159ff. for a proposed interpretation of Art. 51 with precisely this effect.

[35] M. François (*U.N.Doc.* A/CN.4/5 SR.93, para. 19) had pointed to the loopholes in the landing of forces provision in the Soviet definition arising from possible manipulations by the aggressor concerning the consent of the Government of the victim State.

It seems clear, even from the confused reports, that there was a movement of Soviet troops into Hungarian territory in November 1956 to participate in the displacement of the Nagy Government of Hungary. Yet, under the Soviet definition of aggression (Clause 1 (d)) aggression includes the *landing or leading of forces inside the boundaries of another State without the permission of the government of the latter.* Did the Nagy Government invite the Soviet forces in to destroy itself? We leave aside other parts of the definition concerning the violation of the condition of consent to entry, and the duration of stay of such foreign troops. The Soviet argument that her entry was in reaction to "indirect" aggression of other States against Hungary seems also inconsistent with her view on the question whether armed reaction to indirect aggression should be permitted. See *supra* Ch. 3, nn.145, 147. And see on the question whether, under the Soviet definition, consent of the government of the "victim" State negatives aggression, D. A. Loeber, *op. cit. supra* p.2, n.2, and Q. Wright, *op. cit. supra* p.103, at 275.

And despite the Soviet initiative in seeking to have Israel declared an "aggressor" in the Israel-Egypt Affair, the fact was that under the Soviet's own definition Egypt might have had to be regarded as having been in a state of continuing multiple aggression for some considerable time before the Israeli raid on Sinai: (1) As the State first issuing a declaration of war. (Egypt led the Arab States in declaring open war on Israel in 1948, and had continued to insist thereafter on maintaining that state of war.) (2) As having supported or at least not used due diligence to prevent incursions of armed bands into Israel from Egyptian controlled territory. (More than four hundred raids (fedayeen and others) into Israel had been reported up to 1956.) (3) Egypt had under the Soviet definition, been in a state of continuing "economic aggression" for some years by virtue of the economic pressure on Israel by Arab States led and conducted by her. (4) There had been belligerent acts by Egypt against Israeli ships; and (5) Egyptian activities and threats in the Straits of Tiran conceivably involved some form of "naval blockade . . . of the ports of another State" within the Soviet definition.

The Soviet Union's view of the illegality of General Assembly action by dint of usurpation of Security Council functions (see Ch. 9, s.IV) would require that both States at variance could not be bound by General Assembly resolutions without their

by her own petard, had she not been relatively immune as a Great Power from the penal code by which she wished to bind other States.

---

own consent. In fact, because of her partisanship in the recent crisis she only pressed this point in favour of Egypt. (See M. Shepilov (*G.A.O.R. XI,* 592nd Meeting, Nov. 23, 1956, p.265, para. 29, as regards deployment of the U.N.E.F.). *Cf.* on the same point M. Fawzi (Egypt) (A/PV.651, Feb. 2, 1957, pp.72-75).

CHAPTER 7

AGGRESSION AND INTERNATIONAL MORALITY

The Ethical Components

I. AGGRESSION AND A TOLERABLY JUST ORDER BETWEEN STATES.

It must quickly be added that the mere fact that particular offered definitions of aggression reveal a gross subservience to the apparent interests of some States against others, does not rule out the chance that some definition may yet be found which is geared to the common interests of all States. Other difficulties intervene, however, which hinder such consummation.

One difficulty lies in the basic assumption, underlying the demand for definition, that we can control the complex uncertainties of future contingencies within a formula of near-certain operation. This problem, it may be said, also confronts municipal law and constitution making; and does not there prevent the adoption of useful legal formulas. The municipal law analogy, however, is here again treacherous for the international problem. For, first, as contrasted with municipal legal orders, the international order has as yet no reliable collective processes for enforcing observance of legal rights or for legislative adjustment of existing social, legal and political arrangements to the minimal demands of justice in the changing matrix of human life.[1]

Even if it had, however, it has to be pointed out that municipal legal systems never use the notion of "aggression" as a basic concept; that they rarely, indeed, use notions of that character, and that on the rare occasions on which they do, they have similar insuperable difficulties of definition to those which confront us in the notion of aggression. We may find, for example, such notions as "peace, order, and good government" in many municipal constitutional instruments; but the content of such notions is there finally provided from time to time by electors or legislators rather than established by particularised advance definition. Even closer to our subject are such notions as "lack of due process" or "arbitrary, unreasonable, or capricious", in their application to the content of challenged legislation, or challenged procedures, which give rise to repeated judicial applications. For it is well-known that the applications of "lack of due process" cannot be precisely delimited by advance definition; and that those who apply it must suffer the uncertainties of judgment in the full context of each case as it arises.

---

[1] It is thus strangely beside the point to read Professor Pella's indignant incredulity (*La Guerre-Crime* (1946) 43-44), that while in a municipal legal system we can define the most picayune offences, we cannot for international society define "the most monstrous crime that the human imagination can conceive". Notions basic to civilised life are only too often far more difficult to define than minor ones. *Cf. infra* Ch. 9.

When we invoke, indeed, the analogy of the question in American constitutional law whether the range and contents of substantive "due process" can be settled once and for all, we are more likely to reject than support the view that we can answer once and for all, in relation to controversies yet unforeseeable, the question, Which resorts to force are "aggressive" and which justified? The analogy here drawn is not between the respective contents of the notions of "aggression" and "lack of due process", but between their respective conceptual structures. Involved in the application of both are some aspects of the question, What is a just order of disposition from time to time of the world's resources, opportunities and power over others, among its different peoples? Any advance definition of aggression even approaching automatic applicability, would fix, for example, the stigma and penalties of aggression on what may be the only available means either of vindicating legal rights or making *de facto* situations tolerable to great sections of mankind, or even of ensuring survival itself. This is precisely why, as we have shown, most mooted definitions (for instance, in terms of armed crossing of frontiers, or the refusal to obey cease-fire orders) may in particular situations sanctify grave and persistent breaches of international law or justice (or both) by the supposed "victim" of aggression. The moral repugnance to aggression, which we all share, cannot bind us to the grave wrongs which particular offered definitions of it would legitimise and protect, if we accepted them.

Once this aspect of the notion of "aggression", as a delimiting concept for a tolerably effective legal order protecting a tolerably just disposition of the world's resources, opportunities and power, is perceived, the reason for the chronic failure of the clamour for advance definition on the analogy of municipal law may become clearer. No viable municipal legal system attempts to settle *once and for all* the just distribution of the goods of life among its citizens. What a municipal system does, be it flexible or rigid, is to lay down the just distribution for the time being, and provide regular institutionalised organs and processes both for enforcing rights under it, and for redetermining it, on future challenge. Since, in the international legal order there are neither effective collective remedies for violations of existing rights nor collective means for legislative adjustment to deal with the complex and unforeseeable circumstances of the future, the municipal law analogy is of little persuasiveness. So far, indeed, as it is relevant, as in the analogy of "due process" and its negation, "lack of due process", it tends to support the rejection rather than the acceptance of the demand for criteria of aggression for quasi-automatic future application. A municipal system is scarcely conceivable in which there would be no legislature, and no legal means of enforcement of existing legal rights, and of which only one rule of the criminal law was enforceable, namely a rule visiting capital punishment on any citizen who committed a physical assault on another or forcibly entered upon the realty of another. Such a system would place under intolerable handicaps all law-abiding citizens not prone to secret theft, seduction, fraud, defamation, misappropriation and all the other wrongs which can be committed without trespass to person or realty.

II. ETHICAL COMPONENTS IN DUE PROCESS JUDGMENT.

Current controversies surrounding the concept of due process in American constitutional cases and doctrine are indeed so illuminating for the present problem as to merit more extended treatment.[2]

Brandeis J. observed in his famous dissent in *Burnet v. Coronado Oil and Gas Co.*[3] that in "cases under the due process clause when the question is whether a statute is unreasonable, arbitrary or capricious", the decision is in the first instance dependent "upon the determination of what in legal parlance is a fact, as distinguished from the declaration of a rule of law", and that "when the underlying fact has been found, the legal result follows inevitably". In the "fact" here referred to there may clearly be comprised a *very complex set of facts,* interrelated and interpreted, as well as delimited, by reference to the standards of "arbitrariness", "unreasonableness", or "caprice".[4] The notion is, indeed, probably analogous to the *Tatbestand*[4a] familiar to civil lawyers, especially as applied to the underlying complex of

---

2 We are concerned here of course only with certain broad aspects of due process on which see in the recent literature A. Sutherland, *The Law and One Man Among Many* (1956); *id.,* "The Supreme Court and the General Will" (1953) 82 *Proc.Am.Ac. Arts and Sciences* 169; S. H. Kadish, "Methodology and Criteria in Due Process Adjudication—Survey and Criticism" (1957) 57 *Columbia L.R.* 319; P. A. Freund, *On Understanding the Supreme Court* (1949) *passim; Government Under Law* (Marshall Centenary Volume) (1956) *passim;* E. McWhinney, "The Supreme Court and Judicial Policy Making" (1955) 39 *Minn. L.Rev.* 837; E. N. Griswold, *The Fifth Amendment Today* (1955) 36-38. The work of Professors Sutherland and Kadish exposes particularly well those aspects of due process controversies which in the present view run parallel to controversies affecting the definition of aggression.

Thus Professor Kadish's work has the following main themes: (1) The struggle over many years between judicial champions of "fixity"—mainly by enumeration of due process situations (see esp. 321-325)—and those of flexibility (325-327), referring judgment in the new situations to the norms of some kind of "social conscience" or "sense of what is fair and right and just", aided by the gloss of history of English, American, British Commonwealth or other democratic countries (327-333).

(2) The arguments for the attainability and desirability (*cf.* the debate as to "the possibility and desirability" of definition of aggression, *supra* Chs. 3, 4) of a "fixed" due process (335-344) and the rejection of these arguments.

(3) The search for "criteria for interpreting a flexible due process" which shall not be merely subjective (344-358). And see especially on the relevance of the full context of facts and anticipated consequences of decision in a particular case, 358-363, and for the components of decision which I have called "moral evaluations", or the "justice-components", 346-353.

3 285 U.S. 393 (1932). The ruling from which he dissented was reversed in *Helvering v. Mountain Producers,* 303 U.S. 376 (1938).

4 We would therefore make a corresponding comment on G. G. Fitzmaurice's formulation in 1952 (repr. 1 *Int. and Comp. L.Q.* 137, 143): "The truth is that aggression is a question of fact more than a question of law. It is possible to specify certain acts as being *normally* of an aggressive character, but it is not possible to specify any act as being always and in all circumstances aggressive. It is equally possible to specify certain acts as being normally non-aggressive, but many of these acts are acts which are capable of being employed for aggressive purposes or . . . assisting in . . . participation (sic) of aggression." This point is vaguely foreshadowed in S. Glaser, *"Constituye un Crimen la Guerra de Agresión"* (1953) 6 *Revista Española de Derecho Internacional* 539-541, who, however, makes the contrast between municipal and international notions far too stark. And see his stress on 542 on the ethical components of the aggression notion.

4a In these cases perhaps a better phrase would be the *Tat-Wert-Bestand,* if we may

facts and moral judgments involved in the judicial application of such standards as *"contra bonos mores"*, *"Billigkeit"*, *"Treu und Glauben"*, and the like. In this chapter, when referring to the complex of facts, evaluation of facts, and the moral judgments as to what shall be done about the facts, we shall use the phrase "complex of facts and moral judgments" or the simple term "complex".

It is true, of course, as Brandeis J. himself pointed out, that such issues "resemble fundamentally that of reasonable care in negligence cases, the determination of which is ordinarily left to the verdict of the jury". Yet we have to add, with the greatest respect for that fine intellect, that the issue of lack of "due process" also clearly differs from this by the ambit of the "fact-value complex", which is a necessary and sufficient basis of judgment. The complex involved in the jury's determination whether the defendant in a negligence case drove with reasonable care at an intersection is comparatively narrow. It is geographically limited to a locality, it is socially limited to a community, it is demographically limited to the human beings of that community. It is also limited as to the values that are relevant, not only in the sense that they touch but one specialised activity of human life, but that the jury need only look at the legal norms applicable, and possibly at other norms socially accepted in that limited locality, among that limited number of human beings. When, however, we move to the kind of complex that usually underlies a substantive due process judgment as to the validity of legislation, the ambit is so vastly greater as to amount almost to a difference in kind.[5]

The vastness and intractability of this ambit is indeed, perhaps one of the reasons why, in the final analysis of the Brandeis position, the "judgment" involved in the determination of due process is vested primarily and mainly in the responsible legislature, the role of the judicial reviewing tribunal being to determine only whether that legislative "judgment" is palpably baseless and unreasonable. The determination, therefore, what is substantive due process on a particular matter presupposes the confrontation of the full complex of facts and moral judgments by the legislature prior to the embodiment in rules of law of the requirements of justice as legislatively found. It also presupposes sufficient attention to that same complex by the reviewing Court to determine whether this legislative finding is palpably "arbitrary, unreasonable and capricious".

A hint of the wideness of the ambit of the complex thus involved may be given by reference to the famous opinion of Mr. Justice Brandeis in the *Oklahoma Ice Case*,[6] in which in order to meet the grounds taken in argu-

---

be permitted to suggest it. It must be recalled, though I am not here concerned to enter upon the matter, that even the ascertainment of what are the "objective" and "subjective" facts of a situation is affected by unavoidable elements of evaluation in the process of reporting what are believed to be the facts.

[5] On the difficulties affecting "legislative" fact finding in this area, see S. H. Kadish, *op.cit. supra* n.2, 350-363; H. W. Biklé, "Judicial Determination of Questions of Fact Affecting . . . Constitutional Validity . . ." (1924) 38 *Harvard L.R.* 6; Note, "Social and Economic Facts . . ." (1948) 61 *Harvard L.R.* 692.

[6] *New State Ice Co. v. Liebmann*, 285 U.S. 262 (1931).

ment and in the majority judgment,[7] he canvassed at length the factors relevant to the functions both of the legislature and of the reviewing judicial organ. As there sketched, the relevant complex embraced the pattern of life of the entire people of the State, in relation to its climate, habits of work and play, the distribution of wealth in relation to the availability of private refrigeration, and the state of technological development in the production of household refrigerators, and many other factors. It also embraced related evaluations as to the conformity of that fact situation with minimum standards of human life achieved or sought in that community against the background, too, of American society as a whole. According to the kind of legislation challenged under due process, innumerable other complexes are involved, no less formidable in their ambits, and each of which may be quite different from the other, both in content, and in the interrelation of the various elements to each other.

It is precisely here that the notion of substantive lack of due process illuminates so brilliantly the notion of aggression. Clearly the ambit of the "fact-value complex" involved in the judgment of aggression will usually be at least as wide, and often vastly wider than that of lack of substantive due process above described. It will often involve not only the complex conditions of life of a whole people in a whole State, but those of two or more peoples, running possibly into hundreds of millions of human lives. The facts may have no limited geographical or demographical range; and the resources and goods of which the distribution is at stake, and the minimum standards of life to be achieved or sought, may range to the present limits and future potentialities of man's global habitation. Here, too, the exact ambit of relevant facts and standards will vary from case to case; and the variables are so numerous that no advance catalogue can dispense judgment from its responsibility for examining the full context of what is relevant in each case. Yet the notion of aggression in international law seems to demand that this vast ambit, with all its innumerable configurations in the unforeseen future, and without benefit of any preliminary exploration and determinations by an effective international legislature, shall be taken into account by the applying organ in each concrete situation. For the lack of an effective international legislature, and of collective enforcement of legal rights generally, make unavailable to an international applying organ the course charted by Brandeis of not retreading the path of legislative judgment, but merely testing its results by the limiting notions of what is arbitrary and unreasonable on any reading of the whole situation.

III. CORRESPONDING CONTROVERSIES AS TO DEFINITION OF DUE PROCESS.

We have spoken thus far of substantive due process, that is of the standard as applied by the courts to determine the constitutionality of legislative

---

[7] I.e. the substitution of the judicial for the legislative judgment as a basis for holding that "unreasonable . . . interferences or restrictions cannot be saved . . . merely

adjustments of conflicting rights and interests. "Procedural" due process, though the ambit of the complex of facts and moral evaluations which must be confronted in its judicial application to particular situations may not always or even usually be so wide, also affords fruitful reflections for the aggression notion. For in the application of procedural due process, where usually review of a statute is not involved, there has often been no prior legislative exploration and determination of just rules for the conflict. Here, then, the restraint and modesty of the Brandeis attitude to judicial review of legislation cannot serve; and the applying tribunal must itself bear the full burden of dealing with the raw material relevant to the application of the standard in the particular case.[8]

It is the more interesting, in view of this apparent kinship between the notions of "aggression" and lack of "due process", that American constitutional doctrine has presented us in recent times with controversies concerning advance definition and criteria, not too dissimilar from those which are the main subject of this book. Clearly few American lawyers now believe, as Mr. Justice Roberts seemed to believe in 1936,[9] that it is always of much assistance in questions of constitutionality "to lay the article of the Constitution which is invoked beside the statute which is challenged and to decide whether the latter squares with the former". Even more in due process cases, than in the case of State-federal powers to which Justice Roberts was addressing himself, would it be generally agreed that the "due process" provision cannot be (in Arthur Sutherland's recent apt phrasing) [10] "self-defining". Due process rather expresses an "aspiration" and not a rule, and in this area, at any rate, we cannot "find in words a substitute for human judgment".

Among the fascinating controversies which have emerged with the overt recognition, in the post-1937 Supreme Court of the United States, that there are no conceptual escapes from the labyrinth of the complex of facts and moral judgments in due process decision, not the least interesting[11] is a well-

by calling them experimental". See Sutherland, J., for the Court, 285 U.S. 262, at 279 (1931).

[8] The unavailability of preliminary legislative findings is to a degree compensated in these cases by the consideration that the judges may be thought to have some special competence and experience in interpreting the requirements of procedural fairness and decency. This kind of mitigation probably has little applicability to the notion of aggression.

[9] Opinion of the Court in *U.S.* v. *Butler*, 297 U.S. 1, 62 (1936). *Cf.* in Australian constitutional decision Latham, C. J., in the *Uniform Tax Case* (*South Australia* v. *Commonwealth*) (1942) 65 C.L.R. 373, at 409, 426.

[10] Arthur Sutherland, *The Law and One Man Among Many* (1956) 67. I am greatly indebted to this work. as well as to his "Supreme Court and the General Will" (1953) 82 *Proc.Am.Ac. Arts and Sciences* 169 in working out this analogy with the due process notion.

[11] Another, which also has interesting reflections for the debate as to aggression, is the problem whether the single notion of "due process" can properly base differentiation in the standard applied as between, e.g. governmental invasions of property or business interests on the one hand, and civil liberties or human rights, on the other. *Cf. supra* pp.66ff., the suggestion that while there may be "economic" as well as "armed" aggression, equally condemnable as such, forcible self-defence is legitimate against the latter, but not as against the former.

known controversy, running through many cases, between Mr. Justice Frankfurter and Mr. Justice Black.[12] Underlying their controversy, which has arisen mainly in the context of procedural due process,[13] is, we believe, the question whether the "due process" notion is to be applied immediately (in the literal meaning of this adverb) to each situation of challenged governmental power; or whether more precise advance criteria of due process pre-exist each decision, in the form, for instance, of the contents of the federal Bill of Rights. Beneath the American constitutional colour,[14] too, is the issue between judicial acceptance of the duty to confront the full complexity involved in each challenged due process situation, and the demand for more precise criteria, limiting in advance the choice to be made by the Court in relation to the complex which it is to judge.

On the one hand, in *Rochin v. California*,[15] we have Mr. Justice Frankfurter insisting that in the absence of any technical content of the verbal symbol given by "the deposit of history",[16] the "gloss" by which meaning is given to the symbol is "a function of the process of judgment", which "is bound to fall differently at different times and differently at the same time through different judges". He proceeded:

> The vague contours of the Due Process Clause do not leave judges at large. We may not draw on our merely personal and private notions and disregard the limits that bind judges in their judicial function. Even though the concept of due process of law is not final and fixed, these limits are derived from considerations that are fixed in the whole nature of the judicial process. . . . These are considerations deeply rooted in reason and in the compelling traditions of the legal profession.

What deserved, perhaps, to be rendered more explicit in this explanation, is that sound judgment in such cases requires the Court to examine the full ambit of the situation under judgment, and that resort to short cuts by the interposition of more precise advance criteria may obstruct, distort, and even frustrate this examination by cutting off arbitrarily the range of relevance. Stated affirmatively thus, the position would not have been as vulnerable to Mr. Justice Black's mordant comments;[17] and the nature of the demand

---

12 Compare on the relation of the debate between Justices Frankfurter and Black to the long-standing cleavage in American constitutional decision between the judicial drives to "fixity" on the one hand, and "flexibility" on the other, S. H. Kadish, *op.cit. supra* n.2, 321-327, 335-340.

13 The stimulating work of S. H. Kadish, *op.cit. supra* n2, is directed almost exclusively to procedural due process. For the present purpose, however, the significant parallels extend to the area of "substantive" due process, especially in its former more active phases.

14 For example, whether in view of the fact that the Fourteenth Amendment merely repeats for the States the limitations already contained in the Fifth Amendment applicable to the federal government, an interrelation can be correct which would treat the Fifth Amendment (*inter alia*) as a "specific guarantee" of the Fourteenth Amendment identical in terms. See Black, J., dissenting in *Adamson* v. *California*, 332 U.S. 461, 469 (1947).

15 342 U.S. 165 (1952).

16 342 U.S. 165, at 169-170.

17 In *Rochin* v. *California*, 342 U.S. 165, 175ff. (1952), especially upon "the nebulous standards" stated by the majority in terms of what "shocks the conscience", offends "a sense of justice", or runs counter to "the decencies of civilized justice", and of the en-

for precise criteria of due process implicit in the latter's position would itself be exposed for examination.

That demand, stripping it again of local American constitutional colour, is that the testing of a challenged situation by the due process standard should be controlled by advance criteria, in order to prevent the Court from expanding or contracting "constitutional standards to conform to the Court's conception of what at a particular time constitutes 'civilized decency' and 'fundamental liberty and justice' ". By proposing that the civil rights content of the Fourteenth Amendment be based on implied incorporation of the first eight amendments into the Fourteenth Amendment, Mr. Justice Black was urging, on the one hand, that the ambit of the due process and companion clauses of the Fourteenth Amendment, as they applied to civil rights, should be given precision by the adoption of the eight amendments as explicit advance criteria. And, on the other hand, he was also demanding that the ambit of due process beyond the range of such explicit criteria (that is, as it applies to "economic" rather than "civil" or "human" rights) be cut off.[18] And this is quite consistent with his expressed fear that without the specific guarantees "the accordion-like qualities" of the majority's "philosophy" would imperil the individual liberties safeguarded by the Bill of Rights.[19]

---

joinders not to "draw on our merely personal and private notions", to ground judgment on "considerations deeply rooted in reason, on the compelling traditions of the legal profession", on "the community's sense of fair play and decency", on the "traditions and conscience of our people", and on "those canons of decency and fairness which express the notions of justice of English speaking peoples"; and to make an "evaluation based on a disinterested inquiry pursued in the spirit of science on a balanced order of facts".

See for a fuller listing and attempted analysis of the symbols accompanying the attempted immediate application of the due process notion to the full context of the case for decision, S. H. Kadish, *op.cit. supra* n.2, at 325-334, and for a critique of some of the symbols, *id.*, 344-46.

18 Or, in terms of his own assumptions, denied or repudiated. The point, indeed, is almost explicit at moments. See e.g. his opinion in *Rochin* v. *California,* 342 U.S. 165, 177 (1952), where after referring to the former striking down of legislation of an economic regulatory nature, correct by "the evanescent standards of the majority's philosophy," he continued: "What paralyzing role this same philosophy will play in the future economic affairs of this country is impossible to predict."

19 So interpreted the Justice's position is well designed both to immunise individual exercise of "civil rights" or "human rights" from legislative invasion, and to ensure the *exposure* of "economic" rights to such invasion. Violation of the civil liberties embodied in the first eight Amendments is always, whatever the circumstances, to be regarded (in this view) as a violation of due process; while, on the other hand, legislation invading merely "economic rights" is not to be regarded as so violative (as it often was before 1937). Whatever its exegetical demerits this is a position rationally related to ideals of the common welfare which may be shared (as well as differed from) by the rest of the community.

In the moral quality of the ideals sought to be secured, the purpose of the Justice's campaign for definition of due process is therefore worlds apart from that underlying the Soviet campaign for definition of aggression. Yet the analogy in the technical role of definition in securing the ideal sought remains, perhaps, even more illuminating because of the very differences in the ideals sought. For the Soviet draftsmen too there was a double solicitude. On the one hand, their draft was designed to ensure that certain acts of which Soviet interests particularly require the suppression, shall always, whatever the circumstances, be branded and suppressed as aggression. On the other hand, the Soviet draftsmen by expressly declaring in the definition that certain violations

IV. DUE PROCESS AS A SWORD.

No less interesting in its reflection on the aggression notion is the division of opinion in the Supreme Court on the question whether "the civil rights act"[20] (now §20 of the U.S. Criminal Code), making it a federal offence wilfully to deprive a person of any right secured *inter alia* by the due process clause of the Fourteenth Amendment, was itself void as providing "no ascertainable standard of guilt".[21] The argument for striking down the statute was based on the admitted fact that the Court had on many occasions interpreted lack of due process as comprehending any action which "offends some principle of justice so rooted in the traditions of our people as to be ranked as fundamental";[22] as a "scheme of ordered liberty"[23] and as "more fluid" and "less a matter of rule" than the Bill of Rights, and required to be tested by "an appraisal of the totality of facts in a given case", so that "that which may, in one setting, constitute a denial of fundamental fairness may, in other circumstances, and in the light of other considerations, fall short of such a denial".[24]

Mr. Justice Douglas, the Chief Justice, and Justices Black and Reed, in the majority judgment, saved the act on this point by confining §20 "more narrowly" in the rights it purported to protect.[25] They interpreted it to

---

of rights and interests (mostly of an economic nature) can never legally justify any acts of aggression as there defined, would have exposed and left vulnerable to invasion by other States the extensive overseas economic interests of the Western States. See *supra* pp.111-112.

What appears to be a logical inconsistency between his position in *Rochin* v. *California*, and his view in the civil rights acts cases (see *infra* n.20), where Mr. Justice Black seems, by his concurrence, to admit that the evolution of due process cannot be controlled by any precise enumeration of protected rights, may be understood in the light of the first paragraph above, as due to an overriding solicitude for "human rights".

Compare the similar interpretation in S. H. Kadish, *op.cit. supra* 2, 335, 336-340. Professor Kadish adds a refinement with which we agree, namely that even if the contents of the first eight Amendments are made the basis of applied due process, the ostensible aim of setting precise limits on the due process judgment is still not attained. For a number of the Amendments (and incidentally those with which the Justice is most concerned) themselves have constantly changing contours, and are the subject of vigorous divisions of judicial opinion. Although, therefore, the tying of due-process to the Amendments may be "a net tactical gain for the rights of the individual", we agree with Professor Kadish that "it is hardly a triumph of fixed meanings over flexible ones". (339.)

This refinement does not, however, affect the main point on which we are happy to agree with Professor Kadish, that the dual drive to put the Amendments into the due process clause, and to limit its operation to their protection, corresponds to value judgments which on the one hand place the rights of the individual in the "non-economic" field very high and insist on their protection, while putting "economic" rights very low and leaving them without constitutional protection.

20 See, e.g., *Screws* v. *U.S.*, 325 U.S. 9 (1944), which was the first case applying to violations of due process the provisions of s.20 of the U.S. Criminal Code. The substance of s.20 derives from s.2 of the Civil Rights Act, Apr. 9, 1866 (14 *Stat.* 27), amended by s.17 of the Act of May 31, 1870 (16 *Stat.* 144), These and related federal acts were, of course, first introduced after the Civil War with the main object of protecting negroes in their newly granted rights.

21 325 U.S. at 95, *per* Douglas, J.

22 *Snyder* v. *Massachusetts,* 291 U.S. 97, 105 (1934).

23 *Palko* v. *Connecticut,* 302 U.S. 319, 325 (1937).

24 *Betts* v. *Brady,* 316 U.S. 455, 562 (1941), quoted 325 U.S. at 95.

25 See *Screws* v. *U.S.,* 325 U.S. 91, at 100 (1944). *Cf.* Murphy, J.'s, view, dissenting on 136, that the principle against vagueness "does not mean that if a statute is vague

render criminal only such an act which was done "wilfully" in the sense that it had as its purpose to deprive a person of "a specific constitutional right",[26] including in this notion not only what is "specific" in the constitutional text, but what has been made specific (under such provisions as the due process clause) by judicial holdings.[27] The joint dissent of Justices Roberts, Frankfurter and Jackson equivalated §20 in relation to due process to a statute making it punishable to do any act "which the Supreme Court shall find to be a deprivation of any right . . . protected by the Constitution".[28] So far as the dissent turned on the non-severability of that scope of §20 which referred to deprivation of "specific" rights, from that which referred to vague ones, it does not here interest us.[29] In its emphasis, however, on "the vast, undisclosed range of the Fourteenth Amendment", violations of which by State officials "under color of law" §20 would, on its face, turn into offences, the contrast of attitudes to the standard of lack of due process between Justices Frankfurter and Black is clear enough.[30] It presents itself, indeed, in the present context, as rather nearer to the present problems, at least in the respect that (as has been well said) the concept of violation of due process is here being used not as a shield protecting from subjection to arbitrary power, but as a sword to strike by criminal penalties at the violator.[31]

The concluding argument of the minority has an obvious relevance not only to the question whether notions like "aggression" or "violation of due process" can be defined, but to the whole issue whether they can be made a satisfactory basis of criminal punishment of individuals at all. The minority observed: "The Due Process Clause . . . has a content the scope of which this Court declares only as cases come here from time to time and then not without close division and reversals of position".[32] It followed, they thought, that to hold constitutional a statute rendering it an offence to violate whatever rights might fall within the notion, would create "a pliable instrument of prosecution" which could serve "as a dangerous instrument of intimidation and coercion in the hands of those so inclined". They did not think such an objection was removed either by the Congressional power to curb abuse, nor by the use of judges and juries of the localities concerned, nor by any assurance by the executive that it would use the prosecuting power with self-restraint.[33]

---

as to certain criminal acts but definite as to others" the entire statute must fall.

26 325 U.S. at 101, and see 104-105.

27 As to the consistency of Mr. Justice Black's concurrence here with his general position, see *supra* n.19.

28 325 U.S. at 152.

29 See 325 U.S. at 150-151 and contrast Murphy, J.'s, dissent, *supra* n.25.

30 Though, insofar as Mr. Justice Black concurred in the majority ground that the scope of criminal liability for violation of due process rights might depend on the extent to which from time to time these "rights" have been rendered "specific and definite" by judicial holdings, his insistence on advance precision of definition of due process is much less intransigent than that discussed *infra* pp.129ff.

31 A metaphor of the late Mr. Justice Jackson in *Pollack* v. *Williams*, 322 U.S. 4, at 8-9 (1943), quoted in P. A. Freund, "Individual and Commonwealth in the Thought of Mr. Justice Jackson" (1955) 8 *Stanford L. R.* 9, 23.

32 325 U.S. at 158. 33 325 U.S. at 158-161.

We are not here concerned to take sides in these great debates, so much as to suggest that even at the nerve centres of *stable, going, municipal* legal orders, we may also find vague concepts of a most basic nature, for which judges are unwilling or unable to fix precise advance criteria, and for the violation of which they are unwilling to allow criminal punishment to be meted out. And one reason for this, as Professor Sutherland has also recently well stressed, is that the notion of "due process" has come to import into itself whatever we mean by "justice" or "right".[34] This component of due process is "undefinable" in terms of precise directives for future application, for the very good reason that the application of standards of this import must be made in the presence of the relevant complex of facts and moral judgments involved in the instant case, to which "justice" and "right" inevitably refer us.[35] And this reason is, as we have seen, rendered more compelling by the fact that the complex referred to in these areas is of so wide and variable an ambit that advance criteria would inevitably truncate and frustrate, almost in direct proportion to their capacity to dictate decision, the application of the standard to the full context of events. Such advance criteria are inevitably drawn *ex hypothesi* in abstraction from that full context.

V. AGGRESSION MORE DIFFICULT TO DEFINE THAN LACK OF DUE PROCESS.

These due process controversies of municipal constitutional law should be of some comfort to those international lawyers who may view the futile search for precise criteria of aggression as a reflection on their technical skills. The reasons for distrust of such criteria are even more compelling for the notion of aggression, than for that of lack of due process. After all, inadequate criteria of lack of due process can be mitigated in various ways, whether by later reversals or refinements of decision, by new legislation seeking its ends by other less vulnerable means, and always (in theory at any rate) by constitutional amendment.[36] International law lacks any such

---

34 *Op.cit. 65.* Compare the attempted break-down of the value elements involved, and a suggested method of approach to conflicts of values involved in procedural due process, S. H. Kadish, *op.cit. supra* n.2, 346-349.

35 So compare S. H. Kadish, *op.cit. supra* n.2, who rejects the possibility and desirability of "a fixed due process" precisely because of the need for adaptation "to drastically changed and changing social contexts". For this clause is basically related "to the preservation of the conditions of a free society", and in a community committed to judicial review "the residuary guarantee of due process is readily seen to be incompatible with changeless meaning". And see *id.*, 341-44 for illustrations of the manner in which attempted precision of definition must "ignore the unique character in which each generation's problems are presented" (343).

36 Even with these safeguards, some of the most progressive nations as regards protection of civil rights still find difficulties in formulating with final precision the content of basic human rights. Thus proposals in the U.S. Congress to define (even though not exhaustively) the "rights, privileges and immunities" referred to in U.S. Code, title 18, s. 242 have been steadily rejected for some years; but of course problems of definition are certainly not there the decisive ones. See e.g. the latest of a series of proposals by Mr. Celler (85th Congress, 1st Session HR 2145, Jan. 7, 1957) reported out Feb. 28,

collective means for mitigating wrong judgment on an "aggression situation". Judicial enforcement of due process, moreover, is only *one* means for the collective pursuit of an overall minimum justice in American society. But in international society no means exist even of collective redress of the gravest wrongs, whether judicial or private, legal or moral, much less of collective adjustment of law to minimum standards of justice.[37] In such a society, this single notion of "aggression" is being asked to perform within the monstrously wide ambit of all inter-State relations, most of the major tasks of criminal and constitutional law, not to speak of much of the law of property, torts and procedure.[38] It is being asked to do this, moreover, without at the same time throwing out the baby with the bath water; that is, without at the same time overriding those minimum standards of respect for law and justice which lack, in inter-State relations, all other means of assurance than the aggrieved Party's own self-assertion of its rights and interests.

All this we believe is an important part of the explanation of the tragic paradox which has both inspired the enterprise of defining aggression and doomed it to failure. It should perhaps be added that even if major use were made of the concept of "aggression" in municipal law[39] we would often, for instance in investigation of a drunken brawl or of a long smouldering enmity, find it impossible to apply it with confidence. It is situations of this kind which form the more staple analogies for most international conflicts. If we were to try to reduce international conflict to the analogy of inter-individual relations, we would have to speak more often than not of a kind of "perpetual mutual aggression", in which even when physical arms are at rest, the mutual attack continues by ideological and economic weapons, and by armament preparations.[39a] In fact, as we have shown,

---

1957, with the proposed new s.242A on this matter deleted. And *cf.* also, of course, the well-known deadlock on the international level as to the proposed Covenant of Human Rights.

[37] *Cf.* J. Poniatowski, "War and Aggression in Western Eyes" (1953) 6 *Eastern Q.* 27, 31, 32 as to unredressed wrongs.

[38] *Cf.* the related point of R. B. Pal, *International Military Tribunal* (1953) that "even now questions of very great weight in the life of States are left *outside* the system and no State would agree to make them justiciable. . . . *No customary law can develop in respect of them until they are brought within the domain of law.*" (56, and see also 58-59.) And *cf.* J. L. Kunz ("*Bellum Justum* . . ." (1951) 45 *A.J.I.L.* 528, 530), who interestingly points out that the "just war" according to the classical doctrine was "a reaction against a wrong," a procedure either in restitution, or compensation for torts, or broken guarantees, or in criminal law by way of punishment and sanction.

This is not a mere matter of "perfectionism", as Professor Röling implies in his delightful quip that "if the Lord God had been such a perfectionist, He would never have succeeded in formulating the Ten Commandments." (B. V. A. Röling, "On Aggression . . ." (1955) 2 *Nederlands T.Int.R.* 167, 177.) For, on the one hand, the Author of the Ten Commandments did not seek, as do the ardent definers of aggression, to single out one small part of man's duties and leave all the rest to barbarous anarchy. They provided, for their time, a rounded statement of all the main duties of men. And, on the other hand, even their Author did not purport within the rounded Code to support one part by the direct penalties, and leave the observance of all the rest to chance or malice.

[39] It is not, of course; though the concept may play an ancillary role in judging a plea of self-defence.

[39a] For the former Soviet agreement with this view, see *supra* Ch. 6, n.24.

municipal law is built not on the aggression notion, but more on specific offences such as "larceny" or "rape", on which the community has already made its standards definite by specific detailed rules. In international law such specific rules are still largely unformed, and therefore still have to be formulated and agreed before a "crime" of aggression can be given any advance precision of content.[40] We have examined the vain attempts to sidestep this issue by making decisive the priority in time of some defined act such as the first declaration of war, bombardment, or crossing of the frontier. Agreement has not come on those lines; and in a future in which a State's very survival may depend on accurate anticipation of the potential enemy's attack, and each may sincerely feel that only by its own first blow can it hope to survive an impending enemy assault, the prospects of such agreement along such lines are likely to fade rather than otherwise.[41] One result of this lack of consensus is that if we are to use the notion of aggression as a legal notion at all, each application of it prerequires a full assessment in the light of the whole course of the State relations concerned, of the merits of each side of the dispute to which the resort to arms is a climax, including the proportionality of the reaction to the wrong.[42] We thus seem to be thrown back on the hitherto intractable problems of the "just" and "unjust" causes of war,[43] despite two generations of effort to substitute more "sensible", "objective", "externally verifiable" tests, such as use of armed force across a frontier.[44] And it is, as was to be expected, that such tests

---

[40] It is this point which seems inadequately formulated in the comment of Mr. Al Chalabi (Iraq) (A/AC.77/SR.18, p.7) that "the fact that the U.S.S.R. definition amounted to a truism was due to a mistaken approach which gave excessive prominence to the physical act of aggression and neglected the juridical aspect which was the most important".

[41] So *cf.* R. B. Pal (*op.cit.* 115-116) who observes that "emphasis on an arbitrarily fixed *status quo* would certainly not lead us to any understanding of the real conditions of peace and would fail to build any respect for justice. A trial conducted on this basis may be sufficiently unrevealing so as to shut out the essential facts responsible for the world trouble and may, at the same time, afford ample opportunity for a collective expression of retributive and aggressive sentiment."

[42] And including, as C. A. Pompe (*Aggressive War* 177) well points out in relation to Nuremberg not only the full circumstances of starting the war, but the gravity of the consequences thereof, for example, the war crimes and mass murders of the war waged by the Axis Powers.

Cf. G. Podrea, *"L'Agression . . ."* (1952) 30 *R.D.I.* 367, 369; Komarnicki, 43, and citations, *supra* n.38.

The above result coincides with the first of the conceivable classes of tests detected by Professor Wright, "The Concept of Aggression . . ." (1935) 29 *A.J.I.L.* 373, 378ff., namely that which gives weight to "events which occurred before fighting began", and which while perhaps best conforming to the usual conception of justice, are incapable of rapid application since possibly involving hundreds or thousands of events, evaluation of which would require long and laborious analysis. The difficulties, he says, are no less great "whether we centre our interest on the matter of legal rights, or in the military field, and ask who was responsible for starting an armament race, or in the psychological field and ask who had developed a spirit of aggrandizement, or in the procedural field and ask who during the course of controversy had refused to accept reasonable proposals of pacific settlement." (379.)

[43] *Cf.* on the intractability of this question in the context of the old "just war" doctrine, J. L. Kunz, *"Bellum Justum* and *Bellum Legale"* (1951) 45 *A.J.I.L.* 528, 531ff. And see *supra* Ch. 6, n.3.

[44] The most ingenious and diligent analysis is still perhaps that of Quincy Wright, *op.cit.* (1935) at 380ff., who after pointing out the difficulties of full evaluation of the

have never even approached acceptance save subject to qualifications, such as those touching "legitimate" self-defence, or "provocation", which reintroduce by the back door the very questions of justice, which have been vainly ejected through the front door. As with lack of "due process" so with aggression, there is no such easy escape from the duty of seeking just solutions; and the search for such solutions necessarily requires us to consider the full complexity of the situation which is to be judged.[45]

These observations reinforce the suspicion already raised from other standpoints that to make it a pre-condition of peace enforcement that we discover an acceptable definition capable of yielding precise results in future situations, is to put the cart before the horse. We cannot expect this single notion of aggression or any definition of it to provide a substitute for the vast bodies of law, and the complex and sensitive institutions, still required to delimit effectively the *meum* and *tuum* of international life to a degree which will induce States to accept[46] the collective enforcement of the resul-

---

preceding history, points out that "tests confining attention to events which occurred at the time fighting began, conform less to the usual conception of justice, and still raise (though to a lesser degree) difficulties of proof, and objective evaluation, especially in view of the tension at the moment of crisis". "The difficulties," he thinks, "are similar whether we inquire who first invaded someone else's territory, committed other acts of war, or omitted legal formalities in the initiation of hostilities; who first issued a mobilization or other military order rendering an offensive movement inevitable; who, at the moment hostilities began, wanted war and who did not; who, at that moment was ready to arbitrate or conciliate, and who was not." (379.) These difficulties, he admits, render this class of tests "seldom capable of providing the rapid and precise conclusions which a war prevention procedure demands". (See 380, and *cf.* Ch. 9, *infra passim.*)

We are unable (for reasons given *supra* pp.109ff.) to share Professor Wright's greater optimism as to tests based upon events after fighting is in progress. That writer thinks that these tests may make use of events such as a cease-fire order, and the parties' attitudes thereto, which are prepared or observed with the purpose of providing a test of aggression, thus relying on "experimental" rather than "historical" evidence. As shown above (pp.28ff.), modern wars make it even more impossible to support Professor Wright's definition of an aggressor as "a State which is under an obligation not to resort to force, which is employing force against another State, and which refuses to accept an armistice proposed in accordance with a procedure which it has accepted to implement its no-force obligation" (*id.* 381). As to whether League Council practice under Art. 11 of the Covenant really warrants (as the learned writer assumes) his above inferences, see *ibid.*, and also *supra* 38ff.

45 It is, therefore, quite topsy-turvy in relation to the continuing realities of international life, for M. Franklin (*The Conception of Aggression* 8) to claim that by its draft definition "the Soviet Union surpassed Grotius' distinction between just and unjust war", that Grotius remained at the level of "abstraction" because he reflected a "metaphysical natural law conception of war instead of an historical conception thereof", and because the conception of unjust war was an unqualified conception. The true position seems largely the reverse on all counts; except, that is, for that kind of concreteness of the Soviet draft which is a concealed guarantee of its own special interests. (See *supra* Ch. 6.) Professor Franklin indeed almost drops this concealment, when he insists (6) that the Soviet conception of aggression embodies the narrow truth, "aggressive war . . . [results] from imperialism . . . where the means of production [are] privately owned". *Cf.* for a very different interpretation from Mr. Franklin's, L. Schultz, *"Der Sowjetische Begriff der Aggression"* (1956) 2 *Osteuropa-Recht* 274.

46 J. Maktos, *"La Question de la Définition de l'Agression"* (1952) 30 *R.D.I.* 5, 6: *"Il ne s'agit pas de la définition du terme 'aggression' dont il est facile de donner non pas une, mais plusieurs définitions. Il s'agit du développement du droit international."* (This is a summary of the author's remarks as U.S. representative on the Sixth Commission in the debate of Jan. 10, 1952, on the Report of the Third Session, International Law Commission.)

tant *status quo*. Pending the development of such bodies of law, if we were to use the aggression notion at all, progress would rather have to depend on the establishment (necessarily gradual) of appropriate organs to apply the aggression notion as best they can.[47] Finally, however, the fact that no adequate and reliable short cuts to the judgment of "aggression" at the moment of crisis are thus available, must inevitably raise the question whether we are wise to continue to try to base collective peace enforcement action on the notion of "aggression" at all.[48] Preoccupation with the problem of definition of aggression may have to be viewed as a vain abstraction of a single ingredient of a complex problem, and the act of abstraction as itself a serious distortion of a reality in complex flux which only the painful development of complex bodies of law and institutions will ever finally master. These are questions to which we shall return more fully in the final Chapter.

---

[47] *Cf.* D. Sidjanski et S. Castanos, "*'L'Agresseur' et l' 'Agression' au Point de Vue Idéologique et Réel*" (1952) 30 *R.D.I.* 44, 45, who after stressing the imperfect state of the international legal order, including the absence of compulsory jurisdiction over States, observe that the extension of jurisdictional power must have priority over definitional tasks. In this state of the matter (they think) definitions should aim not only at guiding practice, with due account of practice, but at being just in themselves and in the context of their operation, as well as (above all) capable of producing results in our actual situation. "*Ainsi, si la définition de l'agression peut être utile, voire nécessaire en tant qu'orientation, rigide et automatique, elle sera lourde de conséquences néfastes. La question est beaucoup plus complexe qu'on ne désire la croire. Une simple définition ne saurait la résoudre.*" We agree in substance with this position. And *cf.* J. Maktos, article cited, 30 *R.D.I.* 5, 6; and Komarnicki, 43.

Connect also a main point (in the context) of the Chinese view that it was better, instead of attempting to define aggression, to search for means to enforce respect for the Charter provisions. See A/AC.77/SR.18, p.6, and *1956 Sp.Com.Rep.* 12.

[48] It is thus, in the actual world, profoundly self-contradictory to lay down simultaneously as concurrent conditions of peace *both* the demand for change conformable to justice, and the demand for a precise automatically operating definition of aggression, as was common in the League period. See e.g. A. B. Plaunt in Bourquin (ed.), *Collective Security* 295, C. Jordan, *id.* 301-304. And a similar comment is to be made concerning demands for a definition of aggression which shall simultaneously embrace "every act contrary to law and justice", and also be "a solid base" for collective security. See e.g. A. Derying in Bourquin (ed.), *Collective Security* 325.

CHAPTER 8

AGGRESSION AND INDIVIDUAL CRIMINALITY

I. "AGGRESSIVE WAR" AT THE LONDON CONFERENCE, 1945, AND AT NUREMBERG.

While the context of League discussions of aggression shifted between the functions of peace enforcement and disarmament, discussion after World War II opened boldly against the third and comparatively novel background of the trial and punishment of individuals for the crime of "aggressive war-making".[1] By Article 6 of the Charter of the International Military Tribunal, annexed to the London Agreement of August 8, 1945, France, the Soviet Union, the United Kingdom and the United States established an International Military Tribunal for the trial of certain war criminals,[2] on counts *inter alia of* "crimes against peace: namely, planning, preparation, initiation or waging of a war of aggression, or a war in violation of international treaties, agreements or assurances".[3]

At the London Conference, the United States had proposed the inclusion of a definition of aggression in terms broadly of the 1933 Disarmament Conference's Committee formula, itself based on a Soviet proposal; that is, based on the first commission of a declaration of war, territorial invasion, armed attack on territory, ships or aircraft, naval blockade, or support of armed bands.[4] As in its 1933 form the definition would have negatived any "political, military, economic or other considerations as justification for such actions",[5] but it would also have affirmed as a justification "legitimate self-defence, that is to say, resistance to an act of aggression, or action to assist a State which has been subjected to aggression".[6] On the Soviet view

---

[1] We are not here concerned with the wisdom or morality of such trial or punishment, nor with the arguments as to retrospectivity. On the contemporary polemical literature, see *inter alia* R. H. Jackson, *The Nürnberg Case* (1947), S. Glueck, *The Nuremberg Trial and Aggressive War* (1946), R. B. Pal, *International Military Tribunal,* Viscount Maugham, *UNO and War Crimes* (1951), C. A. Pompe, *Aggressive War* 177ff., and other literature collected in Stone, *Conflict* 359. And see the argument of Professor Jahrreiss, for the Defendants at the Trial of the Major War Criminals, International Military Tribunal, *Trial Major War Criminals,* vol. 17, pp.460ff.

For other contemporary polemical literature by German authors see, *inter alia, A. v. Knieriem, Nürnberg, Rechtliche und Menschliche Probleme* (1953); W. Grewe and Otto Küster, *Nürnberg als Rechtsfrage* (1947); H. Laternser, *Verteidigung Deutscher Soldaten* (1950).

For an evaluation of the moral aspect of the Nuremberg Trials from a thomistic point of view, see J. P. Kenny, *Moral Aspects of Nuremberg* (1949).

[2] Those "whose offences had no particular geographical location" (Art. 6).

[3] On the lateness (after the Axis launching of World War II) of proposals for criminal punishment of individuals, see C. A. Pompe, *Aggressive War* 177.

[4] See Report of Robert H. Jackson, U.S. Representative to the Conference on Military Trials, London, 1945, *Dept. of State Publ.* 3080 (1949) 294. And see *supra* Ch. 6, n.22.

[5] *Cf.* the U.S. Prosecutor's argument 2 *Trial Major War Criminals* 149.

[6] This last excuse would probably not have aided many of the major war criminals of that period.

that definition was unnecessary for the instant purpose, and that the London Conference was in any case not an appropriate draftsman, the United States proposal was rejected, no definition of "aggression" at all being provided for the International Military Tribunal.[7] The Soviet view clearly was directed to *ad hoc* action against the particular defeated aggressors, and was opposed to any implication of universality for the future.[8] And this, together with the resulting appearance of *ex post facto* capital punishment, has been a main ground of polemical attacks on the Nuremberg proceedings. The Nuremberg indictments included the following charges against certain defendants,[9] namely: (1) "Aggressive action against Austria and Czechoslovakia". (2) Planning, preparation and initiation of aggressive war against Poland from March, 1939, to September, 1939. (3) Planning and execution of attacks on Denmark, Norway, Belgium, the Netherlands, Luxembourg, Yugoslavia, and Greece: September, 1939, to April, 1941, constituting a "general war of aggression". (4) Invasion of Soviet territory, on June 22, 1941, in violation of the Non-Aggression Pact of August 23, 1939. (5) Collaboration with Italy and Japan and aggressive war against the United States: November, 1936, to December, 1941.[10]

The Tribunal was required, therefore, to determine whether the individual conduct proved amounted to the capitally punishable activities under the "aggressive war" count, without any other further guidance as to the notion of "aggression" itself. The action which it took has three possible bearings on our inquiry. First, it may be regarded as some evidence that the term "aggression" is a useful one, though it has to be added immediately that this point may fade somewhat as we move from the field of punishment of individuals after a war is over, to the prospective value in terms of deterrence and peace enforcement. Second, it may be regarded as evidence that a determination of "aggression" without further criteria by an international body, even of victor States, can command a degree of acceptance by the wisdom and conscience of mankind; though it is to be added here also that acceptance has certainly been far from complete, as evidenced not only in publicists' criticisms, but by dissents on the Tokyo Tribunal.[11] And Judge Röling of the Tokyo Tribunal pointed out in his dissent[12] that it was not

---

[7] Before the rejection the United States had indicated willingness to omit the naval blockade, and support of armed bands, categories of acts. The Soviet attitude in 1945 was later explained by Soviet delegate M. Morozov on Jan. 21, 1952 (*G.A.O.R. VI,* Sixth Committee, 293rd Meeting, p.243) on the ground that General Nikitchenko had not been instructed on "the specific question of defining aggression", as distinct merely from that of "whether or not such a definition should be included" in the Nuremberg Charter. And see *supra* Ch. 6, n.23, on the shifts in the U.S.S.R. and U.S. positions.

[8] See the discussion in C. A. Pompe, *Aggressive War* 177ff., 192ff.

[9] 1 *Trial Major War Criminals* 27, 36ff.

[10] *Id.* 40.

[11] See Judge R. B. Pal *supra* n.1, 14-65, 109-121, Judge Röling, Opinion (Dissenting) of Nov. 12, 1948 (Transcript, Harvard Law School, p.50), quoted Sohn, *Cases on United Nations Law* (1956) 938.

[12] He admitted even that to a degree the impulse leading to wars of conquest might originate partly in the defensive sphere, but said that this could here be left out since the purpose of the trials was not so much retribution for the offence as a measure for protection by elimination of dangerous persons. It is not quite clear whether the

necessary on the facts in either the Nuremberg or Tokyo Trials "to draw a sharp line between aggression and defence. Here, as the evidence shows, we are dealing with wars which can be called wars of conquest, wars of illegal expansion. These wars of conquest certainly come within the scope of illegal aggression, whatever definition might be given".[13]

Third, as the International Law Commission was later to observe,[14] not only were no criteria of aggression provided for the Nuremberg Tribunal, but the Tribunal itself did not formulate any criteria in the course of its determinations. What the Tribunal did was to determine whether aggression had occurred by a review of the historical events, in the full context of the circumstances of alleged aggression and the relations of the States concerned, without resort to any of the much debated pseudo-automatic criteria. Moreover, the search over this area was for both inculpating and exculpating factors. The Tribunal, for example, addressed itself quite flexibly to the related questions whether the invasions of Norway, Belgium, the Netherlands, and Luxembourg, and the Soviet Union could in some way be justified on grounds of self-defence.[15] The only pertinent principle, indeed, which it can be said to have firmly insisted on was that its own determination could not be hampered by the invader's claim to be acting in self-defence. "Whether action under the claim of self-defence was in fact aggressive or defensive must ultimately be subject to investigation and adjudication if international law is ever to be enforced".[16]

The Tribunal found, in fine, that Germany had been guilty of aggression against no less than twelve States, without receiving or formulating any definition of either "aggression" or "self-defence".[17] And it made clear also

---

Judge here meant that the special facts of the Nazi and Japanese adventures made the distinction irrelevant, or whether he is asserting its irrelevance to all criminal proceedings, on the last stated ground.

[13] It is surely only for this "core area" of aggression that we can really accept, in its application to the criminal punishment of individuals, Professor Röling's very strong assertion that ". . . a judge does not need a definition. As easily as he operates with the crime of 'murder' he might operate with the crime of 'aggression'." ("On Aggression . . ." (1955) 2 *Nederlands T.Int.R.* 167, 170.)

[14] See the Commission's formulation of the Nuremberg Principles, *G.A.O.R. V*, Supp. 12 (Doc. A/1316) pp.11-14, under Principle VI:

> The Charter of the Nuremberg Tribunal did not contain any definition of "war of aggression" nor was there any such definition in the judgment of the Tribunal. It was by reviewing the historical events before and during the war that it found that certain of the defendants planned, and waged aggressive wars against twelve nations. . . . According to the Tribunal this made it unnecessary "to discuss the subject in further detail" or to consider whether these aggressive wars were also in violation of international treaties.

[15] See the Judgment, 1 *Trial Major War Criminals* 207-210, 215. It did not wholly exclude the possibility that "preventive" action or even invasion might be consistent, in some circumstances, with a plea of self-defence.

[16] Judgment 208.

[17] The prosecution, though admitting the absence of a definition of aggressive war, and the difficulties of definition, rested on the argument that all the Nazi invasions concerned were "unambiguously aggressive" and that the remote causes invoked by the defendants were "too insincere and inconsistent, too complicated and doctrinaire to be the subject of profitable inquiry in this trial". 2 *Trial Major War Criminals* 149. Insofar as Q. Wright (article cited (1956) 50 *A.J.I.L.* 514, 521-22) suggests that any precise definition was expressed (or can be implied with confidence) from the Judgment, we

that these findings were independent even of the question whether these wars were also wars "in violation of international treaties, agreements or assurances" within its terms of reference. And this is the more striking since the reasons for demanding precise advance criteria of aggression might seem more imperative when trying men for their lives that when a politico-military organ is directing itself to peace enforcement.[18] In criminal proceedings, moreover, which are unlikely to take place while the breach of the peace is actually continuing, there is time to canvass the refinements of the conception of aggression; the opposite is usually the case in peace enforcement action. We are here, as we shall see, confronted with conflicting desiderata. The precise advance criteria which may be necessary to guide individual conduct so as to avoid *ex post facto* criminal punishment, may in peace enforcement be a signpost for the ill-intentioned, and a trap for the unwary State, as well as a serious obstacle to speed and freedom of manoeuvre of the peace-enforcing organ.[19]

II. CONFLICTING DESIDERATA OF CRIMINAL AND PEACE ENFORCEMENT FUNCTIONS.

It is significant that the first impulse of the United Nations towards the enterprise of defining aggression lies precisely in the area of criminal punishment of individuals rather than in that of collective peace enforcement. The mandate given by its resolution of December 11, 1946, to the Committee on Progressive Development of International Law and its Codification opened the way to efforts to formulate the principles of the Charter and Judgment of the Nuremberg Tribunal, and to draft a code of offences against the peace and security of mankind impinging on the present matters.[20] It was (as we have seen) [21] only after 1950 that the matter of definition of aggression in the context of peace enforcement came to dominate and (by reason of failure to distinguish the problems involved) [22] to confuse the debates.

After 1950, in the context of efforts to build up the General Assembly's powers to replace those of the Security Council, the question of defining aggression became a major diplomatic and political issue. And when the

respectfully disagree.

18 See *infra passim,* this Chapter.

19 The above aspects of the Judgment of Oct. 1, 1946, should not be concealed by the fact that they are somewhat overlaid by the precise terms of the Charter as to the "planning, preparing, initiating, and waging" of wars of aggression, as well as by the Tribunal's decision to consider the first count for conspiring or having a common plan to commit crimes against the peace, along with that concerning aggressive war, and by the distinction drawn between "acts of aggression" and a "war of aggression". (See p.186 of the Judgment.)

20 See also Ch. 3, s.III.

21 See also *supra* Ch. 3, s.II.

22 For earlier attempts to distinguish the definitional problems, see Q. Wright, "The Concept of Aggression . . ." (1935) 29 *A.J.I.L.* 373, 376, who proposed a single definition for preventive, deterrent, and remedial as well as punitive purposes. But see *id.* 389 where in the related context of international claims arising from responsibility for hostilities, he fully recognises the discrepant desiderata.

Differentiation of definitions for other purposes was also sometimes proposed in the League period, e.g. as between sanctions procedure and non-aggression treaties (Lord Lytton in Bourquin (ed.), *Collective Security* 329, C. A. W. Manning, *id.* 338), or as between various regions (C. K. Webster, *id.* 335).

International Law Commission abandoned the search for definition proper, and fell back by way of compromise in Article 2 of its Draft Code of Offences against Peace and Security, on mere illustrative non-exhaustive indications of acts which were and acts which were not "acts of aggression",[23] the enterprise of definition moved more into the politico-military peace enforcement context in the General Assembly's Sixth Committee and the two Special Committees of 1953 and 1956.

The "aggression" notion thus moved towards the centre of the post-World War II stage in two distinct roles—the judicial-criminal and the politico-military. The gist at Nuremberg was the punishment of individuals for "the planning, preparation, initiation and waging of a war of aggression, or a war in violation of international treaties".[24] Simultaneously, however, the notion of act of "aggression" had also figured in Article 39 of the Charter as one basis, along with "any threat to the peace, or breach of the peace", for the Security Council's peace enforcement powers.[25] We have seen that the draftsmen both of the Nuremberg and San Francisco Charters deliberately refrained from defining "aggression",[26] and that the latter, by giving the Security Council its full powers on any mere threat to the peace or breach of the peace, probably intended that so far as possible the Security Council should not feel incumbered by the notion at all. Yet as long as the study of the notion of aggression proceeded separately in these two contexts, it was naturally taken for granted that any definition apt for one purpose would also be apt for the other;[28] and this hazardous assumption has only been gradually given its necessary qualifications between 1950 and the present day.

It is the more important to stress the need to distinguish the problems of definition as they affect these distinct functions. On the one hand, in the design to deter individuals from or to punish participation in international aggression, both effectiveness as a deterrent and the policy against *ex post facto* punishment demand precision of advance definition;[29] and the more leisurely judicial enquiry after the event is also tolerant of the refined

---

[23] See Ch. 3, s.III. An "act of aggression" was to include certain acts, the character of which might otherwise be disputable, such as (for example) a threat to resort thereto, the preparation for the employment of armed forces, and the fomentation of civil strife in another State. It was *not* to include an act of collective self-defence, or an act done pursuant to decision or recommendation of a competent organ of the United Nations.

[24] It is immaterial for the present purposes whether such a "crime" existed in 1939 or 1946. It suffices for our purposes that there was at least a movement *de lege ferenda* to create one.

[25] The term also appears in Art. 1(1) and 53. See *supra* Chs. 1 and 5, ss.I-II.

[26] See *supra* pp. 134-135, and Ch. 5, s.I. It has nevertheless often been assumed since that time, that by applying a definition, as compared with applying the notion undefined, action could be expedited. Even if a feasible and acceptable definition were found, however, this is doubtful. See Ch. 4, s.IV, and *infra* pp.154ff.

[27] And see also *supra* Ch. 1, *passim.*

[28] This assumption appears to be implicit in the Secretary-General's Report, *G.A.O.R. VII,* Ann., Item 54. A/2211, *passim* and esp. pp.44ff.; and though it is not attributable to the International Law Commission, it certainly is manifest in the manner in which the General Assembly and its Committees have discussed the various proposed definitions which have come before them.

[29] On Dec. 9, 1948, the General Assembly had adopted the Declaration of Human

enquiries for which the application of definitions may call. On the other hand, in using this notion to base the power of politico-military action of the Security Council or General Assembly for peace enforcement, vagueness rather than precision of definition, seems called for;[30] and, of course, the emergency atmosphere in which this function has usually to be performed, is probably intolerant even of the delays involved in any use at all of the notion of aggression.[31] While it is, of course, as important to States as to individuals that they shall not unjustly be charged with conduct which they could not have known legally to constitute "aggression", these differences between the two functions remain important. They came nearer to recognition by the 1956 Special Committee than in earlier discussions.[32] Some delegates were concerned that differences in definition arising from the different addressees of the norms, and the different sanctions, might raise dangers of contradiction between the definitions directed to the respective functions;[33] some delegates, moreover, thought that definition for the purposes of a criminal code might be easier to achieve, as not involving national interests to the same degree.[34]

III. *MENS REA* IN INTERNATIONAL AGGRESSION.

Closely connected with this contradiction between the desiderata of precision and certainty required by effective deterrence and just administration of criminal law, and of a certain vagueness and flexibility for peace enforcement, is the difficulty of saying what is the *mens rea* involved in the crime of aggression. It certainly seems unthinkable that no *mens rea* should be

---

Rights of which Art. 11 (2) provides that: "No one shall be held guilty of any penal offence on account of any act or omission which did not constitute a penal offence, under national or international law, at the time when it was committed." *Cf.* on this point D. H. N. Johnson, "The Draft Code of Offences against the Peace and Security of Mankind" (1955) 4 *Int. and Comp. L.Q.* 415, 418-49. So Mr. Justice Pal's dissent on the Tokyo Tribunal, holding that "to leave the aggressive character of war to be determined according to 'the popular sense' or (the general moral sense) of humanity is to rob the law of its predictability", is spoken in this context. Though it must be added that in particular cases there may be judicial application without definition, not on the basis of such "shifting opinion and ill-considered thought", but because the particular acts fall within the core area rather than the penumbral area of the concept, thus leaving no serious doubt. See *op.cit. supra* n.1, 112-113.

30 *Cf.* D. H. N. Johnson, *op.cit.* 445, 454. As will be seen, however, I find it difficult to follow Mr. Johnson in thinking (*id.* 460) that the Commission erred "significantly when it resolved to deal with the criminal responsibility of the individuals only, and not with that of States". The point is not merely in the contrast of individual and State, as accused persons, but in the divergence between the tests of criminal punishment and peace enforcement respectively. If, indeed, it were attempted to extend criminal responsibility to States, certain further discriminations might be necessary. It is difficult psychologically to impute guilt or *mens rea* to a State entity, though it may be quite reasonable to impose on a State entity responsibility, e.g. by reparations payment, for the acts or omissions of individuals who have criminal guilt in the ordinary sense. *Cf.* from the psychoanalytical standpoint the problem of imputation of guilt generally, A. MacC. Armstrong, *Philosophy and Phenomenological Research* (1955) 18-44.

31 See *infra* pp.154-160.

32 Some aspects of them had been well pointed out by D. H. N. Johnson, "Code of Offences against Peace and Security of Mankind" (1955) 4 *Int. and Comp L.Q.* 445, 454.

33 *1956 Sp.Com.Rep.* 6.

34 *1956 Sp.Com.Rep.* 7.

required for so grave an individual crime;[35] yet it is difficult also to see how any *mens rea appropriate for this purpose* could also be a satisfactory requirement for the purpose of the peace enforcement function. Even those who are convinced that the aggression notion is an absolutely necessary basis for peace enforcement admit that a requirement of proof of *mens rea* might impede this function,[36] and even frustrate altogether the efforts to recognise and deal with "aggression" as *State* conduct.[37] Definers of aggression, therefore, face the awkwardness that it may be necessary ethically and in terms of the concept of "crime" to require and define the *mens rea* in "aggression" for the purpose of criminal punishment of individuals, and yet also conceptually impossible and practically unwise to do this for the purposes of peace enforcement.[38]

This "necessity" which is also an "impossibility" may, indeed, exist even *within* the peace enforcement function itself. There may well be cases in which it will be impossible, except by reference to the mental element accompanying the warlike action, to distinguish "aggression" from action in

---

[35] *Cf.* C. A. W. Manning in Bourquin (ed.), *Collective Security* 338: "If you are going to compare war to murder, you should surely take account of the state of mind." Logically this need not be so, of course; liability might be absolute as in an expanding area of minor offences in municipal systems, e.g. contraventions of pure food and drug laws. This, however, could scarcely provide the correct analogy.

Cf. in general on the point in the text, G. G. Fitzmaurice, "The Definition of Aggression" repr. (1952) 1 *Int. and Comp. L.Q.* 137, 140, objecting that the Soviet draft "leaves entirely out of account the subjective elements necessarily involved . . ." The question what are these "subjective" elements is of course a different one, which we are here concerned to open further.

[36] *Cf.* Introd., s.III. For the introduction of the term in the U.N. debates see M. Spiropoulos in A/CN.4/44, pp.64ff. G. Scelle, article (1936) cited Introd. n.20, at 379, squarely takes the view in the text. Only the *factum* of the use of force is in his view material. So *cf.* as to the treacherous nature of contemporary expressions or other evidence of opinions and attitudes once hostilities have broken out, Q. Wright, "The Concept of Aggression . . ." (1935) 29 *A.J.I.L.* at 380.

It should be noted that M. Spiropoulos is not always clear as to whether he means by "intention" the deliberate commission of the *factum,* or a *mens rea* additional to the *factum,* e.g. that the act shall not have been done in legitimate defence. At moments he even suggests that there is a right of self-defence against a mere "aggressive intention". See *G.A.O.R. V,* Sixth Committee, 279th Meeting, para. 10, 281st Meeting, para. 13.

[37] The enterprising draftsmen of the proposal in "The Meaning of Aggression in the United Nations Charter" (1954) 33 *Nebraska L.R.* 606, esp. 607-608, seem perhaps insufficiently advertent to this difficulty, and the others later discussed, especially in a definition evidently offered to serve both the politico-military and the judicial functions. According to the commentary their purpose was that of making the conduct defined appear as a "high crime" rather than "a mere tort".

[38] There is an even deeper paradox whose relation to our subject requires further exploration. This is the general assumption, in Sir J. Fischer Williams' words, that "aggression implies a moral stigma" (see his *Chapters* (1934) 119). Yet in psychological and social psychological terms "aggressiveness" usually has a morally neutral meaning. A deficiency in it may, indeed, represent a serious defect of personality, and even be symptomatic (in extreme cases) of insanity or mental deficiency. In psychology, also, the term may be used to cover ability to take the initiative in what the international lawyer and diplomat might well call "legitimate self-defence". And see *supra* Ch. 1, n.2.

As J. L. Kunz observes (*"Bellum Justum . . ."* (1951) 45 *A.J.I.L.* 528, 530), during the period when the *recta intentio* of the monarch directed to the supposedly known "just causes" of war was determinative of guilt, the just war doctrine remained perhaps necessarily "wholly ethical". In theory, under this doctrine, the exaction of terms unrelated to the "just cause" would render the war "unjust" *ab initio* through the *injusta pax.*

legitimate "self-defence" or "defence of rights".[39] Corresponding problems have, of course, arisen, as to *mens rea* of corporations in municipal law,[40] but however it be as to the solutions there adopted, it must be clear that the complexity of the policy-making process in many modern States, renders it most doubtful that there will always be examinable mind or minds the content of which can be imputed to the State, as its *mens rea.* Of course, *mens rea* may have to be constructive or imputed even in relation to *individual* guilt; but while some psychological facts or inferences thereto are there usually available, this cannot be taken for granted in relation to so complex an entity as the modern State.[41] While this does not conclude the question whether imputation of *mens rea* to a State is possible or warranted, it does suggest that this question is not easily answerable, at any rate by merely juristic techniques.

Certainly, we cannot dispose of this matter of State *mens rea* merely by insisting that both the *factum* and *mens rea* of State "aggression" are those of human beings who act for the State. For how are we to fix the *animus aggressionis* of the human beings themselves, except by reference to the notion of "aggression", which, in turn refers us to State conduct and State objectives? Even if, therefore, it were correct to impute the *mens rea* of its human agents to the State, the content of this *mens rea* would still depend on the definition of State "aggression"; and it is precisely that notion (and the role of *mens rea* in it) of which the definition is being sought. And even if such a definition were given, problems would still remain of determining what degree of identification of human agents with the State suffices to ground the imputation of their *mens rea* to the State.[42] Between the unmistakably willed act and *mens rea* of a dictatorial head of State, such as Adolf Hitler, and the acts of a minor official which may be virtually under compulsion of the complex legal order of the State, is a great range of possibilities. There might be little difficulty in reflecting the varying degrees of individual participation in punishments meted out to individuals on the criminal law side of this enterprise; and it might even be possible *thereafter* to make *ex post facto* imputations of *mens rea* to the State concerned. But the question of identification of State aggression for purposes of peace enforcement will usually arise in situations which cannot

---

39 *Cf.* G. G. Fitzmaurice's view, "The Definition of Aggression" repr. (1952) 1 *Int. and Comp. L.Q.* 137, 140.

40 See J. W. C. Turner (ed.), *Kenny's Outlines of Criminal Law* (16 ed., 1952) 's.50, pp.63ff., R. Cross and P. A. Jones, *An Introduction to Criminal Law* (1953) 70.

41 We need not, in taking this position, go quite as far as P. E. Corbett ("Social Basis of a Law of Nations" (1954) 85 *H.R.* 471, 482ff.) who thinks that the real nature of the State as a social process has been distorted by reification, personification, and deification.

42 In considering how far individuals were to be held criminally responsible for State aggression the Nuremberg Tribunal seemed to require both that the individual should have exerted effective influence in planning, etc., aggressive war, and that he should have known that the war was "aggressive". But as observed above they did not render precise the *mens* involved in aggression by States. The International Law Commission, in its Draft Code, seeks to avoid the issue by providing that individuals are criminally liable if "responsible" for aggression by the State. And *cf.* Q. Wright, article cited (1956) 50 *A.J.I.L.* 514, at 522.

be tested by *preliminary* criminal trials of national leaders; and they may even arise in situations in which criminal charges against individuals cannot be brought home at all.

IV. POTENTIALITIES OF CASE TO CASE DETERMINATION.

Lack of agreed definition of aggression may therefore be of different import for the prospects of politico-military peace enforcement, and for judicial-criminal action against individuals respectively; but it is not in itself conclusive as to the prospects of these two functions. In the first place, it is possible and (we have also shown) quite likely, that the notion of aggression is an unnecessary encumbrance of the function of peace enforcement.[43] In the second place, even if it were indispensable, we would have to remember that history has other instances of basic conceptions which were at first impossible to define, but acquired precision of outline in the course of application; we may have been unreasonable to expect to find acceptable definitions at this stage.

This concession is important; but it only reinforces the present thesis concerning the recent campaign to provide an immediate definition. For even if in the peace enforcement sphere an undefined and even changing concept[44] should be acceptable, its value would still depend on the existence of a forum capable of making it concrete by tolerably impartial decision in particular cases. While in the sphere of criminal punishment of individuals accepted ethical principles are generally assumed to require that the conditions for liability are reasonably well indicated in advance. The objective of deterrence produces here a like demand; for it can only be achieved in proportion as the conduct to be discouraged can be identified in advance of action.

Whether, in either sphere, we are entitled to expect that a succession of decisions in time will reveal a sufficient patterning of the conduct and intent to ground a statement of precise principles based on actual practice of States, is beyond present confident prediction. Yet, two indications are disheartening, even at this stage. One is that the juristic enterprise of formulating agreed criteria of aggression is clearly unlikely to yield *quick* results, and that this hard fact is not altered by our sense of its *urgency* for human survival. Another is that the further prospects for this enterprise do not depend merely or evenly mainly on legal analysis based on the conceptions, precepts and techniques of municipal and international law. They depend rather on political, economic and social-psychological factors affecting the limits of effective legal action, as well as on the future role of the State entity in controlling, distorting, or blocking human relations across State frontiers. To some of these factors we must now finally return.

---

43 *Supra* Ch. 1; and *infra* pp.154-158.

44 As was, for example, "the King's peace" for a long period of English legal history

V. OBSTACLES TO JUDGMENT: HISTORICAL TRUTH AND NATIONAL VERSIONS.

We have seen that a central obstacle to the achievement of agreed definition of aggression is that, in order to be feasible, acceptable and desirable, in the present state of the international community, such definition would have to have built into it minimal standards of justice as between the States at variance. And we have seen that, by the same token, the use of even the undefined notion of aggression calls for examination of the merits of the Parties' causes in the full context of action as pre-condition to judgment.[45] It follows that the use of this concept is inevitably affected by certain grave handicaps arising from the state of human knowledge and communication.

In many instances the judgment to be rendered on the aggression issue may pre-require an inquiry so wide and deep as to amount to the writing of the history of a substantial era of the relations of the States affected, and possibly of other States as well.[46] History, Burckhardt has said, "is the most unscientific of the sciences".[47] Even long after the event, when accurate documentation is available, professional historians make a necessary but imprecise distinction between the comparatively simple "events leading up to" and the usually complex "underlying causes" of a war. A judicial tribunal trying men for their lives, and *a fortiori* peace-enforcing organs seeking to fix international responsibility for aggression, could scarcely do less. Moreover few historians would attempt to write, except with firm disclaimers of its finality, the true explanation of an international conflict as it occurs before their contemporary eyes.[48] And what they would disclaim out of concern for their own repute as historians, they would certainly disclaim as a sufficient basis for convicting men of capital offences or for launching peace enforcement actions against particular States and peoples.

This would sufficiently impede quick determination of the issue of aggression in many cases, even if full and accurate evidence were likely to be available on such contemporary events. The future cases, however, are likely to be few in which we may feel as confident, as many of us were at

[45] See *supra passim,* esp. Chs. 1 and 7, and pp.154-158.

[46] We think, however, that it is pushing matters *à outrance* to say with Judge Pal (*International Military Tribunal* 33) that no present war can be "unjust" or "criminal" merely because the present interests of Western Powers in the Eastern hemisphere may have been formerly acquired "mostly through armed violence" and not "just" war. Few roots of title of men would sustain an indefinite tracing back in ultimate time; and the general application of the Judge's view would therefore frustrate at the outset all aspirations to either justice or legal order. We have tried to assess this matter from a position transcending the interests of the Western States. Nor does it meet this point for Judge Pal to say that "the man of violence cannot both genuinely repent of his violence and permanently profit by it". (135.) Who is "the man" to whom he here refers? How far back is any particular man's moral duty to be identified with that of his ancestors, or for that matter the moral right of *the victim* with *his* ancestors?

[47] J. Burckhardt, *Weltgeschichtliche Betrachtungen* (7 ed. 1949) 83. See also *id.* 254.

[48] On this aspect at least of Israeli-Arab controversies it is likely that there would be agreement on all hands with Mr. Rifai (Jordan), who after asking how far one should go in tracing back these problems, concludes "that whenever we try to stop at a certain stage in the past, events will take us to an earlier date" (A/PV.664, 11th Session, Feb. 28, 1957, p.22).

the Nuremberg Trials, that such testimony was in substance available; and few also would be the cases in which we may expect the tribunal to guide itself so scrupulously *in favorem libertatis* in the reception of evidence. For the future, indeed, we are likely to be increasingly confronted by the phenomenon of State manufacture of facts and the fabrication of spurious history. It is supremely in the area where States claim to act in self-defence, that is, where they conceive their vital interests to be involved, that national versions of "truth" flourish like jungle growth to hide the outlines of the landscape of truth. And George Orwell's description of the remaking of history as a normal function of the "Big Brother State" already has a certain foundation for expectancy in the practice of totalitarian States.

It would be optimistic to believe that this disturbing activity of official suppression, distortion and even direct falsification of current events and documents will not increase. For, while it is true that no State is in a position to make over all the facts of an international situation, it is also true that some segment of those facts often lies within the secret archives of each State, at the mercy of its government to suppress, distort and falsify. In these circumstances, even the most impartial international forum required to determine whether particular acts constitute aggressive war-making by a State or its agents, would face the extraordinary difficulties of doing so on the basis of evidence coming from official sources which may have the strongest motives, and the fullest opportunities to present only *those* facts, and to present them only in *that* light, which will further their own interests.

If international judges could be found with supreme skill as historians, and supreme objectivity as judges, they might still reconstruct an approximation to the full truth by gathering together, cross-checking, correcting, and re-integrating the dismembered and distorted national versions created and sponsored by interested States. This is conceivable; but only barely so. And it is at least as likely that the several limbs of dismembered Truth will, like those of the hero of the Finnish Kalevala myth, Lemminkäinen, move steadily down the spacious river of fact and fiction on which men drift towards the sea of oblivion. Unlike the fortunate Lemminkäinen, however, our dismembered Truth may have no devoted Mother to stand with infinite patience on the banks, to retrieve the severed members and restore them with loving care to sentient life.[49] The segments which even our ablest historians could retrieve and reconstruct would too often be those, not of Truth itself, but of a robot or a puppet, which "lives" and "moves" not by the inspiration of human love, but by the digitated strings of State propaganda.[50]

---

[49] In this striking myth even a mother's love and care needed the magic aid of bees, thus perhaps symbolising the indispensable supplementary role of patient, systematic labour. This tale, fills *Runo* (= Canto) XV of the Finnish epos *Kalevala*,.

[50] Only when the above difficulties are overlooked is it correct for Mr. Pompe (*Aggressive War* 58ff.) to recall the view of the German Commission of Experts for the Geneva Protocol that the aggressor could only be determined after the conflict, and after "the disclosure of all sources, the opening of all archives, the hearing of witnesses and experts and the forwarding of all other evidence". Nor does it meet the point for him to say that a solution as to responsibility for war can always be reached if there is "an impartial organ of observation", even if both sides must be considered to have

VI. WHAT FORUM, AND WHEN?

Even, moreover, if we could (as the Writer is convinced that we cannot in any presently foreseeable world) separate the question of aggression from that of the justice of the Parties' causes, it would have to be observed that the moral appeal and the socio-political importance of the *bellum justum* doctrine, has little chance of being effectively displaced by any mere automatically operating modern-type definition of "aggression". A State branded as an "aggressor" has remained and still remains able to invoke the *bellum justum* doctrine, or its version thereof, often with plausibility, and sometimes with widespread support of other States. This fact points to the basic weakness of the "aggression" notion once we attempt, in our existing world, to reduce it to any sets of simple facts, and extrude from it all reference to standards of justice. For if the charge of "aggressive war-making" can be confronted at the crisis of decision with defences of even plausibly higher moral persuasiveness, then the enterprise of making aggression a crime under international law loses much of its power and attractiveness as a rallying point for the common interest of peoples, and the cooperation of States in the tasks of peace enforcement.[51]

In a particular case, of course, the defence of "just war" against a charge of "aggressive war" might be entirely a spurious one, and one which an authoritative international forum (if it existed) might reject altogether. This, however, scarcely disposes of our contemporary difficulties. In our present international situation, the principal antagonists whose relations threaten the world with armed conflict are each surrounded by allies embracing most of the other important States of the world. It thus seems quite impossible to find a forum whose decision would be both objective and likely to win acceptance by the principal parties in conflict, certainly while the verdict of arms was still in the balance. And once the verdict of arms has given the victory to one side, the only forum would be one acceptable to the victor, and one whose objectivity would by that very token be more or less suspect to the other half of mankind, as well as to the careful historians of the future. It would be one, moreover, whose decision would admonish potential aggressors not so much against *waging*, as against *losing*, an aggressive war. And this is, to a degree, none the less the case even if the facts were so plain that even a forum clearly independent and impartial would have reached the same verdict.

Here, then, as at other crucial points in the argument, we are left with the impression of a dreamworld created by the blandishments of municipal criminal law analogies on the one hand, and by the formidable yearnings of all peoples for international peace and security on the other. The protagonists of an international criminal law have been insufficiently aware that the conditions of conflict and its control may be essentially different in international and municipal societies, and that these differences may largely

---

committed aggression or acted in self-defence.

51 Resol. 95 (I), G.A.O.R. I, Second Part of First Session, 23 Oct. to 15 Dec., 1946, p.188.

negate the value of any easy course of appropriating municipal criminal law analogies to international purposes. It may still be that experience of municipal criminal law has much to contribute to the growth of an international criminal law. But what this contribution can be—whether, indeed, and within what limits an international criminal law on this matter is possible at all—can only emerge (and then only with painful gradualness) from a far deeper analysis of the socio-political and psychological structure of inter-State relations, and of the influence of the State-entity on phenomena such as those presupposed by the doctrine of *mens rea,* or by the policy of deterrence in municipal criminal law.[52]

VII. DETERRENCE FROM WHAT? AND AGAINST WHOM?

The prospects for the objective of deterrence in the criminal punishment of individuals for participation in, planning or executing aggressive war also require a certain re-examination. Insofar as the enterprise of establishing an agreed definition or agreed criteria of aggression is directed to deterring individuals from aggressive war-making, it is pertinent to ask to whom the threats are addressed, and what is their psychological weight. If the State as a psychic entity independent of its individual members be the addressee, the whole enterprise turns on the dubious question whether this entity is sensitive to such pressures. The usual assumption, however, is that deterrence is aimed to influence rather the individual human beings, and groups or movements of such, who guide the affairs of the State Leviathan. But to locate and *a fortiori* to control these social forces is no easy task even in a monolithic authoritarian polity; in democratically organised States it may be fantastically difficult.

Even if such persons, groups and movements could be accurately identified, and the deterrent threat addressed unerringly to them, we are still far from assured of its effectiveness in the admitted conditions of the international community. It is easy to say that since the human beings concerned are capable of feeling guilt and fearing threats, they can be deterred from their evil courses. But the fact is that the norms and supporting threats issuing from the international community must struggle for influence over

---

Cf. A. Pompe, *Aggressive War* 100: "Even a superficial glance over post-war disputes . . . makes it already clear that . . . in most conflicts which do not originate from the greed of conquest of a powerful State but from a complicated unsolved situation, both parties can be considered aggressors in the wide sense of the concept. . . ." And see G. F. Kennan, "Lectures on Foreign Policy" (1951) 45 *Ill.L.Rev.* 721, 736-737: "Whoever enters into these unhappy depths looking for right and wrong will find himself wandering in the vale of total confusion and frustration . . . The causes of international conflict are sometimes too profound and too complex to be embraced just by an answer to the question 'who started it?' . . . I am not saying that there is no place for juridical rules in the lives of nations. I am saying that there are limits to the purposes which such rules can be expected to serve. . . ." The fact that we may disagree with the judgments of others on a particular conflict leaves the main point unaffected.

[52] Some of the matters raised in the following pages are often discussed in the form of the more general question whether the conception of crime can exist out of the context of a real international community under the reign of law. See e.g. Pal, *op.cit. supra* n.46, at 48, 70, 83. We hope it may prove useful to take the discussions on to the more concrete levels here preferred.

the conduct of individuals with other norms and threats, as well as powerful pressures and promises, issuing from the individual's own State community. Quite apart from the duties imposed by its legal system, there is also the more diffuse but no less powerful pressure of the shared convictions of the national community. We certainly cannot confidently assume that at the crisis of decision the deterrent pressure of an international criminal law would usually prevail in this struggle, even if all other theoretical problems had been solved and a competent tribunal established. As the world is still, and as it is likely to remain for some time, pressures from the norms and convictions of the municipal community are more likely, at moments of crisis, to prevail over those from an international criminal law.

Municipal society bears down much more immediately on its human members, and it is usually also in a position to give effect to its threats independently of the outcome of any actual or impending international armed conflict. It is because of such circumstances that the threat of international punishment is far more likely to intensify the efforts of leaders to *ensure victory* in war, rather than to deter them from playing their part in what may later be declared by others to be "aggression", but which presents itself to them as mere "defence" of their own State. Whether, and if so by what means, it may become possible to create for an international criminal law against aggression a motivating force superior to the pressures of a State society on its members, raises therefore a question for enquiry transcending merely juristic wisdom and skills. It is a question which must be answered, rather than begged. Until it is answered, sonorous efforts to frame authoritative definitions of aggression, and punishments of aggressive acts, may be but a beating of the juristic air.[53]

VIII. *MENS REA* AND GROUP ETHICAL CONVICTIONS.

We raised above some of the logical-analytical difficulties affecting the nature of the *mens rea* required for a crime of aggression. We must now refer to certain psychological presuppositions of the search for such a *mens rea,* which are no less disturbing than the above reflections on the supposed deterrent powers of an international criminal law. Psychologically speaking, the *mens rea* required for this new kind of criminal liability must be such as to ensure a degree of moral responsibility for choice by the individuals concerned. This in turn presupposes that standards of moral judgment are available to individuals of a national State whereby they can test at any moment the objectives pursued by their State's policies, with a view

[53] The question here raised whether the crime of aggressive war-making can be efficacious in terms of the function proposed for it, is sometimes unwarrantably begged. According to Professor Lauterpacht, for instance, the refusal of writers to take the jump from the *illegality* of such war to its *criminality* "on the part both of the State as such and the individuals responsible for its conduct—has revealed the sterility of an approach which renders impossible the adaptation of specific rules and principles to major changes in the law expressly enacted", and shows disregard of "wider considerations which may reasonably be considered to underlie the will of the legislation". (See H. Lauterpacht, "The Limits on the Operation of the Law of War" (1953) 30 *B.Y.B. Int.L.* 206, 208-209.)

to dissociating themselves from, or at least refraining from furthering, objectives violative of those standards.

We cannot assume that this presupposition will always prove well-based. Men are obviously likely to feel the pressure of shared politico-ethical convictions of their own national community, more intensely than even the most solemn standards established *ab extra*.[54] No doubt we must work to redress this balance, and the solemn adoption of international standards may be regarded as a step in this direction. Yet we must also be aware of the forces which are working against such a redress. Increasingly in our century human judgment is being reduced, within the insulated chambers of State societies, from the free exercise of the intellectual and moral faculties to the acceptance of the version of truth and justice, authoritatively promulgated by the State society, what I have elsewhere termed the "national versions" of truth and justice. Opinion within each State society is increasingly moulded and controlled by the organs of mass communication; and even in democratic communities the versions of truth which these organs do in practice propagate are becoming increasingly limited. These two factors together threaten even the tenuous links which formerly joined men across State frontiers; and not even economic interdependence and rapid travel and communication can fully neutralise their effects. The hackneyed truisms about the shrinking of the physical world under the impact of economic and technological advance, offered to support assertions of the growth of international solidarity, may be worth little in the balance.[55]

This process may have gone further in some countries than in others. It is important, however, to recognise that amid the stress of chronic international tension, and the efforts to convert democratic polities into fortress States, even Western countries may be submitting though more gradually to similar long-term trends. In terms of the intellect and the spirit, this means a reinforcement rather than a weakening of the supernatural accoutrements of the State.[56] By the very token that the dominance of nationalised truth insulates the men and women of one State from those of another, it also deprives the citizens of a State of the moral and legal criteria of international conduct by which they can effectively criticise their own government, or acquire any effective community consciousness transcending their own State frontiers.

Any prognosis, therefore, of the success of the attempt of an international criminal code to bring home to individuals criminal responsibility for

---

[54] Compare N. Maim, *Weltwissenschaft* (1946) 50.: "Nationalism is by its nature something original (native, *urwüchsig*) which arises out of the whole emotional and intellectual life of a people . . . In contrast thereto internationalism is something accessory insofar as the nation is active in the community of nations. Thus nationalism springs from the inner nature, internationalism from the outer situation of the nation."

[55] We must, I fear, still take with great caution on this matter even the most eloquent invocations of "the aspirations of the contemporary juridical conscience" (V. V. Pella, *La Guerra-Crime* (1946) 44, 46) and even President Eisenhower's invocation of "respect for the opinions of mankind", as expressed by the General Assembly's votes, in his speech of Feb. 20, 1957 (*N.Y.T.*, Feb. 21, 1957).

[56] *Cf.* J. Stone, "International Law and International Society" (1952) 30 *Can.B.R.* 164, 170ff., and the related point in R. B. Pal, *op.cit. supra* n.46, at 56-59.

aggressive war-making must take account of these ominous trends. The issue of responsibility for aggressive war is an issue on which, in fact, "truth-finding" is likely to go not by humanity but by nationality. And it is perhaps the most tragic paradox of our century that the first collective attempt to bring home to individuals their responsibility for the scourge of war, should have been made in an age when the attempted appropriation of truth and justice by the State makes the hope of success so desperate.[57] The *mens rea* necessary to base this criminal responsibility presupposes the accused's access to criteria of moral judgment transcending the nationalised "truth" and "justice" of his State, at the very time when that access is being increasingly cut off.[58]

IX. DIFFICULTIES CONFRONTING THE DRAFT CODE OF OFFENCES AGAINST PEACE AND SECURITY.

It will, we believe, be clear that sanguine hopes for any dramatic advance in securing international peace by the establishment of individual liability for the crime of "aggression" are without assured base, even if we leave aside the practical question how we could ensure that justice in these matters could in fact be made to apply equally to victor and vanquished.[59] And it is also clear, in the present view, that this position is not likely to be transformed by the discovery of some new verbal formula for the definition of "aggression". It is therefore a vast understatement of the real obstacles to suggest, as some have done, that progress in the adoption of the draft

[57] Warranted as we may feel the language to be in the particular case, it does not help these long-term problems to seek to enthrone indignation and hatred in the judgment seat, as in the learned writing of the Soviet jurist, M. Trainin (*The Criminal Responsibility of the Hitlerites,* quoted R. B. Pal, *op.cit.* 93): "The monstrous crimes of the Hitlerite butchers have *aroused the most burning and unquenchable hatred,* thirst for severe retributions in the hearts of all the honest people in the world, the masses of all liberty-loving people."

[58] This aspect is perhaps inadequately discussed in the literature, including C. Scelle, *Manuel* . . . (1945) 956-999, P. C. Jessup, "The Crime of Aggression and the Future of International Law" (1947) 62 *Pol.Sc.Q.* 1-10, and Viscount Maugham's bitter attack on "the Nuremberg principles" in his *U.N.O. and War Crimes* (1951) esp. 39. With great respect for the learning there shown, Professor Kelsen's demonstration (*Peace through Law* (1944) 71-124 *passim*) that it is *legally possible* to hold individuals responsible internationally, has little to do with the main thesis he seeks to establish, namely, that such individual responsibility will guarantee peace through law.

The difference of moral climate is perhaps symbolised by contrasting the contemporary scene with that in which the post-medievals were able to say that since the personal sovereign was the sole judge of the justness of a war into which he led his people, he it was who was personally responsible if the cause was not just. See the fascinating study by A. Gardot, *"Le Droit de la Guerre . . . du XVième Siècle"* (1948) 72 *H.R.* 397, at 433. For a divergent view, even on the legal possibilities, see R. B. Pal, *op.cit. supra* n.46, 71-105, esp. 104-105.

[59] On that and other general problems of the "aggressive war" count see Stone, *Conflict,* 98-302, 324-334, 357-363 and literature there cited. And see R. B. Pal, *op.cit. supra* n.46, at 47, 67-68, who observes in this context: "With international law still in its formative state, great care must be taken that the laws and doctrines intended to regulate conduct between State and State do not violate any principles of decency and justice. History shows that this is a field where man pays dearly for mistakes." He adds: "*When the fear of punishment attendant upon a particular conduct does not depend upon law but only upon the fact of defeat in war,* I do not think that law adds anything to the risk of defeat already there in any preparation for war. There is already a greater fear—namely, the power, the might of the victor . . .". And he observes, on

Code of Offences against Peace and Security of Mankind depends on an adequate definition of aggression.[60] The difficulties appear to be of a different and far more formidable order; they may lie rather in the inaptness of the concept of "aggression", however defined,[61] to perform, in our actual world, the functions designed for it by those who have advocated and promoted the proposed international code.[62]

---

p.121, that the term "aggressors" may be "chameleonic", and may only mean "the leaders of the losing State".

Even if Justice Pal's view is questioned in relation to the actual circumstances of the post-World War II Trials (see Stone, *Conflict,* 301-302), and if the two wrongs do not make a right, the difficulty remains as to potential future conflicts. Insofar as it does, we might add that the mere failure of this projected branch of criminal law to attain its objectives is only the lesser part of the danger. More serious is the almost certain abuse of this supposed body of law by a victorious nation, even if it was the aggressor, for "framing" the leaders of the vanquished nations (however innocent), and thus confusing further the moral judgment of mankind.

[60] As does D. H. N. Johnson, *op.cit. supra* n.32, at 448, 466. Mr. Johnson sees this position as analogous to the discovery, in League circles, that disarmament was inextricably bound up with the question of security, and that of security with the question of arbitration. See, as to the genuineness of these latter difficulties, Stone, *Conflict,* 100-102.

[61] Analysis thus suggests that the difficulties are also even greater than those which led Mr. Justice Pal to dissent *inter alia* on this count. (See *op.cit. supra* n.46, at 104.) For he still seems to believe (*op.cit.* 112) that the difficulties could be overcome by provision of an advance definition. But see at 116, where he seems to show insights somewhat inconsistent with such a belief.

Mr. Johnson makes only part of this point when he observes that—"It was perhaps an unwise step to declare 'as the gravest of all crimes' an act (i.e. 'aggression') which was still not defined" (*op.cit. supra* n.32 at 451). See also *id.* 455-58, on the indeterminacy of the term "peace and security" if this is treated, as it probably should be, as an indivisible concept, each limb delimiting the other. See 457 for the views of various authorities to this effect. As an indivisible concept embracing only peace which is also security and security which is also peace, the term "against peace and security" might be an attractive substitute basis for the concept of aggression. But since the term "security" is incapable of definition except in terms of highly controversial ethico-political values, the substitution would scarcely be an apt basis for criminal justice, though it might conceivably (though still not easily) serve for the politico-military purposes of peace enforcement. This indeterminacy is startlingly illustrated by Dr. Manuel Duran's proposal (*U.N. Doc.* A/2162, pp.3-5) that unless the title of the Draft Code were amended to read: "Code of Offences against the Peace, Security and Integrity of Mankind", it could not properly cover the crime of genocide. In Dr. Duran's view, therefore, "peace and security" of mankind could still exist even while States and their agents were engaged in deliberate physical destruction of whole groups of mankind!

[62] It need scarcely be pointed out that the difficulties here presented in rendering individuals liable for the crime of "aggression", would not necessarily arise from the creation of criminal liability for acts defined otherwise than by reference to the aggression notion. Thus some of the ancillary acts proposed to be rendered criminal by paras. 4 (incursion of armed bands), 5 (fomentation of civil strife), 6 (terrorist activities), 7 (violation of disarmament undertakings), 8 (illegal annexation of territory), 9 (coercive intervention), 10 and 11 (genocide and inhumane acts), of Art. 2 of the Draft Code of Offences against the Peace and Security of Mankind (*G.A.O.R. IX,* Suppl. No. 9 (A/2693), c.iii, p.11) might form the basis of individual criminal liability without raising the kind of difficulties with which the present work is concerned.

It illustrates the present point that in the armed bands provision of Art. 2, para. 4, of the Commission's Draft, and the comments thereon, the question of liability of the members of the armed bands is separated off from the question of liability for "aggression" either of those individuals or of the State assisting them. See *G.A.O.R. VI,* Supp. No. 9, A/1838, para. 59, and M. Spiropoulos' comment, *G.A.O.R. VI,* Sixth Committee, 279th Meeting, paras. 16-17.

Cf. a similar point by R. Cassin in Bourquin (ed.), *Collective Security* 330, though he thought that these offences should be created consequentially on the definition of aggression.

CHAPTER 9

AGGRESSION AND THE AUTHORITY OF THE GENERAL ASSEMBLY

I. SUMMARY OF PRECEDING ARGUMENT.

A. Agreed Definition Thus Far Unattainable and Why.

We are fully conscious as we approach this concluding Chapter how deep is the yearning among many noble minds to find criteria of aggression which will express adequately our desire to live in peace and justice with our neighbours, eliminate the agony of individual and collective judgment, as well as quiet the clamour of divergent national interests at the crisis of action. But we still believe that this yearning, even if it were not in any case destined to frustration, would in fact produce dangers and obstacles rather than aid and guidance in the tasks of maintaining peace.

So far as "general" definitions of aggression are concerned, none seem to have the slightest chance of acceptance which do more than restate the questions raised by the notion of "aggression" itself, leaving the agonised judgment still to be confronted, at the moment of crisis, with the usually wide-ranging complex of facts and moral judgments involved in the instant case. As to the so-called "enumerative" definitions, listing concrete acts as quasi-criteria of what constitutes "aggression", insofar as they purport to be exhaustive, that is to fix the collective decision in advance and out of full context of the particular crisis, it is now not seriously disputed even by the most ardent protagonists of definition that they are doubly dangerous. They are a trap for the innocent, branding conduct which in the full circumstances should be held justified, as well as a licence to ingenious aggressors to devise new forms of aggression outside the list.[1] Definitions, whether "enumerative" or "mixed", which are open only at the inculpating end, insofar as the acts they enumerate are deemed to be aggression in all circumstances, are open to all the objections of "enumerative" definitions. Only if they are open at the exculpating as well as the inculpating end, leaving the collective organ free to find aggression in a particular case apart from the enumerated acts, or to find no aggression even in one of the enumerated acts, do they become free of this vice. But by the very same token they then also lose much of the virtue for which precise definition is sought, namely, to make it clear in advance of the particular crisis what the judgment will

[1] This expresses *inter alia* the U.S. as well as the U.K. view for rejecting all types of definitions. See A/AC.77/SR.13, pp.3-4, where the U.S. delegate associated himself with an Indian statement in the Sixth Committee that: "A general definition would be of little value because it would be too vague, an enumerative definition would be dangerous because it might contain too much or too little, and a mixed definition was apt to combine the disadvantages of the other two types." And see *1956 Sp.Com.Rep.* 16.

be, and remove the agony and the conflict of national interests from the moment of decision.

These, among others, are the reasons why simple tests of aggression such as the armed crossing of a frontier, or bombardment of territory or ships, or the failure to obey a cease-fire order, attractive and promising as they seem at first sight, have not come to command even substantial consensus among States. For to apply them in the existing international community regardless of the absence of collective means of redress of wrongs, of the circumstances of provocation by the alleged victim's course of conduct in relation to law and justice, of the effect of the conduct of the alleged victim if unchecked upon the vital interests and even survival of the alleged aggressor, not to speak of the effect of modern weapons,—all this may be to demand (and without certain warrant of law) that governments subject their peoples indefinitely to grievous wrongs, and even to the certainty of destruction. This was one deep reason for the dramatic clash of Soviet and American views when Mr. Sanders, the United States representative, observed on October 29, 1956, in the 1956 Committee that the acts which the proposed Soviet definition listed as acts of aggression by any State which first commits them, "might just as well be considered as acts of self-defence"; and when he went on to say that "only individual circumstances would enable United Nations bodies to decide whether they were faced with an act of aggression",[2] and that "the first act" as a test was "as deceptively simple in appearance as it was unworkable in practice".

B. Lack of Importance for Security Council Peace Enforcement of either the Notion of Aggression itself, or the Problem of Definition.

It has been shown that the vast legal powers of the Security Council under the Charter can be activated by any "threat to the peace, or breach of the peace" as well as by an "act of aggression". Insofar as most authorities agree that at any rate an armed "aggression" can rarely (if ever) occur without either "a threat to the peace or breach of the peace", collective peace enforcement by the Security Council would rarely *require* even the use of the *undefined* notion of "aggression". Any supposed "aggression" could be far more easily brought home as a breach of the peace. So far as the notion need not be used, its definition could scarcely be a matter of urgency; and a case in which it was used, and aggression found, would, in order for all the Permanent Members to be in agreement, be so clear a case that definition would rarely in any event be necessary. It has also been seen, in this connection, that the growth of intense anxiety about the lack of definition of the concept in our own day coincides with the substantial paralysis of Security Council peace enforcement functions after 1950, and with the effort to build in the General Assembly some compensating mechanisms to take their place.

C. Dependence of Effective General Assembly Action on Inspiring Members for Voluntary Cooperation in Recommended Action.

Once we move on to the level of the General Assembly's peace enforce-

---

[2] Doc. A/C.77/S.R. 13, p.7. The Soviet delegate indeed admitted this point except

ment efforts a number of new factors enter into the questions both of the need to use the notion of aggression, and of the need to define it for this purpose. On a Security Council determination of threat to the peace, breach of the peace, or act of aggression under Article 39, and decisions for the taking of measures under Chapter VII generally, the legal obligations of Members to cooperate in measures arose immediately under the Charter, for instance under Article 25 and Article 2 (5). While it would always be desirable that the Members generally should be morally convinced by the Security Council's determination, the obligations under the Charter clearly arose even if they were not.

It is, however, quite otherwise with General Assembly action under the Uniting for Peace Resolutions. The only sure legal characterisation of action thereunder is, in Mr. Cabot Lodge's words, that it is "hortatory and recommendatory";[3] and this is so not only *vis-à-vis* the Members of the United Nations generally, but also even *vis-à-vis* the States in conflict themselves.[4] Members are under no *legal* obligations to heed the exhortation and the recommendation. Whether in fact they will heed them therefore depends on the presence of some non-legal stimulus, or pressure, or inspiration, or common interest, sufficient to serve as an incentive for the assumption of the considerable burdens which may be involved in voluntary cooperation for the restoration or maintenance of peace.

D. *Importance of the Notion of Aggression as a Possible Means or Symbol for Activating Voluntary Cooperation of Members.*

It is, we believe, in this light that we may best understand the widespread

---

that he thought "the principle of priority" removed the ambiguity. See A/AC.77/SR.14, p.9. On this see *supra* Ch. 3, s.X,C.

[3] On Feb. 2, 1957. See A/PV. 650, p.26. See for the fuller context *infra* n.6.

[4] *Cf.* the general analysis in Stone, *Conflict* 234-237, 266-284. And *cf.* recently D. H. N. Johnson, "Effect of Resolutions of the General Assembly . . ." (1955-56) 32 *B.Y.B. Int.L.* 97ff., esp. 122. This author concludes that (1) the term "moral effect", as distinct from "political effect", has "no valid meaning at all in this context"; (2) still, a resolution of the General Assembly always has some "political effect" even if only as inviting displeasure from other Members to a non-complying State, or from the subjects of the latter to its Government; (3) some resolutions "such as those concerned with the internal working of the Organisation" (e.g. as in elections, adoption of budget), are legally binding upon both the Members and other organs; (4) Members may incur legal obligations *by the act of voting* even for other resolutions, *provided there is a clear intention to be so bound;* (5) recommendations addressed to Members who have voted against such resolutions can have legal effect only as a "subsidiary means" (though "very subsidiary indeed") for evidencing rules of law, not as themselves operative to create legal obligations (117), and their weight would depend on the accuracy and persuasiveness of their contents as expressions of the "juridical conscience" of humanity as a whole, "rather than of an incongruous or ephemeral political majority." And see *id.* 101ff., 105ff., where Mr. Johnson collects and discusses some of the relevant judicial and doctrinal authorities.

Cf. as to the nature of recommendations generally Judge Lauterpacht's observation (I.C.J. Reports 1955, p.115) that "although on proper occasions they provide a legal authorization for Members determined to act upon them individually or collectively, they do not create a legal obligation to comply with them." And see *id.* at 118, and 120-121, where the same distinguished judge suggests that States may have the obligations to give "due consideration in good faith" to such recommendations, and to give reasons if they decide to disregard them, even though these appear "intangible" and "almost nominal"; and that finally the more potent sanction in this situation may be "moral

concern with the "aggression" notion as a basis for General Assembly action since 1950, despite the fact that under the Uniting for Peace Resolutions, as under Article 39 of the Charter, not only seisin but also action of the organs may rest equally on "a breach of the peace" as on an "act of aggression".[5] One main reason, at least, for the General Assembly's concentration on the "aggression" notion rather than on the mere notion of "breach of the peace", which would be so much easier to apply, is that the former is a symbol bearing much more emotive power. It is thus better adapted to stimulate or inspire Members to join in and heed the Assembly's hortatory and recommendatory action, and thus to produce the voluntary cooperation and compliance without which General Assembly action cannot be effective, and can only remain a kind of *brutum fulmen*.[6]

E. The Search for Precise Advance Criteria of Aggression in order to Produce Advance Assurance of Member Cooperation and Compliance.

Whatever doubts, therefore, we have been compelled to raise from time to time concerning the cogency and even sincerity of some of the reasons

reprobation following upon non-compliance with a valid recommendation" (121). *Cf.* also, Judge Klaestad (I.C.J. Reports, 1955, 88) that the effects of a General Assembly resolution are of a "moral or political" rather than a legal nature, and that such duties to "consider in good faith" as may arise are scarcely "a true legal obligation", and certainly give rise to no "binding legal obligation to comply".

The Secretary-General's Report of Feb. 11, 1957 (Doc. A/3527), states that the General Assembly (as contrasted with the Security Council) "can only recommend action to Member Governments which, in turn, may follow the recommendations or disregard them", even in action under the "Uniting for Peace" resolution. With respect, we do not see how this legal position is altered by the Report's further point that "recommendations which implement a Charter principle, which in itself is binding on Member States" would have behind them the force of the Charter, "to which collective measures recommended by the General Assembly could add emphasis without, however, changing the legal character of the recommendation." The Members are here bound by the Charter principle, not by any "emphasis" of the Assembly. We do not, indeed, clearly understand what is meant by this "emphasis" unless it be weight as evidence that the given fact situation falls within or without the Charter principle. On this see Stone, *Conflict* 235.

For the general views of the present Writer in relation to the Uniting for Peace Resolutions see Stone, *Conflict* 243-246, 266-284.

5 See *G.A. Resols.* Sept. 19-Dec. 15, 1950, 10-12 *Resol.* 377 (V) A (1) of Nov. 3, 1950. The paragraph asserts seisin by the General Assembly over "threat to the peace" as well, but includes only "breach of the peace" and "act of aggression" as grounds for recommendation for collective "use of armed force".

6 See in the recent crisis Mr. Cabot Lodge's statement (in the context of the sanctions debate) that the General Assembly was "not engaged . . . in running a world government or a super-State, which can adopt legislation having the force of law. We are a forum engaged in passing resolutions which can have great influence, but what we do is hortatory and recommendatory, and the final result is up to the parties." The resolution, he said, will "represent our effort to persuade them . . .". (*G.A.O.R. XI,* Feb. 2, 1957, p.1053, paras. 58-59). So the Uruguayan delegate (*id.* 1067, para. 73) said that it "would be absurd" to regard General Assembly decisions as judgments. And *cf.* the Secretary-General's Reports of Jan. 24, and Feb. 11, 1957, referred to *infra* n.20, and *supra* n.4.

Even during its violent partisanship against Britain, France and Israel in the crises of 1956-57, the Soviet Union still insisted on "the inalienable rights of the Security Council in deciding in each concrete case on the forming and utilisation of armed forces of the United Nations" (M. Shepilov, *G.A.O.R. XI,* 592d Plenary Meeting, Nov. 23, 1956, p.265, para. 29; and, indeed, that the General Assembly's action in forming U.N.E.F. was illegal under the Charter (M. Kuznetsov, *G.A.O.R.* F.E.S.S. 567th Plenary Meeting, Nov. 7, 1956, p.127, para. 291, *G.A.O.R. XI,* Feb. 2, 1957, pp.1077-78, paras. 8,11,17). See also

offered by some States for regarding the definition of aggression as important,[7] we have also been careful to give due weight to the present reason.

Insofar as peace enforcement comes to depend on General Assembly hortation and recommendation the effectiveness of peace enforcement action from case to case would be subject not only to possible uncertainty as to the gaining of the requisite majority in the votes, but also to the individual decisions of Member States thereafter to cooperate or not. Nothing could be more natural, in this context, than the belief and hope that if only Members can agree, in advance of any particular crisis, on precise criteria for determining whether "the gravest crime against mankind" has been committed, this would increase the certainty both that votes will be properly cast at the moment of crisis, and also, and above all, that the sense of moral indignation, justice and concern of Members will be so engaged by the determination as to assure cooperation and compliance in General Assembly action.[8]

We have tried to make this argument in favour of continuing the search for the definition of aggression in terms as strong and as closely geared as possible to special contemporary urgencies, and somewhat stronger even than the related position recently taken by Professor Quincy Wright.[9] But having done so we are also compelled to examine the value of this argument in the light of what has gone before in these pages, and in particular of the history of two generations of this search, and of the analysis of the aggression notion itself. Two capital conclusions seem to follow.

The first conclusion flows from the preceding historical analysis; it is this. Granting the argument its full force, granted that agreement on precise advance criteria *would* make Member cooperation in crisis more assured, we have still to face the fact that such agreed criteria have not been found. Moreover the negligible results of two generations of effort at the highest level make it virtually certain that no criteria will be found in the foreseeable future which will command sufficient acceptance by States, including the major States, to achieve the moral power and inspiration sought.

The second conclusion, flowing this time from the preceding juristic and socio-ethical analysis, is this. Suppose we assume that the near impossible were to happen and that, owing to some sudden and at present unforeseeable conversion of the hearts and minds of many States, sufficient of them did accept and secure adoption by the General Assembly of criteria by which, in advance of future unforeseen crises, they brand certain precisely described acts as "aggression". Still, even then, it would be most unlikely that this

---

M. Zarubin (A/PV. 632, Dec. 21, 1956, p.26).

For the important distinction between the question whether this action was "illegal", and the question whether it produced binding obligations on Members see Stone, *Conflict* 234-236, and *infra* pp.177-181, and Discourse hereto.

7 See, as to other reasons *supra*, esp. Introd., Ch. 1, s.III, and Ch. 8.

8 This point is admirably made by Y. de la Brière, in Frangulis, cited *supra* Introd., n.28, who, however, draws the inference that a definition of aggression must be found and accepted which is capable of certain, immediate and virtually automatic application. He does not address himself to the contingency that the hope of finding such a definition may be chimerical, as it is believed it surely is.

9 See Q. Wright, "The Prevention of Aggression" (1956) 50 *A.J.I.L.* 514-532, the

could guarantee the engagement of the moral convictions of Member States, and therefore their active cooperation in maintaining peace in each future crisis as it arose.

The reason for this, though not simple, flows compellingly from the foregoing analysis. For such criteria to be *precise enough* to control the future judgment of aggression they must, as we have several times shown, constitute a violent abstraction from that full context of the crisis which consideration of the merits of the dispute would require to be taken into account. In any actual crisis, however, it is the fuller context which bears in on the judgment; and the inevitable tendency to frame a judgment on the merits will often dictate a judgment contrary to that called for by the simple criteria of aggression.[10] "Aggression", as defined, will pull one way; the doctrine of the *bellum justum,* as felt and tacitly associated with the aggression notion, will pull the opposite way. In this situation the very precision of the advance criteria, far from assuring a clear and vigorous reaction of Members against the State whose conduct is caught by their terms, is likely rather to confuse and paralyse the moral convictions, and therefore the will to cooperate, of many Members. At worst, it may also range the Members into their opposing *blocs,* the criteria becoming used

---

appearance of which, from the pen of so distinguished a veteran among the students of war and its related concepts, has been of great assistance and stimulus to us, even when we disagree with him. On the present point he clearly bases the need for definition, as does the present Writer, on the paralysis of the Security Council by the veto, and on the corresponding need to stimulate "voluntary action of Members in response to recommendations by the General Assembly under the Uniting for Peace Resolution". To furnish this stimulus he thinks decisions must be based on "a definition of the aggressor which is precise and acceptable to both the jural consciousness and the practical interests of most of the Members of the United Nations." (528, and see 531.) Even then it is strange to find so much of Professor Wright's 1956 discussion centered on Art. 39 and on the Security Council.

It is at this point that our views diverge in respects which will be clear enough from the present study as a whole. "Two main points, however, may here be summarised.

1) Professor Wright, in view of the urgency of the problem of human survival (518-19), thinks that the failure of 30 odd years of effort at definition only means that further effort is called for. He assumes, as it were, that since a suitable definition if it could be found might save us, therefore it must be capable of being found. (He was writing before the further failure of the 1956 Special Committee.) We, for our part, believe that the time has arrived, if our further hopes are pinned on this plan of escape, to seek the reasons for the failure of this enterprise; We believe we have shown that the reasons are such that in fact we have no ground for expecting to succeed where our predecessors failed, and I further maintain that a definition which could stimulate cooperation at the moment of crisis could not be both precise and acceptable.

2) Our second divergence underlies the first. It is an interesting paradox that Professor Wright, who approaches the problem as a political scientist, sees it as a "juridical problem" (517); whilst we, approaching it as a lawyer, feel that its intractability turns rather on the socio-political and ethical presuppositions of definition, and the failure of the actual situation of either international law or international relations to fulfil them. It is these which we have, therefore, sought to expose in this study; no merely "juridical" ingenuity can overcome them, nor even any demonstration (such as Professor Wright attempts on 518-19, 527) that other programmes for security cannot work. One need not believe that our situation is quite so hopeless; but even if one did, that does not prove that despite all the evidence the enterprise of defining aggression is a possible way out.

[10] The final dependence of successful peace enforcement action on due regard for the merits of the disputants' causes was, of course, a constant theme of delegates at

mainly as instruments of political tactics in the struggle between the opposed judgments.[11]

F. If Criteria of Aggression Cannot Be Found Assuring Quick Judgment of Aggression and Inspiration to Positive Cooperation by Members in Recommended Measures, the Aggression Notion Itself Loses Much of its Importance even for General Assembly Action.

If, as was shown under heading E., no criteria of aggression could be relied on to fulfil the desired objectives, the aggression notion, if it were to remain the keystone of General Assembly action, would have to be applied immediately with its built-in reference to what is just in the full context of each crisis as it arose. In the few clear "core" cases of aggression such as came before the Nuremberg Tribunal this would serve well enough; but the likely crises of the future will not always, or even usually have that clarity. Inevitably, therefore, a longer time (and probably a very long time) would be required for canvassing and debating the complex of moral and factual elements involved in applying the aggression notion, even when agreement could be finally reached.[12] It is probable, however, that in many cases agreement in application could not be reached at all on the questions of moral responsibility which the aggression notion raises. In a world in which any threat to the peace or breach of the peace may be the beginning of a chain reaction leading to thermo-nuclear war, action on a breach of the peace should be instantaneous, and should not have to wait upon protracted

the crisis sessions of the General Assembly in 1956-57. See e.g. M. Ortega (Chile) (*G.A.O.R.* 561st Plenary Meeting, Nov. 1, 1956, p.1, para. 6); M. Chamadi (Yemen): "Unless the settlement is just, there can be no peace" (*G.A.O.R.* F.E.S.S., 563rd Plenary Meeting, Nov. 3, 1956, p.58, para. 140); M. Malik (Lebanon) (A/PV. 659, Feb. 22, 1957, p.42); Mr. Pearson (Canada) (*G.A.O.R.* F.E.S.S., 562nd Plenary Meeting, Nov. 1, 1956, p.35, para. 299). On the difficulties involved in applying the justice concept in concrete situations owing to divergent national versions of it, see *infra* pp.169-174.

11 It is by no means fanciful to see the stalemate situation into which the General Assembly degenerated on the question of sanctions against Israel, and as to whether her withdrawal from Gaza and Sharm el Shiekh should be absolutely unconditional, as a presage of this plight. While in that case there was no General Assembly finding of "aggression" against Israel, the simple criterion of aggression as resort to force not under United Nations authority was taken for granted by many Members e.g., of the Soviet and Afro-Asian bloc, in the arguments made for their position. Among the Western States and many South American States the implications of that assumed criterion were rejected in the fuller context of Israeli-Egyptian relations as quite inconsistent with the requirement of minimal justice, in view of "provocations" and "grievances" suffered by Israel under Egypt's declared policy of "driving Israel into the sea", and of the fact that the Gaza strip and the gun emplacements on Sharm el Shiekh were the very main instruments used by Egypt to commit the wrongful acts concerned.

12 This same point is implicit in Professor Lauterpacht's rejection of the idea that the use of prohibited weapons should be licensed as against the aggressor, for the reason that in the absence of "authoritative interpretation" self-defence will certainly be invoked by both sides, and that "in the din of battle the voice of the victim may be drowned by strident and cynical protestations of the aggressor asserting the justification of the resort, on his part, to the illegal weapons". We would add, however, that except in the core cases, this would also be so owing to the lapse of time involved, in the case of a body having a power of authoritative determination, unless its determination were rather arbitrary for so grave a decision. And it is believed that this view also adds strength to the same writer's conclusion that generally where the aggressor cannot be immediately designated and penalised the rules regulating hostilities between a

and tendentious debates inevitably involved in most cases by the attempt to fix moral responsibility.[13]

G. In Fact, the Universal Contemporary Fear of Thermo-Nuclear War May Provide Ample Incentive for Member Cooperation to Arrest Breaches of the Peace, without Reference to the Aggression Notion.

The preceding negative point (F.) that use of the aggression notion cannot provide adequate and prompt incentives to Member cooperation in restoring or maintaining peace, might require us to turn to the much less emotive notion of breach of the peace, even if this could offer (by reason of its less emotive character) little incentive to State cooperation or compliance. In fact, however, this is not the position in our age of thermonuclear weapons. As the 1956 crisis showed, all Members whether Great or Small are intensely sensitive to the threat to themselves of chain reactions to any breach of the peace.[14] In fact, the effective part of the action of the General Assembly in that crisis dramatically demonstrated not only that advance criteria of aggression are not necessary, but that Members can be galvanised into cooperation to halt hostilities[15] even without resort to the conception of aggression at all.

It was, indeed, perhaps at the one point in time at which some Members

---

State which may be an aggressor and its victim cannot differ appreciably from those "usually governing belligerents". See "The Limits on the Operation of the Law of War" (1953) 30 *B.Y.B. Int.L.*, 206, 221, 239. And *cf.* P. Guggenheim, *Lehrbuch des Völkerrechts* (1950) 779; and Stone, *Conflict* 312-13, 695.

Professor Lauterpacht's view, *id.* 233, that a finding of aggression might nevertheless have the legal consequence of rendering void a resultant imposed treaty of peace, also gains more cogency in this way, since *ex hypothesi* the struggle being over, the immediate peace enforcement emergency is also over, so that the requisite time is (in theory at any rate) available for the aggression inquiry. This surely is a better ground for his position than to rely on "the principle *ex injuria jus non oritur*". For in the very same article, (210, 239) he had correctly insisted that in international law, imperfect as it is, that maxim may have to yield to the maxim *ex factis ius oritur*. He must, therefore, surely require some reason *other than the mere iniuria*, for choosing to invoke the former and neglecting the latter maxim, in order to defeat the earlier rule that the duress involved in imposed treaties of peace does not invalidate them.

13 The General Assembly is even less of a "juridical" organ than the Security Council. Insistence on using the aggression notion (defined or not) in such an organ not only involves excessive deliberative delays, but also invites challenges to its findings on technical legal grounds, whether honest or specious. It may be otherwise (but is not always —see *supra* Ch. 7) with municipal judicial organs, where time is not so much of the essence, where more tractable concepts are usually involved, and the judges stand in a special position *vis-à-vis* a stable society.

14 We regret that we are not, however, able to join H. Thirring, *"Was ist Aggression?"* (1952-53) 5 *Oesterreichische Zeitschrift für Oeffentliches Recht* (*N.F.*) 226, 234 in believing that "in view of the danger of effective atomic retaliation of an atomic attack with atomic weapons, the aggressive will cannot be presumed at the present time." See *id.* generally on the influence of atomic weapons on the problem of definition of aggression. This writer does not recognise the difficulties of the programme of depending on the aggression notion and its definitions in the circumstances which he describes well enough.

15 *Cf.* in the 1956 Middle East crisis the dramatic words of Mr. Serrano (Philippines): "Postulates of right and wrong must yield to exigencies of the moment. . . . War—and the inevitable death to which it leads—does not linger on the witness-stand to gaze leisurely at the symbol of justice . . . ." *G.A.O.R.* F.E.S.S. 562nd Plenary Meeting, Nov. 1, 1956, p.13, para. 6). *Cf. id.*, 563rd Plenary Meeting, Nov. 3, 1956, p.50, para. 56);

allowed themselves to act *as if* some simple criterion of aggression were available,[16] that the General Assembly forfeited general cooperation and ceased to be an effective organ of pacification.[17] The reference, of course, is to the insistence, in February-March, 1957, that Israel should hand back *unconditionally* the very bases in the Gaza Strip and Sharm el Sheikh from which Egypt had for years asserted and carried on acts of active belligerence against Israel, without simultaneously dealing with threats to and breaches of the peace arising from this asserted belligerency of Egypt.[18]

H. In the Present View Assembly Action to Engage Cooperation of Members in Securing the Peace Should Not Depend on Findings about Aggression, but Should Proceed on the Bare Finding of Breach of the Peace.

So far is it from the truth that the perils of thermo-nuclear war require that the aggression notion be the keystone of peace enforcement, that the present analysis dictates quite the opposite conclusion. The dangers are too great and urgent for us to let the building of techniques of Member cooperation in peace enforcement wait upon unending debates either on the definition of aggression in general, or on the determination of aggression in the particular case. Techniques should build towards immediate action to restrain and damp down hostilities; and this should be done without foreclosing and without prejudicing any question of the merits of the

---

Mr. Tsiang (China), *G.A.O.R. XI*, Jan. 18, 1957, p.939, para. 119); Sir Percy Spender (Australia), (A/PV. 649, Feb. 1, 1957, p.41); Mr. Carabajal-Victorica (Uruguay), Feb. 2, 1957 (A/PV. 651, p.32). *Cf.* under the League *supra* Ch. 2.

16 The instances in which Anglo-French and Israeli action was actually characterised by individual delegates as "aggression" or "in violation of the Charter" rely, of course, on simple mechanical tests of aggression, which are of no authority, and which mostly serve to score political points, and always to conceal the issues. See, Mr. Baroody (Saudi Arabia): "an immoral act of aggression" against the sovereign State and the principles of the Charter (*G.A.O.R.* F.E.S.S., 562nd Plenary Meeting, Nov. 1, 1957, p.32, para. 25); Mr. Sapoznikiv (Ukraine) ". . . these criminal actions of the aggressors . . ." (*id.* 563rd Plenary Meeting, Nov. 3, 1956, p.74, para. 319); see also MM. Rizk (Lebanon) (*id.* 53, para. 146) "hideous crime of aggression"; Ullrich (Czechoslovakia) (A/PV. 661, Feb. 2, 1957, p.11). And see the interesting formulation of Mr. Gunewardene (Ceylon): "Equitable considerations can be weighed only when you come with clean hands. As an aggressor Israel could hardly claim equity" (*G.A.O.R. XI*, Feb. 2, 1957, p.1062, para. 16).

Contrast the assumptions, which seem at least equally warranted in law in M. Schurmann (Netherlands): "It would be particularly unjust to single out either Israel or France and the United Kingdom and to reproach the one for having taken the action which it considered necessary for its self-defence and survival and the others for having stepped in where the United Nations had failed to act." *G.A.O.R.* F.E.S.S., (563d Plenary Meeting, Nov. 3, 1956, p.49, para. 47). See also Mr. Walker (Australia) (567th Plenary Meeting, Nov. 7, 1956, p.114, para. 116.).

17 See further Sir Percy Spender (Australia): "What precisely do we propose to do to ensure that belligerent rights claimed by one State are not exercised pending a final determination of the issue . . .? Or is it our intention . . . to leave this matter very much up in the air and so to poison further an atmosphere already unhappily charged as it is?" (*G.A.O.R. XI*, Feb. 1, 1957, p.1036, para. 65.) And see generally pp.1036ff.

18 *Cf.* and contrast among the many statements quoted infra n.20 with that of Sir Percy Spender (*G.A.O.R. XI*, Jan. 17, 1957, p.883, para. 67): "Are we to close our eyes and our ears to the wrongs committed by the other side and by doing so place the other side in a privileged position to commit the same wrong again?" And *cf.* M. Georges-Picot (France) who said that it was imprudent to create "by a return to the *status quo ante*", the very situation which was the cause of recent events (*G.A.O.R. XI*, Jan. 19, 1957,

causes of the conflicting Parties, pending the examination of these.[19]

J. It is Important for the Efficacy of this Direct Approach, and in particular for Securing Compliance by Members, that Both Conflicting Parties be Assured that the Action of the General Assembly and the Voluntary Co-operation of Members will Carry Through with Vigour after the Arrest of the Breach of the Peace to Bring about the Reduction of the Grievances of Both Sides to a Minimum Level of Tolerable Justice and National Security.

Only when hostilities are under control can it usually make sense, in a case of any difficulty, for the General Assembly to address itself to the kind of enquiry and debate required by the judgment of aggression. But it is still vital, once hostilities are under control, that this judgment be entered upon with vigour, and with eyes and ears, and hearts also, that are open to the grievances and difficulties of both sides; and, above all, that that vigour and concern should not fade merely because the open conflict has temporarily been stopped.[20]

This procedure, moreover, of postponing the framing of judgment as to the Party responsible will be seen, on careful thought, also to be the more conducive to quick achievement of a cease-fire. A State which has been condemned as an aggressor in advance of full enquiry, on the basis of some oversimple criterion of aggression, has the less to lose by pushing on its military effort in order to consolidate a position from which it can secure

---

p.947, para. 25); Sir Leslie Munro (A/PV.667, 11th Session, Mar. 4, 1957, p.46).

The Israeli case was in effect that the *status quo ante* was not a *status iuris* but a *status iniuriae* on the three issues of access to the Suez Canal, to the Gulf of Aqaba, and the Egyptian raids from the Gaza Strip. (See Mr. Eban (*G.A.O.R. XI,* Jan. 28, 1957, p.982, paras. 16-18).) The present point is not that the Israeli case was correct (though as to the Canal, a Security Council decision clearly supported it), but that it clearly could not be correct (a cease-fire being already in force) to restore Egypt's capacity to resume the alleged wrongs *without full inquiry* into the merits of the respective positions.

Cf. the view of the Consultative Assembly (Council of Europe) that U.N.E.F. should remain in the Middle East pending settlement of the Canal and Arab-Israeli issues. See Recommendation No. 132 (Jan. 11, 1957) 12 *Europa-Archiv* 9699-9700.

[19] *Cf.* the very cogent statements with reference to the League system by Sir J. Fischer Williams (*et al.*), *International Sanctions* (1938) 177. The same position is involved in those writers like P. Mantoux (Bourquin (ed.), *Collective Security* 336) who wish to make a distinction between "the fact of aggression" and "the question of responsibility" for it. "Aggression" is here used misleadingly to mean something like "breach of the peace".

The present view builds on quite a different interpretation of League practice than that given by Q. Wright ("The Concept of Aggression. . . ." (1935) 29 *A.J.I.L.* at 381) insofar as it holds it to be essential not to try to evaluate the breach of the peace at this stage, even if it is persisted in after a cease-fire order, in terms of the "aggression concept". On the reasons for this difference see *supra* p.156.

[20] See e.g. my observation, *supra,* Introd., n.5 on para. 5(a) of the Secretary-General's Report of Jan. 24, 1957 (A/3511). And see the following observations of various delegates, which are open to a similar observation: Mr. Gunewardene (Ceylon) (*G.A.O.R. XI,* Jan. 17, p.880, para. 18): M. Aziz (Afghanistan) (*G.A.O.R. XI,* Jan. 18, 1957, p.914, para. 44; M. Hanifah (Indonesia), who said that "the nullification of advantages seized by aggression is the first thing to be accomplished", but was nevertheless concerned to stress that there could be no going back to the unsatisfactory conditions of the *status quo ante* (*G.A.O.R. XI,* Feb. 1, 1957, p.1042, para. 143). Arab States and those politically aligned with them put no such qualification on the directives they desired from their unproved assumption that aggression had been found. M. Jamali (Iraq) declared that the "aggressor" must be treated as "a criminal"; "either aggression is to be punished and the aggressor put in the dock, or this Organisation cannot function . . ." (A/PV.661,

redress of grievances, and from which it can only with difficulty be dislodged.[21] It may as well be hung for a sheep as a lamb. States, on the other hand, which have reason to expect that the General Assembly and its Members will in due course bring the full vigour of their anxious care and cooperation to assuring them of redress of their more intolerable wrongs, and safeguarding them against the graver dangers by which they feel threatened, may well comply more quickly with the request to cease fire, and thus reduce the risk of spread to general war.[22]

K. No Proposals for Peace Enforcement through Use of the General Assembly's Hortatory and Recommendatory Powers Can Succeed in the Long Run unless the Main Groupings of States in the General Assembly Will Abandon the System of Bloc-Voting and Log-Rolling, at any rate in Cases that Have Involved Breaches of the Peace, and unless most States Become Willing to Address themselves Conscientiously once Hostilities Are Ended to the Merits of Claims to Adjustment Made by either of the Conflicting Parties.

The preceding prescription seems as simple as the preconditions for fulfilling it are difficult. Yet it is very clear that unless we can meet these preconditions efforts to secure peace through the General Assembly are as clearly doomed to failure as the ambitious plans of Chapter VII for the Security Council proved to be. Short of such a drastic change of heart in voting behaviour, or of an equally drastic change in the distribution of voting power, there can be only one of two outcomes of the great design to build in the General Assembly a system of peace enforcement by voluntary cooperation of Members.[23] *At the best,* the General Assembly will move

---

Feb. 26, 1957, pp.32-35) It was perhaps an amusing slip of the tongue which made the distinguished delegate seem to want to punish the alleged criminal even before he was in the dock. *Cf. id.* (A/PV.664, 11th Session, Feb. 28, 1957, p.46), observing that "Israeli aggression should not be rewarded. There is only one thing to be said to Israel: get out—nothing more".

The fallacy was made very clear by Sir Percy Spender's remark, in relation to the Aqaba dispute, that it was the Assembly's duty to ensure that any *modus vivendi* established did not permit action on one side to destroy the claim of right until that claim of right can be determined" (*G.A.O.R. XI,* Jan. 17, 1957, pp.882ff., para. 58). See also Mr. Noble (U.K.) (*G.A.O.R. XI,* Jan. 18, 1957, p.919, para. 114); Mr. Pearson (Canada) (A/PV.660, 11th Session, Feb. 26, 1957, p.21). And see the Secretary-General's rather different position in his subsequent Report, *supra* n.4.

21 *Cf.* Mr. Pearson (Canada) in A/PV.660, 11th Session, Feb. 26, 1957, p.21.

22 We agree with, therefore, but would state much more strongly, the view taken from the standpoint of ethics by M. Sharp, "Aggression: A Study of Values and Law" (1947) 57 *Ethics,* Supp. 16-17, that "The issue of political self-defence, as distinct from the question of the military defensive, is perhaps insoluble in most acute cases. But concern with the issue may contribute in the end to the development of legal and military institutions for the control of war." We would agree too that "the intelligent combination of cooperation and aggression may be thought of as the central problem of our contemporary social order" (37); and if cooperation is taken to include the will to wait, and the will to compromise, that this is also a good statement for the international order.

23 We find Professor Wright's failure to address himself (article cited (1956) 50 *A.J.I.L.* 514, at 531) to this question, when he discusses procedures for rendering General Assembly action effective, very much at odds with the masterly sense of the realities of international life displayed in such *chefs d'oeuvres* as his *Study of War.* It is attributable, perhaps, to his faith as a political scientist in the magic of a hoped-for legal definition of aggression to dispel all the basic difficulties. As a lawyer we cannot share this sanguine faith: any more than we can see an acceptable definition forthcoming. We

into a condition of voting deadlock, in which each side in two generally opposed alignments of voting *blocs* will each command more than one-third of the votes, and thus steadily veto the proposals of the other, thus reproducing in the General Assembly the paralysis of the Security Council. It is possible that we have already witnessed, in the closing days of the Assembly in March, 1957, a rehearsal for this momentous phase. *At the worst,* should the Soviet and Afro-Asian *blocs* be able to develop a political strategy, or should future events be of a tendency such that the issues thrown up are ones on which even many of the Central and South American States might come to vote against the West, the result might be to make any real power of the General Assembly in this area, whether it is *de facto* or *de jure* power, wholly intolerable to Western countries.[24]

For the hard fact now is that of the 82 present United Nations Members, no less than 35[24a] are members of the Afro-Asian and Soviet *blocs* (even apart from Turkey, the Philippines, Japan and Israel) — enough to veto any General Assembly decision favouring the West, even in those cases in which justice might clearly be on the side of the Western States. And on matters—for instance some economic matters—on which Central and South American States might go with the Afro-Asian and Soviet *blocs*—the count could swell to 55, a sufficient two-thirds majority to force through any decisions. While we do not believe that any of the alignments of States, East or West, have any monopoly of virtue or vice, this effect of the constitution and voting system of the General Assembly remains as a hard fact of our present situation.[25]

This hard fact cannot be disposed of by loose talk about the democratic one-State-one-vote principle in the General Assembly. Whatever "democracy" may mean in such a body, representation on a one-State-one-vote principle regardless of size and responsibility, and of form of government, and without the concurrent check of an effective second chamber based on some more adequate principle, is not its full flower. And as for impartiality, it is obvious that wherever any major interest of the numerically dominant

---

cannot, therefore, in the above light, join in his belief that "collective security can be greatly advanced by clear definition of threat to the peace, breach of the peace, and act of aggression, and implementation of the proposals of the Uniting for Peace Resolution, strengthened by supplementary agreements by which States earmark forces to be used when the General Assembly has designated the aggressor." (532.)

24 American opinion tends to assume that Thailand, Pakistan and Iran would be unlikely to vote against the U.S. on major East-West issues. We doubt whether this can be taken as always and permanently so; but even if it were it could still leave an alignment of more than one-third of the Assembly votes. American opinion also thinks hopefully that Ghana, Jordan, Lebanon, Tunisia and Ethiopia might be induced to abstain on such issues. But even then 28 votes of the combined *blocs* would remain. On this kind of basis it is also often expected that the U.S. may continue to count on being able to marshal 25-30 votes on major issues. See e.g. *Frye*, 61. We doubt whether this expectation will continue to be justified unless certain trends are modified. Malaya should, no doubt, now be included (Sept. 1957) in the immediately preceding list.

24a Excluding Malaya. *Cf.* on the main point, E. Stein, " . . . Expanding U.N. Membership", tr. (1957) 12 *Europa-Archiv* 9587, 9592-3.

25 *Cf.* the observation of Mr. Casey (Australia) in the General Assembly that "we cannot afford to continue to paper over the cracks in the United Nations. I believe that this situation will dislocate some old, accepted loyalties and will create new ones—based, I hope, on more realism." (*G.A.O.R. XI,* Nov. 26, 1956, p.319, para. 128); and the same point has been made by Mr. Dulles.

blocs arises, voting may be just a case of "Heads I win, tails you lose", except in the rarest circumstances. And even in the flagrant case of Hungary in 1956 impartiality of voting stopped at the point where the Assembly resolutions would have had any positive effect.[26] On many important issues, the massive steamroller vote could crush the clearest rights of the West, and sanctify the grossest illegalities, if the General Assembly were allowed to wield anything like the big stick originally designed for the Security Council.[27]

If, for example, Panama asserted claims with regard to the Panama Canal analogous to those asserted by Egypt with regard to Suez, and a great Soviet arms build-up and infiltration took place in neighbouring Central and South American countries, Washington would have to face a situation in the Assembly of the following nature. Security Council action would be barred by the Soviet veto. In the General Assembly the Afro-Asian and Soviet *bloc* votes alone could veto any redress. We leave aside as unlikely,

---

[26] Even in the flagrant Hungarian Affair of Nov. 1956 no less than ten Afro-Asian States refused to vote for any resolution critical of the Soviet Union. It may be said, of course, that in any case all Members would draw back at resolutions which implied serious pressure on a Great Power possessing nuclear weapons, by reason of that very fear of general war which is, in other cases, the main hope for securing effective voluntary cooperation of Members. This points up immediately certain outer limits of General Assembly action, as it formerly did of Security Council action.

It is to be added, however, that even on this level impartiality of voting e.g. as between the degree of pressure which might be brought against the United States and the Soviet Union respectively, is most unlikely. It will depend on the assessment by Members of the "provocability" of these two States, and on their habits of respect for law and morality and the opinions of their fellow-men. This quite obviously favoured the Soviet Union in the recent crisis, just as it operated heavily against the U.K., France, and Israel. It is also likely to favour Soviet immunity in the future, and it appears to have helped towards failure of the demand for a Special Meeting of the General Assembly to debate the findings of the General Assembly's Committee of Enquiry on Hungary, in June 1957. President Eisenhower's speech of Feb. 18, 1957, while recognising the discrimination involved, scarcely drew the necessary implications from it.

[27] These dangers are, of course, largely a result of the "package deal" admission of 16 Members in December, 1955, including four Members of the Soviet *bloc*, six of the Afro-Asian *bloc*, and only six of countries generally sympathetic to the West (see *United Nations Review* (1956), Vol. 2, No. 7, p.5); and of five additional Afro-Asian *bloc* States during the Eleventh General Assembly itself (see *United Nations Review* (1956), Vol. 3, No. 6, p.6; (1957), Vol. 3, No. 8, p.28; No. 10, p.30). In the near future four or five further prospective adherents to the Afro-Asian *bloc* may be expected to be admitted, not to speak of the possible addition of the Communist Chinese Government to the Communist *bloc*.

As at present the 28 Afro-Asian votes alone suffice to veto any resolution on which they see a common or log-rolling interest. On disputes which involve the fate of Western economic interests, such as concessions in foreign countries, this number can always be swollen by the ten votes of the Soviet *bloc* and Yugoslavia, and often by sufficient of the 21 Central and South American States, to a possible vote of 59, or 5 more than the requisite two-thirds majority. On some so-called "colonial" issues, also, sufficient of the American votes might be swung to ensure a steady anti-Western two-thirds majority. And at the worst on all other issues, the Afro-Asian *bloc* can always deadlock the Assembly.

On the other hand, there will be few matters chronically in issue between the Western States and Afro-Asian countries on which the 23 remaining Members (including all the Western States) could ever expect, whatever the merits of the issues, to win a two-thirds majority vote. On most of them the best it could hope for is to rally sufficient votes, especially from among the American States, to raise its numbers to more than 27, and thus deadlock the Assembly. Even when it can marshal all the 21 American votes, the West would still be substantially short of the requisite two-thirds majority for any resolution it favoured.

though not wholly inconceivable, that if the Central and South American votes went along with Afro-Asian and Soviet *blocs,* the United States could be forthwith branded an aggressor if it took any measures of self-redress at all likely to succeed.[27a]

It is perfectly true, of course, that insofar as General Assembly action may relate to the use of financial resources to be placed at its disposal by Member States, and insofar as the provision of these resources falls on the generosity of the United States, this latter country may meet hostile *bloc* alignments by simply not providing the requisite funds. It can, however, scarcely be assumed that all the main issues of the future will fall into this pattern: and they are likely more often rather to approximate to the pattern of expropriation of investment or of the means of access to raw materials and other resources, by the territorial sovereign. And while, as to the Panama Canal, the economic strength and influence of the United States would no doubt serve as a restraint, it is far from certain that it will remain an effective restraint in all likely constellations of voting strength. While some may think that we are here taking a pessimistic view of the trends of voting behaviour, and of the consequent unreliability of the Assembly as a political organ, it may be better for us to sharpen our awareness of the danger inherent in the present situation, rather than to hide our heads in the sand.

Clearly the Western Powers would not, in the long run, continue to assist in strengthening the authority of a General Assembly which might become a protective shield for predatory and imperialist designs against them, and an execution chamber for any State that tried to defend itself against these designs.[28] And it is in part these dangers which have led the present Writer repeatedly to stress the importance of remembering that the General Assembly has no *legal* power of *binding* Members by resolutions as to which State is an aggressor, nor, indeed, as to what should be done by any Member in a crisis. But even the power of the General Assembly based

---

[27a] In a declaration dated Jan. 31, 1957, the Panamanian Academy of International Law, after stating certain legal conclusions justifying the Egyptian right to nationalise, was concerned to stress that both as to the sovereign status of the territory and the contract of concession, Panama's rights as regards the Panama Canal were analogous; and that any material differences from the Suez position, e.g. as to Panama's lesser participation in profits, made the claims of Panama even stronger than those of Egypt.

On Mar. 25, 1957, it was reported that a conference of professors and experts in international law was inaugurated at the University of Panama to consider *inter alia* "the nationalisation of canals, the internationalisation of canals, the juridical status of the Suez and Panama Canals, with analogies and differences, and finally the Suez crisis." (*N.Y. Times,* Mar. 26, 1957.) At this Conference (*id.* Mar. 31, 1957) M. O. Fabrego, who headed the Panama negotiations for the Panama-U.S. Treaty of 1955, expressed the view that such agreements in perpetuity should be invalid as inconsistent with the sovereignty of the territorial State. Professor C. Quintero favoured denunciation of the Canal treaties with the support of other Latin American countries. There was some dissent from these views including some from Panamanian scholars, e.g. Dr. F. J. Escobar, there reported. On Apr. 10, 1957, the Soviet Union formally protested against U.S. security checks on Soviet ships while in transit through Panama.

[28] While there was no more than a hint of withdrawal in the recent Middle East crisis (see e.g. Mr. Dodds-Parker's reply of Nov. 12, 1956, to a question as to the possibility of the U.K. withdrawal from the United Nations if she were branded as an

on its claim to represent the conscience of mankind,[29] and its promotion of voluntary action by Members, could also become such a protective shield, if through a regular stacking of votes regardless of the merits it committed a *détournement* of the moral authority of that body.[30]

II. JUSTICE AND THE IMMEDIATE PROBLEMS OF COLLECTIVE SECURITY.

All of us tend to endow the interests which hold our sympathy with the aura of justice, and those which do not with the stigma of violation. We have been the more careful to direct the foregoing admonition to Western as well as to other States. Yet it is believed that the actual position in which the various *blocs* stand to each other in the world as it is, and in the General Assembly as it is, creates some important differences in what the admonition implies.

We refer here in particular to the more dispersed and exposed pattern of distribution in relation to territorial sovereignty of other States, of the interests of most of the Western Powers. And by "interests" here we refer

---

aggressor (560 *Hansard,* 5th series, H.C., col. 542)) the danger might take on different dimensions in situations in which Western States were less disunited.

So *cf.* Sir Winston Churchill's statement of July 6, 1957, that for the U.K. to rely solely on the United Nations would be "disastrous", and his speech to the American Bar Association on Aug. 1, 1957, on the dangers arising from the new responsibilities which the General Assembly sought to assume: "We wish these new nations well . . . but it is anomalous that the vote or prejudice of any small country should effect events involving populations many times exceeding their own numbers, and affect them as momentary self-advantage may direct." He supported an earlier speech of Mr. Menzies on July 8, 1957, in which the latter accused the Assembly of acting hastily and unjustly, and urged that great changes were necessary in procedures and attitudes, especially in voting. "Unless new voting rights can be agreed upon, and I can see all the difficulties, the nations in the General Assembly must have some self-denying ordinance. They must avoid 'ganging up' in order to win votes. . . . Smaller nations must realise that those nations who carry the great weight of responsibility should be heard with respect and their views considered with objectivity."

The Final Communiqué of the Commonwealth Prime Ministers' Conference of July 5, 1957, also referred to "the deficiencies and weaknesses" of the United Nations, though it is clear that not all the participants felt equally strongly about the matter, or agreed on any remedies.

The dissatisfaction of Western States generally with the one-State-one-vote system is well-known. See also John Foster Dulles, *War and Peace* (1950), which significantly in the Preface of its 1957 edition (after the Middle East Crisis) emphasises that the increase of membership since 1950 has accentuated the need for a reformed system of weighted voting. And see among the most carefully worked out proposals of the kind, Grenville Clark and Louis B. Sohn, *op.cit. infra* nn.60,63.

29 For typical views of the General Assembly as expressing the conscience of mankind in the recent crisis, see M. Rodriguez-Fabregat (Uruguay) (the Charter as "the deepest expression of human conscience") (*G.A.O.R.* F.E.S.S., 563rd Plenary Meeting, Nov. 3, 1956, p.55, para. 115); M. Gunawardene (Ceylon) ("the moral authority of this body") (*G.A.O.R. XI,* Feb. 2, 1957, pp.1061-62, paras. 4, 15, 16, and see also Meeting of Nov. 3, 1956, p.64, para. 209); M. Sudajarwo (Indonesia) (*G.A.O.R.* F.E.S.S., 562nd Plenary Meeting, Nov. 1, 1956, p.39, paras. 349, 350, and 563rd Plenary Meeting, Nov. 3, 1956, p.66, para. 230).

And see the critical letter on this point by Frank Altschul, *New York Times,* Feb. 11, 1957.

30 *Cf.* M. Martin Artajo (Spain) who observed in relation to the recent crisis that

not to the interests of the respective States in the loose sense, of what is deemed necessary by each State to consolidate or advance its own position, but to the narrower area of interests which may be said to be legally vested in each State under the existing legal and economic order, for example, in the availability of raw materials. In this sense it seems clear that the African and Asian and Central and South American States now hold within the mercy of their territorial domain more important interests of the Western Powers than *vice versa.* Once it is assumed that the use of force is excluded, these former States, *within* the extent of their territorial domain (and despite the reminiscence of an earlier phase of history), rise to a position of superior power. And this power, thus based on the assumed inviolability of the territorial domain, is even further enhanced once we assume an active General Assembly. For the fact of the superior numerical representation and voting power of those latter States in the General Assembly, gives them a certain power to divert the role of that body to the consolidation of their own interests, and cover over their encroachment on the interests of other States within their territorial domain. Abused in an unrestrained manner, this power could frustrate any promise of long-term participation through the authority of the General Assembly. That might be a disaster to humanity, and to all States, however aligned, which make up humanity; and the search for a path to avoid it is the common burden of all of us.

It is easy to say with so many of our contemporaries, that the path we must find is the path of "justice". The term "justice" has a sense in the literature of international law and relations more general, and no doubt looser than that familiar in philosophy and jurisprudence; and since the present argument is directed to this body of literature and its readers, the term is here used in a similar sense.[31] In that sense we find the term constantly interposed after the words "international law" in a variety of instruments, as well as in political pronouncements ranging from solemn speeches of the President of the United States to the platitudes of the daily public *fora.*[32] Sometimes the prestige of justice is sought to be bolstered by the prestige of law, as when we are first enjoined to remember that *pax justitiae opus,* but that justice in its turn is the work of Law, and our real need is "to get force and Law together".[33] But, of course, this is no service to either man or justice unless we make clear that the "Law" thus referred to is not any existing law, but the desired embodiment of present justice in future law. We have not (despite what some might think) really escaped by the use of the word "Law" from the indeterminacies and relativity of justice into the comforting certainty of a binding code. More often today, how-

---

the ruin of the United Nations was "more likely to be caused by some deviation from its high purposes than by its internal weakness." (*G.A.O.R. XI,* 576th Plenary Meeting, Nov. 13, 1956, p.15, para. 99).

31 On careful consideration we have concluded that it is not essential for the present limited purpose to broach the philosophical and jurisprudential questions involved in this matter of terminology. And see *infra* n.58.

32 See among innumerable illustrations in the recent Middle East crisis the President's speech of Oct. 31, 1956 (*N.Y.T.,* Nov. 1, 1956, p.14). And see quotations *supra* Ch. 3, n.7.

33 H. R. Luce, "Peace is the Work of Justice" (1956) 30 *Conn. Bar J.* 341, 348.

ever, the demands of justice as part of the desiderata of peace are openly acknowledged, whether as with W. E. Rappard in a spirit of despair for their realisation, or as with Lord Davies as a goal which it is still possible to pursue.

Professor Rappard asks with obvious foreboding whether plans for peace enforcement can find any moral basis and therefore any prospect of realisation in a world of which a large part repudiates its fundamental premises.[34] And he thereby challenges the more sanguine summons of Lord Davies to make justice, in the same sense, an indispensable basis of a peace that is still to be hoped and worked for.[35] Lord Davies thinks that justice between States can be thus attained if peoples and individuals are "animated by zeal and enthusiasm for the ideal of justice", so that thus fortified the people can combine to extricate themselves from the shackles of national sovereignty which hitherto have prevented them from following the paths of sanity, justice and peace.[36] The justice, zeal for which is thus to save mankind, Lord Davies finds sufficiently stated in Justinian's "constant and perpetual wish to render everyone his due", expressed in the injunction, "whatsoever ye would that men should do to you, do ye so even unto them"; and he thinks "most of us" believe that it implies "a just, fair and equitable settlement" by appeal (if necessary) to an impartial and disinterested third party.[37] Naturally he recognises that there is risk of miscarriage of justice, since all men are human; but this does not alter the fact that there can be no international justice until an authority has been created with impartial and incorruptible institutions to declare what the law is and to administer, interpret and enforce it.[38] So still, he thought in 1945, as in 1930, that "the preven-

---

[34] W. E. Rappard, *The Quest for Peace: Yesterday and Today* (1954) 41-42: "When justice, to strong and weak alike, is dismissed as an empty outgrown bourgeois prejudice, when the rights and fundamental freedoms of man are derided because his dignity is ignored, when love of peace is no longer pursued for its own sake, but set as a trap for the sincerely pacific by those who deem war inevitable and absolute national sovereignty infrangible, who consequently, condemning to impotence all international organizations not subservient to their own will, maintain preponderant military forces as a threat to would-be recalcitrants, what proximate hope can there be for such institutions of human progress as those which Lord Davies so nobly sought to set up?"

[35] Lord Davies, *The Seven Pillars of Peace* (1945) 20-22: "It is a truism that a peace founded on injustice cannot be durable and, as the framers of the Briand-Kellogg Pact have now discovered, it is not enough merely to outlaw war. A substitute must be found in order that disputes may be settled by a peaceful, not a violent, procedure. Nor is it sufficient to discover a substitute; that substitute must be capable of dealing out justice impartially and guaranteeing its execution.

"Those people whose main preoccupation was to stave off trouble, to patch up settlement, to secure peace for their own day and generation, regardless of grievances, injustice and crime, lived in a fool's paradise. They failed to understand that a sense of injustice can only be removed when the grievance or dispute has been subjected to the process of reasoning and discussion; when the evidence has been carefully sifted and the facts investigated, and when the issues have been adjudicated upon by an impartial court or tribunal. Consequently, until such a procedure had been established, based upon equity and equality in the sight of the law, the sense of injustice will remain, and it will be impossible to prevent a recurrence of war."

[36] *Op.cit.* 24. It is clearer than in Mr. Luce's case that he knows that when he speaks of "the rule of law" in this context, he is not speaking of any present body of binding rules.

[37] *Ibid.*

[38] *Id.* 25-26.

tion of war is, after all, only a negative aspect of our inquiry. The real problem goes deeper: it is the eternal quest for justice . . . an olive of endless age".[39]

There is little doubt that in that general form each of these noble assertions, whether made in despair or in hope, would have widespread agreement and even acclamation anywhere in the world. Yet as a student of law and social institutions, we must add that neither Professor Rappard nor Lord Davies seems to us to have reached the critical practical issues of our day. At the risk of being thought by the latter to be either "a realist" or "a reactionary", and venturing to reject the unfavorable connotations of both these terms, we have to say that the main problem is not men's unwillingness to prefer justice and the rule of law *in general* to war and anarchy *in general,* as he asserts.[41] It arises, indeed, at a stage after the preference is made on that *general* level, when the questions are, Who are the true claimants to international justice? States or human beings? What does justice in its various national versions prescribe in this particular clash of interests?[42] and What are the chances of this or that particular proposed machinery and process attaining it in the existing state of the world? We shall later discuss the value of establishing machinery which may gradually promote the willingness of States to transcend their own interests in matters affecting the maintenance of peace. But it must be said immediately that we are not entitled to expect any quick resolution of the conflict of State claims made in the name of justice by the mere appointment of wise, impartial and incorruptible arbiters. To entertain such a hope may indeed savour somewhat of the ingenious proposal to abolish the congestion of the English "week-end" by changing it from Saturday and Sunday to Thursday and Friday. The trouble with Pandora's Box was not the Box, but what was in it.

Lacking both the bright hope and black despair of these contemporaries, the present Writer believes that we can but do what we can with the institutions available; and also that it behoves us to do what we can. We certainly cannot bring justice down from the heavens to the nations in full and pure measure; yet we may still be able to raise the nations that little

---

39 *The Problem of the Twentieth Century* (1930) 3. Though on the same page he readily acknowledged that "justice in turn is dependent on disarmament", disarmament on security, and security on sanctions. And *cf.* pp.7,9,21 in the 1930 work.

40 *Seven Pillars of Peace* (1945) 24. 41 *Id.* 27.

42 Among the numerous instances of passionate identification of the requirements of justice in general with each of the various national versions of it whose conflict lay behind the outbreak of hostilities, see MM. Jamali (Iraq) (*G.A.O.R. XI,* Nov. 26, 1956, p.340, para. 183; *G.A.O.R. XI,* Jan. 17, 1957, p.906, para. 137); Dejany (Saudi Arabia) (*G.A.O.R. XI,* Jan. 18, 1957, p.927, paras. 20, 23); Ullrich (Czechoslovakia) (A/PV.661, Feb. 26, 1957, p.11); and Mr. Eban (Israel) (*G.A.O.R.* F.E.S.S., 562nd Plenary Meeting, pp.20ff., and 563rd Plenary Meeting, Nov. 3, 1956, p.61). M. Ritter Aislan (Panama) aptly observed as to many of these invocations that—"It would appear that to some minds the words 'peace', 'fraternity', 'tolerance', 'justice' and 'understanding' are merely words with lyrical resonance and artificial meaning, and not sacred objectives to which all our efforts should be directed." (*G.A.O.R. XI,* Jan. 19, 1957, p.951, para. 62.)

Yet the main difficulty may still arise even when these ideals are sincerely held as "sacred objectives". M. Malik (Lebanon) struck nearer home when he said that "justice is most important—but even more important than justice is truth, for without truth justice becomes false. . . . Only by an honest, humble, complete, courageous, real facing

towards justice which may allow them to survive together. We may not be able to resolve the pluralism and relativism of men's ideas of what is just in concrete situations into a broad consensus; yet it may still be worthwhile to seek sufficiently to abate the conflict of versions, so that no State need feel its claims to survival and the opportunity so wholly denied as to make it prefer the risk of war and general destruction. It may be, as Lord Davies' idealism declares, that "peace at any price usually means war in the long run";[43] but it is an even more urgent truth that justice at any price (at any rate in any particular human version of it) is likely today to mean war and human immolation in the short run. The General Assembly may be a very defective organ to secure justice in particular cases, and there may be not the slightest hope of it ever being the organ of which Lord Davies (and the present Writer also) dream; yet if it can be raised that modest little which promises dedication at least to the securing of minimal levels of survival and opportunity for all States, that is worth having. Staving off trouble, and patching up settlements conformably to this modest standard, which we may despise as a shameful parody of justice, may yet be as much as we can attain; and by that token what we ought therefore to strive for.[44]

For the same basic reasons, too, namely the implied demand for perfection in goal, and the desire to set out as from a dreamed-of rather than the actual human situation, we cannot fully accept the pessimism of M. Rappard. We must recognise the importance, as conditions of success of the United Nations plan for collective security, of a sufficient sense of common urgency of the need to avoid war, of willingness of all States to grant the requisite power to the "grand alliance for peace", and of ensuring that the *status quo* is such that men may think it worth sacrifice to preserve it.[45] And we must admit, too, that both in theory and practice these conditions were far from met in 1945, and that they remain unmet, and that as M. Rappard properly claims, there are deep-centred contradictions and hypocrisies in the United Nations Charter.[46] We are not yet prepared, however, as he appears to be, to write of that institution in the past tense,[47] so long as there is any possibility of remoulding it even little by little into a means towards a minimal survival and opportunity for the world's peoples. Even apart from men's conscious efforts, the degree of fulfilment of some of the conditions of success may be increased by the urgent desire to avoid war, for example, as a result of the threat of thermo-nuclear weapons. As already indicated, the present

of the whole truth, in which we hide nothing, are we going to pull out of the mess into which we have all, so unhappily and so smugly, got ourselves in the Near East. . . ." (*id.* A/PV. 659, Nov. 22, 1956, p.41). Yet even truth as a practical criterion does not easily overcome the obstacles created by the national versions of it. See *supra* pp.143-144.

[43] *The Problem of the Twentieth Century* (1930) 8.

[44] Lord Davies *op.cit.* 8. We also dissent, therefore, from his apparent view that "justice" must come before friendship (38-39), if that is intended to mean what it says. If all that he means is that some degree of trust must precede friendship that, of course, would be a different matter.

We also dissent from this kind of absolutism in reverse, as when C. Jordan observed "that Right can wait, and that Peace cannot". (Bourquin (ed.), *Collective Security* 305.) For beyond a certain point "Rights" *cannot* wait precisely because "Peace" *will not* wait.

[45] *The Quest for Peace* (1954) 35.

[46] *Id.* 30, 31, 38.

[47] *Ibid.*

Writer's position would change, once it became clear beyond doubt that the Member States will use the institution without regard to other interests than the self-regard of steadily aligned *blocs*. For then, indeed, the United Nations must become a contrivance which could only accelerate the dissolution of mankind. Until then, however, we must struggle, though without illusions, to reverse the trends towards consolidation of these *blocs*.

We say without illusions: for we agree with Professor Rappard that "easy intellectual optimism is for the mind a dangerous habit-forming drug".[48] We need to face the full terror and perplexity of the human situation. We must be prepared to admit, with the grand gentleness of a Max Huber, after a lifetime dedicated to these problems,[49] that what we have so far achieved in the United Nations is still not even a foreshadowing of the basic type of group-communities, whether of family, fellowship or state-society, in which individual members have learned to "meet each other in love", to recognise a common good which may not be their separate goods and a justice which may not be their versions of justice. We must recognise that we have as yet no basis for pretending that the United Nations is any more than a system of State relations in more or less friendly and unstable equilibrium, and that there is no prospect of changing this by activating those parts of the Charter which seemed to many to promise a more organic degree of international community. We must also recognise, in the company of the same fine intellect, that relations of States cannot be moved onto the higher level of community, without the profoundest change in the relations of the human beings of whom they consist. We cannot, finally, reform mankind without reforming men. "The community of States finally must depend on an ethos which has its source in the moral responsibility of the individual".[50] It follows that unless this is achieved "all merely legal, organisational and economic measures" are a labour of Danaides. And we must follow him also to the bitter acknowledgment that though some men may always have had this insight, from the Hebrew prophets onwards, and though incipient movements for acting on it may be observable, we cannot pin any faith for the foreseeable future on the moral reformation of enough individual men as a means of saving mankind. We must, in short, have the courage to admit with him that "seen from a human intellectual point of view our situation seems to be hopelessly difficult", and yet also to affirm that we cannot and ought not to despair, but rather to let hope still spring from the vistas of time and history that transcend our situation, and faith from the awareness that disappointments must come in the pursuit of the greater goals.[51]

If we are asked to say what all this means in terms of the possible mission of the General Assembly in its double aspect of preserving peace, and fol-

---

48 *Op.cit.* 11.

49 M. Huber, *"Koexistenz und Gemeinschaft, völkerrechtliche Erinnerungen aus sechs Jahrzehnten"* (1955) 12 *Schweizerisches Jahrbuch für Internationales Recht* 11, 30ff.

50 *Op.cit.* 32.

51 We have taken some liberties in rendering the sense of *"aus dem Blick über den Horizont der Zeit und Geschichte hinaus in eine Welt, wo Gott sein wird Alles in Allem"* (32).

lowing through to the merits of the causes of the States at variance, we must say as follows.

First, we must exclude on this ground, as we have already done on practical grounds, the idea that peace can be preserved by mere cease-fires if the Assembly thereafter fails to follow through to the merits of the causes of the Parties. This is the deep truth of the truism that peace and justice finally, though two ideals, are mutually dependent ideals.[52] Perhaps it would be better stated in the terms that collective action must not be such *as to ignore or override systematically* claims which are sincerely urged and may be warranted in terms of justice. And it is because (in our concrete situation) over-simplifications of the problem by mechanical identification of resort to force with aggression involve this mortal sin that they must be rejected.[53]

Second, it must immediately be added that in the existing relations of States the ideal of justice generally involved is not available as a practical standard for application by an organ such as the General Assembly. Nor is this merely a matter of the obstructive role of power relations; it is as much or even more a function of the plurality of national convictions as

---

[52] See *supra* n.35, and *cf.* W. Schätzel, *"Frieden und Gerechtigkeit"* (1950-51) 50 *Friedens-Warte* 97, 106; and see his interesting analogy to the relation in Roman law, of the protection of the possessor by the interdict *uti possidetis* against violent dispossession, to the follow-through protection of the person finally entitled (106).

It is feared that we cannot escape this reality by concluding with J. L. Kunz (*"Bellum Justum . . ."* (1951) 45 *A.J.I.L.* 528, 533) that in the conflict "between the two juridical values of security and justice, security is the lower, but most basic value", and must therefore prevail. This seems to be an undemonstrated conclusion on whatever ground we place it. If the ground is that security is somehow a *more basic,* as it were a *preordinating value,* the argument seems oversimplified, since these notions of hierarchical structure may express some tendencies in the realm of values, but certainly give us no ethical or even sociological imperative for all groups. As made by Hobbes for municipal societies the simplification may serve. But where the units of a supposed society include many States each of which has at any point sufficient power to subvert the society if it feels sufficiently outraged and oppressed in its claims to just treatment, then justice at some minimal level may in some sense also have to be regarded as a preordinating value for security.

It is important to remember the multi-dimensional character of the realm of values defying simple description and calculation, and producing not unilinear relations of determination but rather interpenetration and reciprocal determination. In Greek mythology Hesychia, the Goddess of Serenity, was a daughter of Dike, the Goddess of Justice, and Eirene, the Goddess of Peace, was her sister. While we shall here have to suggest that justice is not at this time an apt basis for the General Assembly's use in penetrating to the merits of conflicts, we have rejected throughout this work (we believe correctly) the idea that it is either possible or necessary to prefer security to justice so far as to welcome or even create injustice, for the sake of security. As will shortly be suggested, the question rather is, What is the minimal adjustment of each concrete conflict which will reduce tension to a sufferable level? And what is the maximal adjustment which most States can be led by anxious care to press hard upon the Parties in conflict, and the Parties to yield? We can probably not find axiotically neutral concepts to work with; but we should get as near to this as possible.

[53] Some of the most active delegations in the recent crises were fully advertent to the sterility of arresting collective action at mere cease-fire and return to *status quo ante.* So Mr. Lester Pearson (Canada) said that the Canadian view from the very start had been that "there must be no return . . . to the conditions which helped to provoke the initial military action . . . Such a return would not be to a position of security . . . but would be a return to terror, bloodshed, strife, incidents, charges and counter-charges, and ultimately another explosion . . ." (And *cf. id. G.A.O.R.,* F.E.S.S., 562d Plenary

to what is just, which emerges as soon as that general notion is brought down to the level of concrete conflicts to be adjusted.[54]

Third, we have insisted that it may still be possible even then to nourish and develop, in the forcing atmosphere of our thermo-nuclear age, some approach which will serve to transcend national interests and national power sufficiently to allow the Assembly to right at least the gravest wrongs, and afford minimal assurance of survival to each State by abating the direst fears.[55] It is not really necessary that the General Assembly should reach consensus on a judgment of final justice in the Egyptian-Israeli affair, in order to quiet fears of mutual invasion by a mined system of dividing fences in the Gaza area; or to secure appropriate contributions by Israel and other States for resettlement of the Arab refugees; or to assure Egyptian security claims in the Suez Canal, or Israeli claims to have *some* assured

---

Meeting, Nov. 1, 1956, pp.35ff.) *Cf.* Mr. Dulles' view of the priorities (with which we agree) that the first task was to "ensure that this fire which has started shall not spread but shall be promptly extinguished; and then to turn with renewed vigour to curing the injustices out of which this trouble has arisen" (*G.A.O.R.*, F.E.S.S., 561st Plenary Meeting, Nov. 1, 1956, p.12, para. 158.) The Burmese delegate, U Win, described the necessity for follow through to the merits after the cease-fire in precisely similar terms: (*G.A.O.R.*, F.E.S.S., 562d Plenary Meeting, Nov. 1, 1956, p.43, para. 411). And *cf.* Sir Percy Spender (Australia) (*G.A.O.R. XI*, Jan. 17, 1957, p.883, para. 67; Sir Leslie Munro (*G.A.O.R. XI*, Jan. 17, 1957, p.903, para. 101; M. Georges-Picot (France) (*G.A.O.R. XI*, Jan. 19, 1957, p.947, para. 25). And see A/PV.660, 11th Session, Feb. 6, 1957, p.21, where Mr. Pearson said that the problem is one of securing a fair and agreed basis for the withdrawal of Israel . . . which can be used to increase security. . . . It is a question of associating the withdrawal of Israel with arrangements which should remove the necessity, or at least minimize the possibility, of facing this same problem a year or two from now."

[54] The difficulty in this regard has probably increased since the days of the *bellum justum doctrine*, as to which J. L. Kunz properly observes ("*Bellum Justum* . . . (1951) 45 *A.J.I.L.* 528, 531) that "in its purity, even if it might have been or were a norm of positive international law, [it] would be practically valueless because of the grave objections against its workability." We say the difficulty has probably increased since, after all, the monarchs of Vitoria's century did still share a largely common heritage of Christianity-and-chivalry-textured values. The heterogeneous heritages of the Members of the United Nations scarcely need stressing.

[55] The imperative nature of this follow-through duty received clear verbal recognition even amid the solid support for the cease-fire resolution of the First Emergency Special Session on Nov. 1, 1956. Mr. Dulles spoke of the duty, after the prompt extinction of "this fire" to turn with renewed vigour to "curing the injustices out of which this trouble has arisen". (See *G.A.O.R.*, F.E.S.S., 561st Plenary Meeting, Nov. 1, 1956, p.12, para. 158.)

Cf. also, Sir Leslie Munro (N.Z.): "Whatever our vote here tonight, let us not regard our work in this place as finished . . . the whole problem of Arab-Israel relations should be fully and effectively considered at the forthcoming General Assembly." (*id.* 562nd Plenary Meeting, Nov. 1, 1956, p.34, para. 285); and Mr. Casey (Australia): "The events of recent weeks have taught us that the world cannot afford to continue latent sources of international infection. . . . I believe that we cannot afford to continue to paper over the cracks in the United Nations." (*G.A.O.R.*, F.E.S.S., 562nd Plenary Meeting, Nov. 1, 1956, p.35, paras. 299, 304); M. van Langenhove (Belgium) (*id.* p.37, para. 326); Mr. Cañas (Costa Rica) (*id.*, 563rd Plenary Meeting, Nov. 3, 1956, p.64, para. 201); M. Sarasin (*G.A.O.R. XI*, Jan. 18, 1957, p.911, para. 5); M. Eskelund (Denmark) (*G.A.O.R. XI*, Jan. 18, 1957, p.940, para. 126); Mr. Carabajal-Victorica (Uruguay) (*G.A.O.R. XI*, Jan. 18, 1957, 941ff., paras. 141, 147); M. Schurmann (Netherlands) (*G.A.O.R. XI*, Jan. 19, 1957 p.946, paras. 7, 9); Mr. Serrano (Philippines) (*G.A.O.R. XI*, Jan. 28, 1957, p.992, para. 143). On the same problem M. Spaak (Belgium) observed, quoting Cavour: ". . . unsolved questions are merciless to Governments and peoples" (*G.A.O.R. XI*, 594th Plenary Meeting, Nov. 24, 1956, p.296, para. 12.)

means of access to the Red Sea.[56] Measures which might be effective on each of these heads might well be regarded by one side or another as not doing "justice" to its claims; but taken each in turn and all together, with other similar measures, they might nevertheless still reduce the sense of injustice and insecurity to a point permitting a tolerable coexistence.[57]

For this kind of approach to the merits of the Parties' causes we do not have to assume that consensus can suddenly be produced overnight as to what justice demands, resolving the differences between the many versions of justice which different peoples apply to the same concrete situation.[58] We do not have to assume any greater displacement of the national interest by the common interest than what is implied in the need of all nations to survive, so that they may continue to have national interests. Nor need we assume that mutual fear and hate can be turned suddenly to love, except to the extent that men are finally united by the love of life itself, and that their hold on life depends in our age on their willingness to acknowledge at least the bare right to live of others as well.

There is not presupposed in short by this projection of a possible constructive role of the Assembly any achievement of consensus among these divided peoples beyond a recognition of their shared danger, and their shared inability to escape the danger. If to recognise this, and modify the pursuit of national interests to the extent which this recognition requires, be regarded as still a kind of justice at the marginal level, we would have no objection. What is important is not what name we give to this marginal standard, but that we acknowledge that its application should not be confused with the aspiration to achieve some quick harmonisation of national interests and ideals in the full sense. What it may be possible to hope is that such a more modest approach may, if aided by the kind of example of immolation of national interests given in recent months by some of the Powers, assist

---

56 While there is, of course, room for the full statement of claims and counter-claims in terms of law and justice on each *legal* problem as such (see e.g. recently from the Israeli standpoint, L. M. Bloomfield, *Egypt, Israel and the Gulf of Aqaba* (1957) *passim* and esp. 72-79, 164ff.) we would regard it as more profitable for Assembly action to address itself to the Suez and Aqaba questions together, as one concrete part of the total merits, in the above terms and for the above reasons. But see certain contrary arguments *id.* 79-80.

57 The breaking up of the problem into units smaller and more concrete than the total merits is important, even though problems of priority as between these lesser units will remain. See e.g. as to priority between the problems of Arab refugees, of Gaza, Aqaba and Suez, the exchange between M. Schurmann (Netherlands) (*G.A.O.R. XI*, Jan. 19, 1957, p.945ff., paras. 7, 9), and M. Jamali (Iraq) (A/PV. 646, Jan. 29, 1957, p.17.)

58 The main position here taken does not, we believe, depend upon any particular theory of justice, or of the nature of justice, and we have not, therefore, found it necessary to re-canvass here for the international society the problems of justice and its criteria which I have elsewhere explored in relation to municipal societies. (See e.g. Stone, *Province* cc. 8-16, 27.) We may perhaps observe, however, in view of the recent appearance of Hans Kelsen's *What is Justice* (1957) that the modest guides to minimal adjustment for the purposes of peace enforcement which we are here proposing should not be confused with that distinguished writer's "relativist" theory of justice.

It will be apparent that we agree with him that the idea of justice in an absolute sense can contribute little to the immediate problems of preserving international peace, and that justice as appealed to among men presents itself as a conflict of competing

in generating a will to wait, and a will to compromise among States in conflict. To envisage this possibility (we again stress) is not to envisage the General Assembly as suddenly transformed into a company whose Members agree upon what justice demands, and seek to bring it about. It is merely to envisage the possibility that out of the ineluctable common helplessness and perplexity may come a sufficient degree of anxious care to restrain the deeper intransigencies of national interests, postures, and *bloc* alignments, to a degree which is manifestly indispensable for common survival.[59] And above all it is to draw the necessary inferences from the plight in which all nations find themselves: a plight in which the peril of common destruction is so near that we simply dare not let our response wait upon the far distant hope of harmonising the claims which men and nations make in the name of justice.

III. THE NEED TO CULTIVATE THE INSTITUTIONS AND BEHAVIOUR PATTERNS FOR INTERNATIONAL ADJUSTMENT.

It is not, of course, the purpose of this study to design any structure for converting the United Nations into an international community in the full sense, endowed through an effective disarmament plan, an international peace force, and organs with general compulsory jurisdiction over international disputes, including those requiring legislative adjustment, with a true community monopoly of the means of coercion. All proposals to these ends are worthy of close study and warm sympathy. But they require above all a cold and assiduous inquiry concerning steps which must be taken if humanity is ever to move into a position from which such proposals can be given

values (*op.cit.* 4ff.), though the Writer would rather leave ultimate questions a little open by speaking of a conflict of men's competing versions of justice.

The important point, however, is that Professor Kelsen's relativity theory, whatever its value for purposes of municipal societies, does not seem to help us in our present international problems. It is that writer's view that the very "subjectivity" which he finds in all judgment of justice heightens rather than destroys individual moral responsibility (23), and that his relativism includes the "moral principle" of "tolerance", of "sympathetic understanding of the religious and political beliefs of others". This "moral principle" is obviously essential if Kelsen's relativism is to work as a basis of social life (23). (If, incidentally, a workable relativism implies this principle, does not this principle itself carry us beyond what is relative, to a kind of absolute procedural principle of justice? *Cf.* Stone, *Province* 785.) Kelsen also makes the point, crucial for international purposes, "that no absolute tolerance can be commended by a relativistic philosophy of values; only tolerance within an established legal order guaranteeing peace by prohibiting and preventing the use of force among those subjected to the order. . . ." (*Id.* 23.) Clearly in the context he is directing himself here to the problems of justice in settled stable municipal societies. A relativist theory of justice thus finally dependent on the existence of "an established legal order guaranteeing peace" and excluding the use of private force, can obviously make little immediate contribution to our pressing problems of peace enforcement in an international legal order which clearly does *not* guarantee peace in the sense stated. Insofar as (in Kelsen's view) the social operability of a relativist theory presupposes that such a guarantee of peace already exists, it can scarcely be used to bring about what it already presupposes.

59 Certainly this assumes that the pressure of national interest must stop short of denying the right of other States to continue to exist. And it is in this respect that the Israeli-Egyptian problem is particularly obstinate. The Egyptian Government's intention to destroy Israel has been openly expressed; and this intention is the steady background of the Israeli complaints that "every single right, every amenity, every advantage which Israel had a claim to enjoy under the 1949 Agreement was effectively denied . . . At

a practical trial.[60] It is with this last mentioned inquiry that the present work has been concerned, and in particular with the question of what steps are *now* open to us which may help to avoid premature annihilation, and move us somewhat nearer to a promising point of departure for the more long-term planning.

Few will disagree with the view that the problems of third party settlement, of maintaining the peace, and of disarmament, are finally interdependent and must for full success be concurrently approached. Yet it is important to recall also that this truth became a central slogan of the policy of most States and of the League of Nations in the last generation, in the form "Arbitration, Security and Disarmament"; and that the emergence of this vast indivisible programme in the 'twenties and 'thirties heralded a period of failure and retrogression in the tasks of maintaining peace.[61] That, of course, in no way proves that the programme cannot succeed now; but neither does it encourage us to believe that it can. And it suggests, at any rate, that it would be well to try to reinsure against a repetition of failure by transitional measures more modest in their demands for reformation of the established State system and for conversion of the human race from its hitherto inveterate courses.

What is here proposed is that we address ourselves to the central problem of preventing breaches of the peace as such, without trying to beg those questions of ultimate justice, and those questions of preference between competing national versions of justice, which we are as yet quite unable to solve in very many cases. It is the present inability to solve these questions which has led us to the conclusion that the aggression notion, unless it be used in a merely morally neutral sense to mean a breach of the peace, cannot serve as a sufficient conceptual basis for an effective peace enforcement system. It has at the same time been recognised that immediate and automatic General Assembly action in arrest of breach of the peace will not be effective for this limited purpose, unless disputants have a certain degree of assurance that their more intolerable grievances and dangers will thereafter receive consideration at the hands of those who have restrained them from forceful self-redress. We have made clear in this connection that we cannot expect this consideration to attain immediately the level of "the doing of justice"; we believe it to be crying for the moon to ask for an early

---

the same time Egypt claimed, and sometimes received, international support in its efforts to secure respect of the agreement by Israel" (*G.A.O.R. XI,* Jan. 28, 1957, p.984, para. 45, and *cf. id.* p.986, paras. 68-69). "Egypt . . . has stood in belligerency, and Egyptian belligerency has prevailed on land and on sea as a legal doctrine and in the whole spirit and emotion of Egypt's relations with Israel. It was here that there arose a paradox impossible to resolve—how to achieve peaceful conditions on the basis of a state of war. Belligerency and progress to peace were deemed capable of living together side by side". (*G.A.O.R. XI,* Feb. 2, 1957, p.1090, para. 174.) And *cf.* Sir Percy Spender (*G.A.O.R. XI,* Jan. 1, 1957, pp.1035,1039, paras. 49, 107.)

60 Among the most thoughtful and up to date of these studies, though perhaps still insufficiently directed to the need for intervening steps, see Grenville Clark and Louis B. Sohn, *Peace Through Disarmament and Charter Revision* (1953) and Supp. (1956). And see *infra* n.63.

61 See on this slogan in its historical context, and for some references to the literature, Stone, *Conflict* 100-102.

emergence among the 82 members of the United Nations of agreement as to what justice demands in the main situations of tension which confront us. The practical next steps are rather, without systematically denying claims in title of justice, to appeal to States to transcend their own versions of it on a plane which has hope of being heard.

And while, in general, this work is not concerned with proposals for long-term reform of the United Nations, we must add a few words concerning one proposal which seems deeply relevant precisely to the problem of the next steps on which this study is centred. Proposals for an International Equity Tribunal, to determine disputes of which the gist is a demand for change in the legal *status quo* may of course be of varied character. In terms of a resort with compulsory jurisdiction and power to make binding decisions which are then enforced by collective authority, such proposals seem to us too far in advance of present possibilities, in respects much discussed in this study.[62] Yet a carefully qualified plan for such a resort may provide a valuable means by which States might learn gradually and experimentally that it may be possible to transcend their national interests to the degree required by common survival.

A carefully designed process, for example, whereby political debate and voting in the General Assembly would proceed within the context of recommendations made after careful enquiry by a standing tribunal of as impartial and expert a nature as we can create, and the interplay between these two bodies, might be an excellent medium for cultivating the modest degree of transcendence of national interests here aimed at.[63] The existence of such a standing tribunal or commission for dealing with non-legal disputes might tend to sustain the interest of Members in reducing grievances of disputants even after the guns have ceased to fire, without frightening off State cooperation with the threat of binding recommendations. The ideal of impartial third party judgment would have its steady symbol, around which, if we have the will to wait, loyalty would have a chance to grow. The freedom of Members to make their own appreciation of the findings of such a Tribunal, might help to emancipate debate somewhat from the intractable realms of competing national versions of justice; and might promote awareness both of the possibility and the urgent need to find some middle course between merely self-centred or *bloc*-centred voting, on the one hand, and the ideals of full self-abnegation, on the other.

No one, of course, could guarantee such gains, but they appear to be

---

[62] In at least three major respects. First, they assume that States can be induced in one great step, to move from attempted control each of their own destiny to full surrender to an impartial third party of the power to determine the basic conditions on which their destiny may depend. Second, they assume that there are available the personnel necessary to provide the wise arbiters of which such a Tribunal must, in order to succeed, consist. Third, they assume that the ideas of "justice" or "equity" in their present form will provide a standard usable by the Tribunal and acceptable to the Parties. And see generally Chs. 4, 7 and 8.

[63] Grenville Clark and Louis Sohn, (*op.cit. supra* n.60, 1957 revision, under title *World Peace Through World Law* (1957), Art. 36 and comment thereto) have proposed that the appropriate United Nations political organ might refer disputes likely to endanger peace, and not resolvable on the basis of applicable law, to a newly established standing "World Conciliation Board", for investigation and mediation. In default

within present reach if we can make the effort. This way at least may lie some hope of a path towards sanity and survival which it may be within our power to reach.

IV. AN INTERNATIONAL PEACE FORCE FOR THE GENERAL ASSEMBLY?

Amid the tangle of events which made up the recent crisis, the issues as to the legal nature and functions of the 6,000 strong United Nations Emergency Force, which entered the Canal Zone and later Gaza and Sharm el Sheik after the cease-fire and concurrently with the Anglo-French and Israeli withdrawals, are deeply relevant to an assessment of the authority of the General Assembly. And the question, What are appropriate next steps for increasing that authority for securing international peace? must also take account of this creation of what the Secretary-General termed a "truly international force" as a "subsidiary organ" of the General Assembly.[64] Bearing in mind, therefore, we are only concerned with this special aspect of U.N.E.F. problems,[65] we have devoted a Discourse following this Chapter to the

---

of agreed settlement after a stated period the General Assembly might, by a three-fifths majority of votes of the representatives, refer such non-legal questions to a World Equity Tribunal, also of a standing nature, after, however, obtaining rulings on any important legal questions involved from the present Court.

The Equity Tribunal after due hearing and investigation would submit recommendations for just and fair solution to the Assembly. The General Assembly would then promptly consider such recommendations and vote upon them in their entirety, the vote required for approval being carefully designed to ensure overwhelming agreement by the representatives of the more important States (according to the system adopted as a basis of representation in the Clark-Sohn project), and by a majority of those of other States. If the General Assembly so approves, and finds that the danger to peace is likely to continue unless the recommendations are carried out, it would then call for acceptance by the States concerned, and would (by the Clark Sohn project) have power to decide on measures (including enforcement measures under Arts. 41 and 42 of the Charter) to ensure compliance. In case the Tribunal's recommendations were not approved "in their entirety" by the General Assembly, the Assembly might refer the questions back to the Tribunal for further consideration, or might itself make recommendations in the light of those of the Tribunal, or propose other procedures for settlement.

The Clark-Sohn proposal on this matter above sketched is, of course, part of a comprehensive plan for revision of the structure of the United Nations. As such it is predicated on the adoption of a proposed system of weighted representation of States in the General Assembly, and on the adoption there of a system of free voting by representatives rather than by States. We do not believe that such changes in the constitution and voting system of the Assembly are attainable in time to avert present dangers; and it is for that reason that we would reject for the present those aspects of the Equity Tribunal proposal which would make recommendations binding on and enforceable against the Parties. This would still, as indicated in the text, leave valuable suggestions for an institutional structure appropriate to the purposes here in mind.

64 See his statement reported *N.Y.T.*, Apr. 11, 1957, p.13, and the Regulations of the United Nations Emergency Force of Feb. 20, 1957 (*U.N. Doc.* ST/SGB/UNEF/1). Reg. 6 refers to the Force as "a subsidiary organ of the United Nations", but his covering Memorandum (Doc. A/3552), as "a subsidiary organ of the General Assembly". And see the Discourse hereafter.

65 On the wider problems of an international police force see among the most notable modern works, Lord Davies, *The Problem of the Twentieth Century* (1930), and the full bibliography up to 1950 in L. B. Sohn, *Cases and Other Materials on World Law* (1950) 852-53. And see the proposals for a "United Nations peace force" in G. Clark and L. B. Sohn, *op.cit. supra* n.63. And see the 1947 Report of the Military Staff Committee and other documentation cited in the Discourse, *infra* p.184. *Cf.* the conclusions in *Frye*

problem of "A United Nations Peace Force and the Authority of the General Assembly".[66]

That analysis leads, in the present submission, to the following conclusions: (1) It would exceed the constitutional power of the Assembly to establish a United Nations Emergency Force with peace enforcement functions strictly so-called. (2) The Assembly cannot by its own resolutions (not even by the Uniting for Peace Resolutions) give itself this power which it does not have under the Charter. (3) Member-States cannot, either, validate the General Assembly's assumption of such extra-constitutional power by consenting thereto, except by constitutional amendment. (4) This constitutional disability of the Assembly does not legally prevent Member States who believe that a case of armed attack has arisen from coordinating their measures of individual or collective defence, and, perhaps, even from receiving for that purpose encouragement and certain organisational facilities from the General Assembly.[67] Such a coordinated self-defence, however, is a military instrument of the Members concerned acting under the licence either of Article 51 or of customary international law, and not a peace-enforcement organ of the General Assembly. (5) The General Assembly's lack of power to create a military organ of peace enforcement does not entail the illegality of the United Nations Emergency Force created in 1956, unless that Force purports to be such an organ. (6) In fact, close examination of its functions indicates that it does not purport to be such an organ, and indeed that the Force is little more than an observer corps. Its modest functions fall easily within what is properly incidental to the Assembly's powers under Article 11, of making recommendations on questions relating to the "maintenance" (as distinct from the enforcement) of international peace. (7) This method of demonstrating the constitutional legitimacy of U.N.E.F. as either a subsidiary organ of the United Nations or the General Assembly, or as an administrative unit of the Secretariat, requires us in turn to acknowledge the modesty of its proper functions, and the limits on its contribution to peace thereby implied. (8) Finally, this modesty of functions involved in its constitutional legitimation implies a correspondingly modest limit on the size of any future force that is to be similarly legitimated.

Obviously those for whom the next step on the road to international peace is the creation of an international military force capable of enforcing peace against (at any rate) all but the greatest Powers, will draw little comfort from the present analysis. It will offer, perhaps, even less comfort to any who hail the United Nations Emergency Force as a harbinger, shortly to be followed by such a full-fledged international peace-enforcing instrument.[68] For such hopes and expectations fail to take account of the indicated limits

---

which reached me in typed form as this volume comes off the press. The general concurrences of independently reached results following upon our conferences in May-June, 1957, are most welcome to the present Writer. See *infra* pp.184ff. *Cf.* the able analysis in L. M. Goodrich and G. E. Rosner, "U.N.E.F." (1957) 11 *Int. Org.* 413.

[66] *Ibid.*

[67] E.g. the services of the Secretariat, and the premises of the General Assembly. It is unnecessary for the present purpose to examine the doubts which may arise even on this point.

[68] See e.g. Mr. Sasorith (Laos), *G.A.O.R. XI,* Nov. 29, 1956, p.431.

of function and size necessary for a United Nations Emergency Force which can stand its legal ground. They also ignore certain other even more indubitable truths. One is that if a "force" promoted by the General Assembly is to be more than temporary and disbandable at the will of the contributing States, enough States must agree to place substantial forces permanently at the disposal of the General Assembly. (This is even apart from the constitutional difficulties already mentioned.) Nor does it remove this obstacle to formulate plans, as did Pakistani Foreign Minister Noon on November 29, 1956,[69] in terms of establishing on a permanent basis "the international force envisaged in Chapter VII . . .". This route, too, prerequires the agreement of the contributing States, a requirement that should not be concealed by wishful and wistful hopes that "the force should eventually be recruited and paid for by the Organisation . . .".

It has always been open to Members to enter into special agreements with the Security Council to provide contingents for standing United Nations armed forces under Chapter VII. And since 1950 it has been open to Members to agree to earmark units for service under the Uniting for Peace Resolutions. No such agreements have been forthcoming; and it must surely be for any statesman or writer whose plans depend on their being forthcoming, to explain how and why they think that State attitudes are now so transformed as to make such proposals feasible. The Writer sees no evidence of such transformation.

The reasons why consent and cooperation of Member States for establishing effective permanent peace enforcement armed forces is not forthcoming, are no doubt many and complex. But, in important part, they are certainly related to the reasons examined in the present work for the failure of the enterprise of finding an agreed definition of aggression capable of immediate and certain application to future crises. These reasons were seen to lie deep in the deficiencies of the international legal order which man at present endures, in the absence of orderly means of collective vindication of rights, and of collective adjustment of legal rights in a changing world, as well as in the unpredictability of future situations, and in the dominance of national versions of truth and justice over any such values as are at present shared by mankind in common. In this light it should scarcely surprise us that the unease and insecurity which prevent States from firmly branding particular concrete acts as aggression, out of the as yet unknown contexts of their future occurrence, may also prevent them from voluntarily creating a standing instrument of coercion which, in some future contingency, might be manipulated against themselves by some self-interested alignment of States, even within a United Nations organ.

It may be said that the need for unanimity of the Permanent Members removes any serious danger of abuse in the Security Council. The point may have truth, but it is self-defeating. For even if by a miracle such a force as Foreign Minister Noon envisaged were established, the need for Great Power unanimity would rarely if ever allow it to fulfil its mission. It is *very* rarely that conflict even between small Powers does not also align the Great; and

[69] *G.A.O.R. XI,* Nov. 29, 1956, p.417.

the advocates of Security Council armed forces do not explain how the permanent armed forces, even if established, would be brought into operation in each crisis over the hurdle of the veto. In the General Assembly, at any rate, with its alignments, its patterns of voting behaviour and blockages of communication so often manifest, the dangers in question are clear enough. The failure of Members to earmark units under the Uniting for Peace Resolutions, and the way in which they drew back even in the recent crisis from permitting any peace enforcement role to U.N.E.F., are eloquent enough as to the obstinacy of this sector of reality.

Compared with all this, the particularisation of legal devices and arguments aimed to bring a "truly international force" with peace enforcement functions into existence, are of only collateral interest.[70] The conclusion is, for the present Writer, quite inescapable that hopes of enforcing peace by the quick establishment of a permanent effective international force are not well-based; and that U.N.E.F., certainly, is not now and cannot quickly (even if it could ever legally) be transformed into such a force.

Yet here again, as with proposals for an international equity tribunal, wisdom requires us to seize upon whatever aspects of impractical dreams may give a basis for practical next steps. Measured by the aspirations which we have here had to question, U.N.E.F. was and is a weak, emasculated kind of international "force". Yet it was, after all, this very weakness and emasculation, the absence of real military functions, the subjection of its birth, and even its practical survival, to the consent of the contributing States, and of its operations to that of the territorial sovereigns—these were among the essential features which permitted it to come into being and operation under openly international command, and even show a modicum of success. If this be so, then, in the present view, the next step is to seek to consolidate this tiny but significant advance into the wilderness of international life, rather than to seek, from such a slender base, to subdue in one swoop the vast unconquered jungle which bars the way to real international peace enforcement.

Whether in time the modest U.N.E.F. enterprise can be exchanged for an effective instrument of peace enforcement, depends on whether and when sufficient Member States are willing to provide the standing resources of men and money, and to accept the risks of diversion to unacceptable purposes of the power thus granted. And this remains the final question, whatever the constitutional form of the force—whether Security Council armed forces under Chapter VII, Members' coordinated self-defence under the Uniting for Peace Resolutions, a General Assembly peace-enforcing organ claiming authority (but of dubious constitutionality) under the same Resolutions, or a functionally more modest and constitutionally proper "para-military" quasi-observer organ of the General Assembly or the United Nations, or unit of the Secretariat, under the various Charter provisions already mentioned. Whether, in turn, State willingness will grow is not predictable with assurance. But it can at least be said that its growth must depend in substantial part on the possibility of cultivating among the Member States that modicum

[70] See, however, the Discourse *infra* pp.184ff. for a fuller analysis of these aspects.

of restraint of the deeper intransigencies of national interests and *bloc* alignments, and transcendence of these in voting behaviour, required by common survival in the thermo-nuclear age.

Meanwhile a subsidiary international organ of the modest functions and size of U.N.E.F., which has proved factually and constitutionally viable, while it may not realise ambitious objectives of an enforced world order, does good service in symbolising the community interest which now broods between the battle lines at every breach of the peace. It may also be a valuable damper on passions, a softener of the humiliations which so often obstruct peaceful settlement, and a model of international intervention around which acceptance of the full role of the community interest may grow. It may thus lay some of the foundations capable of carrying more powerful international structures at some future time. Other, perhaps more important, parts of these foundations may have to be sought elsewhere, in the no less significant model presented by the Korean type of multi-national coordinated self-defence forces stimulated into existence by General Assembly activity. The fact that, in the present view, the former may be a United Nations organ proper, while the latter is an emergency device legally extraneous to the United Nations, should not conceal the opportunities of mutual reinforcement of the two models in progress towards an effective peace enforcement system.

Yet finally, we must repeat, neither drafting ingenuity nor constitutional improvisation will decide whether such a consummation is possible, or at what rate. Here as with the definition of aggression, and the international equity tribunal, the critical questions lie on a different level, amenable neither to simple idealism, verbal evasion, nor to the juristic or diplomatic *tour de force*.

V. PRIORITY OF THE TASKS OF PEACE ENFORCEMENT AND ADJUSTMENT AND BASIC ETHICAL IMPERATIVES.

Humanity may still survive particular criminal acts of war-like aggression, but the time may already have arrived when it cannot afford a major world conflict, unjust or just, aggressive or defensive, whether as an instrument of national or of international policy. The mass annihilation of innocents, the destruction of civilisation, and of life on the earth itself, may now proceed from the initiative of States whose war is just, as well as from those whose cause is unjust or aggressive. Even if justice between States were a precise and known measure (and we have seen that it is not), mercy as well as justice, and firm and open-eyed patience as a handmaid of mercy, would still be part of the wisdom essential for our times.

To leap from this, however, to the erroneous conclusion that we can brand as "aggression" and *ipso facto* unlawful and unjust every State resort to force by way of self-help against wrongs other than armed attack, would be only to restart the vicious circle which has kept the debate on definition of aggression in such endless deadlock. The correct inference is rather that first priority in peace enforcement must be given to the arrest of any breach of the peace as such by immediate pressure applied regardless of the merits;

but that this must then be followed through if either conflicting Party requests it, to the recommendation of measures and the giving of assurances necessary to reduce to tolerable proportions the wrongs and dangers complained of. Mere arrest of hostilities without the growth of a pattern of grievance-handling will not succeed even in the shorter long run. States will break out of such situations as soon as it becomes clear that the General Assembly cannot or will not use its authority also to protect their rights and legitimate interests, which suppression of forcible self-redress must otherwise leave naked and exposed to the rapacity, malice or irresponsibility of other States. They will assuredly break out once it is clear that this moral suasion is so appropriated to the selfish interests of any coalition of votes as to override steadily the minimal demands of elementary justice.[71]

And it is because a definition of aggression which systematically ignores demands sincerely made in the name of justice is thus not operationally viable, while an agreed definition that is precise enough to guide us and yet flexible enough to take these demands into account is beyond our reach, that the hope of basing peace enforcement on a definition of aggression has gradually faded. The argument that it is ethically imperative to define aggression on the ground that such definition is vital to human survival, loses most of its force once it is shown, as we believe has been shown in these pages, that such a definition even if found and if accepted by most States would not fulfil its assumed purpose.

It is, finally, just because we continue to regard as pre-eminent the questions raised by men's yearning for a just world, and their constant search to realise it through their many competing versions of what justice requires, that it has been here urged that we should not let the immediate here-and-now tasks of maintaining peace wait upon the answers to them. We must, of course, bend increasing efforts towards these ultimate tasks of understanding; the Writer has elsewhere stressed the importance of these tasks and examined the conditions and range of effective work on them. But this present study is directed not to the conditions of humanity's ultimate salvation, but to the conditions of its immediate survival, without which there can be no hope of ultimate salvation. These conditions of immediate survival are set by the exigencies of our actual situation in a world threatened by thermonuclear weapons.

In such a world and at such a phase the main task is to buy time: to buy time involves inevitably facing facts as they are, and suspending courses which experience has shown to be illusory and even dangerous to peace. One danger has been in the tendency to interpret our situation in terms of impossible choices, whether between Expediency and Morality, Power and Justice, of Perdition and Perfection, State Sovereignty and World Government. To leave men only with such alternatives may bring comfort and a sense of confident righteousness to individual hearts, and even individual peoples, but only to each according to their respective interpretations of these concepts. But it is also to undermine moderation, understanding and

[71] And see *supra* nn.15, 35, 42.

tolerance and to cause human communication to become increasingly clipped, and perverted. By such a course we may increasingly lose not merely the will to live and let live, but also the will to wait, and the will to buy the time in which to wait. For such illusory alternatives tend too often to confront particular nations with the plausible duty of solving the international problem once and for all for the vindication of its own version of the preferred moral values.[72] And above all they tend to blind each nation and State to the availability of the kind of middle course, which we are concerned here to press.

This middle course, of moderation and anxious care in the pursuit of its interests and those of its *bloc*-fellows, does not call for the abandonment or surrender of any nation's version of justice. It calls only for a readiness not to press this, or to abate it at the point where it cannot be realised without the creation for other States of conditions which are inconsistent with their stable survival. It calls for this as the only basis on which we can expect the United Nations, and especially the General Assembly, to consolidate its authority to arrest breaches of the peace before these spread into a holocaust for mankind.

It would not be impossible to rationalize this precept in terms of some ambitious theory of justice. At the least it could be stated as a moral imperative dictated by the need of survival in our actual situation. We prefer to state it in the paradoxical form of a plea that States should, in this situation, set limits on their pursuit of what they regard as justice. For, whatever version of justice we may cleave to, its compulsiveness should certainly not take us to the point when we have to argue that it demands the sacrifice of the whole human race. Our age is perhaps the first in which men have been asked to take with stark literalness the admonition, *"Fiat justitia, ruat coelum."* For our age is the first in recorded history in which this maxim may be tested literally; now for the first time *ruat coelum* may mean the actual end of man. If it were clear that the course here urged involved the final abandonment of men's aspiration to achieve justice in their relations with each other, we might take pause even then. That is not here in issue however; what is rather asked is that men and States learn to say humbly with an ancient sage: "It is not for thee to finish the task; neither art thou free to desist from it." Through such moderation, too, we might even hope to achieve a more sensible adjustment between the interests of our own and of future generations, acknowledging the vastly expanded temporal dimension of moral responsibilities which spring from the new powers we have seized over the human future.[73]

---

72 See generally Stone, *Conflict*, Introduction, and *supra* pp. 143ff.

73 Cf. J. Stone, "International Law and Contemporary Social Trends: Some Reflections" (1957) 29 *Rocky Mountain Law Review* 149, esp. 156ff., 163ff.

A DISCOURSE
ON
A UNITED NATIONS PEACE FORCE AND THE AUTHORITY OF THE GENERAL ASSEMBLY

I. CONTEXT OF "PEACE FORCE" PROPOSALS.

The prospects for the establishment of the authority of the General Assembly are often thought to depend on equipping that body with a military arm to enforce the peace, with an international "police" or "peace" force. Aspirations of this sort have naturally been much stimulated by the role of the United Nations Emergency Force in the crisis of 1956-57.

Here again it is necessary, if we are to make any advance, or even to hold any ground gained, that dreaming should not too far outrun intellection. This certainly was a vice in the original design of the Charter for United Nations forces to be placed at the disposition of the Security Council, under its Military Staff Committee, as a permanent military organ of the United Nations. That Committee was (in design) to advise the Security Council on military requirements for peace enforcement, on the employment and command of its forces, and was to be responsible for the strategic direction of those forces.

It is a stale story that these and related provisions of Chapter VII of the Charter have never moved from the shadows of Charter exegetics into the light of practical affairs. No State has concluded any special agreement under Chapter VII to place forces at the Council's disposal. The military "teeth" which many attributed to the Charter[1] were never cut, much less can they bite. The "internationalism" of the Military Staff Committee, consisting of the Chiefs of Staff of the Permanent Members, proved entirely illusory. For those who proceeded by thought rather than by dreams, it should have been clear from the start that neither a Great Power nor its Chief of Staff could be expected to put into the hands of an international organ, not controlled by that Power, a military instrument which had any chance of successful use against itself or its friends or allies. It should scarcely have been a matter of surprise that the Military Staff Committee reported in 1947 that it was not practical to create a force capable of restraining any threat to the peace, breach of the peace or act of aggression emanating from a Permanent Member.[2]

The spread of paralysis to the Security Council peace enforcement functions led to an attempt by the General Assembly first through the establishment of "the Little Assembly",[3] and then more successfully through the Uniting for Peace Resolutions in 1950,[4] to assume some of the derelict

---

[1] *Cf.* e.g. the *Report,* by M. P. Boncour, Rapporteur of Committee III/3 of the San Francisco Conference, June 10, 1945, 12 *U.N.C.I.O. Docs.* 502ff., esp. 513.

[2] *Report,* Apr. 30, 1947, *U.N. Doc.* S/336, *S.C.O.R.,* Second Year, Sp. Supp. No. 1. And see Stone, *Conflict* 199, and other documents there cited.

[3] Established by Resol. III(II) of the General Assembly, Nov. 13, 1947 (*U.N. Doc.* A/454); and re-established Dec. 3, 1948 (*U.N. Doc.* A/740). For literature see L. B. Sohn, *World Law* (1950) 454.

[4] See Stone, *Conflict* 266-284, and literature there cited. And see *supra* n.2.

functions. Resolution A(8) recommended that Members maintain units in their respective armed forces suitable for United Nations service on the recommendation of the Security Council or the General Assembly; and the stage began to be set for the great legal and political debates which have surrounded proposals for a standing United Nations force.[5] If such proposals are not to meet the final fate of the Security Council's vast powers, they must be better tested against realities in which they would have to be implemented.

II. BIRTH AND PEDIGREE OF U.N.E.F.

Among the powers which may be vested in a collective international organ, the power of peace enforcement stands near the summit; and among the powers which may be conferred for the purpose of peace enforcement, the power to constitute, maintain, and employ military forces are obviously central. For that reason proposals for the establishment of a United Nations force are inevitably entangled with the problems of the constitutional power of the General Assembly.

Yet as soon as we begin to talk about the "powers" of the General Assembly, we are faced with pitfalls of language which, unless avoided, must abort fruitful discussion. Loosely used, the word "power" conceals at least three quite different meanings. We have "power" in the layman's sense to twiddle our thumbs, symbolising by that an activity which affects neither the factual interests nor the legal rights of other persons.[6] Since, *ex hypothesi*, powers of this type do not materially affect State rights and interests, they are of little importance for the controversies surrounding proposals for a permanent United Nations Force. Yet there is a constant tendency in the

---

[5] Among these recent proposals there may be mentioned the following:
1. The Canadian proposal for "a permanent mechanism by which units of the armed forces of member countries could be endowed with the authority of the United Nations and made available at short notice for supervisory police duties". See L. Pearson, "Force for U.N." (1957) 35 *Foreign Affairs* 395. The author's initiative in relation to U.N.E.F. is well known. He also pointed out that Canada had earlier offered to keep available its special force raised for Korea for carrying out its obligations elsewhere (pp.399-400).
2. The Brazilian suggestion for implementing the Uniting for Peace Resolutions, so that in future "the requisitioning of troops in obedience to resolutions adopted by either the Security Council or the General Assembly would come to be regarded as normal procedure". (*G.A.O.R. XI*, Plenary Meetings, p.86.)
3. The Iraqi declaration in favour of "a strong police force . . . available to enforce or supervise the enforcement of United Nations decisions". (*Id.* p.90.)
4. The Norwegian proposal for "a permanent basis of United Nations forces in readiness for emergencies". (*Id.* 366.)
5. The Laotian proposal to develop U.N.E.F. into "a world police force", "an effective instrument of action, a real armed force in the service of peace". (*Id.* 431.)
6. The Chilean hope "that the United Nations will organize a permanent armed force ready to step in . . . to deter aggression by any State in disregard of its Charter obligations". (*Id. 401.*)
7. The Pakastani proposal cited *supra* pp.179-180.

Among private discussions see G. Clark and L. B. Sohn, works cited *supra* Ch. 9, nn.60, 63, H. F. Armstrong, "The U.N. Experience in Gaza" (1957) 35 *Foreign Affairs* 600, 618-19, and the new basic study here cited as *Frye*. On the older U.N. guards proposal (1948) see *infra* n.30; on the report of the Security Council's Military Staff Committee *supra* p. 186, and for a full account L. Goodrich in *Frye* 175-184.

[6] Of course, occasionally even this activity might in an unusual case prejudice the interests or rights of others. The usual case is here assumed.

debates to move from the assertion that the General Assembly has "power" in this first sense (which we may term "non-operational power") to the second and third, much more substantial, senses, and thus beg the very questions which have to be decided.

The second of these senses, which we may call "legally enforced power", applies where the Assembly may by its action not only affect the interests of a Member, as by requesting it to take or desist from certain action, but also thereby impose upon the Member a corresponding legal obligation to comply. It goes without saying that the action gives the obliged Member no legal ground of protest or remedy against such action. This is one form of "operational power". The third sense of power here distinguished is also operational power, but with legal consequences somewhat less drastic. We may term it "legally licensed power". Under such a power also the General Assembly may act prejudicially to the interests of a Member, in the sense that such action gives no valid ground of legal protest or remedy to the Member. Yet this third kind of power falls short of "legally enforced power" in that the Assembly action here imposes on the Member no legal obligation to comply. The Member here has not any ground for legal complaint against the exercise of this kind of power; but neither has it any legal duty to submit to it.

Thus the General Assembly has "power" in the first sense—non-operational power—to make recommendations under Article 10 of the Charter on any question or matter within the scope of the Charter. It has power in the second sense—of legally enforced power—to adopt a budget and fix the contributions of Members. As regards the *enforcement* of peace and security only the Security Council has legally enforced power over the peace-breaking State, that is, the power to impose on that State whose interests are prejudiced by the peace-enforcing action, and the legal obligation to submit thereto. The General Assembly has no such enforcement power. It has, perhaps, power in the third sense—of legally licensed power—to offer certain facilities to Member States who wish to organise and coordinate the exercise of their own licensed powers of individual and collective self-defence under Article 51 of the Charter or under customary international law. This Writer has shown elsewhere[7] that this is probably the only interpretation which will reconcile the "Uniting for Peace" system with the United Nations Charter. And it is for this reason, as became very clear during the Middle East crisis, despite much loose talk to the contrary, that the General Assembly could not impose sanctions in any sense legally compelling the State concerned to submit thereto.[8] The State against which individual Members may join in the exercise of their alleged rights of self-defence under the Uniting for Peace Resolutions has no legal obligation to submit to such hostile action, even though that hostile action may be provisionally deemed to be legally

[7] See Stone, *Conflict* 243-46. It is here assumed, of course, that the Security Council has neither taken measures necessary to maintain "international peace and security", within Art. 51, nor is otherwise exercising its authority in the matter.

[8] See my letter to the *N.Y.T.* of Feb. 8, 1957. More complex questions (into which it is here unnecessary to enter) may arise in the case of legal injuries of a non-physical character, e.g. repudiation of contracts in force under claim of sanctions measures.

licensed. Military "sanctions", in this situation, can only mean measures voluntarily undertaken by the cooperating Members of the United Nations under a claim of individual and collective self-defence, which the object of the measure is also free to resist. Moreover, since the General Assembly has no power to determine authoritatively the claim of self-defence, even this provisional licensed power may be subject to nullification if the claim is subsequently rejected by a competent forum, such as the Security Council.

This is a vital and impassable boundary of General Assembly power. The General Assembly has no authority, similar to that of the Security Council, to "determine" with legal consequences under the Charter the existence of a threat to the peace, breach of the peace or act of aggression. Nor has it the consequential authority to enforce peace after such determination.[9] A General Assembly resolution overwhelmingly adopted may create a strong factual presumption that some such event has occurred, and may thus lay a provisional basis for individual or collective self-defence by Members which the Assembly may then perhaps help to stimulate and coordinate.[10] But such a resolution is not an exercise of any power to affect the rights and obligations of Members; it is not "legally enforced power" but only (at most) "legally licensed power". All this bears immediately on the General Assembly's creation of U.N.E.F. For if the General Assembly lacks power to make such a binding determination, it can scarcely be competent to establish a peace enforcement force to give effect to such a determination. Nor can the consent of some Members extend this competence other than by the due process of Charter amendment; for the establishment of such an organ would inevitably also affect the rights and obligations of Members other than those consenting. Contrarily the scrupulous attention of the General Assembly to the need for consent of States affected, including Egypt and Israel to the operation of the Force on their territory, seems quite incongruous with the idea that its function was peace enforcement. And it would be consistent with this view that the Assembly refrained from any formal assertion of aggression or even forceful breach of the Charter.

III. FUNCTION AND SOURCE OF AUTHORITY.

It was within this historical and legal context that the recent hostilities between Israel and Egypt, and the Anglo-French intervention, stimulated the establishment of the United Nations Emergency Force[11] after rejection

---

9 For the fuller grounds of this view, and other views and authorities, see Stone, *Conflict* 266ff.

10 See *id.* 235.

11 A "United Nations Command for an Emergency International Force" was established by Resol. 1000 (E-1) of the General Assembly, 5 Nov., 1956 (*G.A.O.R.* F.E.S.S. Supp. 1 (A/3354) pp.2-3). The guiding principles for the Force as suggested in parts of the *Second and Final Report of the Sec.-Gen. on the Plan for an Emergency International United Nations Force,* Nov. 6, 1956 (A/3302, *G.A.O.R.* F.E.S.S. Ann., Agenda Item 5, pp.19-22, here cited as *"Final U.N.E.F. Report"*), were approved by Resol. 1001 (ES-I) of the General Assembly Nov. 7, 1956 (*G.A.O.R.* F.E.S.S., Supp. 1 (A/3354), p.3).

On this authority, and after consultation with the Advisory Committee established under Resol. 1001, the Sec.-Gen. issued *Regulations for the United Nations Emergency Force*

of a Soviet request that the Security Council[12] authorise that State and the United States under Article 42 of the Charter, to send "naval and air forces, military units, volunteers, military instructors and other forms of assistance" to Egypt. This crisis, as has been seen, exposed dramatically the parlous state of the debate on the definition of aggression; it bore no less dramatically on proposals for an international police force. And an ironic twist was given to the issues by the Anglo-French claim that these Governments were intervening on behalf of the United Nations as a kind of "police" action of a preventive nature.[12a] And when the Secretary-General referred to U.N.E.F. as "the first . . . truly international force",[13] his meaning, too, (so far as it went beyond rhetoric) challenged clarification.

If clarity is to be brought to the conception of an international or United Nations force, it is essential always to specify, first, what are the precise functions to be performed by the force under whatever authority, and second, which is the principal organ under whose authority the force purports to be created and act. The functions range, *in terms of talk,* from a group of guards armed with batons at United Nations Headquarters,[14] to a major combat force equipped with the most modern weapons for large-scale hostilities.[15] And even in the historical practice of the United Nations at least four types of force can be detected in terms of function. One is the Headquarters guard in whose tasks the need for the use of force is, to say the least, rather subsidiary. A second is the small armed bodyguard unit for the protection of United Nations officials abroad,[16] where possible use of force is more distinct but on a tiny scale. A third is the unit of the observer function, usually with some admixture of control function, for instance for the administration of truce terms in Palestine or Korea.[17] A

---

on Feb. 20, 1957 (*U.N. Doc.* ST/SGB/UNEF/1). Additional regulations became applicable through the U.N.-Egypt agreement on the status of the Force there. (See the Exchange of Letters of Feb. 8, 1957 (*U.N. Doc.* A/3526, supplementing an *Aide-Mémoire* on the subject approved by the General Assembly on Nov. 24, 1956 (G.A. Resol. 1121(XI), A/Res./411.)

For the texts of Agreements between the Sec.-Gen. and States contributing units to the Force see the Annex to the Final U.N.E.F. Report.

12 *Cf. Doc.* S/3736, *S.C.O.R.,* 755th Meeting, pp.4-14.

12a This was the intended gist of para. 2 of the text of the joint Anglo-French Statement read in the House of Commons on Nov. 3, 1956. For the original "Pearson Plan" to use the intervening British and French troops as a U.N. police force, see *Frye* 1-2.

13 See *N.Y.T.* Apr. 11, 1957, p.13. Cf. the Eisenhower Doctrine as finally adopted s.4 (Public Law 85-7, 85th Congress, H .J. Res. 117, Mch. 9, 1957).

14 *Cf.* in this connection Art. VI on "Police Protection of the Headquarters District" of the Headquarters of the United Nations Agreement between the U.N. and the U.S., June 26, 1947 (11 *U.N.T.S.* No. 147, p.12).

15 *Cf.* e.g. G. Clark and L. B. Sohn, *Peace through Disarmament and Charter Revision,* Supp. (Feb. 1956), esp. Ann. II, "United Nations Peace Force", and *id. op.cit. supra* Ch. 9, n.63.

16 After the tragic death of the U.N. Mediator, Count F. Bernadotte, the General Assembly expressly stated that the Sec.-Gen. "will provide a limited number of guards for the protection of the staff and premises" of the U.N. Conciliation Commission for Palestine. (See s.12 of the General Assembly resolution of Dec. 11, 1948, *Doc.* A/807.)

17 The U.N. Field Service and especially the panel of Field Observers illustrate this functional type. It should be noted, however, that these officers may also exercise guard functions. See *Report of the Special Committee on a United Nations Guard,* Oct. 10, 1949 (*G.A.O.R. IV,* Supp. No. 13 (*Doc.* A/959), pp.2-4,6-7; G.A. Resol. 297 (IV), *G.A.O.R. IV, Doc.* A/1251, pp.21-22).

fourth in United Nations practice might be the "para-military" unit for the execution of certain "military" functions short of actual hostilities,[18] such as the patrolling of a troubled or disputed area, as recently Gaza or Sharm el Sheikh. The function of peace enforcement against a threat to or a breach of the peace or act of aggression is only to be found in United Nations practice in the debatable form of the Korean action. These are the principal modalities in function as manifest in United Nations practice[19] which, it will be obvious, must be held in mind also in the discussion of the legal authority to create a force.

As to the purported source of authority for creation and operation of the unit, some of the listed functions might properly proceed from the authority either of the General Assembly, the Security Council, or even the Secretary-General, depending on what these functions are. And some complexities arise by reason of devious courses that have had to be followed in some instances by reason of the paralysis of functions in a particular organ. Thus, in the Korean Affair, though the "United Nations" force was empowered by Security Council resolution of July 7, 1950 to fly the United Nations flag, it consisted merely of national units voluntarily contributed under a unified command headed by the United States, and in fact controlled by the United States Command. These were certainly not the "armed forces" or the command contemplated by Article 47 of the Charter, or by Chapter VII generally. The Writer has elsewhere shown,[20] that the source of legal authority of the Korean force must probably be traced to the licence of States either under Article 51 or under customary international law, to engage in hostilities so far as Charter provisions do not forbid. This matter will also be considered somewhat more fully in the next Section.

This case of a nationally contributed combat force, created and operating by legal authority of the contributing States even though ostensibly approved as international by the Security Council or General Assembly, should be distinguished from two others. One is the possible case of a force operating for individual and collective self-defence without such approval (or even after disapproval by non-binding "action" of the Security Council or the General Assembly); this might for instance occur under the North Atlantic Treaty Organisation or the Warsaw Pact systems. At the other extreme, is the case of a force such as U.N.E.F. which, though still not the "armed forces" contemplated by Chapter VII, and still consisting of national units voluntarily contributed, is organised and operated on the initiative of the United Nations organ concerned, purportedly under its authority and under United Nations command. An understanding of the legal basis of U.N.E.F. and therefore of its relation to the authority of the General Assembly, will require simultaneous consideration both of the

18 See, however, *infra* s.VIB for doubts as to whether this function is really distinguishable from the third.

19 Of course, as already seen, more than one function may be found in a single unit.
Under the League there was also experience of an international police force in charge of the ordinary police administration of a territory, for instance, the Saar and Danzig. Proposals for such a U.N. administration of Trieste were, of course, abortive.

20 See Stone, *Conflict* 234ff.

functions of the force and the legal powers of the Assembly in relation to those functions. We should avoid speaking at large about the lawfulness of a "United Nations" or "international" force, and the mere addition of terms such as "peace", or "police"[21] or "emergency" in no way removes the need for careful differentiation of functions and source of constitutional powers of the respective United Nations organs.

IV. LIMITATIONS ON "CONSENT" FORCES.

The years have made clear that a meeting of international "policemen",[22] as Roosevelt at Teheran thought the Security Council ought to be, is not necessarily an effective international police force. But for present purposes it is important to stress that the failure of the Security Council in its primary responsibility for international peace and security is not (as is often implied) merely the result of the Great Power veto.[23] Even if the veto were abolished, or the Security Council were unanimous, its decisions could still not oblige any Member State to contribute to a United Nations force, whether of a standing or *ad hoc* nature. The decisions which Article 25 obliges all Members "to accept and carry out" extend only to those taken "in accordance with the Charter". Under the Charter no Member is obliged to make national contingents available except in accordance with a special agreement or agreements with the Security Council (Article 45). Neither big nor small Powers agreed at San Francisco to subject their military forces to use by an international body without their advance agreement; and thus far no such agreements have been concluded under Article 43.

The stark clarity of this position should not be concealed by the legal obscurities of the Korean action, during which, on July 7, 1950, the Security Council recommended that Members providing military or other assistance to the Republic of South Korea should make the same available to a unified command under the United States. In the analysis elsewhere[24] of the legal standing of the action of Members making military contributions to the force in Korea, there were shown to be grave legal obstacles to regarding these measures as Security Council enforcement action under Chapter VII, or the forces concerned as the armed forces thereunder. But it was also shown (contrary to the Soviet view) that this action may nevertheless be legally well-based as action taken in "individual or collective self-defence" infringing any no-force obligation of Members under the Charter.

This view of the Korean operation as voluntary action of Members within their legally licensed power under the Charter and customary international law, avoids dangerous and (in the present view) impossible overstrain of Article 27 of the Charter on voting in the Security Council. Yet

---

21 The term "police" is also sometimes used to escape constitutional limitations, e.g. in the U.S. as to Congressional participation in declaration of war. It is also sometimes aimed (e.g. in the Korean affair) to escape problems of recognition of a belligerent as a State; or (as in the Dutch-Indonesian affair) to support pleas of domestic jurisdiction.

22 *Cf.* 2 R. E. Sherwood, *The White House Papers of Harry L. Hopkins* (1949) 780.

23 For fuller treatments of the veto and consent problems see Stone, *Conflict* 221ff.

24 Stone, *Conflict* 228ff.

it may be essential to bear it in mind also because, quite apart from the voting rules, Members unwilling to conclude the agreements necessary to bring into being the United Nations forces envisaged in Chapter VII, may (as the Korean action showed) still be willing to join forces on that other basis.

The forces in Korea operated not under the command of the United Nations or any of its organs, but under that of the United States.[25] In 1956, in the later context of the creation of U.N.E.F., the Secretary-General described it as a case where the United Nations charged "a country or a group of countries, with the responsibility to provide independently for an emergency international force serving for purposes determined by the United Nations".[26] He carefully distinguished it from a force "set up on the basis of principles reflected in the constitution of the United Nations itself", of which the commander-in-chief would be appointed by the United Nations and responsible ultimately to its competent organs.[27]

The return of the Soviet representative to the Security Council in August, 1950, ended for the time being any serious speculation as to the exercise of the Security Council's powers with respect to the Korean operation. Subsequent efforts were channelled towards developing substitute "peace enforcement" procedures and instrumentalities through the "Uniting for Peace Resolutions" adopted by the General Assembly on United States sponsorship, on November 3, 1950. The procedures envisaged included "the use of armed force when necessary", and the Assembly also recommended that "each Member maintain within its national forces elements so trained, organized and equipped that they could promptly be made available . . . for service as a United Nations unit or units upon recommendation by the Security Council or the General Assembly."[28]

The Writer has shown elsewhere[29] that with the Uniting for Peace system, as with the Korean action, the anarchic liberty of self-defence, whether under Article 51 of the Charter, or under customary international law, is the only plausible basis of legality. Even on this level, however, the implementation of the Uniting for Peace system has not proceeded to the point that many States have accepted the recommendation to earmark national contingents[29a] for use under the resolution. In short, whatever U.N.E.F. may be, it is not the "United Nations unit or units" envisaged in A(8) of the Uniting for Peace Resolutions, any more than it is the "armed forces" at the Security Council's disposal under Chapter VII. What the Uniting for Peace Resolution A(1), as incorporated in the General Assembly's rules of procedure did do, was to permit the convocation of the First Emergency session within forty-eight hours of the outbreak of the Middle East crisis and the no less rapid produc-

---

25 *Cf.* the Security Council Resol. of July 7, 1950 (*Doc.* S/1588). As to the incoming U.S. Administration's "sacrifice" of the United Nations "moral umbrella" in the peace negotiations, see *Frye* 57.

26 *Cf. Final U.N.E.F. Report.*

27 *Ibid.*

28 See *supra* n.4.

29 Stone, *Conflict* 234ff., 272ff.

29a See as to the limited action of Canada, Denmark, Greece, Norway, Thailand and Uruguay, *Frye*, 59, and *supra* n.5.

tion by the Secretary-General[30] of a "plan for the setting up, *with the consent of the nations concerned,* of an emergency international United Nations Force to *secure and supervise* the cessation of hostilities in accordance with all the terms" of Resolution 997.[31]

V. THE UNITED NATIONS EMERGENCY FORCE AND PEACE ENFORCEMENT.

On the basis of the Secretary-General's plan, the General Assembly established "a United Nations Command for an emergency international force" and approved "the guiding principles for the organisation and functioning of the emergency international United Nations Force". And it approved the Secretary-General's suggestion that this Force would function "on the basis of a decision reached under the terms of the Resolution 334(V) "Uniting for Peace", and that the generally recognised rules of international law as to the requirement of consent of the parties concerned should apply to the operations of the Force. The Secretary-General also pointed out that "while the General Assembly is enabled to *establish* the Force with the consent of those parties which contributed units to the Force, it could not request the Force to be *stationed* or *operate* on the territory of a given country without the consent of the Government of that country".[32] Despite the euphemism of this formulation, it will shortly be seen that the implied distinction between the requirements for valid creation, and those for lawful stationing and operation, may not be the decisive one for constitutional purposes.[33]

The Secretary-General thought the preceding principle did not "exclude the possibility that the Security Council could use such a Force within the wider margins provided under Chapter VII of the United Nations Charter".[34] If this meant that it could be so used without the consent of the contributing Member States, the reasons already canvassed in relation to armed forces

---

30 In no derogation of admiration from this rapid action it may be recalled that essential features of U.N.E.F. were already elaborated in the *Report of the Secretary-General of Sept. 28, 1948 on the Establishment of a United Nations Guard* (*U.N. Doc.* A/656.) (This is hereafter cited as *"Guard Report"*). This was a somewhat less bold version of his earlier project for "a small United Nations Guard Force". See the *Annual Report of the Secretary-General,* 1947-1948, *G.A.O.R. III,* Supp. No. 1 (*Doc.* A/565).

31 Resol. 998 of the General Assembly, Nov. 4, 1956, *G.A.O.R.* F.E.S.S., Supp. 1 (A/3354). By that resolution the General Assembly had asked "the Parties to the armistice agreements promptly to withdraw all forces behind the armistice lines, to desist from raids across the armistice lines into neighbouring territory, and to observe scrupulously the provisions of the armistice agreements".

32 *Final U.N.E.F. Report,* para. 9.

33 For some important support for this doubt see *infra* n.41.

34 *Ibid.* Some of the confusions as to the function of the force may have arisen from such passages. The above sentence was left standing by the authorising General Assembly resolution in spite of the Philippine delegate's protest that such a possibility "was far from the mind of the Assembly when it approved the establishment of such a force". He expressed apprehension "lest the force might thereafter be converted to another purpose".

Presumably the Sec.-Gen.'s statement would require it to be implied that he negotiated with the contributing States on behalf of the General Assembly, and that that body in turn was acting as agent of the Security Council. But (1) the maxim *delegatus non potest delegare* may present a difficulty; (2) it is strained to say that the contributing States thought they were negotiating with the Security Council; and (3) as the Sec.-Gen. himself later pointed out, the Force was not to be available for "peace enforcement".

under Chapter VII would make it gravely questionable. Insofar, moreover, as it suggests that the mere consent of the contributing States sufficed to allow the creation of U.N.E.F. as "a truly international force" under the authority of the General Assembly, it seems, with respect, to make insufficiently explicit the cardinal principle that the General Assembly's authority to establish a "force" cannot be predicated without reference to the precise functions entrusted to the force.

Insofar as the functions of U.N.E.F. were to be regarded as peace enforcement in the sense of Chapter VII of the Charter, and insofar as the view must be adopted that the General Assembly cannot as such exercise functions attributed by the Charter only to the Security Council,[35] it is clear that the Assembly could not, for example, conclude those special agreements by which under Article 43 of the Charter Members may contribute armed contingents to a true United Nations force. The question then arises whether some Members of the United Nations can, by agreements *inter se,* even in the form of purported General Assembly resolutions, or by agreements with the Secretary-General as agent for that body, constitutionally confer upon the General Assembly, other than by Charter amendment proper, powers other than those granted in the Charter. Despite the hazardous analogies from some recent practice of States or international organisations,[36] it is believed that such agreements could not overcome the constitutional difficulties involved.[37]

These Charter principles, moreover, equally control action in the Assembly under the Uniting for Peace Resolutions. It is presumed that the Secretary-General was not asserting the contrary when he referred to those resolutions as the basis on which U.N.E.F. was to be established as a "truly

35 See citations *supra* nn.20,23 and s.III *passim.*

36 Agreeing to accept as binding, acts of an international organ which in terms of that organ's constitution are not binding. Thus the Italian peace treaty and certain agreements between the General Assembly and Specialised Agencies, as well as I.L.O. constitutional arrangements, provide that advisory opinions of the International Court of Justice shall be binding in certain cases of dispute between the parties concerned. (See Stone, *Conflict* 118n.) The analogy is hazardous insofar as in the given instances only the obligations of the assenting States are modified; whereas to convert the forces of individual States into an organ of the General Assembly of the Security Council would also obviously affect the legal rights of non-assenting Members. If all U.N. Members assented, *aliter,* perhaps; though the question would then be rather unreal insofar as the Charter could be amended.

37 This view is confirmed by the common insertion of express provisions in international constitutions if it is desired to permit the extension of an organ's jurisdiction by action of one or more Members, without formal amendment.

The superficially contrary instances mentioned in n.36 are better seen, not as extending the constitutional power of the organ involved, but as the exercise by the particular States concerned of the liberty to bind themselves by agreement to undertake certain obligations if a certain event occurs, whether this event be the award of an arbitral tribunal, or the utterance of the Delphic oracle, a majority decision of the General Assembly, or an advisory opinion of the International Court. By the same token, the parties may terminate these obligations by agreement, thus displaying the adventitious nature of the additional "powers" apparently conferred on the organ concerned. Moreover, some of the above instances, like the Agreement between the General Assembly and certain Specialised Agencies for Assembly recommendations to be binding, may in any case be sufficiently based on the Charter as it stands and the implied relations of the Specialised Agencies to the United Nations.

The point in the text, as to limits on an organ's constitutional powers, should not be confused with the question whether States can assume international obligations through

international force". For, behind the question whether the Uniting for Peace Resolutions can be interpreted so as to accommodate the establishment of "a truly international force", stands the overriding question whether as so interpreted those resolutions would themselves be consistent with the Charter.[38] In the present clear view, these Resolutions can only be interpreted so as to make them and action under them consistent with the Charter, by reading them as providing for the coordination of self-defence of Members. But insofar as they must be so read, they cannot authorise the establishment of a "truly international force" by the General Assembly. And the protagonists of the contrary view, if they are proceeding on the assumption that the Resolutions are a legitimate and conclusive act of auto-interpretation by the General Assembly of its own powers, have the unsustained burden of showing either that the *Willkuer* of this power of auto-interpretation is boundless, or that this particular exercise of it falls within the dubious limits permitted by law.

VI. FUNCTIONS OTHER THAN UNITED NATIONS PEACE ENFORCEMENT.

We must now quickly remind ourselves that U.N.E.F. may still be lawfully created, and lawfully operate, even if it is not as "a truly international force" created under authority of the General Assembly. For it may constitute merely a manifestation of concerted action by Member States in exercise of the right of collective self-defence. And we must also add the further point that it may even be lawfully created, and also operate by and under the authority of the General Assembly as a "truly international force", as soon as (and so long as) it is clear that its actual functions remain within the needs implicit in the constitutional powers of the General Assembly under the Charter. These do not, as we have seen, include peace enforcement.[38a]

A. *U.N.E.F. as a Coordinated Self-Defence Force.*

The first question is whether any legal obstacle prevents our regarding U.N.E.F. in the same way as, in the present view, the Korean action, the Uniting for Peace Resolutions and action thereunder, are all best regarded, namely, as a form of coordination of self-defence measures of individual Member States. And insofar as all the States involved in the recent crisis were Members of the United Nations, this action may be even more readily

resolutions of that organ. See on this narrower point the rather inconclusive formulations by H. Lauterpacht (1 Oppenheim, *International Law* (1948) 139), A. Leriche, (*"L'Evolution Récente . . . [des] Traités Multilatéraux"* (1951) 29 *R.D.Int. . . . Sciences Pol. Dip. . . .* 16, at 23), and L. B. Sohn ("The Second Year of United Nations Legislation" (1948) 34 *A.B.A. Jo.* 315). And see *supra* Ch. 9, n.4, where the literature is cited, on the "binding power" of General Assembly resolutions.

[38] Some oversight on this matter seems clear in the Sec.-Gen.'s assertion (*G.A.O.R.* F.E.S.S. 83) that the Force was sufficiently based on "the legal fact created by the vote taken . . . by the Assembly". The basic legal question is whether an Assembly resolution can be such an operative legal fact if unbased on the Charter.

[38a] This is one important legal *caveat* on the suggestion in *Frye*, 55, for the transfer of Security Council powers to the General Assembly without Charter amendment, as a means towards "universal collective security".

attributed to self-defence as delimited in Article 51 than was the Korean action.

Here, as in those cases, a careful lawyer must remember that States Members of the United Nations did not surrender to the United Nations all their liberty of action—not even all their liberty of forcible action. And beyond doubt, the Charter reserved to them—reserved, not granted—their "inherent right of individual and collective self-defence". It did this for self-defence as delimited by Article 51, notwithstanding any otherwise contrary provisions of the Charter. Self-defence when not otherwise contrary to the Charter remains of course licensed under customary law. In exercising these rights of self-defence, they act on their own behalf as States, not as organs of the General Assembly, nor even of the United Nations; and the acting States themselves, and not the United Nations, are responsible for such action.[39]

The temporary character which the General Assembly and the Secretary-General were sometimes at pains to attribute to the Emergency Force lend some additional, though not conclusive, colour to this view of the nature of the Force,[40] as an instrument of coordinated self-defence. Even if, as submitted above, the Force is not well grounded as a peace enforcement instrument created by the General Assembly, neither the mere fact that its command was favoured with the description of a unified United Nations command, nor the role played by the Secretary-General and the General Assembly's Special Advisory Sub-Committee in its mobilisation and deployment, prevent it being more adequately based on coordinated self-defence.

There is, however, a graver obstacle to grounding U.N.E.F. on coordinated self-defence. This is that all the contributing States (which would on this hypothesis have to be regarded as acting in collective self-defence) seem to have insisted that the consent both of Israel and Egypt was necessary for the stationing and operation of U.N.E.F. within their respective territories.[41] Such an insistence seems difficult to reconcile with either an actual (or even a constructive) posture of self-defence. It is, as seen in Section II, rather incongruous with "peace enforcement" to make such action subject to consent of the States in conflict. But it is even more incongruous to think of a Member State deciding that a situation requires it to take military action in self-defence, and yet insisting that it will not so act unless all the States involved in the hostilities agree to it so acting. The insistence of the supposedly self-defending States on the consents both

39 *Cf.* as to this, and also as to the incidence of cost of operation, Resol. of Dec. 21, 1956 (A/Res/448) reserving the final determination of these matters. We are also aware that this would have important implications as regards acts by U.N.E.F. units or elements violating the rights of other States, e.g. by negligent or malicious killings of their nationals. It seems, however, inescapable on this interpretation.

40 *Final U.N.E.F. Report,* esp. para. 8.

41 Thus the Swedish Government presumed in making its contribution "that the Swedish unit shall not be stationed in foreign territory without the consent of the State concerned". (A/3302, Ann. 5, *G.A.O.R.* F.E.S.S. Ann., Agenda Item 5, p.22.) The Indian Government seemed to go further by making its contribution conditional on Egypt's consent both to the establishment of the Force and its functioning on Egyptian territory (*id.* pp.23-24). And see the debates in the General Assembly, *G.A.O.R.* F.E.S.S., Plenary, esp. El Salvador at p.69, Israel at p.83, and Colombia at p.87.

of Israel and Egypt thus affords grounds for doubting whether they are to be regarded as engaged in an act of collective self-defence. Yet it may also be argued that there is no reason why, when a breach of the peace has undoubtedly arisen, but third States are unable to make up their minds which State is defending itself, these third States may not regard themselves provisionally as in a condition of collective defence with both sides. And if this were conceivable, the insistence that the interposed contributed units should not engage in hostilities, and that both combatants should agree to their stationing and operation in their respective territories, might be a natural manifestation of suspended judgment in the course of common defence.

It must be admitted, however, that this involves a very strained interpretation of collective self-defence under Article 51, even if it has slightly more plausibility as an exercise of the vaguer residual liberty of action of Members under customary law consistently with Charter inhibitions.

B. *U.N.E.F. as an Assembly or other United Nations Subsidiary Organ with Non-Peace-Enforcing Functions.*

Thus far the legal basis of the Emergency Force has been sought on the assumption that the Force is either charged with peace enforcement functions under Chapter VII or some pretended General Assembly substitute, or is a coordinated collected self-defence instrument of Members. Even if all these are rejected, it is still open to seek a basis for the Force by regarding it as engaged in functions not involving peace-enforcement, or indeed combative functions at all. For despite its name and despite some loose language concerning military functions of the Force and its possible use by the Security Council, the functions of the Emergency Force certainly fall short of making it a military or peace enforcement instrument in the sense of Chapter VII of the Charter. The mere fact that a too pretentious label has been attached to this product should not bar inquiry whether the contents are not in fact more licit than the label suggests.[42]

It is clear that there may be established under Article 7 of the Charter such "subsidiary organs" of the United Nations "as may be found necessary", that the General Assembly itself may under Article 22 "establish such subsidiary organs as it may deem necessary for the performance of its functions", and that under Article 107 (2) appropriate staffs, as a part of the Secretariat, may be permanently assigned to any organ of the United Nations. Moreover, among the Secretary-General's somewhat variegated conceptions of his foster-child, he described it in his Regulations of February 20, 1957 as "a subsidiary organ of the United Nations".[43] In a Memorandum the next day, he even stated that "the Regulations affirm the international character of the Force as a subsidiary organ of the General Assembly".[44] The General

[42] The flat Soviet charge of illegality of the Force, as involving General Assembly usurpation of Security Council powers (*G.A.O.R.* F.E.S.S., Plenary, p.127) ignores this possibility, and thus begs one of the main legal questions involved in this tangled area.

[43] *Doc.* ST/SGB/UNEF/1, Reg. 6.

[44] Doc. A/3552. So also in the Exchange of Letters between the Secretary-General and

Assembly exercises its authority over the Force through an Advisory Committee chaired by the Secretary-General, the latter being authorised "to issue all regulations and instructions which may be essential to the effective functioning of the Force, following consultation with the [Advisory] Committee . . ., and to take all other necessary administrative and executive action".[45] On this basis, the Secretary-General's Regulations give him "authority for all administrative, executive and financial matters affecting the Force", and responsibility for "the negotiation and conclusion of agreements with Governments concerning the Force". The Commander-in-Chief has "full command authority over the force" and "direct authority for the operation of the Force and for the provision of facilities, supplies and auxiliary services".[46]

This conception of this Emergency Force as a subsidiary organ of the General Assembly would place it on a legal basis similar to that of the somewhat controversial "Interim Committee" of the General Assembly, or the recently established Administrative Tribunal of the United Nations. The International Court majority advised that the General Assembly had power to create this latter jüdicial organ, as involved in performing effectively the Assembly's power under Article 101 to make regulations for United Nations staff, even though it could itself not perform this judicial function.[47] And on a similar basis the question to be raised as to the Emergency Force would be whether the actual functions allotted to it were reasonably necessary for effective exercise of the proper powers of the Assembly, and in particular, its power under Article 11, para. 2 "to make recommendations" with regard to "questions relating to the maintenance of international peace and security brought before it by any Member or by the Security Council".

Penetrating therefore behind name to functions there must first be recalled the unquestioned statement of the Secretary-General that it was not part of the functions of that Force to be used for "enforcement action directed against a Member country".[48] There seems on the contrary to have been a wide measure of agreement that U.N.E.F. was not a military force in the classical sense, neither tasks of attacking an enemy, nor of defence

---

the Minister for Foreign Affairs of Egypt of Feb. 8, 1957 (*U.N. Doc.* A/3526), where U.N.E.F. is described as "an organ of the General Assembly of the United Nations established in accordance with Article 22 of the Charter".

45 Res. 1001 (F.E.S.S.) of the General Assembly, Nov. 7, 1956 (*G.A.O.R.* F.E.S.S., Supp. 1 (A/3354), p.3).

46 Cited *supra* n.43, esp. paras. 11, 15 and 16.

47 See the Opinion of July 13, 1954 on "Effects of Awards of Compensation made by the United Nations Administrative Tribunal" I.C.J. Reports, 1954, p.71. The controversies in this case are a salutary reminder that in international, as in municipal, constitutional interpretation, the line between what is *intra vires* or *ultra vires* of an organ may be hard to demonstrate. Vital decisions may depend on the choice of one from among alternative starting-points within a complex body of provisions (here the Assembly's power of regulation), and the attribution of higher value thereto as compared with the other alternatives.

The argument in A. Rossignol, ". . . *Sécurité Collective* . . ." (1954) 58 *R.G.D.*1, n.6, p.84, 124, seems unsustainable.

It is not believed that the fact that the issue in the above case was intra-organisational excludes the application of the principles of the Opinion in the present context of the relations between the Organisation and its Member States.

48 See the *Final U.N.E.F. Report,* and also the Sec.-Gen.'s Report of Jan. 24, 1957

against an attacking enemy, being assigned to it.[49]

The functions which Resolution 998 did ascribe were "to secure and supervise the cessation of hostilities", but the non-combatant ambit of this task was ensured by pre-requiring "the consent of the nations concerned", and also that the Force should exercise its functions "in accordance with all the terms" of that resolution. The resolution urged all parties now involved in hostilities in the area to agree to an immediate cease-fire, to halt movement of forces and arms into the area, and "to withdraw all forces behind the armistice lines". According to the Secretary-General's view, later approved by the General Assembly, this means that *"when a cease-fire is being established* U.N.E.F. should enter Egyptian territory with Egyptian consent in order to help maintain quiet during and after the withdrawal of non-Egyptian troops, and to secure compliance with the other terms" of the resolution. The Force would, on his view, "be more than an observers' corps, but in no way a military force temporarily controlling the territory in which it is stationed". It would have no military functions beyond those necessary to secure peaceful conditions *"on the assumption that* the parties to the conflict take all necessary steps for compliance . . .".[50] Its function was not to enforce a withdrawal of forces, but only "to secure the cessation of hostilities, with a withdrawal of forces".[50a] In this and other respects (he thought) the Force differed from the observers of the United Nations Truce Supervision Organisation: it was, "although para-military in nature, not a Force with military objectives".

However, we may describe the functions thus delineated, they certainly do not include peace enforcement, or enforcement of international decisions, or even police action to maintain peace. These are excluded, not only by the specific negations quoted, but also by the overall requirements of con-

---

(*Doc.* A/3512) esp. para. 5(b).

It may be recalled that in 1948 the then Sec.-Gen. (Trygve Lie) asserted that the then proposed U.N. Guard could not legally be used for enforcement purposes under the Charter, nor "for the purpose of maintaining law and order in an area". He explained this view in the Appendix to his report on the ground that "armed action [under Art. 42] may be undertaken only in accordance with special agreements contemplated by Article 43" (or under Art. 106—not here relevant). See his *Guard Report.*

This assumes that the conclusion of the special agreements are a condition, not only of the use of Members' contributed contingents (i.e. a "consent force"), but even of a non-contributed U.N. Force of directly recruited individuals. The present Writer dissents from this view. Assuming that such a force were raised by proper decision of the Security Council, with budget duly provided for, this Writer sees no such difficulty as M. Lie envisaged.

Curiously enough M. Lie's successor, in asserting that the Security Council could use U.N.E.F. (which is obviously a "consent force" contributed by Members) "within the wider margins provided under Chapter VII", seems, with respect, to commit the converse error. See *Doc.* A/3302, para. 9, and *Final U.N.E.F. Report*; and *supra* n.34.

The principles here involved are not clarified by the rather confused and abortive discussions of proposals for a "U.N. Legion", on which see S. M. Schwebel's Paper (s.vii) appended to *Frye,* and literature there cited. But see for a Polish argument against the legality of a Force recruited directly by the Security Council, *id.* n.30.

49 See, however, *supra* nn.34,47.

50 *Final U.N.E.F. Report,* para. 12.

50a *Id.* para. 10. The contrast is clear enough in terms of the foregoing analysis though the Sec.-Gen.'s language may not have been wholly designed to point it. So *cf.* Mr. Pearson's account, *op. cit. supra* n.5, at 401.

sent of both the contributing States and the conflicting States whose territory was involved, to the operations of the Force.[51] A unit set up by the voluntary contributions of some Member States, operating only within the limits of consent of the territorial sovereigns affected, subject probably to instant withdrawal of the component troops by the contributing States, and of the permission to stay of the territorial sovereign,[52] can scarcely be engaged in peace enforcement under Chapter VII. If, as the Secretary-General thinks, this is "a para-military organisation", its para-military functions seem to be limited to that of a buffer between the withdrawn belligerents, a United Nations symbol approaching no nearer to a military function than the steady maintenance of the inert but receptive posture of a sandbag.[53]

The question thus becomes whether, with the peace-enforcing and policing functions thus excluded, and with the consent requisites above enumerated, the Emergency Force could lawfully be created by the General Assembly in performance of that body's proper functions. Assuming the force to be simply an observer corps, then its propriety under the Court's *Administrative Tribunal Opinion* would seem beyond doubt. It may clearly be essential for effective exercise of the Assembly's power to recommend on questions of maintaining peace and security under Article 11, that it have first-hand knowledge which can only be obtained by sending such subsidiary organs to places of potential or actual international tension. The Secretary-General, however, suggested that the Emergency Force is more than an observer corps. If this be correct, it would raise the question whether insofar as its functions go beyond this, they are such as take its creation out of the legitimate frame of the Assembly's Charter powers. Since the preceding analysis has shown that this Force's functions do not entrench on peace enforcement proper, the answer is believed to be negative.

Indeed, even the suggestion that the United Nations Emergency Force is more than an observer corps may have to be questioned altogether. In view of the limits on its use of force, its functions seem finally to reduce themselves to mere supervision and patrol of territory where actual hostili-

---

51 These two elements coincided in the instant case. Interesting further questions as to consents may arise as to those States in conflict whose territory is not involved in the operations, e.g. perhaps, the U.K. and France in the 1956 crisis.

52 *Cf.* as to the elements of control by the contributing States, H. F. Armstrong, "The United Nations Experience in Gaza" (1957) 35 *Foreign Affairs* 600, 608; and as to its subjection in Gaza to the Egyptian Government's view of Egyptian interests, *ibid.*

53 We agree on this with an unpublished paper of Professor L. B. Sohn on "The Establishment of the United Nations Emergency Force" kindly made available to us. Professor Sohn thinks that the Force was to use arms only "in exceptional circumstances". Even this limited authority has to be implied, the circumstances certainly not having been clearly designated. The relevant resolutions and regulations make no express provision about the use of armed force by U.N.E.F. No doubt "exceptional circumstances" would cover the liberty of members of the Force to defend themselves if attacked, which might go no further than that of any group of foreign servicemen, present and carrying arms by consent of the host State. So *cf.* on this matter, L. Pearson, "Force for U.N." (1957) 35 *Foreign Affairs* 394, 403, and H. F. Armstrong, "The United Nations Experience in Gaza" (1957) 35 *Foreign Affairs* 600, 616. *Cf.* also on this matter Sec.-Gen. Lie's *Guard Report*, esp. App. B, para. 4, and the Conclusions in *Frye*. On the abortive attempt among the Secretary-General, General Burns, the contributing States, and Israel and Egypt, to settle the limits of such self-defence by the Force see also *Frye*, 15. And see *supra* Ch. 9, n.65.

ties have stopped.[54] It is difficult to see here any substantial distinction from an international observer corps to supervise execution of an armistice agreement or the like. It is true that the Assembly Resolution 998 of November 4, 1956[55] referred to a task of "securing . . . the cessation of hostilities" of the Force: yet it is also difficult to see which of its specific functions fall within this description, aside from the legal, moral, and political effects *of its very presence itself*. In view of all this, it seems an over-estimation to regard the Force as even a defensive shield placed between the Parties; its design and present form is such as to render it unable to resist even the slightest military assault of the States involved. If this Force is a shield, it is one wrought not in martial steel, but in the less material substance of the symbolisation by its mere presence of the possible humanity-wide concern with any situation which threatens international peace.[56] The fact that, by its mere presence, an observer corps may restrain potential belligerents, can scarcely impair the Assembly's power to create such a corps. And while it is true that 6,000 men seems incongruously large for a corps of observers, it is no less true that such a Force, very lightly equipped as it is, is even more incongruously small for any functions which go much beyond this.[57]

Yet even if U.N.E.F. functions be thought to go beyond those of a rather novel type of observer corps, the excess still leaves this organ, in the present view, within the range of what is necessary for the effective performance of the General Assembly's function of making recommendations, under Article 11, para. 2, on "questions relating to the maintenance of peace and security". Insofar as they do, the present conclusion is that this Force, within the functional limits above displayed, is legally created as a subsidiary organ of the General Assembly under Article 22, or of the United Nations as a whole under Article 7, para. 2, or even perhaps as a unit of the Secretariat appropriate to be assigned to the organs of the United Nations under Article 101(2).[58]

---

[54] *Cf.* the view of U.N.E.F. proposals as merely combining "observer" with "supervisory" unctions in L. Pearson, *op.cit. supra* n.53, at 404. So also *Frye* sets the "restoration", as distinct from the "preservation" of peace, outside the ambit of the Peace Force there proposed. *Cf.* his Conclusions, 93, with p.13, wherein he seems for this purpose to equivalate 'preservation of peace" with "peaceful settlement".

[55] *G.A.O.R.* F.E.S.S., Nov. 4, 1956, Supp. 1 (A/3354) p.2.

[56] *Cf.* on the exiguity of U.N.E.F. functions apart from its mere presence, H. F. Armstrong, *op.cit. supra* n.53, at 600, 613, 617. Mr. Frye, in his conclusions, seems even to press this to the point of saying that if there is any fighting his proposed "Peace Force" must be careful to keep out of it. *Cf.* also Mr. Pearson's proposal of Oct. 21, 1957 for a small unarmed force on the Syrian-Turkish frontier.

[57] Propriety of size for a particular function must obviously depend on the concrete historical situation, and there may well be recalled in this context the actual difficulties which confronted General Burns in supervision of the armistice immediately before the outbreak of large-scale hostilities. Former Sec.-Gen. Lie's *Guard Report* contemplated final numbers running into several thousands. Insofar as the present Sec.-Gen. implied in one statement (*N.Y.T.*, Apr. 11, 1957, p.13) that only the aim (and not the size) of the force was subject to constitutional limits, we respectfully dissent.

[58] The broader questions, consequential on this analysis, of the actual and potential significance of the creation of the United Nations Emergency Force for development of the authority of the General Assembly in the maintenance of international security, have already been examined in Section IV of Chapter 9.

APPENDIX

SELECTED DRAFT DEFINITIONS OF AGGRESSION

PART I

DRAFTS PRESENTED TO THE GENERAL ASSEMBLY'S SPECIAL COMMITTEE ON THE DEFINITION OF AGGRESSION, 1956.

DEFINITION PROPOSED BY THE DELEGATION OF THE UNION OF SOVIET SOCIALIST REPUBLICS TO THE UNITED NATIONS 1956 SPECIAL COMMITTEE.[1]

[*This is substantially similar to the Soviet Draft of 1933, supra pp.34-35, except for the following:*

Para. 1(a) For "aggressor" read "attacker".

Para. 1(b) Add "even" before "without declaration of war".

Para. 1(f) is additional as follows:]

(f) Support of armed bands organized in its own territory which invade the territory of another State, or refusal, on being requested by the invaded State, to take in its own territory any action within its power to deny such bands any aid or protection.

[*Paras. 2, 3, 4 and 5 are new, as follows:*]

2. That State shall be declared to have committed an act of indirect aggression which:

(a) Encourages subversive activity against another State (acts of terrorism, diversionary acts, etc.);

(b) Promotes the fomenting of civil war within another State;

(c) Promotes an internal upheaval in another State or a change of policy in favour of the aggressor.

3. That State shall be declared to have committed an act of economic aggression which first commits one of the following acts:

(a) Takes against another State measures of economic pressure violating its sovereignty and economic independence and threatening the bases of its economic life;

(b) Takes against another State measures preventing it from exploiting or nationalizing its own natural riches;

(c) Subjects another State to an economic blockade.

---

1 Doc. A/AC.77/L.4, repr. *1956 Sp.Com.Rep.*, Ann. II, pp.30-31.

4. That State shall be declared to have committed an act of ideological aggression which:

(a) Encourages war propaganda;

(b) Encourages propaganda in favour of using atomic, bacterial, chemical and other weapons of mass destruction;

(c) Promotes the propagation of fascist-nazi views, of racial and national exclusiveness, and of hatred and contempt for other peoples.

5. Acts committed by a State other than those listed in the preceding paragraphs may be deemed to constitute aggression if declared by decision of the Security Council in a particular case to be an attack or an act of economic, ideological or indirect aggression.

[Para. 2 of 1933 becomes para. 6 of 1956, and its negations of justification apply as regards all the acts now mentioned in new paras. 1-4.

Para. 3 of 1933 becomes para. 7 of 1956.]

DEFINITION PROPOSED BY THE DELEGATION OF PARAGUAY TO THE UNITED NATIONS 1956 SPECIAL COMMITTEE.[2]

1. A State (or States) commits (or commit) armed aggression if it (or they) provokes (or provoke) a breach or disturbance of international peace and security through the employment of armed force against the territory, population, armed forces or the sovereignty and political independence of another State (or other States), or against the people, the territory or the armed forces of a Non-Self-Governing Territory.

2. Without prejudice to the provisions of Article 39 of the Charter, the General Assembly recommends that in addition to other acts of aggression the following acts shall be deemed to constitute armed aggression:

(a) A declaration of war by one State against another (or others) in contravention of Articles 1 and 2 of the Charter;

(b) The organization by a State within its territory of armed bands intended to take action against other States, either within or outside the territory of such States; or the encouragement, support or the mere toleration of the formation or action of such armed bands in its territory.

Nevertheless, a State shall not be considered to be an aggressor if, being unable to suppress the activities of such bands in its territory or having justifiable reasons for not undertaking their suppression, it reports the matter to the competent organ of the United Nations and offers its co-operation.

. . . . . .

DEFINITION SUBMITTED JOINTLY BY THE DELEGATIONS OF IRAN AND PANAMA AT THE NINTH SESSION OF THE GENERAL ASSEMBLY AND CIRCULATED AT THE REQUEST OF THE REPRESENTATIVE OF PERU IN THE UNITED NATIONS 1956 SPECIAL COMMITTEE.[3]

1. Aggression is the use of armed force by a State against another State for any purpose other than the exercise of the inherent right of individual or collective self-defence or in pursuance of a decision or recommendation of a competent organ of the United Nations.

2. In accordance with the foregoing definition, in addition to any other acts which such international bodies as may be called upon to determine the

---

[2] Doc. A/AC.77/L.7, repr. *id.* p.31.

[3] Doc. A/AC.77/L.9, repr. *ibid.*

aggressor may declare to constitute aggression, the following are acts of aggression in all cases:

(a) Invasion by the armed forces of a State of territory belonging to another State or under the effective jurisdiction of another State;

(b) Armed attack against the territory, population or land, sea or air forces of a State by the land, sea or air forces of another State;

(c) Blockade of the coast or ports of any other part of the territory of a State by the land, sea or air forces of another State;

(d) The organization, or the encouragement of the organization, by a State, of armed bands within its territory or any other territory for incursions into the territory of another State, or the toleration of the organization of such bands in its own territory, or the toleration of the use of such armed bands of its territory as a base of operations or as a point of departure for incursions into the territory of another State, as well as direct participation in or support of such incursions.

. . . . . .

DEFINITION PROPOSED BY THE DELEGATION OF MEXICO TO THE UNITED NATIONS 1956 SPECIAL COMMITTEE.[4]

In an international conflict, the direct or indirect use of force by the authorities of a State taking the initiative for the purpose of attacking the territorial integrity or political independence of another State, or for any purpose other than individual or collective self-defence or compliance with a decision or recommendation of a competent organ of the United Nations, shall be regarded as aggression.

In particular, the commission of any of the following acts shall be regarded as aggression:

(a) invasion by the armed forces of one State of territory belonging to, or under the effective jurisdiction of, another State;

(b) armed attack against the territory or population or the land, sea or air forces of one State by the land, sea or air forces of another State;

(c) the blocking of the coast or ports or any other part of the territory of one State by the land, sea or air forces of another State;

(d) the organization, or the encouragement of the organization, by one State, of armed bands within its territory or any other territory for incursions into the territory of another State; or the toleration of the organization of such bands in its own territory, or the toleration of the use by such armed bands of its territory as a base of operations or as a point of departure for incursions into the territory of another State, as well as direct participation in or support of such incursions.

In no event may an act constituting aggression be justified by any considerations of a political, economic, strategic or social nature.

[The rest of this Draft incorporates the substance of the two sub-paras. "A" and "B" of para. 2 of the Soviet 1933 Draft (supra pp.34-35) save that B (a) is omitted, and B (b) -B (j) become B (a) -B (i) .]

---

[4] Doc. A/AC.77/L.10, repr. *id.* p.32.

DEFINITION PROPOSED BY THE DELEGATION OF IRAQ TO THE UNITED NATIONS 1956 SPECIAL COMMITTEE (CONTAINED IN THE REVISED DRAFT RESOLUTION OF IRAQ.[5]

Aggression, within the meaning of both Article 39 and Article 51, is the use of force by a State or group of States, or by a Government or group of Governments, against the territorial integrity or independence of a State or group of States, or against the conditions of existence of the people and the territories of a Government or group of Governments, in any manner, by any method and for any purpose whatever, other than that of enforcement action in pursuance of a decision or recommendation of a competent organ of the United Nations, or than that of individual or collective self-defence against an armed attack which is aimed at, or results in, a change in the international juridical situation and a disturbance of international peace and security and with respect to which the competent organ of the United Nations has not taken measures necessary to maintain international peace and security and to enable it to take the place of the party possessed of the right of individual or collective self-defence.

. . . . . .

DEFINITION OF ARMED ATTACK PROPOSED BY BERNARD V. A. ROELING TO THE UNITED NATIONS 1956 SPECIAL COMMITTEE.[6]

Armed attack as this term is used in Article 51 is any use of armed force which leaves the State against which it is directed no means other than military means to preserve its territorial integrity or political independence; it being understood that the definition may never be construed to comprise acts of legitimate individual or collective self-defence or any act in pursuance of a decision or recommendation by a competent organ of the United Nations.

. . . . . .

DEFINITION PROPOSED BY THE DELEGATION OF DOMINICAN REPUBLIC, MEXICO, PARAGUAY AND PERU TO THE UNITED NATIONS 1956 SPECIAL COMMITTEE.[7]

1. Any use of force by a State (or States) against the territorial integrity or inviolability or the sovereignty or political independence of another State (or States), or against a territory under the effective jurisdiction of another State, or for any purpose other than the exercise of the inherent right of individual or collective self-defence or the execution of a decision or recommendation of a competent organ of the United Nations, shall be regarded as aggression.

2. In accordance with the foregoing definition, and without prejudice to the power of the competent international organs to determine the existence of, or take a decision upon, an act of aggression, the following shall be acts of aggression in all cases:

(a) declaration of war by one State against another State (or States) in violation of the Charter of the United Nations;

(b) the invasion by the armed forces of the territory of another State or of a territory under the effective jurisdiction of another State;

(c) armed attack against the territory or population or the land, sea or air forces of one State by the land, sea or air forces of another State;

---

5 Doc. A/AC.77/L.8/Rev. 1, repr. *id.* p.31-32.

6 *1956 Sp.Com.Rep.* 25.

7 A/AC.77/L.11, repr. *id.*, Ann. II, p.33.

(d) the blockading of the coast or ports or any other part of the territory of one State by the land, sea or air forces of another State; and

(e) incursions into the territory of one State by armed bands organized by, or with the participation or direct assistance of another State.

In no event may aggression be justified by any considerations of a political, economic or social nature.

PART II

SELECTED DRAFTS AT THE SAN FRANCISCO CONFERENCE 1945

DEFINITION CONTAINED IN BOLIVIAN PROPOSALS CONCERNING THE DUMBARTON OAKS PROPOSAL SUBMITTED TO COMMITTEE 3 OF THE THIRD COMMISSION OF THE SAN FRANCISCO CONFERENCE.[8]

A State shall be designated an aggressor if it has committed any of the following acts to the detriment of another State:

a) Invasion of another State's territory by armed forces.

b) Declaration of war.

c) Attack by land, sea, or air forces, with or without declaration of war, on another State's territory, shipping, or aircraft.

d) Support given to armed bands for the purpose of invasion.

e) Intervention in another State's internal or foreign affairs.

f) Refusal to submit the matter which has caused a dispute to the peaceful means provided for its settlement.

g) Refusal to comply with a judicial decision lawfully pronounced by an international Court.

. . . .

DEFINITION CONTAINED IN THE PROPOSED AMENDMENTS TO THE DUMBARTON OAKS PROPOSALS SUBMITTED BY THE PHILIPPINE DELEGATION TO COMMITTEE 3 OF THE THIRD COMMISSION OF THE SAN FRANCISCO CONFERENCE.[9]

Any nation should be considered as threatening the peace or as an aggressor, if it should be the first party to commit any of the following acts: (1) To declare war against another nation; (2) To invade or attack, with or without declaration of war, the territory, public vessel, or public aircraft of another nation; (3) To subject another nation to naval, land or air blockade; and (4) To interfere with the internal affairs of another nation by supplying arms, ammunition, money or other forms of aid to any armed band, faction or group, or by establishing agencies in that nation to conduct propaganda subversive of the institutions of that nation.

PART III

DRAFTS BEFORE UNITED NATIONS ORGANS

DETERMINATION OF AGGRESSION IMPLIED IN ARTICLE 2(1) OF THE DRAFT CODE OF OFFENCES AGAINST THE PEACE AND SECURITY OF MANKIND.[10]

---

8 3 *U.N.C.I.O. Docs.* 585.

9 3 *id.* 538.

10 *G.A.O.R. IX*, Supp. No. 9 (A/2693), c.iii, p.2. Art. 2(1) imports a non-exhaustive

Article 2: The following acts are offences against the peace and security of mankind:

(1) Any act of aggression, including the employment by the authorities of a State of armed force against another State for any purpose other than national or collective self-defence or in pursuance of a decision or recommendation of a competent organ of the United Nations.

(3) The preparation by the authorities of a State of the employment of armed force against another State for any purpose other than national or collective self-defence or in pursuance of a decision or recommendation of a competent organ of the United Nations.

(4) The organization, or the encouragement of the organization by the authorities of a State, of armed bands within its territory or any other territory for incursions into the territory of another State, or the toleration of the organization of such bands in its own territory, or the toleration of the use by such armed bands of its territory as a base of operations or as a point of departure for incursions into the territory of another State, as well as direct participation in or support of such incursions.

(5) The undertaking or encouragement by the authorities of a State of activities calculated to foment civil strife in another State, or the toleration by the authorities of a State of organized activities calculated to foment civil strife in another State.

(6) The undertaking or encouragement by the authorities of a State of terrorist activities in another State, or the toleration by the authorities of a State of organized activities calculated to carry out terrorist acts in another State.

(7) Acts by the authorities of a State in violation of its obligations under a treaty which is designed to ensure international peace and security by means of restrictions or limitations on armaments, or on military training, or on fortifications, or of other restrictions of the same character.

(8) The annexation by the authorities of a State of territory belonging to another State, by means of acts contrary to international law.

(9) The intervention by the authorities of a State in the internal or external affairs of another State by means of coercive measures of an economic or political character in order to force its will and thereby obtain advantages of any kind.

---

determination rather than a definition as indicated by the word "including". And see I.L.C., *Report Covering the Work of the Third Session . . .* (*G.A.O.R. VI,* Supp. No. 9 (A/1858), c.iv, p.11: "While every act of aggression constitutes a crime under paragraph (1), no attempt is made to enumerate such acts exhaustively. It is expressly provided that the employment of armed force in the circumstances specified in the paragraph is an act of aggression. It is, however, possible that aggression can be committed also by other acts, including some of those referred to in other paragraphs of Article 2." It will be apparent that even all the relevant paragraphs of Art. 2 are not intended to constitute a definition.

Art. 2(2) providing that "any threat by the authorities of a State to resort to an act of aggression against another State" and Art. 2(10) and (11) (crimes against the integrity of population) and 2(12) (acts in violation of the laws or customs of war), add nothing to the present aspect.

DEFINITION SUBMITTED BY M. AMADO TO THE THIRD SESSION OF THE INTERNATIONAL LAW COMMISSION (16 MAY-27 JULY 1951).[11]

Any war not waged in exercise of the right of self-defence or in application of the provisions of Article 42 of the Charter of the United Nations [is] an aggressive war.

. . . .

DEFINITION SUBMITTED BY M. YEPES TO THE THIRD SESSION OF THE INTERNATIONAL LAW COMMISSION (16 MAY-27 JULY 1951).[12]

For the purposes of Article 39 of the United Nations Charter an act of aggression shall be understood to mean any direct or indirect use of violence (force) by a State or group of States against the territorial integrity or political independence of another State or group of States.

Violence (force) exercised by irregular bands organized within the territory with the active or passive complicity of that State shall be considered as aggression within the meaning of the preceding paragraph.

The use of violence (force) in the exercise of the right of individual or collective self-defence recognized by Article 51 of the Charter or in the execution of a decision duly adopted by a competent organ of the United Nations shall not be held to constitute an act of aggression.

No political, economic, military or other consideration may serve as an excuse or justification for an act of aggression.

. . . .

DEFINITION SUBMITTED BY MR. HSU TO THE THIRD SESSION OF THE INTERNATIONAL LAW COMMISSION (16 MAY-27 JULY 1951).[13]

Aggression, which is a crime under international law, is the hostile act of a State against another State, committed by (a) the employment of armed force other than in self-defence or the implementation of United Nations enforcement action; or (b) the arming of organized bands or of third States, hostile to the victim State, for offensive purposes; or (*c*) the fomenting of civil strife in the victim State in the interest of some foreign State; or (d) any other illegal resort to force, openly or otherwise.

. . . .

DEFINITION SUBMITTED BY M. CORDOVA TO THE THIRD SESSION OF THE INTERNATIONAL LAW COMMISSION (16 MAY-27 JULY 1951).[14]

Aggression is the direct or indirect employment by the authorities of a State of armed force against another State for any purpose other than national or collective self-defence or execution of a decision by a competent organ of the United Nations.

The threat of aggression should also be deemed to be a crime under this Article.

. . . .

DEFINITION SUBMITTED BY M. ALFARO TO THE THIRD SESSION OF THE INTERNATIONAL LAW COMMISSION (16 MAY-27 JULY 1951) AND TAKEN BY THE COMMISSION AS A BASIS OF DISCUSSION.[15]

Aggression is the use of force by one State or group of States, or by any government or group of governments, against the territory and people of

---

11 *G.A.O.R.* VI, Supp. No. 9 (A/1858), p.8 (A/CN.4/L.6 and Corr. 1).
12 *Id.* p.9 (A/CN.4/L.7).
13 *Ibid.* (A/CN.4/L.11 and Corr. 1).
14 *Ibid.* (A/CN.4/L.10).
15 *Ibid.* (A/CN.4/L.8).

other States or governments, in any manner, by any methods, for any reasons and for any purposes, except individual or collective self-defence against armed attack or coercive action by the United Nations.

. . . .

DEFINITION SUBMITTED BY M. ALFARO AND AMENDED BY THE INTERNATIONAL LAW COMMISSION BUT NOT ADOPTED BY IT (THIRD SESSION OF I.L.C. 16 MAY-27 JULY 1951).[16]

Aggression is the threat or use of force by a State or government against another State, in any manner, whatever the weapons employed and whether openly or otherwise, for any reason or for any purpose other than individual or collective self-defence or in pursuance of a decision or recommendation by a competent organ of the United Nations.

. . . .

DEFINITION SUBMITTED BY M. SCELLE TO THE THIRD SESSION OF THE INTERNATIONAL LAW COMMISSION (16 MAY-27 JULY 1957).[17]

Aggression is an offence against the peace and security of mankind. This offence consists in any resort to force contrary to the provisions of the Charter of the United Nations, for the purpose of modifying the state of positive international law in force or resulting in the disturbance of public order.

. . . .

DEFINITION CONTAINED IN THE REVISED DRAFT RESOLUTION OF CHINA OF 10 NOVEMBER 1954.[18]

. . . aggression is the unlawful use of force by a State against another State, whether directly or indirectly, such as:

(a) Attack or invasion by armed force;

(b) Organization or support of incursion of armed bands;

(c) Promotion or support of organized activities in another State aiming at the overthrow by violence of its political or social institutions;

". . . the use of force is lawful when it is in pursuance of a decision or recommendation by a competent organ of the United Nations, or is in self-defence against armed attack until a competent organ of the United Nations has taken the measures necessary to maintain international peace and security;

". . . the employment of measures, other than armed attack, necessary to remove the danger arising from an indirect use of force is likewise lawful until a competent organ of the United Nations has taken steps to remove such danger.

. . . .

DEFINITION CONTAINED IN THE DRAFT RESOLUTION OF PARAGUAY OF 28 OCTOBER 1954.[19]

[This definition is identical with the one submitted to the 1956 Special Committee, Part I above.]

. . . .

DEFINITION CONTAINED IN THE REVISED DRAFT RESOLUTION OF IRAN AND PANAMA OF 6 NOVEMBER 1954.[20]

[This definition is identical with the one submitted to the 1956 Special Committee, Part I above.]

---

16 *Ibid.*

17 *Id.* p.10 (A/CN.4/L.19 and Corr. 1).

18 *G.A.O.R. IX,* Ann. Item 51, p.8 (A/C.6/L.336/Rev. 2).

19 *Id.* p.7 (A/C.6/L.334/Rev. 1).

20 *Ibid.* (A/C.6/L.335/Rev. 1).

DEFINITION PROPOSED BY BOLIVIA TO THE 1953 SPECIAL COMMITTEE ON THE QUESTION OF AGGRESSION.[21]

1. Independently of acts of aggression designated as such by the competent international organs of the United Nations, the invasion by one State of the territory of another State across the frontiers established by treaties or judicial or arbitral decisions and demarcated in accordance therewith, or, in the absence of marked frontiers, an invasion affecting territories under the effective jurisdiction of a State shall in all cases be deemed to constitute an act of aggression.

2. A declaration of war, an armed attack with land, sea or air forces against the territory, ships or aircraft of another State, support given to armed bands for purposes of invasion, and the overt or covert inciting of the people of one State by another State to rebellion for the purpose of disturbing law and order in the interests of a foreign Power shall also be defined as acts of aggression.

3. Any threat or use of force against the territorial integrity or political independence of any State or in any other manner incompatible with the purposes of the United Nations, including unilateral action whereby a State is deprived of economic resources derived from the proper conduct of international trade or its basic economy is endangered so that its security is affected and it is rendered unable to act in its own defence or to co-operate in the collective defense of peace shall likewise be deemed to constitute an act of aggression.

4. Apart from the cases provided for in paragraphs 1 and 2, which shall constitute sufficient grounds for the automatic exercise of the right of collective self-defense, other acts of aggression shall be defined as such, when they take place, by the competent organs established by the United Nations Charter and in conformity with its provisions.

PART IV

LEAGUE OF NATIONS DRAFTS

SIGNS WHICH BETOKEN AN IMPENDING AGGRESSION ENUMERATED IN AN OPINION SUBMITTED JOINTLY BY THE BELGIAN, BRAZILIAN, FRENCH AND SWEDISH DELEGATIONS IN THE PERMANENT ADVISORY COMMISSION OF THE LEAGUE OF NATIONS IN 1923.[22]

. . . It may be taken that the signs [of aggression] would appear in the following order:

1. Organisation on paper of industrial mobilisation.
2. Actual organisation of industrial mobilisation.
3. Collection of stocks of raw materials.

---

21 *G.A.O.R. IX*, Supp. No. 11, p.15 (A/AC.66/L.9).

22 Opinion of the Permanent Advisory Commission . . . *L.N.O.J.* Sp.Supp. No. 16, (*Records of the Fourth Assembly,* Third Committee, Ann.), pp.116ff. at 117.

4. Setting-on-foot of war industries.
5. Preparation for military mobilisation.
6. Actual military mobilisation.
7. Hostilities.

. . . .

FACTORS ON WHICH GOVERNMENTS CAN BASE THE IMPRESSION OF AN AGGRESSIVE INTENTION CONTAINED IN A COMMENTARY PREPARED BY THE SPECIAL COMMITTEE OF THE TEMPORARY MIXED COMMISSION OF THE LEAGUE OF NATIONS IN 1923.[23]

In the absence of any indisputable test, Governments can only judge by an *impression* based upon the most various factors, such as:

The political attitude of the possible aggressor;

His propaganda;

The attitude of his press and population;

His policy on the international market, etc.

. . . .

DEFINITION OF NON-AGGRESSION CONTAINED IN ARTICLE 1 OF THE DRAFT TREATY OF MUTUAL ASSISTANCE OF 1923.[24]

A war shall not be considered as a war of aggression if waged by a State which is party to a dispute and has accepted the unanimous recommendation of the Council, the verdict of the Permanent Court of International Justice, or an arbitral award against a High Contracting Party which has not accepted it, provided, however, that the first State does not intend to violate the political independence or the territorial integrity of the High Contracting Party.

. . . .

THE DEFINITION OF AGGRESSION CONTAINED IN THE DRAFT (GENEVA) PROTOCOL FOR THE PACIFIC SETTLEMENT OF INTERNATIONAL DISPUTES OF OCTOBER 2, 1924.[25]

Article 10 (1): Every State which resorts to war in violation of the undertakings contained in the Covenant or in the present Protocol is an aggressor. Violation of the rules laid down for a demilitarised zone shall be held equivalent to resort to war.

In the event of hostilities having broken out, any State shall be presumed to be an aggressor, unless a decision of the Council, which must be taken unanimously, shall otherwise declare:

1. If it has refused to submit the dispute to the procedure of pacific settlement provided by Articles 13 and 15 of the Covenant as amplified by the present Protocol, or to comply with a judicial sentence or arbitral award or with a unanimous recommendation of the Council, or has disregarded a unanimous report of the Council, a judicial sentence or an arbitral award recognising that the dispute between it and the other belligerent State arises out of a matter which by international law is solely within the domestic jurisdiction of the latter State; nevertheless, in the last case the State shall only be presumed to be an aggressor if it has not previously submitted the

---

23 *Id.* 184.
24 *Id.* 203.
25 *L.N.O.J.* Sp.Supp. No. 24, Ann. 18, pp.138-39.

question to the Council or the Assembly, in accordance with Article II of the Covenant.

2. If it has violated provisional measures enjoined by the Council for the period while the proceedings are in progress as contemplated by Article 7 of the present Protocol.

Apart from the cases dealt with in paragraphs 1 and 2 of the present Article, if the Council does not at once succeed in determining the aggressor, it shall be bound to enjoin upon the belligerents an armistice, and shall fix the terms, acting, if need be, by a two-thirds majority and shall supervise its execution.

Any belligerent which has refused to accept the armistice or has violated its terms shall be deemed an aggressor.

The Council shall call upon the signatory States to apply forthwith against the aggressor the sanctions provided by Article II of the present Protocol, and any signatory State thus called upon shall thereupon be entitled to exercise the rights of a belligerent.

. . . .

DEFINITION OF AGGRESSION CONTAINED IN THE COMMENT OF M. POLITIS ON ART. 10 OF THE GENEVA PROTOCOL.[26]

. . . any State is the aggressor which resorts in any shape or form to force in violation of the engagements contracted by it either under the Covenant . . . or under the present Protocol . . .

. . . .

PROPOSAL FOR THE DEFINITION OF AGGRESSION SUBMITTED TO THE GENERAL COMMISSION OF THE DISARMAMENT CONFERENCE OF 1932-1933 BY THE DELEGATION OF THE U.S.S.R.[27]

[*See for the text of this Draft, supra pp.34-35.*]

DEFINITION DRAFTED BY THE COMMITTEE ON SECURITY QUESTIONS OF THE DISARMAMENT CONFERENCE, 1932-1933.[28]

Article 1: The aggressor in an international conflict shall, subject to the agreements in force between the parties to the dispute, be considered to be that State which is the first to commit any of the following actions:

(1) Declaration of war upon another State;

(2) Invasion by its armed forces, with or without a declaration of war, of the territory of another State;

(3) Attack by its land, naval or air forces, with or without a declaration of war, on the territory, vessels or aircraft of another State;

(4) Naval blockade of the coasts or ports of another State;

(5) Provision of support to armed bands formed in its territory which have invaded the territory of another State, or refusal, notwithstanding the request of the invaded State, to take in its own territory all the measures in its power to deprive those bands of all assistance or protection.

Article 2: No political, military, economic or other consideration may serve as an excuse or justification for the aggression referred to in Article 1.

Article 3: The present Act shall form an integral part of the General Convention for the Reduction and Limitation of Armaments. . . .

---

[26] *Id.* 127.

[27] Repr. *G.A.O.R. VII,* Ann., Item 54, Sec.-Gen.'s Report (A/2211) para. 76, pp.34ff.

[28] Repr. *id.* para. 78, p.35 and see *Sp.Com.Rep.* Ann. 1.

Protocol Annexed to Article 2 of the Act relating to the Definition of the Aggressor by which the High Contracting Parties—

Desiring, subject to the express reservation that the absolute validity of the rule laid down in Article 2 of that Act shall be in no way restricted, to furnish certain indication for the guidance of the international bodies that may be called upon to determine the aggressor:

Declare that no act of aggression within the meaning of Article 1 of that Act can be justified on either of the following grounds, among others:

A. The Internal Condition of a State:

E.g., its political, economic or social structure; alleged defects in its administration; disturbances due to strikes, revolutions, counter-revolutions or civil war.

B. The International Conduct of a State:

E.g., the violation or threatened violation of the material or moral rights or interests of a foreign State or its nationals; the rupture of diplomatic or economic relations; economic or financial boycotts; disputes relating to economic, financial or other obligations towards foreign States; frontier incidents not forming any of the cases of aggression specified in Article 1.

The High Contracting Parties further agree to recognize that the present Protocol can never legitimate any violations of international law that may be implied in the circumstances comprised in the above list.

PART V

SELECTED PROVISIONS OF NON-AGGRESSION, REGIONAL AND SECURITY TREATIES

DEFINITION CONTAINED IN THE TREATY BETWEEN FINLAND AND THE UNION OF SOVIET SOCIALIST REPUBLICS, JANUARY 21, 1932.[29]

Article 1: Any act of violence attacking the integrity and inviolability of the territory or the political independence of the other High Contracting Party shall be regarded as an act of aggression, even if it is committed without declaration of war and avoids warlike manifestations.

. . . . . .

DEFINITION CONTAINED IN THE PACT OF NON-AGGRESSION BETWEEN POLAND AND THE UNION OF SOVIET SOCIALIST REPUBLICS, SIGNED AT MOSCOW, JULY 25, 1932.[30]

Article 1: The two Contracting Parties, recording the fact that they have renounced war as an instrument of national policy in their mutual relations, reciprocally undertake to refrain from taking any aggressive action against or invading the territory of the other Party, either alone or in conjunction with other Powers.

Any act of violence attacking the integrity and inviolability of the territory or the political independence of the other Contracting Party shall be regarded as contrary to the undertakings contained in the present Article, even if such acts are committed without declaration of war and avoid all warlike manifestations as far as possible.

---

[29] 157 *L.N.T.S.* No. 831.
[30] 136 *L.N.T.S.* 49.

DEFINITION CONTAINED IN THE CONVENTION FOR THE DEFINITION OF AGGRESSION BETWEEN AFGHANISTAN, ESTONIA, LATVIA, PERSIA, POLAND, ROUMANIA, UNION OF SOVIET SOCIALIST REPUBLICS AND TURKEY, SIGNED AT LONDON, JULY 3rd, 1933.[31]

[Arts. II and III are identical with Arts. 1 and 2 of the Committee on Security Questions Draft, supra p.214.]

ANNEX: . . . no act of aggression within the meaning of Article II of that Convention can be justified on either of the following grounds, among others:

A. *The internal condition of a State*:

E.g., its political, economic or social structure; alleged defects in its administration; disturbances due to strikes, revolutions, counter-revolutions, or civil war.

B. *The international conduct of a State*:

E.g., the violation or threatened violation of the material or moral rights or interests of a foreign State or its nationals; the rupture of diplomatic or economic relations; economic or financial boycotts; disputes relating to economic, financial or other obligations towards foreign States; frontier incidents not forming any of the cases of aggression specified in Article II.

The High Contracting Parties further agree to recognise that the present Convention can never legitimate any violations of international law that may be implied in the circumstances comprised in the above list.

. . . . . .

DEFINITION CONTAINED IN THE RESERVATION OF THE DELEGATION OF COLOMBIA TO THE CONVENTION BETWEEN THE UNITED STATES OF AMERICA AND OTHER AMERICAN REPUBLICS. SIGNED AT BUENOS AIRES, DECEMBER 23, 1936.[32]

That State shall be considered as an aggressor which becomes responsible for one or several of the following acts:

a) That its armed forces, to whatever branch they may belong, illegally cross the land, sea or air frontiers of other States. When the violation of the territory of a State has been effected by irresponsible bands organized within or outside of its territory and which have received direct or indirect help from another State, such violation shall be considered equivalent, for the purposes of the present Article, to that effected by the regular forces of the State responsible for the aggression;

b) That it has intervened in a unilateral or illegal way in the internal or external affairs of another State;

c) That it has refused to fulfil a legally given arbitral decision or sentence of international justice.

---

31 147 *L.N.T.S.* No. 3391, pp.71,73,75.

Definitions identical with the one above are contained in the Convention for the Definition of Aggression, and Annex, concluded between Lithuania and the U.S.S.R., signed at London, July 5, 1933 (148 *L.N.T.S.* No. 3405), and a definition identical to the one above is contained also in the Convention for the Definition of Aggression between Roumania, the U.S.S.R., Czechoslovakia, Turkey and Yugoslavia, signed at London, July 4, 1933 (148 *L.N.T.S.* No. 3414). See also the incorporation by reference of this definition in the Protocol-Annex of the Pact of Balkan Entente, signed at Athens, Feb. 9, 1934 (153 *L.N.T.S.* No. 3514, Protocol-Annex, p.157) (English translation).

32 *U.S.T.S.* No. 926, p.7.

DEFINITION CONTAINED IN THE TREATY OF NON-AGGRESSION BETWEEN AFGHANISTAN, IRAQ, IRAN AND TURKEY, SIGNED AT TEHERAN, JULY 8, 1937.[33]

Article 4: The following shall be deemed to be acts of aggression:

1. Declaration of war;
2. Invasion by the armed forces of one State, with or without a declaration of war, of the territory of another State;
3. An attack by the land, naval or air forces of one State, with or without a declaration of war, on the territory, vessels or aircraft of another State;
4. Directly or indirectly aiding or assisting an aggressor.

The following shall not constitute acts of aggression:

1. The exercise of the right of legitimate self-defence, that is to say, resistance to an act of aggression as defined above;
2. Action under Article 16 of the Covenant of the League of Nations;
3. Action in pursuance of a decision of the Assembly or Council of the League of Nations, or under Article 15, paragraph 7, of the Covenant of the League of Nations, provided always that in the latter case such action is directed against the State which was the first to attack;
4. Action to assist a State subjected to attack, invasion or recourse to war by another of the High Contracting Parties, in violation of the Treaty for Renunciation of War signed in Paris on August 27th, 1928.

. . . . . .

DEFINITION CONTAINED IN THE ACT OF CHAPULTEPEC SIGNED BY ALL THE AMERICAN REPUBLICS ON MARCH 8, 1945.[34]

Preamble, j) : . . . any attempt on the part of a non-American State against the integrity or inviolability of the territory, the sovereignty or the political independence of an American State shall be considered as an act of aggression against all the American States.

Part I, 3: That every attack of a State against the integrity or the inviolability of the territory, or against the sovereignty or political independence of an American State, shall, conformably to Part III hereof, be considered as an act of aggression against the other States which sign this Act. In any case invasion by armed forces of one State into the territory of another trespassing boundaries established by treaty and demarcated in accordance therewith shall constitute an act of aggression.

(Part III: The above Declaration and Recommendation constitute a regional arrangement for dealing with such matters relating to the maintenance of international peace and security as are appropriate for regional action in this Hemisphere. The said arrangement, and the pertinent activities and procedures, shall be consistent with the purposes and principles of the general international organization, when established.)

. . . . . .

DEFINITION CONTAINED IN THE TREATY OF BROTHERHOOD AND ALLIANCE BETWEEN IRAQ AND TRANSJORDAN, SIGNED AT BAGHDAD ON APRIL 14, 1947.[35]

Article 5: . . . (b) The following shall be deemed acts of aggression:

(1) The declaration of war.

(2) The seizure by an armed force of a third State, or territory belonging

[33] 190 *L.N.T.S.* No. 4402, p.21.

[34] *U.S. Treaties and Other International Acts Series* No. 153, p.12, 9 Hudson, *Int. Leg.* No. 647, pp.286-288.

[35] 23 *U.N.T.S.* No. 345, pp.156ff., 158.

to either High Contracting Party even without a declaration of war.

(3) An attack on the territory, land, naval or air forces of either High Contracting Party by the land, naval or air forces of a third State, even without a declaration of war.

(4) Direct or indirect support or assistance to the aggressor.

(c) The following shall not be deemed acts of aggression:

(1) The exercise of the right of legitimate defence, i.e., resisting any act of aggression as defined above.

(2) Actions taken to implement the provisions of the Charter of the United Nations.

. . . . . .

DEFINITION CONTAINED IN THE INTER-AMERICAN TREATY OF RECIPROCAL ASSISTANCE BETWEEN THE UNITED STATES OF AMERICA AND OTHER AMERICAN REPUBLICS, SIGNED AT RIO DE JANEIRO, SEPTEMBER 2, 1947.[36]

Article 1: The High Contracting Parties formally condemn war and undertake in their international relations not to resort to the threat or the use of force in any manner inconsistent with the provisions of the Charter of the United Nations or this Treaty.

Article 3 (1): The High Contracting Parties agree that an armed attack by any State against an American State shall be considered as an attack against all the American States and, consequently, each one of the said Contracting Parties undertakes to assist in meeting the attack in the exercise of the inherent right of individual or collective self-defense recognized by Article 51 of the Charter of the United Nations.

Article 9: In addition to other acts which the Organ of Consultation may characterize as aggression, the following shall be considered as such:

a. Unprovoked armed attack by a State against the territory, the people, or the land, sea or air forces of another State;

b. Invasion, by the armed forces of a State, or the territory of an American State, through the trespassing of boundaries demarcated in accordance with a treaty, judicial decision, or arbitral award, or, in the absence of frontiers thus demarcated, invasion affecting a region which is under the effective jurisdiction of another State.

. . . . . .

ROOSEVELT DECLARATION OF DECEMBER 23, 1933.[36a]

A simple declaration that no nation will permit any of its armed forces to cross its own borders into the territory of another nation. Such an act would be regarded by humanity as an act of aggression, and as an act therefore that would call for condemnation by humanity.

. . . . . .

HARVARD RESEARCH IN INTERNATIONAL LAW, DRAFT CONVENTION ON RIGHTS AND DUTIES OF STATES IN CASE OF AGGRESSION.[36b]

Article 1 (c): In this Convention the term "aggression" means "a resort to

---

[36] *U.S. Treaties and Other International Acts Series* No. 1838, pp.24-26, 21 *U.N.T.S* No. 324, pp.95,99.

[36a] Quoted Bourquin (ed.), *Collective Security* 296.

[36b] (1939) 33 *A.J.I.L.* Supp. pt. iii, p.827.

armed force by a State when such resort has been duly determined, by a means which that State is bound to accept, to constitute a violation of an obligation.

PART VI

SELECTED SCHOLARLY DRAFTS

DEFINITION BY H. THIRRING.[37]

Eine Aggression begeht, wer militärische Operationen kriegerischer Natur im Gebiet eines fremden Staates ausfuehrt, ohne vorher den Vereinigten Nationen auf Grund evidenter Tatbestände bewiesen zu haben, dass dieser Staat selbst eine kriegerische Aggression begangen hat und weiterzufuehren droht, gegen die der Betroffene sich nur durch Massnahmen wehren kann, die ueber die eigene Grenze hinausgreifen.

[Translation: An aggression is committed by the entity which carries out military operations of a warlike nature in the territory of a foreign State, without having proved previously to the United Nations on the basis of evident facts that this State itself had committed warlike aggression and had threatened to continue it, against which the entity concerned can defend itself only by measures which extend beyond its own border.]

. . . .

DEFINITION BY R. THÉRY.[38]

. . . *l'agression, c'est une contrainte indûment exercée par un Etat sur la personne d'un autre Etat.*

. . . .

DEFINITION BY GEORGES SCELLE.[39]

. . . *tout recours à la violence = guerre; toute guerre = agression.*

. . . .

DEFINITION BY ROBERT H. JACKSON.[40]

. . . An "aggressor" is . . . that State which is the first to commit any of the following actions:

(1) Declaration of war upon another State;

(2) Invasion by its armed forces, with or without a declaration of war, of the territory of another State;

(3) Attack by its land, naval, or air forces, with or without a declaration of war, on the territory, vessels, or aircraft of another State;

(4) Provision of support to armed bands formed in the territory of another State, or refusal, notwithstanding the request of the invaded State, to take in its own territory, all the measures in its power to deprive those bands of all assistance or protection.

---

37 H. Thirring, *"Was ist Aggression?"* (1952-53) 5 *Oesterreichische Zeitschrift für öffentliches Recht* (*N.F.*) 226, at 241. Thirring's definition was intended as an improvement to the Soviet draft definition (A/C.6/L.208). He proposed to place it before the Soviet definition as a general formula.

38 R. Théry, *La Notion d'Agression en Droit International* (1937) 239.

39 G. Scelle, *"L'Agression et la Légitime Défense dans les Rapports Internationaux"* (1936) 10 *L'Esprit International* 372, at 378.

40 R. H. Jackson, *The Nürnberg Case* (1947) 86.

DEFINITIONS BY QUINCY WRIGHT

1935 Text:[41] (. . . the conception of aggression in terms of its consequences . . .)
"An aggressor is a State which may be subjected to preventive, deterrent or remedial measures by other States because of its violation of an obligation not to resort to force."
". . . an aggressor is a State which is under an obligation not to resort to force, which is employing force against another State, and which refuses to accept an armistice proposed in accordance with a procedure which it has accepted to implement its no-force obligation."
1956 Text: [42]An act of aggression is the use or threat to use force across an internationally recognized frontier, for which a government, *de facto* or *de jure,* is responsible because of act or negligence, unless justified by a necessity for individual or collective self-defence, by the authority of the United Nations to restore international peace and security, or by consent of the State within whose territory armed force is being used.

. . . .

DEFINITIONS BY THE INTERNATIONAL LAW SEMINAR, COLLEGE OF LAW, UNIVERSITY OF NEBRASKA, 1954.[43]

The Seminar makes no attempt here to define "aggression" generally, but only "aggression" within our understanding of the meaning of that term as used in the United Nations Charter.

An act of State A which is intended to and which in fact does contribute to or result in a substantial encroachment upon the independence of State B or the security of the people of State B in their right to be free from political repression is an act of aggression within the meaning of the Charter of the United Nations.

. . . .

DEFINITION BY C. A. POMPE.[44]

The use or imminent threat of force on the part of a State, whether acting openly or indirectly, which leaves the State against which it is directed no other than military means to preserve its territorial integrity or political independence, or which disturbs the international *status quo* in such a way that only a military reaction can maintain the status of territories under an international regime or under the effective jurisdiction of a State.

---

41 Q. Wright, "The Concept of Aggression in International Law" (1935) *A.J.I.L.* 373, at 375, 381.
42 Q. Wright, "The Prevention of Aggression" (1956) 50 *A.J.I.L.* 514, at 526.
43 "Meaning of 'Aggression' in the United Nations Charter" (1954) 33 *Nebraska L.R.* 606, 607, 612.
44 C. A. Pompe, *Aggressive War* 113.

INDEX OF NAMES

(Note: This Index is ancillary to the Index of Subjects.)

INDEX OF SUBJECTS[1]

Note: The following additional abbreviations are used in this Index:

"ag." = "aggression"
"B." = "Briand"
"Com." = "committee" or "commission"
"decl." = "declaration"
"def." = "definition" or "define"
"int." = "international"
"Int. E.T." = "International Equity Tribunal"
"Int. M.T." = "International Military Tribunal"
"K." = "Kellogg"
"M.E." = "Middle East"
"p." = "peace"
"S.F." = "San Francisco"
"Sec.-Gen." = "Secretary-General"

[1] The Writer is indebted to H. -J. Stieringer for assistance in preparation of this Index.

D

E

F

www.ingramcontent.com/pod-product-compliance
Ingram Content Group UK Ltd.
Pitfield, Milton Keynes, MK11 3LW, UK
UKHW050945290926
15470UKWH00005B/1655

9 781584 7